International Journal on Advances in Security

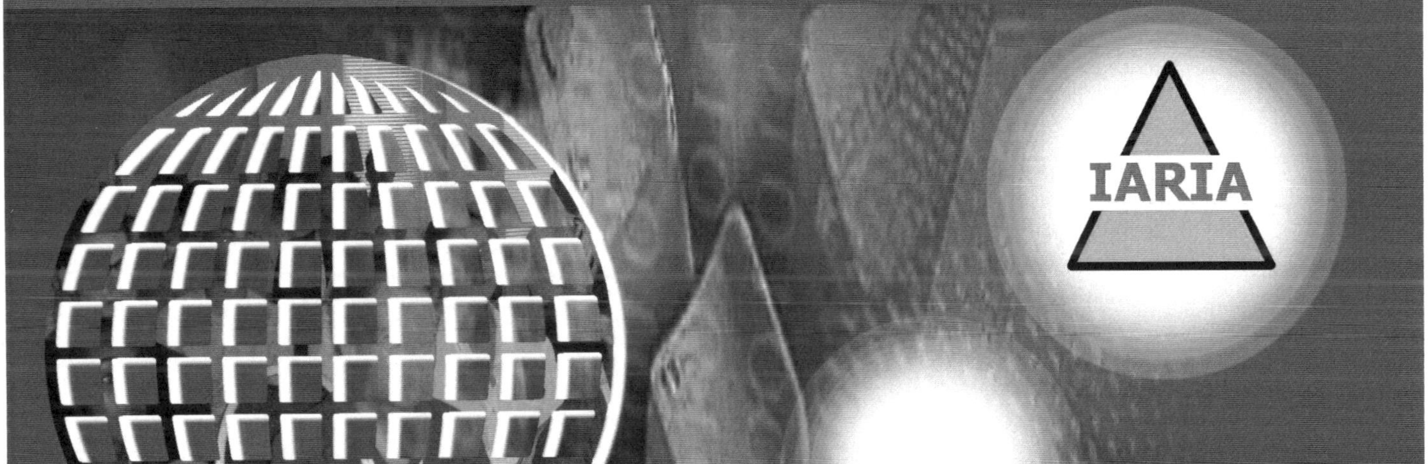

2017 vol. 10 nr. 1&2

Printed from e-media with permission by:

Curran Associates, Inc.
57 Morehouse Lane
Red Hook, NY 12571

Some format issues inherent in the e-media version may also appear in this print version.

Printed by Curran Associates, Inc. (2018)

International Academy, Research, and Industry Association (IARIA)
412 Derby Way
Wilmington, DE 19810

Phone: (408) 893-6407
Fax: (408) 527-6351

petre@iaria.org

Additional copies of this publication are available from:

Curran Associates, Inc.
57 Morehouse Lane
Red Hook, NY 12571 USA
Phone: 845-758-0400
Fax: 845-758-2633
Email: curran@proceedings.com
Web: www.proceedings.com

The *International Journal on Advances in Security* is published by IARIA.
ISSN: 1942-2636
journals site: http://www.iariajournals.org
contact: petre@iaria.org

Reference should mention:

International Journal on Advances in Security, issn 1942-2636
vol. 10, no. 1 & 2, year 2017, http://www.iariajournals.org/security/

Reference to an article in the journal is as follows:

<Author list>, "<Article title>"
International Journal on Advances in Security, issn 1942-2636
vol. 10, no. 1 & 2, year 2017, <start page>:<end page> , http://www.iariajournals.org/security/

Sponsored by IARIA
www.iaria.org

International Journal on Advances in Security
Volume 10, Number 1 & 2, 2017

Vladimir Stantchev, Institute of Information Systems, SRH University Berlin, Germany
Lars Strand, Nofas, Norway
Young-Joo Suh, Pohang University of Science and Technology (POSTECH), Korea
Jani Suomalainen, VTT Technical Research Centre of Finland, Finland
Enrico Thomae, Ruhr-University Bochum, Germany
Tony Thomas, Indian Institute of Information Technology and Management - Kerala, India
Panagiotis Trimintzios, ENISA, EU
Peter Tröger, Hasso Plattner Institute, University of Potsdam, Germany
Simon Tsang, Applied Communication Sciences, USA
Marco Vallini, Politecnico di Torino, Italy
Bruno Vavala, Carnegie Mellon University, USA
Mthulisi Velempini, North-West University, South Africa
Miroslav Velev, Aries Design Automation, USA
Salvador E. Venegas-Andraca, Tecnológico de Monterrey / Texia, SA de CV, Mexico
Szu-Chi Wang, National Cheng Kung University, Tainan City, Taiwan R.O.C.
Steffen Wendzel, Fraunhofer FKIE, Bonn, Germany
Piyi Yang, University of Shanghai for Science and Technology, P. R. China
Rong Yang, Western Kentucky University , USA
Hee Yong Youn, Sungkyunkwan University, Korea
Bruno Bogaz Zarpelao, State University of Londrina (UEL), Brazil
Wenbing Zhao, Cleveland State University, USA

International Journal on Advances in Security
Volume 10, Numbers 1 & 2, 2017

CONTENTS

Aspects of Security Update Handling for IoT-devices

Geir M. Køien

Institute of ICT
University of Agder, Norway
Email: geir.koien@uia.no

Abstract—**There is a fast-growing number of quite capable Internet-of-Things (IoT) devices out there. These devices are generally unattended, often exposed and frequently vulnerable. The current practice of deploying, and then leaving the devices unattended and unmanaged is not future proof. There is an urgent need for well-defined security update management procedures for these devices. Sufficient, sensible and secure default settings, as well as built-in privacy must be included. This paper presents a brief overview of the IoT threat landscape, argues for the necessity of security update provisioning for the IoT devices. As such, it is a call for action. Finally, an outline of a privacy-aware security update provisioning model is given. We have included incident management as well in the outline, but is only very rudimentary sketch of what one would need to provide. Suffice to say that there may be a need for these capabilities too, but it can probably only be justified for relatively capable devices.**

Keywords–Security update; Internet-of-Things; Incident reporting; Security maintenance; Privacy; Security management.

I. Introduction

A. Background and Motivation

This paper is based on the paper "Security Update and Incident Handling for IoT-devices; A Privacy-Aware Approach" [1], presented at SecurWare 2016.

It was noted that there is a growing number of relatively capable devices being designed and deployed. We only concern our selves with this class of devices in this paper. These devices, although quite simple, tend to have sufficient hardware support to be able to provide cryptographic functionality. It is thus feasible to design security schemes for these devices.

A central argument of the above paper was that IoT devices should be properly managed. It was postulated that the majority of the IoT device owners will be unable to adequately manage the devices, and furthermore they would generally be ill-equipped to understand and respond to security and privacy requirements. To solve these problems, IoT devices will need to have fully-automated security update capabilities. No user intervention should be required, although one must permit knowledgable users to configure the mechanisms. The security maxim should be "Security-by-Default", where sensible security defaults are applied and enabled. Of course, privacy must also be catered for, and one may here look to the "Privacy-by-Design" initiative for high-level guidelines [2].

Since the original paper was published in July 2016, we have witnessed a number of high-publicity Internet infrastructure attacks facilitated by IoT devices with poor or non-existent security. These include, amongst others, large scale Distributed Denial-of-Service (DDoS) attacks using web cameras. With a proper security update solution in place, these cameras would have been substantially less vulnerable, and the DDoS attack by the Mirai-based malware would likely had been a lot less effective or maybe even fully prevented. We shall provide an update on some real-world attacks on unattended and generally unprotected IoT devices in Subsection II-D.

We have further updated the original paper on a concrete and practical firmware (FW) update schemes already in place. This scheme will serve as an example of the basic firmware update capability that is often provided with uncommissioned devices. Generally, it seems that the basic FW update functionalities may be reasonably complete by themselves, by that the trust assumptions are fairly naive. Furthermore, the schemes are often quite limited in scope and cannot provide anything other than a basic rudimentary update functionality. That is, there is hardly an overall solution in place, which provides credible security, roll-back, etc.

We must stress that to provide basic capabilities is not enough. The solution must be automated, completely transparent to the user, and it must provide credible security and privacy. Of course, the security update scheme must also be trustworthy and honest with respect to agreed capabilities and attributes. There has recently been reports of abuse of such schemes [3]. The scheme in [3] was not a security update scheme, but a fully automated firmware-based App downloader. It was also covert, and it did carry out software installation and updating without any user interaction. It may best be described as a persistent App installation scheme, reinstalling and updating unwanted Apps irrespective of user actions.

There needs to be a level of assurance and some measure of enforcement in place, and while a technologically basis must be provided, one likely also need support from jurisdictional and regulatory authorities. That is, there must a) exists pressures to provide honest and effective security update services and b) there must exists authorities which can react to protect end-users when update functionality has been used in subversive ways. We note that legal and regulatory control is slow acting and that they only seem to react after-the-fact.

We note that a properly implemented security update scheme will look a lot like a so-called "command & control" structure that is typically employed by botnets. And, clearly also quite similar to the scheme in [3]. However, the control servers for a security update scheme should be fully visible and official, so traffic to/from a security update server would not be confused with botnet control plane traffic (which may also be obfuscated to hinder intrusion detection systems (IDS) from noticing it).

B. Outline of our Proposed Security Update Model

The security update management and a minimal security incident and anomaly reporting service presented in this paper is not intended as a realistic model or proposal. The aim of proposal is rather to identify and highlight aspects of a possible solution, and thus to identify and illustrate requirements.

An important aspect of the model is to demonstrate technical feasibility. This is in line with the article itself, which aim to demonstrate the urgent need for security update services. The suggested architecture model features three information planes:

- User Services Plane (USP)
- User Management Plane (UMP)
- Security Management Plane (SMP)

The services will be realized by a two-tier architecture, separating global and local components, with clear division of authority and assumed trust between them.

The USP and UMP service planes may have cloud-based components, but whatever the case, these planes will have "local" termination with respect to the IoT device. The SMP service will be centralized and "global" in scope.

Privacy is a required property, and our design aim to adhere to the Privacy-by-Design (PbD) [2] tenets. We have therefore taken steps to make the model privacy-aware and privacy respecting, by introducing separation of duties and being particular at what kind of trust is placed in which architectural component/layer.

C. Related Work and Relevant Standards

The field is not yet settled, and the number of papers and proposed standards, of all types, is large and growing. We expect security and privacy to become even more important for IoT in the future. Our paper highlight the needs for secure management, and provide pointers as to how one could design such system.

1) Related Work: A few examples.

The survey paper "Security, privacy and trust in Internet of Things: The road ahead" [4] contains a broad overview over the challenges to IoT security. It emphasises that the IoT vision is characterized by heterogeneity, in terms of technologies, usages and application domains. It is also a fast phased and dynamic environment. Traditional security measures still play a large role, but the paper highlights that these are not always complete, sufficient or even appropriate. The authors also point out that scalability and flexibility is essential in this domain.

Another paper which also highlights open issues more than solutions is found in [5]. Also, the authors discusses these and related issues, like vulnerability, threats, intruders and attacks, in [6]. Both papers take a relatively high-level perspective. Other relevant works include [7]–[11].

In [12], the authors claim that "And as IoT contains three layers: perception layer, transportation layer and application layer, this paper will analyze the security problems of each layer separately and try to find new problems and solutions.". In the end, the authors conclude that IoT devices are more exposed and less capable than other network elements, and that therefore the challenges are both different and more urgent. Trust related to IoT devices, both in software and hardware, is discussed in [13].

2) Relevant Standards: There is no shortage of formal standards and industrial standards concerning IoT and security for IoT. The following is an incomplete selected set of standards. There is a bias in the selection towards wireless and cellular communications standards. We feel this is well justified given that very large proportion of the IoT devices will have WLAN and/or cellular capabilities built-in. Others will probably have Bluetooth (Low Energy) or some similar short-range access technology that in turn enables access to the internet.

– 3GPP TS 33.401: 4G Security Architecture

This standard is about the 3GPP 4G security architecture and it encompasses security for the eNodeB (eNB) base (tranceiver) stations (chapter 5.3 in [14]). In a 4G network, to achieve sufficient spatial ($[bit/s]/m^2$) capacity, one needs a densely distributed network of eNB's. There will therefore be a large number of eNB's, and the scenario may be somewhat reminiscent of a managed IoT network. Security for updating and managing the highly distritbuted base stations may be different from many IoT scenarios, but we believe there are many similarities and lessons to be learned here.

– 3GPP TS 33.310: Authentication Framework

This standard [14] specifies, amongst others, roll-out of digital certificates to the 3GPP eNB base stations, using the Certificate Management Protocol (CMP) [15]. This part is highly relevant for IoT devices too, since many of them will indeed be capable of handling asymmetric crypto and digital certificates. Indeed, even the humble SIM card (smart card) is able to do so, and we therefore postulate that this capacity is fully feasible for any IoT device that needs to handle security sensitive data and/or privacy sensitive data. Moore's law also implies that this capacity will only be cheaper over time, and so we fully expect that such capabilities will be commonplace.

– 3GPP TS 33.187: Machine-Type Communications

This standard [16] encompasses security for the so-called Machine-Type Communications (MTC). The standard defines how to allow IoT and machine-to-machine (m2m) devices be connected to a Service Capability Exposure Function (SCEF). Specifically, TS 33.187 requires "integrity protection, replay protection, confidentiality protection and privacy protection for communication between the SCEF and 3GPP Network Entity shall be supported" (Chapter 4.1 in [16]). These aspects are important for all IoT devices and this standard may serve as design input for non-3GPP cases too.

– GSMA CLP.11: IoT Security Guidelines Overview

This document [17] by the GSM Association is a non-binding guidelines document, and is as such not a normative standards document. It may still be quite influential since the GSM Association does have great reach within the community of cellular operators and vendors. The document identifies a set of grand challenges for IoT, and then proceeds to propose possible solutions. The challenges listed are:

A) Availability
B) Identity
C) Privacy
D) Security

Provisioning of scalable and flexible identifier structures is at the heart of the problem. Similarly, availability and security normally presupposes that the entities (the IoT devices) can be identified. Privacy then adds to this, but presupposing strong security [2] *and* requiring that the long-term identifiers are never exposed in clear (amongst others).

The document pays considerable attention to life-cycle aspects issues. The document also includes a chapter on risk assessment, an aspect which is all too often neglected in standards documents. Would-be IoT system designers are well advised to take this document into consideration. The document seems inspired by the "assumptions must be stated" idea, in a similar vein to the "Prudent Engineering Practice for Cryptographic Protocols" [18] paper. We strongly approve of the need for being explicit about assumptions and conditions.

– **NIST:** Cyber-Physical Systems (CPS) Framework

The NIST "Framework for Cyber-Physical Systems" document is an ambitious document which is expected to have considerable influence over future products [19]. The CSP Framework is largely oriented around the notion of systems-of-systems.

We also note that NIST has initiated work on "IoT-Enabled Smart City Framework" (abridged to "IES-City Framwork"). The framework is developed by a consortium, and started in earnest March 2016. Currently, only a white paper has been released by the working group [20].

3) Emerging Standards: International Mobile Telecommunications (IMT) is a framework for international mobile systems. It is mainly oriented towards defining capabilities, and have previously been defining framework for 3G (IMT 2000) and 4G (IMT-Advanced) mobil systems. The coming standards for 5G mobile systems, based upon the International Telecommunication Union (ITU) so-called "IMT for 2020 and beyond" vision, will have substantial support for "machine type communications (MTC)" [21]. The 3GPP, which is a consortium that includes standards development bodies, telecom operators and vendors, develops the concrete technical specifications based on the IMT vision. The 3GPP has stated that the basic technical standards for the IMT-2020 vision should be ready during 2020, and that some of the more advanced features are scheduled for 2021. Products, 5G compliant nodes/components and devices, will start arriving shortly after this. Experimental- and pilot deployment of parts of the 5G architecture already takes place.

Figure 1 depicts the 5G service triangle, where two of the three sides will have a strong focus on MTC services:

- **Enhanced Mobile Broadband:** Mainly focusing on bandwidth and to some extent user mobility
- **Ultra-reliable and Low Latency Communications:** This axis also encompasses the so-called "Critical MTC (cMTC)" type of communications. Strong security and hard requirements on bit error probabilities are part of this vision, and also fog computing (due to stringent round-loop latency requirements).
- **Massive Machine Type Communications (mMTC):** Low system/device overhead is main priority (extremely low power, small and infrequent payloads, upto 10^6 devices per km^2)

It is early days for IMT 2020 and 5G, but we expect important standards to emerge from for instance the 3GPP work on 5G, and some of these will no doubt have an impact on future IoT security.

D. Paper Layout

In Section II, we provide a high-level problem description. This includes the main aspects and high-level requirements. In particular, we provide a basic outline of the threats and real-world attacks that a IoT security scheme will have to face.

In Section III, we continue our investigation with a focus on underlying assumptions and premises concerning the devices and the detailed security service needs. This includes details concerning device capabilities, concerning firm ware updating and concerning device identifiers and location/identity privacy concerns.

In Section IV, we provide an outline of the proposed security management plane model. Here we outline the logical planes, network components and interfaces.

In Section V, we discuss the achievements and in Section VI we round off with a Summary and Conclusion.

II. High-Level Problem Description

A. Security for IoT Truisms

In the article "Click Here to Kill Everyone" [22], the author postulates that the IoT may be seen as a world-size robot and that it is about time to get it under control. The article is a bit alarmist, but maybe rightly so.

A cental point to the article is that there is an arms race between information assurance and the people who want to exploit the IoT devices for their own illicit goals. Based on these observations, the author outlines a set of truisms. Awareness of these truisms, which may or may not be tautological to the various IoT actors, will help us better protect the IoT devices and the associated infrastructures.

Schneier's IoT security truisms:

1) On the internet, attack is easier than defense.
2) Most software is poorly written and insecure.
3) Connecting everything to each other via the internet will expose new vulnerabilities.
4) Everybody has to stop the best attackers in the world.
5) Laws inhibit security research.

One may or may not agree with this set of truisms, or one may find it inconsistent, overlapping or incomplete, but the obvious lesson here is that we sorely need professional security management for IoT devices and IoT infrastructure.

B. User Interaction, Security Fatigue and Informed Consent

As a general rule, we believe that it is unrealistic to expect the end-users to configure or carry out much in terms of security setup of IoT devices. Likewise, we believe that it is equally unrealistic to expect the end-users to act on information pertaining intrusion attempts and similar. Partially, this can be attributed the phenomenon of "security fatigue" [23], but it can also be attributed to the fact that, to most ordinary end-users, information concerning security configuration, setup or intrusion alerts, simply must be considered "non-actionable". That is, there is no realistic way that the end-user would know what he or she should do. As such, information, warnings

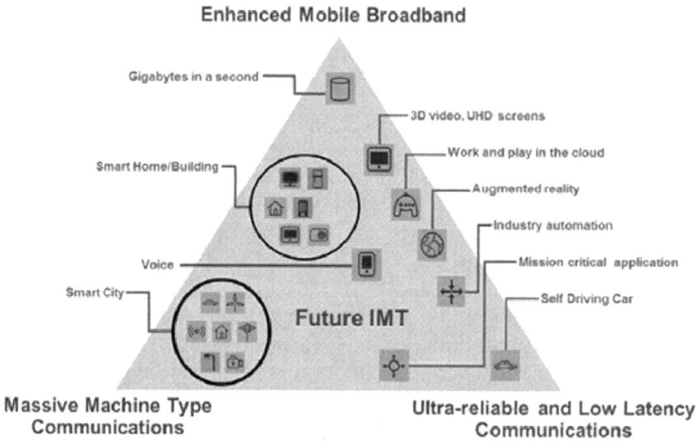

Figure 1. Usage secenarios of IMT for 2020 and beyond (Source: Fig.2 in ITU-R M.2083).

and alerts directed towards the end-user, that he or she cannot realistically be expected to know how to deal with, will only contribute towards "security fatigue". This would be analogous to the concept of non-actionable news, in which the meaning of the provided news items degenerates into mere entertainment [24]. Security related non-actionable information would have no entertainment value, but would contribute to cause stress and the before mentioned "security fatigue".

The problem with non-actionable information is also somewhat reminiscent of the problems with "informed consent". There are many papers highlighting these problems [25], [26], and one main objection is that one cannot easily expect anyone but experts to be truly informed.

We therefore conclude that while IoT devices should be managed, we cannot expect end-users to be able to do this except for possibly assisting a management system with very basic actions and decisions ("reset device","turn off device"). To ask users for permission to carry out various actions, the "informed consent" part, is likewise not very useful. It may serve a legal need, but this is pretence and has for the most part little to do with true informed consent.

C. Threat Landscape

The "European Union Agency for Network and Information Security" (ENISA) annually publishes so-called "ENISA Threat Landscape" (ETL) reports, the most recent being the 2015 report [27]. They also publish topic-orient threat landscape reports, but there is no report dedicated to IoT.

In chapter 3.2 Malware in ETL-2015 [27] it is noted that:

> "Rather than complexity, cyber-criminals are focussing on efficiency. In the reporting period we have seen the revival of infection techniques employed almost 20 years ago...."

We believe that this opportunistic cyber attack strategy is quite effective towards IoT devices, since they generally seems to have poorly designed and poorly implemented security functions.

We may ourselves briefly outline the basics of a threat landscape. The basic premises for assessing the threat landscape consists minimally of the following parameters:

- Asset identification and attributed value
- Asset exposure (per design)
- Attack surface and Vulnerability exposure
- Baseline security features
- Detection and Response capabilities
- Threat Agents (Intruder/Attacker)
- Attack Vectors
- Manifest Threats/Actual attacks

1) Asset identification and attributed value: What is it that has value? The physical device may have some value, but it is often the case that the data on the device has more value than the device itself. Understanding where the value actually is, is of course paramount.

2) Asset Exposure: For IoT the exposure or "visibility" is both through local physical exposure and through global connectivity exposure by means of the internet access. The local exposure, severe as it may be, does not scale and as such is of lesser importance. The global connectivity exposure is through the IP interface, and commonly though some sort of web server on the IoT device.

3) Attack surface and Vulnerability exposure: The attack surface is generally the whole of the exposed part of the asset. For our case, we define this to be the IP address(es) and the port range visible on the internet. The vulnerabilities would be associated with flaws or weaknesses in the information handling over the available attack surface. Exploitation of vulnerabilities is generally not straight forward, and it is not obvious that one can create attack vectors from a set of vulnerabilities. Or indeed, that the vulnerabilities are known to a threat agent.

4) Baseline Security features: The IoT device may or may not have some built-in security, but it is common to at least have some sort of password based scheme in place. The security in place will effectively mitigate vulnerabilities and remove or mitigate attack vectors.

Ideally, the configuration of the device would also include proper security hardening, and removal of all unneeded functionality and closing down all unneeded ports. This would reduce the attack surface and invariably also reduce the vulnerabilities, leaving less possible attack vectors available.

Advanced persistent threats (APT) is of course also a concern, but realistically these types are much less common and they are also far more difficult to protect against.

We therefore postulate that the baseline security ought to be able to fend off most of the trivial attacks. If the security measures are cost-effective, then certainly the baseline security should do more, but we cannot realistically require a simple IoT device to be able to withstand APT attcks.

5) Detection and Response capabilities: Low-cost IoT devices seldom have much in terms of detection and response capabilities. This is a problem, and it makes it substantially harder to recover from an intrusion event. This situation can actually be improved upon, and even low cost devices could have basic detection and response mechanisms in place. We return to this topic later in the paper (Section III).

6) Threat Agents (Intruder/Attacker): In this paper we will mostly consider relatively opportunistic threat agents. As was mentioned in the ENISA ETL-2015 quote, cyber criminals are more concerned with efficiency than demonstrating technical competency. That is, they are more concerned with goals than methods. It is therefore no surprise then that attacks as simple targeting devices with default administrator accounts with default passwords are popular. Script kiddies would probably also mostly use quite simple methods, or whatever methods easily available to them.

APT intruders are obviously also possible, but to protect against these are not part of the scope of this paper. At best, one can hope to make attacks costlier to these types of intruders, and thereby prevent or mtigate scalability of the attacks. This is important, since form a system perspective, to prevent attack scalability is an important goal.

7) Attack Vectors: Attack vectors are simply possible recipes to carry out a successful attack on a system, utilizing whatever exposed vulnerabilities there are. We note that what constitutes "success" is defined by the threat agent.

8) Manifest Threats/Actual attacks: Classification wise, this is actual attacks that has succeeded, using one or more of the available attack vectors. Success is here relative to the intruder goals, and these are detrimental to the security and privacy goals. Note that the intruder goals may not be aligned with what the end-user perceives to be the most valuable aspect of the IoT-device/service.

D. Real-World Experiences with Unprotected IoT Devices

During 2016 we have witness a new trend, in which cyber criminals systematically search out vulnerable IoT devices. The devices are attacked *en masse* and infected with botnet malware. A couple of rather high-profile DDoS attacks were conducted with the Mirai botnet malware.

In one instance, the web site of Brian Krebs, known as **KrebsOnSecurity**, were attacked [28]. By itself, an attack on a single host would be inconsequential and of little general interest, but in this case the attack was on an unprecedented scale, and caused internet giant Akamai to terminate the pro-bono hosting contract with Brian Krebs. They simply could not afford to stand up to the record breaking torrent of 620 Gigabits of traffic per second. Brian Krebs himself is a security researcher and blogger who does in-depth research and analysis of cybercrime worldwide. His reporting on DDoS attacks and the perpetrators apparently made him the target of the DDoS attack. The KrebsOnSecurity site is now hosted behind Google's **Project Shield**, which according to Google is "...is a free service that uses Google technology to protect news sites and free expression from DDoS attacks on the web" (https://projectshield.withgoogle.com/public/). The particular attack on KrebsOnSecurity seems to have been conducted by compromised routers, security cameras, printers and digital video recorder (DVRs). Default account names and passwords seems to be the common denominator for the infection process.

The Mirai source code was published subsequent to the attack on KrebsOnSecurity, which ironically makes it "open source" code [28]. Since then, Mirai has been used in other attacks, by other botnets. There was also a large scale attack on the French hosting firm OHV, and there was an attack on the company Dyn, who provides Domain Name System (DNS) services. The Dyn attack effectively prevent name resolution and thereby reachability for services such as Twitter, SoundCloud, Spotify and Reddit amongst others [29], [30].

The infection stage of Mirai have evolved after it was made public, and by now there are many variants of Mirai. The evolved versions are exploiting different vulnerabilities, and at least on strain seems to be specializing on infecting routers [28]. Mirai, of course, are just one type of botnet which attacks IoT devices. At this years DEF CON there was considerable attention on IoT security, and there results were abysmal. During DEF CON 47 new vulnerabilities were found in a total of 23 different devices [31]. One example includes solar panel. Several security issues were found, including a hard-coded password, a command injection flaw, an open access point connection and a lack of network segmentation [32].

E. Device Capabilities

Many of the devices, if power is not too much of a constraint, will be enjoying 32-bit processing, relatively large amounts of memory and even more flash memory. A typical mid-level IoT platform these days would be based on the ARM Cortex M family of processors. Here we have the relatively powerful ARM M4 processor (w/floating point and DSP functionality), being both very affordable and surprisingly power efficient [33], [34]. These devices typically provide 32-256KB SRAM memory and up to 1GB flash memory. We assume a device of roughly this capability in our design. However, the flexibility that comes with updatable software may also turn out to be an Achilles heal unless properly managed.

F. Lightweight, Minimality and Modularity

The core IoT architecture should be lightweight, including the base protocols. Correctness and efficiency is likely to benefit from this. Basic security and privacy functionality must be included in the core architecture.

Extensibility and additional features will be needed, and this must be designed to be modular. Restraint in adding features is necessary, but is clear that any successful architecture will over time grow more complex and encompass new areas [35]. We advocate a design reminiscent of the microkernel approach to operating systems design [36], in which only a minimal set of functional are at the core, running in supervisor mode, and where other component may be added and where strict rules concerning use of well-defined interfaces and protocols are adhered to. This will, amongst others, facilitate security hardening and it will enable the systems to be deployed on less capable devices.

G. Connectivity and Exposure

Commonly the devices will have bluetooth low energy connectivity, WLAN connectivity or even fixed LAN or cellular access. That is, they are reachable over the internet. This also exposes the devices to a whole range of threats, and whenever a device, or a class of devices, gains popularity they are prone to become a target. It is therefore prudent to assume that our IoT devices will, sooner-or-later, become targets.

H. Scalability

Needless to say, any solution that must be able to cope with a large, and fast growing number of devices, must be scalable. That is, the cost model for adding devices/users must be linear and with a low constant factor. The upper limit on the number of devices must be very high as to not prohibit future growth. The IMT-2020 vision for mMTC devices highlight this, with a requirement to serve in the order of a million devices per km^2. This calls for a redesign of the current access signalling schemes and for a new way of handling identifiers and access security. To combine solid security and credible identity/location privacy at the same time is not trivial.

I. Explicitness

As a rule, all requirements, including the security and privacy requirements must be explicit. Also, all conditions and premises must be made explicit. Explicitness is also a main lesson from [18] (being essential to Principles 1, 2, 4, 6, 10 and 11 in that paper).

J. Security and Privacy Requirements

Due to the exposure, the devices will need security protection, security supervision and security updating to remove, reduce and mitigate the risks. The devices will need basic capabilities regarding device integrity assurance, and for handling entity authentication, data confidentiality and data integrity.

It is quite likely that the devices will capture, store and transmit privacy sensitive data. Since there is a considerable chance that this may be so, it is prudent practice to take this into consideration. We therefore require that a PbD regime should be adhered to [2]. As noted in [37], [38], PbD does not come about all by itself, and considered and careful design, implementation and maintenance is required to create credible privacy solutions.

When it comes to communications security there are several options, depending on needs and what the devices actually communicates. We have typically the following possibilities:

- L2 Link layer protection
- L3 IP layer protection
- L4 Transport layer protection
- – No device support

The link layer protection support is often supported directly by the link layer hardware, whether it be Bluetooth, Zigbee, or some flavour of WLAN. Adequate configuration is still an issue, but the most up-to-date support found is often adequate and sufficient. There are notable exceptions though, and some chip sets do not support security at all.

There is generally very few devices which support IPsec directly. The IPsec code base is relatively large and this makes IPsec less well suited for many IoT devices.

There are transport layer solutions available, supporting https connection. This is quite reasonable since many IoT devices do provide a web based interface. Use of https is also on the increase, and it seems well justified to support https. Https support is also greatly facilitated by the efforts of the "Let's Encrypt" initiative, which is a free public Certificate Authority (CA) service [39].

K. Cryptographic Requirements

To be able to offer strong security and credible privacy, it is essential that the IoT device be able to support strong cryptographic algorithms and protocols. Additionally, there must be support for a secure execution environment and secure storage (more on this later). The basic requirements today is for "128-bit" security or better, and for "strong" algorithms. What is considered "strong" is a moving target, but as of February 2017 we have for instance that the commonly used SHA-1 algorithm has actually been broken [40]. Of course, there is SHA-256 and there is SHA-3 for hash functions, and there is the AES algorithm for confidentiality (with various well-defined mode-of-operation options available).

Quantum machines, which may become a practical reality within the next 10 years, will be uniquely able to break existing asymmetric cryptographic primitives. It is noted that standard cryptographic hash functions and symmetric crypto primitives will will be affected too. However, here it is believed that a doubling of key length (block length) will suffice to mitigate the effect of quantum computers. The National Institute of Standards and Technology (NIST) has published an overview of the problems associated with quantum computers and cryptography [41].

To the extent possible and practical, quantum-safe cryptography should be used.

L. Automation and Autonomy

We cannot expect that the end-users will provide security management for the devices. In fact, the end-user may increasingly be unaware of the presence of the IoT-devices. Effective security management of unattended and highly distributed devices will necessarily have to be automated and autonomous.

M. Challenges

As already mentioned, the GSM Association has recognized four main challenges created by IoT: *availability*, *identity*, *privacy* and *security* [17]. An autonomous security update and incident management system will need to address all these aspects, and provide at least a partial solution to the security aspect. We note that strong security is effectively a prerequisite for availability and privacy.

Trust and trustworthiness are essential elements and even prerequisites for widespread IoT adoption. Trust is a complex matter [13], but suffice to say that credible security management should instill confidence and thereby trust. Trustworthiness is hard to prove, but good security management should provide a measure of assurance.

N. Scope

The proposal made in this paper is an architectural proposal concerning security updating and incident and anomaly reporting. The proposal is, however, not a proposal for a fully fledged architecture, but rather for an architectural component. The proposal may therefore be compatible with other IoT architectures, but may of course also overlap with them or even be at odds with them.

In this respect, more is not going to be better, and defense-in-depth, which often means that there is benefit in multiple and possibly overlapping schemes, probably does not apply.

III. Assumptions and Premises

This paper makes a few assumptions about the IoT devices.

A. Internet Connectivity

We assume that the device is connected to the Internet. Locally, the connection may be wireless (Bluetooth, WLAN) or wired. It may also be a cellular connection. Preferably, there will be a hub/proxy device with firewall functionality etc., but this is not required.

B. Hardened OS

The OS is assumed to be hardened. Hardening is also assumed to be carried out when the OS is compiled and built with the program, as is often the case for embedded devices. Unnecessary protocols and services must removed or disabled, and only a minimal set of software be present. A local IPtables firewall may be deployed. There is a growing market for security hardened OS implementations [42].

C. Security Capabilities

The devices are assumed to have a trusted platform module (TPM), with basic crypto processing support and secure storage. Preferably, they adhere to standards such as ISO/IEC 11889-1:2015 [43]. A vendor issued device certificate is assumed to be available, or some similar identification that may be used for bootstrapping the CMPv2 protocol [15].

In late 2015, ARM released the ARMv8-M architecture, which is the new baseline Cortex-M architecture [44]. It introduces support for ARM's TrustZone TPM for the Cortex-M processors, and is as such an important step towards credible security for IoT devices. As of yet, there are no commercially available designs, but it is expected that there soon be a plethora of available processors targeted for the security sensitive IoT markets.

D. Power, Processing and Memory Capabilities

The device may have limited capabilities, but we shall assume that the device is not too restricted. That is, we assume it to be roughly at least as powerful as the lower end of the ARM Cortex M3/M4 processor families.

E. Secure Bootloading and Software/Firmware Attestation

A secure bootloader is necessary, and it will likely be using TPM functionality. All software, including firmware and patches, must be signed. All software packages shall have version numbers, and this includes firmware and patches. A TPM may facilitate attestation, but alternatives exists [45].

F. Firmware Over-the-Air

1) "Firmware Over-the-Air" (FOTA): is a firmware updating concept designed by Nordic Semiconductors. The FOTA scheme is targeted for Bluetooth Low Energy (BLE) enabled devices/chips, like the nRF52 device [33]. Here one have the so-called "Device Firmware Update" scheme. In particular, there is the "BLE Secure DFU Bootloader". The user guide, applying the "BLE Secure DFU Bootloader", is quite instructive [46]. The update FW package should be signed, and here one uses one of the available signature schemes. These are generally elliptic curve cryptography (ECC) oriented and using SHA-256. The ECC library used is the open source micro-ecc [47].

2) Secure Bootloader.: Nordic Semiconductors provides a secure bootloader scheme. The "BLE Secure DFU Bootloader" is not very easy to use or deploy, but it is still a useful tool for competent designers and developers. While Bluetooth connectivity is the main goal, the scheme also works over serial line protocols. It must also be mentioned that the ability to have roll-back and similar functionality is not quite there. There is the possibility to store multiple images, but the update functionality is still quite limited.

3) DFU bootloader.: The DFU bootloader supports updating the firmware of the device. This includes updating your application, the SoftDevice (which is the BLE handler) or even the bootloader. At startup, the DFU bootloader will check if a valid application already exists on the device. If there is no application present, the bootloader simply initiates the transfer of a FW image.

If there is a valid application present, the DFU bootloader will either start the application or go to DFU mode. There are several options, but only when in DFU mode will the bootloader actually install the new FW image. Having entered DFU mode, the DFU bootloader initializes the DFU transport module, which is responsible for receiving the new FW image at the chip. The downloaded image is validated and copied to the correct location in memory, before being activated. The device must be restarted to actually start executing the newly updated firmware. An outline of the process flow is presented in figure 2.

4) Omissions and Shortcomings.: The above described firmware updating scheme may be fairly typical, and we do not want to single out Nordic Semiconductors as being particularly bad. The secure bootloader scheme does provide basic update functionality and it has reasonable security with respect to the firmware image. That is, to the authenticity and data integrity of the image.

There is no data confidentiality provided, although that would not be too hard to facilitate. Given the lack of confidentiality, there can be no privacy protection for sensitive data. The scheme therefore cannot be used as-is to provide secure data backups, since it obviously allows information embedded in the image to be exposed.

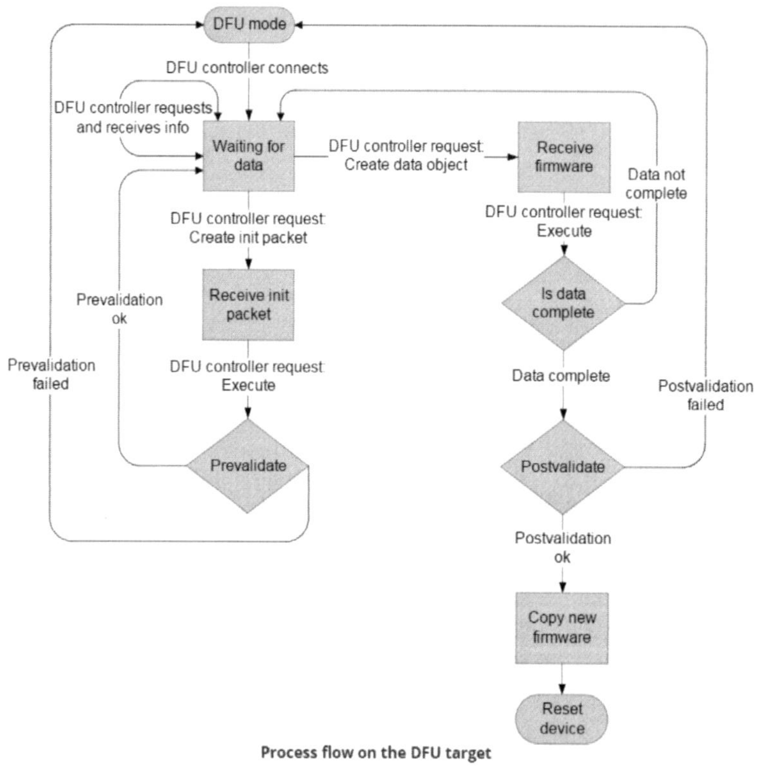

Figure 2. Process flow on the DFU target (Source: Nordic Semiconductors)

For a complete scheme we clearly also need more fine grained control with respect to permission and authorization. The secure bootloader update granularity is coarse, basically covering the image, although it is possible to differentiate somewhat (update the bootloader, update the application and update the Soft Device). There is for instance no way to read/write/delete application configuration data separately. Another aspect is that there is no framework for distinguishing between purely functional updates and security updates. While we strongly advocate automated security updating, this is not the case for functional updates. Tools and support for functional updates is important, but the end-user (or authorized manager) may have many good reasons for not wanting to implement new functionality.

The scheme is limited to serial line communications, which is also how it is implemented on top of the Bluetooth link. This limits the usefulness of the scheme for devices that ought to be able to communicate over the internet. Having said this, it must be acknowledged that the secure bootloader scheme limits the exposure of the scheme to to the local BLE range or serial line range.

G. Device Recovery

The device shall feature a secure loader, which facilitates a basic boot strap procedure that can securely rebuild the device software. We expect this to be part of the TPM functionality.

H. Device Identifier

The device must have a unique device identifier. This identifier is assumed to be used in the device certificate, but we shall otherwise be agnostic about the nature of the identifier. The device may also have, or use, higher-layer identifiers, but this is considered outside the scope of this contribution. An example would be a dropbox account identifier.

The device may also have network addresses and cellular identifiers. These *may* uniquely identify the device, but we do not in general consider these to be appropriate for identifying the device (observe the *explicitness* rule).

I. Identifiers and Privacy

A fundamental part of privacy is that there is sensitive data that is linked to a person. That is, usually we are concerned with linkability. If one can break the linkage between the person and the sensitive data, then leakage of the data would not necessarily be (privacy) critical.

We must assume that an intruder will be able to link plaintext device identifiers with the person(s) associated with the device. This capability is after all the core business for enterprises like Google. Consequently, we must assume that the intruder will be able to correlate unprotected data.

It is thus necessary to conceal the permanent device identifier such that no outsider will be able to associate the device identifer with the device or the user/owner. There are several ways to do this, including those described in [48], [49].

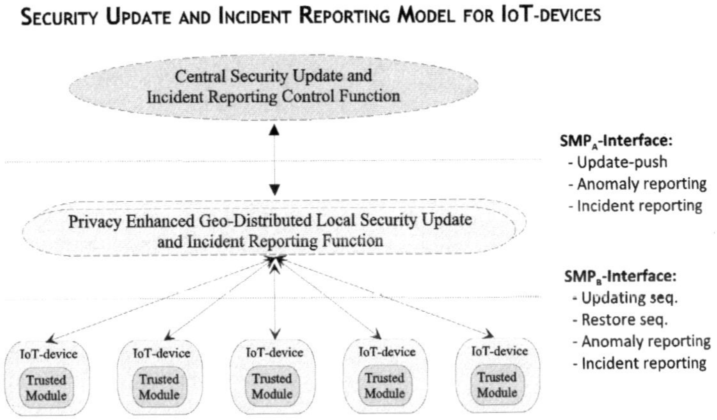

Figure 3. Outline of the Security Management Plane Model.

The functional split between the global and local services are very much reminiscent of split found in the cellular networks, where the local component necessarily must know the location and where the central component must necessarily know the permanent identity. Here, it has been shown that with proper setup one may achieve both location- and identity privacy [50]. In this paper, we shall ignore the specifics, but we do require that identifier and location privacy is part of the design.

IV. OUTLINE OF THE SECURITY MANAGEMENT PLANE MODEL

Figure 3 depicts an outline of the Security Management Plane (SMP) model. We have already introduced the logical planes, but shall now take a closer look at how they are arranged. We shall primarily investigate the SMP plane and the associated services.

A. *Trust Assumptions and Trust Relationships*

We have the following principal entities in our model:

- **USER:** The user and/or owner of the IoT-device.
- **LOCAL:** The local SMP component.
- **GLOBAL** The global (centralized) SMP component.

We assume that the USER is an entity entitled to privacy protection according to the local laws. The GLOBAL entity is assumed to be operated by the IoT device manufacturer or some entity operating on behalf of the device manufacturer. It may also be operated by the software manufacturer. This would be similar to patch update services operated by Microsoft, Google and others. A standard, such as "Cortex Microcontroller Software Interface Standard" (CMSIS) [51], might also be extended in the future to cover support for patch management tools and facilities.

The LOCAL entity is assumed to be operated by a local entity, perhaps a local branch of the IoT manufacturer or some authority which is legally responsibly, warranties etc., for the IoT devices. It is required that the LOCAL and GLOBAL entities strictly observe the SMP model with regard to information exchange. We have observed that in the post-Snowden era, local authorities have increasingly required critical services to be hosted locally. We therefore have reason to believe that similar requirements may surface for IoT-devices too, or that such services are seen as commercially important to reassure the end-users (building confidence and perceived trustworthiness). We have the following trust assumptions:

- **USER vs. LOCAL**

  The USER trust LOCAL with respect to provided services. This is an asymmetric dependence trust.

- **LOCAL**

  The LOCAL entity must have security trust in the GLOBAL entity. The LOCAL entity shall not trust the GLOBAL entity with respect to USER privacy. The LOCAL entity cannot fully trust the USER. The LOCAL entity trust the incident- and anomaly reports, but do not place high significance in individual reports.

- **GLOBAL**

  The GLOBAL entity trust the LOCAL entity with respect to security, but not blindly so. The GLOBAL entity trust the incident- and anomaly reports, mediated by the LOCAL entity, but need not trust any single report and/or report from any single device.

B. The Logical Planes

1) The User Services Plane (USP): USP consists of the data associated with services provided by the IoT-device. The data forwarded here may end up at an App, at a local web service or at a cloud-hosted web service. We shall not be further concerned with the USP in this paper.

2) The User Management Plane (UMP): UMP consists of the device setup and configuration services provided by the IoT-device. The UMP is specifically about setting up the device end-user functionality. It does not cover basic security or privacy related setup or configuration. The data associated with UMP may end up at an App, at a local web service or at a cloud-hosted web service. The data *may* be privacy sensitive, and the design must reflect this. We shall not be further concerned with the UMP in this paper.

3) The Security Management Plane: The *security management plane* (SMP) is the crux of this paper. It consists of:

- Security setup and configuration
- Security update functionality
- Security incident and anomaly reporting, including local aggregation
- Secure restore functionality
- Identity- and Location Privacy handling

There will be a division of labor:

- Local SMP handling
- Centralized SMP handling

This will facilitate privacy and provide geo-distributed services. Localized processing may easier satisfy national regulatory requirements, while centralized analysis and handling of incidents will provide scalability and efficiency benefits.

C. The Network Components

The division or labor implies a LOCAL component and a centralized GLOBAL component. We observe that the local component will need to have provisions for geographical assurance. Implementation-wise, it will be a matter of policy if there is a need to comply with jurisdictional and regulatory requirements that dictate location of the local SMP handling.

1) The Central/Global SMP Component: The central security update and incident management control function will facilitate both security update production and distribution, and security incident and anomaly analysis.

This function does not need to know the device identifiers, nor does it need to know the associated IoT-device owner or user(s). It may need to know the software version status and any report on incidents and security anomalies associated with the devices. For the purpose of the incident analysis, we restrict this function to know the device class and the identity of the local SMP handling component. The true device identifier must never be divulged to the central SMP component.

2) The Local SMP Component: This function handles interactions with the IoT-devices within its geographical coverage area. We expect this area to coincide with regulatory or jurisdictional borders. The local SMP component may or may not be cloud-hosted, but in any case geo-location assurance must be possible.

The IoT-devices will communicate with the local SMP component. The local component will therefore know both the IP-address and the device identifier. The IP-address may be concealed if one uses Tor services [52], but the device identifier must be known to the local SMP component.

The local SMP component will communicate with the central SMP component, and it will receive protected security patches and software packages from the central SMP component. The local SMP component will aggregate and anonymize incident- and security anomaly reports from the IoT-devices before forwarding them to the central SMP component. The local SMP component may use temporary synthetic alias identifiers for a device, if there is a need for device references. This identifier must never be allowed to become an emergent identifier, and it must be fully de-correlated from the true device identifier. The de-correlation must be complete with respect to the full context given by the message exchange.

D. The SMP-Interfaces

1) The SMP_A-interface: This is a fully authenticated and security protected interface between the local SMP component and the central SMP component, as depicted in Figure 3.

2) The SMP_B-interface: This is a fully authenticated and security protected interface between the IoT-device and the local SMP component, as depicted in Figure 3.

3) Realization: The abstract SMP protocols should be agnostic about the underlying security transport protocol. Suffice to say, that strong security and credible privacy must be assured. The ENISA recommendations for cryptographic protocols, algorithms and key lengths provides good advice in this respect [53], [54]. ENISA is an EU agency, and the recommendation therefore carry some significance.

E. The SMP Services

1) Security Update – Local provisioning: One can have both push and pull mechanisms for security updates, but for IoT devices we do not generally recommend push solutions since it probably require more resources from the device. Push solutions may of course be appropriate for zero-day vulnerabilities, but scheduled pull solutions would likely suffice for patches that are less urgent and less critical. The scheduled pull frequency should reflect the security policy for the particular device class and according to usage, availability, etc. That is, IoT devices with sufficient processing power and no restrictions concerning power, may also use push services.

In either case, signed security updates will be received by the IoT device. All updates must be numbered, and the device will log the date/time and update number before implementing it. The local SMP shall not maintain logs about device status unless required to do so by the IoT device.

2) Security Update – Central provisioning: Whenever a security update patch is produced, the central SMP component will distribute the security update to the local SMP components. We recommend update frequencies to reflect the common vulnerability scoring system (CVSS) [55], although the CVSS system has been criticized for not properly reflect IoT devices [56]. The normal "serious vulnerability" score of 7 may therefore not properly reflect IoT concerns.

3) Incident- and Anomaly Reporting: Security incidents and anomalies are detected and reported by the TPM. This information is used by the SMP components to uncover large scale attacks and emerging attack trends. The ENISA publication [57] provides valuable guidance as to EU regulatory input on incident reporting.

4) Local Incident and Anomaly Reporting: This service will include software status, including patch levels etc. The device identifier is part of the security context, but should not be part of the incident/event report itself. A synthetic referential identifier may be provided by the local SMP.

It may, subject to authorization, be beneficial to store the incident history of the devices at the local SMP. This may allow the local SMP to detect if certain devices are specifically targeted. If so, one may speculate that the IoT device is an advanced persistent threat (APT) target. This in turn may trigger increased supervision and alarms.

5) Central Incident and Anomaly Reporting: The local SMP component will forward incident reports to the central SMP component. The local SMP component shall take steps to replace identifiers, if any, such that the central component never learns the true device identifier behind a reported incident. The local component *may* aggregate certain events and may delay reports to provide further de-correlations.

6) Device Attestation: The IoT device may request attestation services from the local SMP component. This service will need to be based on TPM functionality and permitting the local SMP component to survey the state of the IoT device. It may be part of a forensics service or a device recovery service.

7) Device Recovery: The IoT device may subscribe to recovery services at the local SMP component. As a minimum the local SMP should provide services to restore the device to a pristine condition, with all recent security update patches being implemented. The services may also account for security backup, with configuration data etc. being included in the restore procedure.

8) Device Backup: The local SMP component may provide a secure backup procedure, covering all or selected data elements. This procedure must permit to backup an entire device image and later restore the image. The device image must never leave the device in unprotected form. The device backup data should be encrypted and protected by the TPM, using unique device specific keys. Only the TPM should be able to restore the backup data.

9) Device Decommissioning: Life cycle considerations implies that one will need an explicit way of clearing all information on the target device. This will in effect clear all data and restore initial factory settings. This procedure must be resilient enough to withstand efforts from ordinary forensic tools to restore the information. The procedure may be triggered by a request via the local SMP component. The TPM should be responsible for carrying out the task.

V. Discussion

This paper describes an outline of an architectural component. Quite a few of the characteristics described below cannot be fully judged on the basis of the outline.

A. Lightweight, Minimality and Modularity

Our architectural component outline is both lightweight and relatively minimal. It is also modular, in the sense that it will build upon basic identifier structures and cryptographic capabilities, and delivers higher-level services.

B. Explicitness

This is related to requirements and conditions, including preconditions and postcondition. Essentially we have a "Mean what you say and say what you mean" situation. Use of formal methods may help verifying that captured requirements are adhered to, but these tools cannot in general help out with the "capturing" part. Explicitness must be enforced in any further development of the architectural component and in any implementation.

C. Scalability and Exposure

The division into a local-global split will facilitate scalability, as well as improving error resilience and thereby improving availability. Exposure is a necessary evil, but conscious design and appropriate use of cryptographic protocols can significantly reduce the unwanted effects of exposure.

D. Security and Privacy

The concrete security mechanisms is not specified in our proposal. Hence, more work is needed here for a concrete realization. However, there is no grand challenge here, only work that must be done precisely and consistently. Identity privacy and unlinkablity is mainly addressed through the local-global functional split. Data privacy is primarily by means of encryption. The requirements for the split is important, and schemes and measures that enforce the split must be encouraged. It would seem prudent to have this as a contractual requirement, and local regulatory requirements may also be an instrument in enforcing the functional split. Still, in the end, there must also be an economical incentive to manage and run both the local and the global infrastructure.

How credible is the privacy?

Clearly, it depends on the split between the local and global component being fully respected. There exists other solutions that would avoid this. These would be *privacy-preserving* and tend to be based on secure-multiparty computation and/or homomorphic cryptography. However, as argued in [58], strong irrevocable encryption may in the end provide less security and privacy. Governments are claimed to act a long the lines of "If we cannot break the crypto for a specific criminal on demand, we will preemptively break it for everybody." [58]. So, privacy must be balanced and possibly revoked, and this is achieved in our proposal.

E. Challenges: Availability, Identity, Privacy and Security

"Identity" is the only aspect that has not been addressed by our proposal. That is, we have identified this as a building block that our proposal depends upon.

F. Scope and Completeness

The scope is limited to a high-level model. Within the scope the proposal is reasonably complete, but there are many parts to be resolved, and the details have not yet been fully worked out.

G. Further Work

The model presented is an architectural component of a security architecture. Further work is needed to fit this component into a complete architecture. In particular, the concrete implementation of the security requirements should be aligned to the use in other areas. This is particularly relevant for identifiers and for basic services such as entity authentication, and integrity and confidentiality services.

Key agreement and key distribution must also be addressed and aligned to the overall security architecture. Preferably, one also wants to have a well-defined, effective and efficient security protocol to be the backbone of the services. As of today, one is often advised to use the Transport Layer Security (TLS) protocol [59] or the IPsec security protocols [60]. However, these are poor choices for IoT, and many version and implementations of TLS are also broken [61], [62].

That is, a dedicated, effective and efficient privacy-aware security protocol would probably be beneficial, provided that it would have wide-spread support. This archive this will be a difficult task, but following advise from [18], [53] and applying state of the art tools, it is also clearly doable on the technical level. Privacy, if it is to be credible, must be strongly aligned and be consistent over the full architecture to avoid leakage of sensitive data.

Smart metering or remote home monitoring would be examples of IoT systems that could benefit from the capabilities of the model. As such they would make good candidates for a pilot implementation to feature the model architecture.

VI. Summary and Conclusions

In this paper, we have identified the need for autonomous security update and incident/anomaly reporting for IoT-devices. In particular, we have addressed relatively capable IoT devices that ordinarily will be unattended devices, very much in line with a significant segment of the smart home devices.

This paper has provided a rough outline of a model in which IoT security update and incident handling is separated from normal user functionality, including user functionality setup and configuration. We believe that this is necessary since security management is becoming too complex to handle for end-users, and that the consequence of not managing security will be too severe. The current deploy-and-forget regime does not play out well for security functionality.

We have also provided a model in which there is a clear distinction between the centralized function and the local function. The main benefits of this arrangement is that one can more easily adhere to local regulatory requirements and one can provide identity- and location privacy solutions. This facilitates unlinkability, which is essential for credible privacy. It also enables scalability, which is ever so important for the IoT domain.

This paper represents an initial investigation of a new model for security update and incident handling for IoT devices. The model is not devised to be implemented as-is, but to serve as basis for discussions and further work.

References

[1] G. M. Køien, "Security Update and Incident Handling for IoT-devices; A Privacy-Aware Approach," in The Tenth International Conference on Emerging Security Information, Systems and Technologies (SECURWARE 2016), C. MerkleWestphall, H.-J. Hof, G. M. Køien, L. Králík, M. Hromada, and D. Lapkova, Eds. IARIA, 07 2016, pp. 309–315.

[2] A. Cavoukian, "Privacy by design; the 7 foundational principles," [retrieved: 06-2016] www.ipc.on.ca/images/Resources/7foundationalprinciples.pdf, 01 2011.

[3] D. Goodin, "Covert downloaders found preinstalled on dozens of low-cost Android phone models," Ars Technica, http://arstechnica.com/, 12 2016.

[4] S. Sicari, A. Rizzardi, L. A. Grieco, and A. Coen-Porisini, "Security, privacy and trust in internet of things: The road ahead," Computer Networks, vol. 76, 2015, pp. 146–164.

[5] M. Abomhara and G. M. Køien, "Security and privacy in the internet of things: Current status and open issues," in Privacy and Security in Mobile Systems (PRISMS), 2014 International Conference on. IEEE, 2014, pp. 1–8.

[6] ——, "Cyber security and the internet of things: Vulnerabilities, threats, intruders and attacks," Journal of Cyber Security, vol. 4, 2015, pp. 65–88.

[7] L. Patra and U. P. Rao, "Internet of thingsarchitecture, applications, security and other major challenges," in Computing for Sustainable Global Development (INDIACom), 2016 3rd International Conference on. IEEE, 2016, pp. 1201–1206.

[8] R. Roman, J. Zhou, and J. Lopez, "On the features and challenges of security and privacy in distributed internet of things," Computer Networks, vol. 57, no. 10, 2013, pp. 2266–2279.

[9] Z.-K. Zhang, M. C. Y. Cho, C.-W. Wang, C.-W. Hsu, C.-K. Chen, and S. Shieh, "Iot security: ongoing challenges and research opportunities," in Service-Oriented Computing and Applications (SOCA), 2014 IEEE 7th International Conference on. IEEE, 2014, pp. 230–234.

[10] M. M. Hossain, M. Fotouhi, and R. Hasan, "Towards an analysis of security issues, challenges, and open problems in the internet of things," in Services (SERVICES), 2015 IEEE World Congress on. IEEE, 2015, pp. 21–28.

[11] J. Granjal, E. Monteiro, and J. S. Silva, "Security for the internet of things: a survey of existing protocols and open research issues," IEEE Communications Surveys & Tutorials, vol. 17, no. 3, 2015, pp. 1294–1312.

[12] Q. Jing, A. V. Vasilakos, J. Wan, J. Lu, and D. Qiu, "Security of the internet of things: Perspectives and challenges," Wireless Networks, vol. 20, no. 8, 2014, pp. 2481–2501.

[13] G. M. Køien, "Reflections on trust in devices: an informal survey of human trust in an internet-of-things context," Wireless Personal Communications, vol. 61, no. 3, 2011, pp. 495–510.

[14] 3GPP TSG SA3, "3GPP System Architecture Evolution (SAE); Security architecture (Release 13)," 3GPP, TS 33.401, 03 2016.

[15] T. Kause and M. Peylo, "Internet X.509 Public Key Infrastructure – HTTP Transfer for the Certificate Management Protocol (CMP)," IETF, RFC 6712, 09 2012.

[16] 3GPP TSG SA3, "Security aspects of Machine-Type Communications (MTC) and other mobile data applications communications enhancements (Release 13)," 3GPP, TS 33.187, 01 2016.

[17] GSM Association, "IoT Security Guidelines Overview Document; CLP.11, Ver.1," [retrieved: 06-2016] www.gsma.com/connectedliving/wp-content/uploads/2016/02/CLP.11-v1.1.pdf, 02 2016.

[18] M. Abadi and R. Needham, "Prudent engineering practice for cryptographic protocols," IEEE Transactions on Software Engineering, vol. 22, no. 1, 1996, pp. 6–15.

[19] Cyber Physical Systems Public Working Group, "Framework for Cyber-Physical Systems," NIST, USA, Framework Release 1.0, 05 2016.

[20] IES-City consortium, "IoT-Enabled Smart City Framework," 02 2016.

[21] ITU-R, "IMT Vision - Framework and overall objectives of the future development of IMT for 2020 and beyond," ITU, Geneva, Switzerland, Recommendation M.2083-0, 09 2015.

[22] B. Schneier, "Click Here to Kill Everyone; With the Internet of Things, were building a world-size robot. How are we going to control it?" New York Magazine, 01 2017.

[23] B. Stanton, M. F. Theofanos, S. S. Prettyman, and S. Furman, "Security fatigue," IT Professional, vol. 18, no. 5, 2016, pp. 26–32.

[24] N. Postman, Amusing ourselves to death: Public discourse in the age of television, 1985.

[25] E. Sedenberg and A. L. Hoffmann, "Recovering the history of informed consent for data science and internet industry research ethics," 2016.

[26] T. Ploug and S. Holm, "Informed consent and routinisation," Journal of Medical Ethics, vol. 39, no. 4, 2013, pp. 214–218.

[27] L. Marinos, A. Belmonte, and E. Rekleitis, "Enisa threat landscape 2015," ENISA, Report ETL-2015, 1 2016.

[28] US-CERT, "Alert (TA16-288A): Heightened DDoS Threat Posed by Mirai and Other Botnets," https://www.us-cert.gov/ncas/alerts/TA16-288A, 10 2016, [retrieved 12-2016].

[29] C. Williams, "Today the web was broken by countless hacked devices your 60-second summary," The Register, http://www.theregister.co.uk/, 10 2016.

[30] B. Krebs, "DDoS on Dyn Impacts Twitter, Spotify, Reddit," KrebsOnSecurity, https://krebsonsecurity.com/, 10 2016.

[31] L. Constantin, "Hackers found 47 new vulnerabilities in 23 IoT devices at DEF CON," CSO Online, http://www.csoonline.com/, 09 2016.

[32] F. Bret-Mounet, "All Your Solar Panels are belong to Me," DEF CON, https://media.defcon.org/, 08 2016.

[33] Nordic Semiconductor ASA, "nRF51822 Product Specification," Access: www.nordicsemi.com/eng/nordic/download_resource/20339/13/85365517, 2016.

[34] ARM Ltd., "Cortex-M4 Processor," [retrieved: 06-2016] www.arm.com/products/processors/cortex-m/cortex-m4-processor.php, 2016.

[35] G. M. Køien, "Reflections on evolving large-scale security architectures," International Journal on Advances in Security Volume 8, Number 1 & 2, 2015, 2015, pp. 60–78.

[36] A. S. Tanenbaum, "Lessons learned from 30 years of minix," Communications of the ACM, vol. 59, no. 3, 2016, pp. 70–78.

[37] S. Spiekermann, "The challenges of privacy by design," Communications of the ACM, vol. 55, no. 7, 2012, pp. 38–40.

[38] D. Le Métayer, "Privacy by design: a formal framework for the analysis of architectural choices," in Proceedings of the third ACM conference on Data and application security and privacy. ACM, 2013, pp. 95–104.

[39] Internet Security Research Group (ISRG), "Let's encrypt," Accessed March 2017: https://Letsencrypt.org, 03 2017.

[40] M. Stevens, E. Burzstein, P. Karpman, A. Albertini, and Y. Markov, "The first collision for full sha-1," Shattered IO, 02 2017.

[41] L. Chen et al., "Report on post-quantum cryptography," National Institute of Standards and Technology Internal Report, vol. 8105, 2016.

[42] Symantex, "Embedded security: Critical system protection," Access: www.symantec.com/content/en/us/enterprise/fact_sheets/b-sescsp-ds-21345379.pdf, 11 2015.

[43] ISO/IEC, "ISO/IEC 11889-1:2015," ISO, Geneva, Switzerland, Standard 11889-1:2015, 08 2015.

[44] ARM Connected Community., "Whitepaper - ARMv8-M Architecture Technical Overview," [retrieved: 06-2016] https://community.arm.com/docs/DOC-10896, 2015.

[45] F. Armknecht, A.-R. Sadeghi, S. Schulz, and C. Wachsmann, "A security framework for the analysis and design of software attestation," in Proceedings of the 2013 ACM SIGSAC Conference on Computer Communications Security, ser. CCS '13. New York, NY, USA: ACM, 2013, pp. 1–12.

[46] Nordic Semiconductors, "nrfutil User Guide v1.0," 09 2016.

[47] K. MacKay, "micro-ecc: ECDH and ECDSA for 8-bit, 32-bit, and 64-bit processors," 07 2016.

[48] G. M. Køien and V. A. Oleshchuk, Aspects of Personal Privacy in Communications-Problems, Technology and Solutions. River Publishers, 2013.

[49] G. M. Køien, "A privacy enhanced device access protocol for an iot context," Security and Communication Networks, vol. 9, no. 5, 03 2016, pp. 440–450.

[50] ——, "Privacy enhanced cellular access security," in Proceedings of the 4th ACM Workshop on Wireless Security, ser. WiSe '05. New York, NY, USA: ACM, 2005, pp. 57–66.

[51] ARM Ltd, "CMSIS MCU Software Standard 4.5," 2016.

[52] "The Tor Project," [retrieved: 06-2016] www.torproject.org, 2016.

[53] N. P. Smart, V. Rijmen, M. Stam, B. Warinschi, and G. Watson, "Study on cryptographic protocols," ENISA, Report TP-06-14-085-EN-N, 11 2014.

[54] N. P. Smart et al., "Algorithms, key size and parameters report 2014," ENISA, Report TP-05-14-084-EN-N, 11 2014.

[55] First, "Common vulnerability scoring system, v3," [retrieved: 06-2016] https://www.first.org/cvss, 06 2015.

[56] D. J. Klinedinst, "CVSS and the Internet of Things," SEI Insights, [retrieved: 06-2016] insights.sei.cmu.edu/cert/, 09 2015.

[57] M. Dekker and C. Karsberg, "Technical guidance on the incident reporting in article 13a (ver.2.1)," ENISA, Report, 10 2014.

[58] P.-H. Kamp, "More encryption means less privacy," Commuications of the ACM, vol. 59, no. 4, 04 2016, pp. 40–42.

[59] T. Dierks and E. Rescorla, "The Transport Layer Security (TLS) Protocol; Version 1.2," IETF, RFC 5246, 08 2008.

[60] S. Kent and K. Seo, "Security Architecture for the Internet Protocol," IETF, RFC 4301, 12 2005.

[61] H. Krawczyk, K. G. Paterson, and H. Wee, "On the security of the tls protocol: A systematic analysis," in Advances in Cryptology–CRYPTO 2013. Springer, 2013, pp. 429–448.

[62] C. Hlauschek, M. Gruber, F. Fankhauser, and C. Schanes, "Prying open pandora's box: Kci attacks against tls," in 9th USENIX Workshop on Offensive Technologies (WOOT 15), 2015, pp. 1–15.

Visualization and Prioritization of Privacy Risks in Software Systems

George O. M. Yee
Computer Research Lab, Aptusinnova Inc., Ottawa, Canada
Dept. of Systems and Computer Engineering, Carleton University, Ottawa, Canada
email: george@aptusinnova.com, gmyee@sce.carleton.ca

Abstract—**Software systems are ubiquitous in almost every aspect of our lives, as can be seen in social media, online banking and shopping, as well as electronic health monitoring. This widespread involvement of software in our lives has led to the need to protect privacy, as the use of the software often requires us to input our personal information. However, before privacy can be protected, it is necessary to understand the risks to privacy that can be found in the software system. In addition, it is important to understand how the risks can be prioritized since budgetary constraints usually mean that not all risks will be mitigated. Indeed, understanding the risks and prioritizing them is key to protecting privacy throughout the system's range of application. This paper presents straightforward methods for effectively visualizing, identifying, and prioritizing privacy risks in software systems, and illustrates the methods with examples.**

Keywords-software; system; privacy; risks; visualization; prioritization.

I. INTRODUCTION

The rapid growth of the Internet has been accompanied by numerous software systems targeting consumers. Software systems are available for banking, shopping, learning, healthcare, and Government Online. However, most of these systems require a consumer's personal information in one form or another, leading to concerns over privacy. For these systems to be successful, privacy must be protected.

This work extends Yee [1] by expanding the sections on privacy and risk visualization. Further, a new section on risk prioritization has been added.

Various approaches have been used to protect personal information, including data anonymization [2] and pseudonym technology [3]. Other approaches for privacy protection include treating privacy protection as an access problem and then bringing the tools of access control to bear for privacy control [4]. However, these approaches presume to know where and what protection is needed. They presume that some sort of analysis has been done that answers the question of "where" and "what" with respect to privacy risks. Without such answers, the effectiveness of the protection comes into question. The total risks to data depends both on the number of vulnerable locations of the data (where) and on the severity of each vulnerability (what). For example, protection against house break-ins is ineffective if the owner only secures the front door without securing other vulnerable spots such as windows. An effective break-in risk analysis would have identified the windows as additional locations having break-in risks (where and what) and would have led to the windows also being secured. The result is a house that is better protected against break-ins. In the same way, privacy risk identification considering "where" and "what" is essential to effective privacy protection - this work proposes a visual method for such identification.

The objectives of this paper are to a) propose an effective method for visualizing privacy risks in software systems to identify where and what risks are present, b) propose a straightforward method for prioritizing the risks for mitigation, since not all risks can be mitigated due to financial constraints, and c) illustrate the method using examples.

In the literature, there are significant works on security threat analysis but very little work on privacy risk identification using visualization. In fact, the only works that are directly related to privacy risk identification appear to be those on "privacy impact assessment (PIA)", originating from government policy [5]. PIA is meant to evaluate the impact to privacy of new government programs, services, and initiatives. PIA can also be applied to existing government services undergoing transformation or re-design. However, PIA is a long manual process consisting mainly of self-administered questionnaires. It is not focused on software systems nor does it employ visual techniques as proposed in this work.

This paper is organized as follows. Section II defines privacy, privacy preferences, privacy risks, and what they mean for software systems. Section III presents the proposed method for privacy risk visualization, together with examples. Section IV presents the method for prioritizing privacy risks. Section V examines the strengths and weaknesses of the approach, including potential improvements. Section VI discusses related work. Section VII presents conclusions and future work.

II. PRIVACY

As defined by Goldberg et al. in 1997 [6], privacy refers to the ability of individuals to *control* the collection, retention, and distribution of information about themselves. This leads to the following definition of privacy for this work.

DEFINITION 1: *Privacy* refers to the ability of individuals to *control* the collection, purpose, retention, and distribution of information about themselves.

Definition 1 is the same as given by Goldberg et al. except that it also includes "purpose". To see that "purpose" is needed, consider, for example, that one may agree to give out one's email address for the purpose of friends to send email but not for the purpose of spammers to send spam. This definition also suggests that "personal information", "private information" or "private data" is any information that can be linked to a person; otherwise, the information would not be "about" the person. Thus, another term for private information is "personally identifiable information (PII)". These terms are used interchangeably in this paper. In addition, controlling the "collection" of information implies controlling *who* collects *what* information. Controlling the "retention" of information is really about controlling the *retention time* of information, i.e. how long the information can be retained before being destroyed. Controlling the "distribution" of information is controlling to which other parties the information can be *disclosed-to*. These considerations motivate the following definitions.

DEFINITION 2: A user's *privacy preference* expresses the user's desired control over a) *PII* - what the item of personal information is, b) *collector* - who can collect it, c) *purpose* - the purpose for collecting it, d) *retention time* - the amount of time the information is kept, and e) *disclosed-to* - which other parties the information can be disclosed-to.

DEFINITION 3: A *privacy risk* is the potential occurrence of any action or circumstance that will result in a violation of any of the components PII, collector, purpose, retention time, and disclosed-to in a user's privacy preference.

For example, Alice uses an online pharmacy and has the following privacy preference:

PII: name, address, telephone number
Collector: A-Z Drugs
Purpose: identification
Retention Time: 2 years
Disclosed-To: none

This preference states that Alice allows A-Z Drugs to collect her name, address, and telephone number, and that A-Z Drugs must: use the information only to identify her, not keep the information for more than 2 years, and not disclose the information to any other party.

This work considers only privacy risks as defined in Definition 3. The privacy preference components PII, collector, purpose, retention time, and disclosed-to have, in fact, been standardized by the Canadian Standards Association in its Model Code for the Protection of Personal Information [7]. The Model Code is based on ten privacy principles as given in Table I. As can be seen in Table I, PII is reflected in principle 3 (which PII requires consent), collector is seen in principle 1 (collector's accountability) and principle 5 (disclosure to other collectors), purpose is contained in principles 2 and 4, and finally, retention time and disclosed-to are seen in principle 5. Further, these privacy preference components have been enacted by privacy legislation as fully describing the privacy rights of individuals in many countries, including Canada, the United States, the European Union, and Australia [8]. Thus, this work is consistent with privacy legislation, and treating only privacy risks defined by Definition 3 does not overly reduce the generality of this work.

TABLE I. Ten Privacy Principles Forming Basis of Model Code

Principle	Description
1. Accountability	An organization is responsible for personal information under its control and shall designate an individual or individuals accountable for the organization's compliance with the privacy principles.
2. Identifying Purposes	The purposes for which personal information is collected shall be identified by the organization at or before the time the information is collected.
3. Consent	The knowledge and consent of the individual are required for the collection, use or disclosure of personal information, except when inappropriate.
4. Limiting Collection	The collection of personal information shall be limited to that which is necessary for the purposes identified by the organization. Information shall be collected by fair and lawful means.
5. Limiting Use, Disclosure, and Retention	Personal information shall not be used or disclosed for purposes other than those for which it was collected, except with the consent of the individual or as required by the law. In addition, personal information shall be retained only as long as necessary for fulfillment of those purposes.
6. Accuracy	Personal information shall be as accurate, complete, and up-to-date as is necessary for the purposes for which it is to be used.
7. Safeguards	Security safeguards appropriate to the sensitivity of the information shall be used to protect personal information.
8. Openness	An organization shall make readily available to individuals specific information about its policies and practices relating to the management of personal information.
9. Individual Access	Upon request, an individual shall be informed of the existence, use and disclosure of his or her personal information and shall be given access to that information. An individual shall be able to challenge the accuracy and completeness of the information and have it amended as appropriate.
10. Challenging Compliance	An individual shall be able to address a challenge concerning compliance with the above principles to the designated individual or individuals accountable for the organization's compliance.

The following works show the importance of privacy in the online world: Tene [9], Kambourakis [10], Ruiz-Martinez [11], and Ren and Wu [12]. In addition, Pfitzmann and Hansen [13] present some terminology for talking about privacy, e.g., "anonymity", "unlinkability".

III. METHOD FOR PRIVACY RISK VISUALIZATION

The proposed method for privacy risk visualization assumes the following common characteristics of a software system:

a) The software system requires the user's personal information in order to carry out its function. For example, an online bookseller requires the user's address for shipping purposes.
b) The software system may transmit the information (e.g., move it from one group to another within the software system's organization), store the information (e.g., store the information in a data base), and make use of the information to carry out its function (e.g., print out shipping labels with the user's address).

The method is based on the notion that the *location* of personal information gives rise to privacy risks. The importance of location is reflected in physical security, where sensitive paper documents are kept in a locked safe (a location) to protect privacy, rather than being left on a desk (a location). For a software system, storing the user's personal information in an encrypted database with secure access controls is the equivalent of storing it in a safe, with corresponding reduced privacy risks. The method employs notation, as given in Table II.

TABLE II. Notation for Visualizing Privacy Risks

Element	Description
Use Circle	Identifies where PII is used. Labeled with a letter together with a description of the use in a legend.
Data Store	Identifies where PII is stored. Labeled with a letter together with a description of the data store in a legend.
Same Physical Platform	Identifies use circles and data stores that execute on the same computing platform.
PII Data Flo w	Identifies the movement of PII from one location to another. Labeled with a number together with a description of the data in a legend.
Non-PII Data Flow	Identifies the movement of non-PII from one location to another. Labeled with a number together with a description of the data in a legend.
Legend	Descriptions corresponding to the letters or numbers with which the above notational elements were labeled.

The method, then, consists of i) determining all the possible locations in the software system where the user's personal information could reside, and ii) visualizing at each of these locations the possible ways in which the user's privacy preferences could be violated. The complete method is as follows:

A. Method for Privacy Risk Visualization

1. Draw the paths of all personal information flows within the software system, based on characteristic b) above, namely, that personal information can be transmitted, stored, and used. Use a solid arrow to represent the transmission of personal information items that are described by privacy preferences. Label the arrow with numbers, where each arrow number corresponds to a description of a personal data item in a legend. Use a square to represent the storage of personal information. Use a circle to denote the use of the information. Use a dashed rectangle to enclose circles or squares into physically distinct units. For example, two circles representing two uses would be enclosed by a dashed square if both uses run on the same computing platform. Physically separate units allow the identification of risks for any data flow between them. Circles or squares not enclosed by a dashed rectangle are understood to be already physically separate units. Label the squares and circles with letters. Each such label corresponds to a description of the type of storage or the type of use as indicated in the legend.
2. Use dashed arrows, numbered in the same way as the solid arrows in Step 1, to add to the drawing all non-personal information flows, if any, that are involved with the transmission, storage and use of the personal information. Non-personal information is information that is not personal or not private, i.e., information that cannot identify any particular individual, e.g., the price of something. The resulting drawing is called a Personal Information Map (PIM). Figure 1 illustrates steps 1 and 2 for the software system of an online seller of merchandise, e.g., Amazon.com, that requires the user's name, address, merchandise selection, and credit card number. These are considered as three personal information items where name and address together are considered as one item. Figure 1 also shows three non-personal information flows (4, 5, 6). The dashed rectangle enclosing A, B, and C indicates that A, B, and C all run on the same physical computing platform.
3. Inspect the PIM resulting from step 2, and for each location (flow arrow, storage square, and use circle) and each personal information item, visualize the possible ways in which a privacy preference may be violated in terms of violations of any of *PII*, *collector*, *purpose*, *retention time*, and *disclose-to* (see Section II). This may be achieved by asking risk questions for each component, as proposed in Table III, and drawing conclusions based on security and systems knowledge and experience. The risk questions are "how" questions, based on the idea that a risk arises where there is some way (i.e. how) for a violation to occur. This step actually calls for visualization since one is tasked with exploring the possible risks in conjunction with a visual notation, the PIM. Record the results in a Privacy Risks Table containing two columns: the left column for records of the form "(PII_1, PII_2, …/ locations)" and the right column containing the corresponding privacy risks. The Privacy Risks Table is the goal of the method. Table IV illustrates this step for the online seller of Fig. 1.

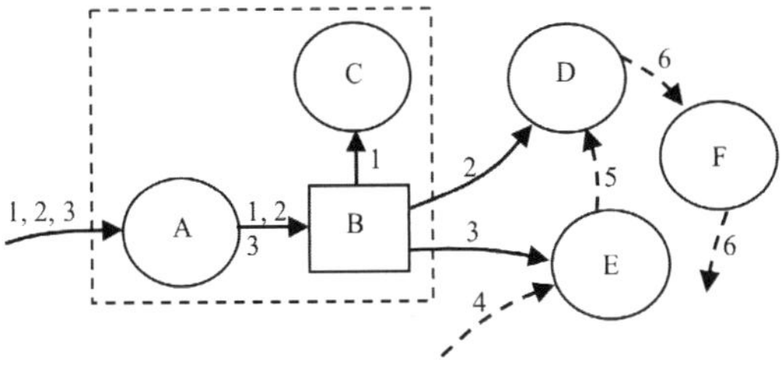

Legend:
A: receive and store data
B: database
C: print shipping label
D: pack item for shipping
E: charge credit card
F: send shipping status to buyer

1: name and address
2: item selected
3: credit card number
4: company account number
5: payment status
6: shipping status

Figure 1. PIM for an online seller of merchandise.

TABLE III. Risk Questions

Component	Risk Questions
PII	How can the user be asked for other PII, either intentionally or inadvertently?
collector	How can the PII be received by an unintended collector, either in addition to or in place of the intended collector?
purpose	How can the PII be used for other purposes?
retention time	How can the PII retention time be violated?
disclose-to	How can the PII be disclosed either intentionally or inadvertently to an unintended recipient?

TABLE IV. Partial Privacy Risks Table Corresponding to Fig. 1

(PIIs / locations)	Privacy Risks
(1, 2, 3 / path into A); (2 / path into D); (3 / path into E)	Man-in-the-middle attack violates *collector, purpose, retention time* and *disclose-to*.
(1, 2, 3 / A)	User could be asked for personal information that violates *PII*, i.e. asked for personal information other than as specified in the user's privacy preferences.
(1, 2, 3 / A); (1 / C); (2 / D); (3 / E)	Trojan horse, hacker attack use circles violating *collector, purpose, retention time*, and *disclose-to*.
(1, 2, 3 / B)	SQL attack on B violates *collector, purpose, retention time*, and *disclose-to*.
(1, 2, 3 / B)	*PII* in B could be kept past its *retention time*.

It is important to note that the PIM resulting from Step 2 is not a program logic flow diagram and one should not try to interpret it as such. It shows *what* PII is required, *where* PII goes, *where* PII is stored, and *where* PII is used, corresponding to the notion that the location of personal information is key to understanding privacy risks, as mentioned above.

Privacy risks and security risks are conceptually different. However, a privacy risk may be due to a security risk, and vice versa. For example, the privacy risk associated with a man-in-the-middle attack in Table IV is really due to the security risk of a man-in-the-middle attack. Again in Table IV, a higher security risk of theft can be attributed to the privacy risk of PII being kept past its retention time, since the longer the PII is retained, the greater the security risk of it being stolen.

Adding non-personal information flows in Step 2 is important to help identify potential unintended leakages of PII. For example, consider a "produce report" use circle that "anonymizes" (any obvious links to the information owner removed) PII and combines the result with non-personal information to produce a report for public distribution. The fact that both PII and non-PII flow into "produce report" could lead to identifying a personal information leakage risk.

It is recommended that this method be applied by a privacy risks identification team, consisting of no more than three or four people, selected for their technical knowledge of the software system and the work procedures and processes of the software system's organization. Good candidates for the team include the software system's design manager, test manager, and other line managers with the required knowledge. The team should be led by a privacy and security analyst, who must also be knowledgeable about the software system, and who must have the support of upper management to carry out the privacy risks identification. A definite advantage of the team approach would accrue to step 3, where the visualization would be more thorough by virtue of more people being involved.

B. *First Application Example*

Consider PatientBilling, a patient billing system running in a doctor's office. PatientBilling makes use of two business software systems: an accounting system PatientAccounting and an online payment system PatientPay.

Table V shows the user's personal information required by each system. The user provides her private information to PatientBilling which then discloses this information to PatientAccounting and PatientPay.

TABLE V. Personal Information Required

Software System	Patient Personal Information Required
PatientBilling	name and address, health complaint (patient name, health problem, health problem resolution), method of payment details (name, credit card number, credit card expiry date, health insurance number, health insurance expiry date)
PatientAccounting	name and address, health complaint (as above)
PatientPay	method of payment details (as above)

The proposed method for privacy risks visualization is carried out as follows:

Steps 1 and 2: Draw the PIM for each software system (see Fig. 2**).** As shown in Figure 2, the following uses of personal information are extra to the core function of each system. First, both PatientAccounting (M) and PatientPay

(L) send activity reports back to PatientBilling that contain personal information. These reports contain selections and re-arrangements of personal data (15, 16). Second, PatientBilling produces a publically accessible report for the medical association, giving statistics on the patients seen. To produce this report, PatientBilling (N) selects, re-arranges, and anonymizes personal data (13). Third, PatientAccounting allows its employees to partially work from home (G). Finally, the patient's method of payment details are used without being stored in databases.

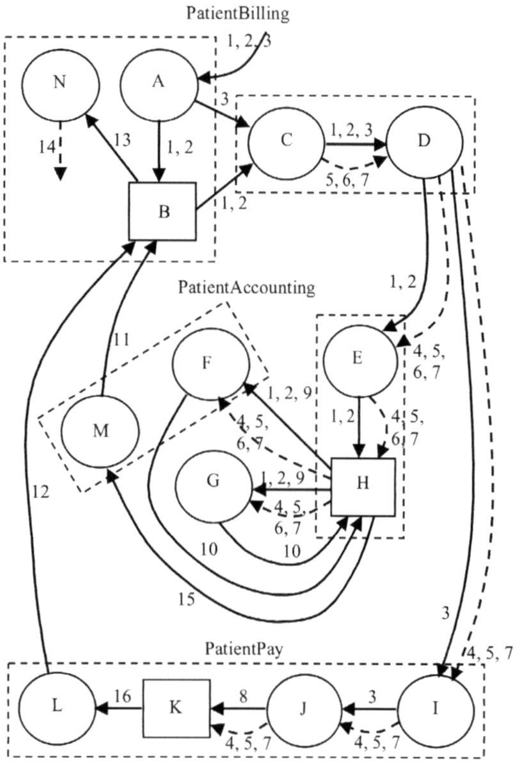

Legend:
A: receive and store data
B: database
C: process billing
D: disclose data
1: name and address
2: health complaint
3: method of payment details
4: doctor id
5: billing id
6: time spent with patient
7: billing amount
8: doctor account update
9: current ledger record
10: updated ledger record
11: accounting report
12: payment report
13: patients seen data
E: receive and store data
F: update ledgers at work
G: update ledgers at home
H: database
I: receive and forward data
J: charge credit card or insurance; update doctor's account
K: database
L: compose payment report
M: compose accounting report
N: compose report for medical association
14: anonymized report for medical association
15: accounting data
16: payment data

Figure 2. PIM for PatientBilling, PatientAccounting, and PatientPay.

Step 3: Visualize privacy risks at private information locations. Table VI gives a partial Privacy Risk Table for locations in Fig. 2 that have interesting or serious privacy risks. The theft of personal information means that the information is under the control of an unintended party. Clearly, this can violate the corresponding privacy preference or preferences in terms of violating *collector*, *purpose*, *retention time*, and *disclose-to*. The risk of personal information theft arises so often that it is convenient to call it *CPRD-risk*, from the first letters of collector, purpose, retention time, and disclose-to.

TABLE VI. Partial Privacy Risks Table Corresponding to Fig. 2

(PIIs / locations)	Privacy Risks
(1, 2, 3 / path into A); (1, 2 / path between B and C, path between D and E); (3 / path between A and C, path between D and I); (12 / path between L and B); (11 / path between M and B)	Man-in-the-middle attacks lead to CPRD-risk.
(1, 2, 3 / A)	The patient could be asked for personal information that violates PII (i.e. asked for PII other than 1, 2, 3).
(1, 2, 3 / A, C, D); (13 / N); (1, 2 / E); (1, 2, 9 / F, G); (15 / M); (3 / J); (16 / L)	Trojan horse, or hacker attacks on the personal information use circles lead to CPRD-risk.
(1, 2, 11, 12 / B); (1, 2, 10 / H); (8 / K)	Potential SQL attacks on B, H, and K lead to CPRD-risk.
(13 / N)	A bad anonymization algorithm can expose personal information, leading to CPRD-risk.
(1, 2, 9 / G)	An insecure home environment, e.g., people looking over the shoulder or printed personal information lying on a desk in the clear, can also lead to CPRD-risk.
(1, 2, 9 / G)	If an employee works from home on a laptop and carries the laptop between home and work, possible theft or loss of the laptop can also lead to CPRD-risk for any of 1, 2, or 9 that might be temporarily stored in the laptop.
(1, 2, 9 / G)	If an employee works from home on a home PC and stores 1, 2, 9 on a flash memory stick, carrying the memory stick between home and work, possible theft or loss of the memory stick can also lead to CPRD-risk.

To illustrate this step, the risks in the first 3 rows of Table VI were obtained as follows. For the first row, it was noticed that the personal information flows through transmission paths connecting physically distinct units. The risk questions of Table III were then considered, leading to possible man-in-the-middle attacks that give rise to CPRD-risk. For the second row, violations of PII are always possible unless strict controls are in place against it. For the third row, it was observed that the associated personal data are input to information use processes (e.g., A, C, D). The risk questions of Table III were again considered, leading to possible Trojan horse or hacker attacks that again give rise to CPRD-risk. For the fourth row, it was noticed that personal data are stored in databases. Once again the risk questions were considered, leading to possible SQL attacks against the databases, giving rise to CPRD-risk. In each of these four cases, knowledge of the system (personal data locations) and knowledge of information security (possible attacks) were needed to identify the risks. The remaining risks in Table VI were derived in a similar fashion.

B. *Second Application Example*

Consider an airline reservation system called AccuReserve offered by a Canadian airline with headquarters in Toronto, Canada. AccuReserve is a globally distributed system with modules in Canada, the United States, and Germany (serving the European Union).

Table VII shows the user's personal information required by the country specific modules of AccuReserve. The user provides her private information to each of these modules when she makes a travel reservation.

TABLE VII. Personal Information Required

Software Module	Patient Personal Information Required
Canada	Identification details (name, address, telephone number, nationality, passport number); payment details (credit card name, credit card number, credit card expiry date, credit card verification code)
United States	Same as above
Germany	Same as above

The proposed method for privacy risks visualization is carried out as follows:

Steps 1 and 2: The PIM for AccuReserve is shown in Fig. 3, and was obtained by drawing the PIM for each module (Main, Mod-US, and Mod-EU) and then linking the modules together with communication links. Main runs in Canada, Mod-US in the United States, and Mod-EU in Germany.

Step 3: Table VIII gives a partial Data Risk Table for locations in Fig. 3 that have PII risks. The privacy risks in Table VIII were obtained as follows. For the first and second rows, it was noticed that the personal information flows through transmission paths connecting physically distinct units. The risk questions of Table III were then considered, leading to possible man-in-the-middle attacks that give rise to CPRD-risk. Notice that "(1, 2, 3 / path between A and D)" is excluded because A and D both run on the same platform (so the path is not very accessible to attack). For the third row, violations of PII are always possible unless strict controls are in place against it. For the fourth row, it was observed that private data are input to information use processes A, I, L, C, K, O. The risk questions of Table III were again considered, leading to

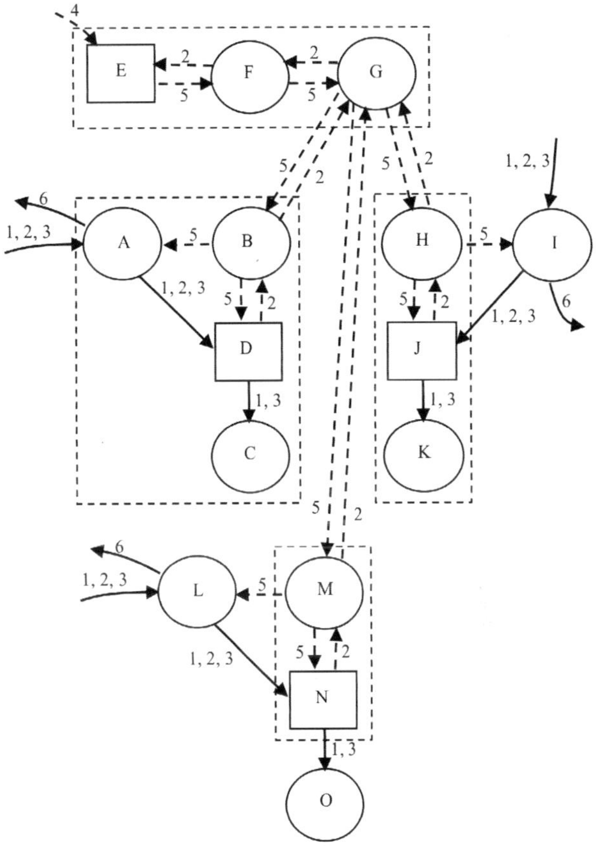

Legend:

A, I, L: receive and store data	1: identification details (PII)
B, H, M: communicate with G	2: flight details requested (non-PII, non-SD)
C, K, O: charge credit card	3: payment details (PII)
E: flights database (SD)	4: flight availability updates (SD)
D, J, N: customer databases	5: flight details assigned (non-PII, non-SD)
F: flight availability manager	6: travel itinerary (PII)
G: communicate with countries	

Figure 3. PIM for AccuReserve; Main consists of E, F, G, A, B, D, and C; Mod-US consists of L, M, N, and O; Mod-EU consists of H, I, J, and K.

possible Trojan horse or hacker attacks that again give rise to CPRD-risk. For the fifth row, it was noticed that private data are stored in databases. Once again the risk questions were considered, leading to possible SQL attacks against the databases, giving rise to CPRD-risk. For the sixth row, it was noticed that private information stored in databases could be subject to insider attacks. For the seventh row, it was observed that the private data stored in the databases could be kept past their retention times. It should be noted that the links between G and B, G and M, and G and H are also vulnerable to man-in-the-middle attacks, but these attacks would not be privacy attacks, since these links are not used for private information.

IV. METHOD FOR PRIVACY RISK PRIORITIZATION

In this work, the concept behind privacy risk prioritization is that once a set of n privacy risks have been identified, we want to prioritize or select a subset k, $k < n$, of those risks for mitigation, given that we do not have sufficient financial resources to mitigate all n of the risks.

NOTATION: Let R be the set of identified privacy risks. Let P, $P \subset R$, be a subset of risks to be mitigated. Let ρ be the prioritization mapping such that $\rho: R \longrightarrow P$.

Our purpose in this section is to define the prioritization mapping ρ. In other words, we seek a method for selecting risks for mitigation (determining the set P). Intuitively, one would want to mitigate risks that are highly probable to be realized, and that once realized, would result in very costly damages. Due to financial budgetary constraints, we feel that we can ignore the risks that tend not to be realized and even if realized would cause very little damage. Determining which risks to mitigate may be assisted though weighting the risks according to certain criteria.

TABLE VIII. Partial Data Risks Table Corresponding to Fig. 3

(PIIs / locations)	Privacy Risks
(1, 2, 3 / path into A); (1, 2, 3 / path into I); (1, 2, 3 / path into L); (6 / path from A); (6 / path from I); (6 / path from L)	Man-in-the-middle attacks lead to CPRD-risk.
(1, 2, 3 / path between I and J); (1, 2, 3 / path between L and N); (1, 3 / path between N and O)	Man-in-the-middle attacks lead to CPRD-risk.
(1, 2, 3 / path into A); (1, 2, 3 / path into I); (1, 2, 3 / path into L)	The user could be asked for personal information that violates PII (i.e. asked for PII other than 1, 2, 3).
(1, 2, 3 / A, I, L); (1, 3 / C, K, O)	Trojan horse, or hacker attacks on the personal information use circles lead to CPRD-risk.
(1, 2, 3 / D, J, N)	Potential SQL attacks on D, J, and N lead to CPRD-risk.
(1, 2, 3 / D, J, N)	Potential insider attack steals private information from D, J, and N resulting in CPRD-risk.
(1, 2, 3 / D, J, N)	Private information in D, J, and N could be kept past the retention time.

Salter et al. [14] proposed a method for applying weights to various forms of attacks in order to determine if a particular attack would be probable. They focused on three aspects of an attack, namely "risk", "access", and "cost", where "risk" is risk to the safety of the attacker, "access" is the ease with which the attacker can access the system under attack, and "cost" is the monetary cost to the attacker to mount the attack. To avoid confusion between "risk" to the safety of the attacker and "risk" to privacy, we use "safety" for "risk" to the safety of the attacker. The weight values are simply "L", "M", and "H" for Low, Medium, and High, respectively. These attack aspects can be represented using a 3-tuple, as [safety, access, cost] and so [H, M, L] would be an instance of the weights. For example, consider a physical attack such as a mugging incident in a park. In this case, the risk to the safety of the attacker would be high (the person being mugged could be an undercover police officer), the attacker's ease of access would be high (people stroll through the park all the time), and the attacker's cost would be low (not much needed to mount the attack). Thus, this attack has the weights [H, H, L].

In this work, we add a fourth aspect of an attack, namely the resulting damages from the attack. Thus, we use the 4-tuple [safety, access, cost, damages] with the same weight values L, M, and H. Hence, we would definitely want to defend against privacy risks leading to attacks with weights [L, H, L, H]. We feel that we can ignore privacy risks having attacks with weights [H, L, H, L]. In reality, there is a spectrum of weights between these two boundaries, where a decision to defend or ignore may not be clear, and ultimately a judgment, perhaps based on other factors, may be needed. For example, it is not clear whether or not a privacy risk with associated weights [L, L, H, H] should be ignored, and one would decide to defend if one believes that no matter how improbable the attack, the resulting damages must never be allowed to occur.

The uncertainty of deciding which risks to mitigate using the weights may be remedied through the use of a Prioritization Policy, which would be developed by the privacy and security analyst (see Section IIIA). This policy would identify the 4-tuples of weights whose associated risks are to be prioritized or mitigated. For example, the policy might state that risks with associated 4-tuples [L, *, *, H] and [L, *, *, M] are to be mitigated, where "*" indicates possibilities L, M, and H. We are now ready to define ρ.

DEFINITION 4: (Method for Privacy Risk Prioritization, ρ) Apply weights to the privacy risks in R using the procedure described in Section IV above. Select the risks for prioritization (or mitigation) based on the Prioritization Policy.

Prioritization Examples

Examples of the application of Definition 4 may be obtained by re-visiting and prioritizing the risks found in the privacy risk tables above (Tables IV, VI, and VIII). Two extra columns are added to each privacy risk table: one column for the weights, and one column identifying P, the set of risks that have been prioritized.

Re-visiting Table IV, adding the weights, and prioritizing using a Prioritization Policy that states "only prioritize (mitigate) risks with weights [*, *, L, H]", where * admits possibilities L, M, H gives Table IX.

The weights in Table IX were assigned by the privacy and security analyst as follows. For the man-in-the-middle attack, the risks to the attacker's safety is low since he or she is attacking at a distance; the access is high since it's the Internet; the cost is low as not much equipment is needed; the damages would be high since the attacker could post the private information leading to heavy damages to the company's reputation. Similar considerations apply to the weight assigned to the Trojan horse or hacker attack. For the

SQL attack on B, accessibility was assigned as low and cost as high because improvements to the database user interface were recently carried out to guard against SQL attacks. The risk of the user being asked for information violating PII and the risk of information kept past the retention time were considered as potential accidents caused by the company itself. Therefore, the risk to safety, the accessibility, and the costs were deemed to be low, high, and low respectively. The resulting damages were considered to be medium because the accidents would likely be quickly discovered through auditing and remedied.

TABLE IX. Partial Prioritized Privacy Risks Table Corresponding to Fig. 1

(PIIs / locations)	Privacy Risks	Weights	In *P*
(1, 2, 3 / path into A); (2 / path into D); (3 / path into E)	Man-in-the-middle attack violates *collector*, *purpose*, *retention time* and *disclose-to*.	[L, H, L, H]	Yes
(1, 2, 3 / A)	User could be asked for personal information that violates *PII*, i.e. asked for personal information other than as specified in the user's privacy preferences.	[L, H, L, M]	No
(1, 2, 3 / A); (1 / C); (2 / D); (3 / E)	Trojan horse, hacker attack use circles violating *collector*, *purpose*, *retention time*, and *disclose-to*.	[L, H, L, H]	Yes
(1, 2, 3 / B)	SQL attack on B violates *collector*, *purpose*, *retention time*, and *disclose-to*.	[L, L, H, H]	No
(1, 2, 3 / B)	*PII* in B could be kept past its *retention time*.	[L, H, L, M]	No

Table VI is prioritized next giving Table X. This time the Prioritization Policy used states "only prioritize (mitigate) risks with weights [*, H, L, H]" where * admits possibilities L, M, H. The analyst assigned the weights in Table X as follows. The weights for the man-in-the-middle attack, the violation of PII, and the Trojan horse or hacker attack are the same as in Table IX since they are the same attacks. The SQL attack was assigned the same weight as the Trojan horse or hacker attack since they have similar safety, access, and cost requirements, and the aftermath of which would also be highly damaging. The bad anonymization algorithm is considered as accidental and is assigned the same weight as the violation of PII, which is also considered accidental. The insecure home environment is assigned H for safety since the attacker could be easily caught, M for access since it's a private home, L for cost since it does not cost anything to look, and H for damages since lost of the information is highly damaging. The theft of the laptop (theft is considered here rather than accidental loss) is assigned H for safety since the thief could be observed and caught, M for access since the laptop can be a

TABLE X. Partial Prioritized Privacy Risks Table Corresponding to Fig. 2

(PIIs / locations)	Privacy Risks	Weights	In *P*
(1, 2, 3 / path into A); (1, 2 / path between B and C, path between D and E); (3 / path between A and C, path between D and I); (12 / path between L and B); (11 / path between M and B)	Man-in-the-middle attacks lead to CPRD-risk.	[L, H, L, H]	Yes
(1, 2, 3 / A)	The patient could be asked for personal information that violates PII (i.e. asked for PII other than 1, 2, 3).	[L, H, L, M]	No
(1, 2, 3 / A, C, D); (13 / N); (1, 2 / E); (1, 2, 9 / F, G); (15 / M); (3 / J); (16 / L)	Trojan horse, or hacker attacks on the personal information use circles lead to CPRD-risk.	[L, H, L, H]	Yes
(1, 2, 11, 12 / B); (1, 2, 10 / H); (8 / K)	Potential SQL attacks on B, H, and K lead to CPRD-risk.	[L, H, L, H]	Yes
(13 / N)	A bad anonymization algorithm can expose personal information, leading to CPRD-risk.	[L, H, L, M]	No
(1, 2, 9 / G)	An insecure home environment, e.g., people looking over the shoulder or printed personal information lying on a desk in the clear, can also lead to CPRD-risk.	[H, M, L, H]	No
(1, 2, 9 / G)	If an employee works from home on a laptop and carries the laptop between home and work, possible theft or loss of the laptop can also lead to CPRD-risk for any of 1, 2, or 9 that might be temporarily stored in the laptop.	[H, M, L, H]	No
(1, 2, 9 / G)	If an employee works from home on a home PC and stores 1, 2, 9 on a flash memory stick, carrying the memory stick between home and work, possible theft or loss of the memory stick can also lead to CPRD-risk.	[H, M, L, H]	No

little difficult to get to (e.g., inside a car), L for cost since it does not cost much to execute, and H for damages as again such a loss would be very damaging. The theft of the memory stick (theft is considered rather than loss) is assigned the same weights as the theft of the laptop since they have similar dangers and requirements for the attacker, and is also very damaging.

Table VIII is the last privacy risks table to be prioritized, giving Table XI. This time the Prioritization Policy used states "only prioritize (mitigate) risks with weights [L, *, *, H]" where * admits possibilities L, M, H. The analyst assigned the weights in Table XI as follows.

TABLE XI. Partial Prioritized Data Risks Table Corresponding to Fig. 3

(PIIs / locations)	Privacy Risks	Weights	In *P*
(1, 2, 3 / path into A); (1, 2, 3 / path into I); (1, 2, 3 / path into L); (6 / path from A); (6 / path from I); (6 / path from L)	Man-in-the-middle attacks lead to CPRD-risk.	[L, H, L, H]	Yes
(1, 2, 3 / path between I and J); (1, 2, 3 / path between L and N); (1, 3 / path between N and O)	Man-in-the-middle attacks lead to CPRD-risk.	[M, M, L, H]	No
(1, 2, 3 / path into A); (1, 2, 3 / path into I); (1, 2, 3 / path into L)	The user could be asked for personal information that violates PII (i.e. asked for PII other than 1, 2, 3).	[L, H, L, M]	No
(1, 2, 3 / A, I, L); (1, 3 / C, K, O)	Trojan horse, or hacker attacks on the personal information use circles lead to CPRD-risk.	[L, H, L, H]	Yes
(1, 2, 3 / D, J, N)	Potential SQL attacks on D, J, and N lead to CPRD-risk.	[L, H, L, H]	Yes
(1, 2, 3 / D, J, N)	Potential insider attack steals private information from D, J, and N resulting in CPRD-risk.	[L, H, L, H]	Yes
(1, 2, 3 / D, J, N)	Private information in D, J, and N could be kept past the retention time.	[L, H, L, M]	No

A weight of [L, H, L, H] was assigned to the first row after the same considerations as that described for man-in-the-middle attacks in Table IX. A weight of [M, M, L, H] was assigned to the second row since the paths in this row are relatively short (connecting components in the same module), leading to greater risk for the attacker (greater risk of being seen) and lower accessibility (fewer places to access the link). A weight of [L, H, L, M] was assigned to the third and last rows out of the same considerations as in Table IX, for the risk of the user being asked for information that violates PII and the risk of private information kept past the retention time. A weight of [L, H, L, H] was assigned to the Trojan horse or hacker attack in the fourth row and the SQL attacks in the fifth row since the attacker could operate from a distance with easy access through the Internet and with relatively low costs. A weight of [L, H, L, H] was assigned to the risk of an insider attack in the sixth row since an insider can hide in plain sight, has high access by virtue of being an insider, and carry out the attack at zero cost to herself.

V. DISCUSSION OF STRENGTHS, WEAKNESSES, AND IMPROVEMENTS

Some of the strengths of the approach include: a) provides a structured straightforward way to identify and prioritize privacy risks, b) user friendly common sense graphical notation, and c) based on the locations that involve PII, a concept that is easily understood.

Some weaknesses of the method are: a) drawing the PIM, filling out the Privacy Risks Table, and prioritizing the risks require expertise in how personal information is used as well as expertise in security and privacy, b) drawing the PIM is manual and is prone to error, c) the prioritization is partly subjective, and d) the method can never identify all the risks. Weakness a) is unavoidable as the expertise must be available somehow. This requirement for expertise is common to many technical endeavors, e.g., software engineering. Weakness b) can be addressed by building tools for automatically drawing the PIM. Similar tools already exist for rendering a software architecture diagram from the reverse engineering of code, e.g., Nanthaamornphong et al. [15]. Furthermore, automated analysis of the PIM should be feasible by using a rules engine to automate the visualization or enumeration of privacy risks, based on machine understanding of the graphical notation in this work. These automations should improve both the accuracy of the PIM and the identification of the privacy risks. Weakness c) may be attenuated by having a team of experts assign the weights through consensus. The accuracy of the prioritization may also be improved by considering other factors such as the nature and frequency of recent attacks, as well as the cost of mitigating a risk. Weakness d) may also be unavoidable, as it is mostly due to the nature of security, that no system can be completely secure. However, the above automated tools and rules engine should improve risk coverage.

VI. RELATED WORK

The literature on works by other authors, dealing *directly* with privacy risk visualization for software systems, appears to be non-existent. However, the following authors have written on topics that are related to privacy risk analysis. Hong et al. [16] propose the use of privacy risk models to help designers design ubiquitous computing applications that have a reasonable level of privacy protection. Their privacy risk model consists of two parts: a privacy risk analysis part and a privacy risk management part. The risk analysis identifies the privacy risks while the risk management part is a cost-benefit analysis to prioritize the risks and design artifacts to manage the risks. Visualization is not used.

A second class of related work applies privacy risk analysis to specific application areas. Biega et al. [17] propose a new privacy model to help users manage privacy risks in their Internet search histories. They assume a powerful adversary who makes informed probabilistic inferences about sensitive data in search histories and aim for a tool that simulates the adversary, predicts privacy risks, and guides the user. Paintsil [18] presents an extended misuse case model and a tool that can be used to check the presence of known misuse cases and their effect on security and privacy risks in identity management systems. Das and Zhang [19] propose new design principles to lessen privacy risks in health databases due to aggregate disclosure. None of these works employ visualization.

A third class of related work is of course the work on privacy impact analysis (PIA) [5] (Section I). There are also works that support PIA. Meis and Heisel [20] present a method with tool support, based on a requirements model, that facilitates the PIA process. Tancock et al. [21] describe plans for a PIA tool that can be employed in a cloud environment to identify potential privacy risks and compliance. Joyee De and Le Métayer [22] present a Privacy Risk Analysis Methodology (PRIAM) for conducting privacy risk analysis in a systematic and traceable way, suitable for application in a PIA.

A fourth class of related work consists of security and privacy threat analysis, e.g., Nematzadeh and Camp [23]. Security and privacy threats are related risks. For example, a Trojan horse attack (security threat) can lead directly to the lost of private data (privacy threat). These works also do not use visualization as described here.

A fifth class of related work concerns earlier work on privacy visualization by this author. Yee [24] presents a notation for representing the software and hardware components of a computer system as well as the data flows between the components. It then checks each component for vulnerabilities that could violate a privacy policy. It differs from this work in terms of the notation (lower level than this work), the method of identifying vulnerabilities, and the use of privacy policies. Yee [25] featured the first use of the PIM but for web services only and involved privacy policies. In this work, we have extended the PIM to software systems in general and removed the need to work with privacy policies.

A sixth class of related work also involves visualization of risks but with different goals than in this work. They are works on the visualization of information intended to assist the decision making process under risk or improve the understanding of system security and risks. They differ from this work as follows: a) they concern the visualization of *security* risks rather than privacy risks, b) their goals are to assist in decision making or improve security understanding, whereas the goal of this work is to identify privacy vulnerabilities, and c) their visualizations are lower level in general and resemble more the objects being visualized, whereas this work uses a high level more abstract visualization. Three works representative of this class are Daradkeh [26], Takahashi et al. [27], and Kai et al. [28]. Daradkeh evaluates an information visualization tool for the support of decision making under uncertainty and risk. Takahashi et al. discuss the architecture of a tool for security risk visualization and alerting to increase security awareness. Kai et al. present a security visualization system for cloud computing that displays security levels computed over information gathered at monitoring points. Their visualization system is similar to visualizations provided by a security information and event management system (SIEM) [29].

A seventh class of related works deals with privacy by design. Guerriero et al. [30] provide a tool prototype to assist the process of continuous architecting of data intensive applications for the purpose of offering privacy by design guarantees. They also present a research roadmap for ensuring privacy by design for Big Data DevOps. Spiekermann [31] writes about the challenges of privacy by design. Le Métayer [32] presents a formal framework for use in the design phase of privacy by design, which checks if an architecture meets the requirements, including privacy requirements, of the parties involved with a system. Perera et al. [33] offer a conceptual framework with guidelines that employ privacy by design principles to direct software engineers in systematically assessing the privacy capabilities of Internet of Things applications and platforms.

Finally, no references were found that deals directly with the prioritization of privacy risks. However, abundant work exists on the assessment of security risks, which is closely related to prioritizing privacy risks. Alizadeh and Zannone [34] present a risk-based framework that facilitates the analysis of business process executions. The framework detects non-conforming process behaviors and ranks them according to criticality, which is determined by the execution's impact on organizational goals. The criticality ranking enables a security analyst to prioritize the most severe incidents. Jorgensen et al. [35] propose decomposing risk associated with a mobile application into several risk types that are more easily understood by the application's users and that a mid-level risk summary be presented that is made up of the dimensions of personal information privacy, monetary risk, device availability/stability risk, and data integrity risk. Their work suggests that privacy risk prioritization, as in this work, may be facilitated by decomposing the risks into more easily understandable categories or dimensions. Islam et al. [36] present a framework for threat analysis and risk assessment of automotive embedded systems to systematically tackle security risks and determine security impact levels. The latter serve to prioritize the severity of the risks. The framework aligns with several industrial standards.

VII. CONCLUSION AND FUTURE WORK

This work has proposed a straightforward method for visualizing and prioritizing privacy risks applicable to software systems, based on locations involving PII. Such locations are important for risk evaluation because they represent varying levels of vulnerabilities or risks, and they contribute to total risks. Although the approach has weaknesses, the weaknesses can be remedied, as described in Section V.

Future work includes the automations and improvements to the method for risk prioritization mentioned in Section V, along with a validation of the effectiveness of the approach. For this validation, it is envisioned that a software system with known privacy risks and prioritization (reference risks and prioritization) would be defined to act as the reference system. Different teams of privacy and security experts who do not have prior knowledge of the reference risks and prioritization would then be invited to apply the approach to the reference system. Their results would be compared to the reference risks and prioritization to gage the effectiveness of the approach. If the effectiveness was found to be inadequate, a follow-up analysis could point to the reasons for the discrepancy and could give insight into ways to improve the approach.

REFERENCES

[1] G. Yee, "Visualization of Privacy Risks in Software Systems," Proceedings of the Tenth International Conference on Emerging Security Information, Systems and Technologies (SECURWARE 2016), pp. 289-294, 2016.

[2] V. S. Iyengar, "Transforming Data to Satisfy Privacy Constraints," Proceedings of the 8th ACM SIGKDD International Conference on Knowledge Discovery and Data Mining (KDD'02), Edmonton, Alberta, pp. 279-288, 2002.

[3] R. Song, L. Korba, and G. Yee, "Pseudonym Technology for E-Services," chapter in Privacy Protection for E-Services, edited by G. Yee, Idea Group, Inc., 2006.

[4] C. Adams and K. Barbieri, "Privacy Enforcement in E-Services Environments," chapter in Privacy Protection for E-Services, edited by G. Yee, Idea Group, Inc., 2006.

[5] Treasury Board of Canada Secretariat, "Directive on Privacy Impact Assessment," available on March 27, 2016 at: http://www.tbs-sct.gc.ca/pol/doc-eng.aspx?id=18308

[6] I. Goldberg, D. Wagner, and E. Brewer, "Privacy-Enhancing Technologies for the Internet," IEEE COMPCON'97, pp. 103-109, 1997.

[7] CIPP Guide, "CSA Model Code," available on Feb. 22, 2017 at: https://www.cippguide.org/2010/06/29/csa-model-code/

[8] G. Yee, L. Korba, and R. Song, "Legislative Bases for Personal Privacy Policy Specification," chapter in Privacy Protection for E-Services, edited by G. Yee, Idea Group, Inc., 2006.

[9] O. Tene, "Privacy: The New Generations," International Data Privacy Law, Vol. 1, Issue 1, pp. 15-27, February 2011. Available on May 31, 2017 at: https://academic.oup.com/ idpl/article-lookup/doi/10.1093/idpl/ipq003

[10] G. Kambourakis, "Anonymity and Closely Related Terms in the Cyberspace: An Analysis by Example," Journal of Information Security and Applications, Vol. 19, Issue 1, pp. 2-17, Elsevier, February 2014.

[11] A. Ruiz-Martinez, "A Survey on Solutions and Main Free Tools for Privacy Enhancing Web Communications," Journal of Network and Computer Applications, Vol. 35, Issue 5, pp. 1473-1492, Elsevier, September 2012.

[12] J. Ren and J. Wu, "Survey on Anonymous Communications in Computer Networks," Computer Communications, Vol. 33, Issue 4, pp. 420-431, Elsevier, March 2010.

[13] A. Pfitzmann and M. Hansen, "A Terminology for Talking About Privacy by Data Minimization: Anonymity, Unlinkability, Undetectability, Unobservability, Pseudonymity, and Identity Management," Version v0.34, 98 pages, Aug. 10, 2010. Available on May 31, 2017 at: https://dud.inf.tu-dresden.de/literatur/Anon_Terminology_v0.34.pdf

[14] C. Salter, O. S. Saydjari, B. Schneier, and J. Wallner, "Toward A Secure System Engineering Methodology," Proceedings of the New Security Paradigms Workshop, pp. 2-10, 1998.

[15] A. Nanthaamornphong, K. Morris, and S. Filippone, "Extracting UML Class Diagrams from Object-Oriented Fortran: ForUML," Proceedings of the 1st International Workshop on Software Engineering for High Performance Computing in Computational Science and Engineering (SE-HPCCSE'13), pp. 9-16, 2013.

[16] J. I. Hong, J. D. Ng, S. Lederer, and J. A. Landay, "Privacy Risk Models for Designing Privacy-Sensitive Ubiquitous Computing Systems," Proceedings, 2004 Conference on Designing Interactive Systems: Processes, Practices, Methods, and Techniques, Cambridge, MA, USA, pp. 91-100, 2004.

[17] J. Biega, I. Mele, and G. Weikum, "Probabilistic Prediction of Privacy Risks in User Search Histories," Proceedings of the 1st International Workshop on Privacy and Security of Big Data, pp. 29-36, Nov. 2014.

[18] E. Paintsil, "A Model for Privacy and Security Risks Analysis," Proceedings of the 5th International Conference on New Technologies, Mobility and Security (NTMS), pp. 1-8, May 2012.

[19] 14-G. Das and N. Zhang, "Privacy Risks in Health Databases From Aggregate Disclosure," Proceedings of the 2nd ACM International Conference on Pervasive Technologies Related to Assistive Environments (PETRA'09), article no. 74, June 2009.

[20] R. Meis and M. Heisel, "Supporting Privacy Impact Assessments Using Problem-Based Privacy Analysis (Technical Report)." Available on May 31, 2017 at: https://www.uni-due.de/imperia/md/content/swe/pia-formal.pdf

[21] D. Tancock, S. Pearson, and A. Charlesworth, "A Privacy Impact Assessment Tool for Cloud Computing," Proceedings of the 2nd IEEE International Conference on Cloud Computing Technology and Science, pp. 667-676, 2010. Available on May 30, 2017 at: http://barbie.uta.edu/~hdfeng/CloudComputing/cc/cc47.pdf

[22] S. Joyee De and D. Le Métayer, "PRIAM: A Privacy Risk Analysis Methodology," Research Report RR-8876, Inria - Research Centre Genoble - Rhône-Alpes, 51 pages, 2016. Available on May 31, 2017 at: https://hal.inria.fr/hal-01302541/document

[23] A. Nematzadeh and L. J. Camp, "Threat Analysis of Online Health Information System," Proceedings of the 3rd International Conference on Pervasive Technologies Related to Assistive Environments (PETRA'10), article no. 31, June 2010.

[24] G. Yee, "Visualization for Privacy Compliance," Proceedings of the 3rd International Workshop on Visualization for Computer Security (VizSEC'06), pp. 117-122, Nov. 2006.

[25] G. Yee, "Visual Analysis of Privacy Risks in Web Services," Proceedings of the IEEE International Conference on Web Services (ICWS 2007), pp. 671-678, July 2007.

[26] M. Daradkeh, "Exploring the Use of an Information Visualization Tool for Decision Support under Uncertainty and Risk," Proceedings of the International Conference on Engineering & MIS 2015 (ICEMIS'15), article no. 41, 2015.

[27] T. Takahashi, K. Emura, A. Kanaoka, S. Matsuo, and T. Minowa, "Risk Visualization and Alerting System: Architecture and Proof-of-Concept Implementation," Proceedings of the First International Workshop on Security in Embedded Systems and Smartphones (SESP'13), pp. 3-10, 2013.

[28] S. Kai, T. Shigemoto, T. Kito, S. Takemoto, and T. Kaji, "Development of Qualification of Security Status Suitable for Cloud Computing System," Proceedings of the 4th International Workshop on Security Measurements and Metrics (MetriSec'12), pp. 17-24, 2012.

[29] Wikipedia, "Security information and event management," available on June 12, 2016 at: https://en.wikipedia.org/wiki/Security_information_and_event_management

[30] M. Guerriero, D. Tamburri, Y. Ridene, F. Marconi, M. Bersani, and M. Artac, "Towards DevOps for Privacy-by-Design in Data-Intensive Applications: A Research Roadmap," Proceedings of the 8th ACM/SPEC on International Conference on Performance Engineering Companion (ICPE '17), pp. 139-144, April 2017.

[31] S. Spiekermann, "The Challenges of Privacy by Design," Communications of the ACM, Vol. 55, Issue 7, pp. 38-40, July 2012.

[32] D. Le Métayer, "Privacy by Design: A Formal Framework for the Analysis of Architectural Choices," Proceedings of the 3rd ACM Conference on Data and Application Security and Privacy (CODASPY '13), pp. 95-104, 2013.

[33] C. Perera, C. McCormick, A. Bandara, B. Price, and B. Nuseibeh, "Privacy-by-Design Framework for Assessing Internet of Things Applications and Platforms," Proceedings of the 6th International Conference on the Internet of Things (IoT '16), pp. 83-92, November 2016.

[34] M. Alizadeh and N. Zannone, "Risk-based Analysis of Business Process Executions," Proceedings of the 6th ACM Conference on Data and Application Security and Privacy (CODASPY'16), pp. 130-132, 2016.

[35] Z. Jorgensen, J. Chen, C. Gates, N. Li, R. Proctor, and T. Yu, "Dimensions of Risk in Mobile Applications: A User Study," Proceedings of the 5th ACM Conference on Data and Application Security and Privacy (CODASPY'15), pp. 49-60, 2015.

[36] M. Islam, A. Lautenbach, C. Sandberg, and T. Olovsson, "A Risk Assessment Framework for Automotive Embedded Systems," Proceedings of the 2nd ACM International Workshop on Cyber-Physical System Security (CPSS'16), pp. 3-14, 2016.

A Formalised Approach to Designing Sonification Systems for Network-Security Monitoring

Louise Axon, Jason R. C. Nurse, Michael Goldsmith, Sadie Creese

Department of Computer Science, University of Oxford,
Parks Road, Oxford, UK
Email: {louise.axon, jason.nurse, michael.goldsmith, sadie.creese}@cs.ox.ac.uk

***Abstract*—Sonification systems, in which data are represented through sound, have the potential to be useful in a number of network-security monitoring applications in Security Operations Centres (SOCs). Security analysts working in SOCs generally monitor networks using a combination of anomaly-detection techniques, Intrusion Detection Systems and data presented in visual and text-based forms. In the last two decades significant progress has been made in developing novel sonification systems to further support network-monitoring tasks, but many of these systems have not been sufficiently validated, and there is a lack of uptake in SOCs. Furthermore, little guidance exists on design requirements for the sonification of network data. In this paper, we identify the key role that sonification, if implemented correctly, could play in addressing shortcomings of traditional network-monitoring methods. Based on a review of prior research, we propose an approach to developing sonification systems for network monitoring. This approach involves the formalisation of a model for designing sonifications in this space; identification of sonification design aesthetics suitable for real-time network monitoring; and system refinement and validation through comprehensive user testing. As an initial step in this system development, we present a formalised model for designing sonifications for network-security monitoring. The application of this model is demonstrated through our development of prototype sonification systems for two different use-cases within network-security monitoring.**

***Keywords*–Sonification; Network Security; Anomaly Detection; Network Monitoring; Formalised Model; Situational Awareness.**

I. INTRODUCTION

The cybersecurity of enterprises crucially depends on the monitoring capabilities of the Security Operations Centres (SOCs) operating on their behalf, aiming to maintain network and systems security; in particular, their ability to detect and respond to cyber-attack. Organisations today are frequently the target of cyber-attacks, the nature of which varies widely from ransomware to denial-of-service (DoS) attacks to the exfiltration of sensitive data by insiders, for example. These attacks can be highly damaging both financially, and in terms of the reputation of the organisation. In the face of a constantly evolving set of threats and attack vectors, and changing business operations, there is a constant requirement for effective monitoring tools in SOCs to both automatically and semi-automatically detect attacks.

One of the key challenges that SOCs face in monitoring large networks is the huge volume of data and metadata that can be present on the network. This consists of both the data created by the day-to-day operations of the enterprise, and the data created by security tools. For real-time monitoring, tools that present this data in a form that can be processed in negligible time are essential [1]. Intrusion Detection Systems (IDSs) and visualisations are general examples of classes of tools that are widely used to convey information pertaining to network security in a form that can be easily understood by analysts. The detection algorithms that usually underlie such tools have certain limitations, and can produce false-positive and false-negative results [2,3]. Detecting attacks, and recognising which risks must be prioritised over other attacks and malign activities is difficult, and the degree of inaccuracy in detection systems can make it even more so.

Sonification can provide a potential solution to the challenges of network-security monitoring in SOCs. Sonification is the presentation of data in an audio (generally non-speech) form. Over the last two decades, the incorporation of sonification systems into the monitoring activity of SOCs has been considered [1]. A range of systems has been proposed in which sonified data are presented to support security analysts in their network-monitoring tasks. Some prior work has provided strong evidence of the role sonification could play in improving SOC monitoring capabilities. It has already been shown, for example, that using sonification techniques enables users to detect false-positives from IDSs more quickly [4]. However, the use of sonification systems in this context has not been sufficiently validated, and there is a lack of uptake in SOCs. Sonification has not yet been used operationally in SOCs to our knowledge. Based on the current state of the art, there are clear needs for further research and testing to validate the usefulness of sonification for efficient network monitoring, and to develop appropriate and effective sonifications to enhance network-monitoring capabilities.

This paper is an extension of a survey paper by Axon et al. [1]. In that paper, the major developments over the last two decades in sonification and multimodal systems for network monitoring were reviewed, with particular focus on approaches to design and user testing. That article also contributed a research agenda for advancing the field. This agenda included comprehensive user testing to assess the extent to which, and ways in which, sonification techniques can be useful for network-monitoring tasks in SOCs; the development of aesthetic sonifications appropriate for use in continuous network-monitoring tasks; and the formalisation of an approach to sonifying network-security data. In this paper, we extend that work by proposing an approach to designing sonification systems for network-security monitoring, and presenting a formalised sonification model as part of that approach. We illustrate the application of the model by using it to design two different sonification-system prototypes.

The remainder of this paper is structured in six sections: in Section II, we present traditional approaches to network monitoring and detail their shortcomings. Section III presents a review of prior work in using sonification for network monitoring, and highlights outstanding challenges in the field. In Section IV, we propose an approach to developing sonification systems for real-time network monitoring. We present our initial work in a part of this approach – the formalisation of a sonification design model – in Section V. In Section VI we apply this model to develop prototype sonification systems for two different use-cases within network-security monitoring. We conclude in Section VII, and indicate directions for future work.

II. Traditional Approaches to Network-Security Monitoring

Network-security monitoring is generally conducted by security analysts, who observe activity on the network – usually using a variety of tools – in order to detect security breaches. According to the UK government's Cyber Security Breaches Survey for companies across the UK, published in May 2016, two-thirds (65%) of large organisations reported that they had detected a security breach in the last twelve months, with the most costly single breach experienced by an organisation during that time purported to have cost £3 million [5]. In the face of such frequent and potentially costly breaches, network-monitoring and attack-detection capabilities are of extremely high importance.

A variety of tools are used in network monitoring: IDSs, Intrusion Prevention Systems (IPSs), visualisations, textual presentations, and firewalls are some of the tools with which analysts conduct their monitoring tasks. The subject of our research is primarily detection, rather than prevention capabilities. We therefore focus on IDSs and anomaly-detection techniques. We also describe the data-presentation methods generally used to convey network-security monitoring information to security analysts – security visualisation tools, and text-based interfaces.

Network monitoring is largely based on alerts given by IDSs. Many IDSs have been based on Denning's model [6]. In general, there are two types of IDS. Anomaly-based IDSs monitor network traffic, and compare it against an established baseline (based on bandwidth, protocols, ports, devices, and connections that are "normal"). Signature-based IDSs, on the other hand, compare packets monitored on the network against a database of signatures or attributes from known malicious threats [2]. Leading SOCs typically craft their own signatures, defined by analysts in the form of rules. Recent advances automate the collection and analysis of data from a range of sources such as logs and IDS alerts using novel Machine Learning and Data Mining approaches.

Anomaly-detection techniques describe methods for the detection of changes in systems that may indicate the presence of threat, and so be of interest from a monitoring perspective. In contrast with signature- or rule-based detection, which relies on comparison with known attack signatures, in anomaly detection, the state of the network is monitored and compared with a "normal" baseline. Anomalous activity is that which exceeds an acceptable threshold difference from this baseline. Anomaly detection often informs the output of IDSs and visualisations. There are several reports reflecting on the state of the art in anomaly-detection techniques [2,7,8]. In general, we can divide anomaly-detection methods into three categories [2,9]: detection methods based on Statistics, in which values are compared against a defined acceptable range for deviation [10,11]; detection methods based on Knowledge Systems, in which the current activity of the system is compared against a rule-based "normal" activity [12]; and detection methods based on Machine Learning, automated methods in which systems learn about activities and detect whether these are anomalous through supervised or unsupervised learning [7,13].

Data-presentation techniques convey network-security monitoring information to security analysts. Command-line interfaces are commonly used mediums for presenting the output of network-monitoring appliances such as IDSs and network firewalls. Security visualisations are another widely-used class of tool that convey the output of automated detection tools, and may also present information about the raw network data. While some security-visualisation systems are very basic, there are a number of recent surveys of the state of the art in visualising complex network data. Zhang et al. [14] and Etoty et al. [15] present reviews as of 2012 and 2014 respectively, reporting research into improving graphical-layout and user-interaction techniques [16,17]. Visualisations generally work by mapping network-data parameters to visual parameters, such that analysts can observe the changes in the visualisation presented and from this deduce changes in, and information about, the network. The design of effective visualisation involves identifying mappings that represent the data in a way that can be understood by security analysts, in SOCs for example, without inducing cognitive overload, and can clearly convey information pertaining to the security of the network.

There are certain drawbacks to current approaches to the monitoring and analysis of security data. Existing automated techniques can be unreliable or inaccurate. Signature-based IDSs may suffer from poorly-defined signatures, and are limited to detecting only those attacks for which signatures are known. The algorithms underlying anomaly-detection techniques using Statistics or Machine Learning also produce false-positives and false-negatives [2,3]. There is, therefore, a requirement to identify improved anomaly-detection methods. Alongside ongoing research into improving the accuracy of automated detection methods, one avenue that has been researched in security-visualisation work is the detection of anomalies by humans observing aspects of the network data [18].

Given the potential inaccuracy of the alerts produced by the automated detection-system used, it is important that the human analyst has situational awareness and an understanding of the network state, in order that he can interpret alerts and accurately decide their validity; this is one of the key roles of data-presentation techniques. A shortcoming of existing text-based and visualisation-based network-monitoring systems is the requirement that operators dedicate their full attention to the display in order to ensure that no information is missed – for real-time monitoring especially – which can restrict their ability to perform other tasks. Furthermore, the number of visual dimensions and properties onto which data can be mapped is limited [19], and the presentation of large amounts of information visually may put strain on the visual capacity of security analysts.

III. Network Monitoring Using Sonification

Based on the shortcomings we identify in existing monitoring techniques, we believe that sonification may have the potential to improve monitoring capabilities in SOCs, in a number of ways. While many promising advances have been made recently in novel data-analytics approaches in particular, we highlight that automated network-monitoring systems do not always produce reliable outputs. Presenting network-monitoring information as a continuous sonification could improve analysts' awareness of the network-security state, aiding their interpretation of the alerts given by automated systems. Such awareness could also enable analysts to detect patterns, recognise anomalous activity and prioritise risks differently from the way their systems do, acting as a human anomaly-detector of sorts.

Sonification could also offer a solution to the shortcomings of current data-presentation techniques – in particular, text-based presentation and security visualisations – as an extra interface that requires humans to use their sense of hearing rather than vision. It is important to design representations of large volumes of network data that are as easy as possible for analysts to use, understand and act on. A potential advantage of using sonification in this context is that sound can be presented for peripheral listening. This means that, if designed correctly, sonification could enable analysts to monitor the network-security state as a non-primary task, whilst performing other main tasks. Furthermore, using sound offers another set of dimensions in addition to visual dimensions onto which data can be mapped. The addition of sonification to existing visualisation-based or text-based data presentation approaches could provide a useable method of monitoring highly complex, multivariate network data.

A. *Sonification: a Background*

Sonification is the presentation of data in an audio (generally non-speech) form. It is used in numerous fields, such as financial markets, medicine (Electroencephalography (EEG) monitoring [20], image analysis [21]) and astronomy. User testing has validated that the presentation of sonified data can improve certain capabilities in a number of applications: improved accuracy in monitoring the movement of volatile market indices by financial traders [22], and improved capabilities for exploratory analysis of EEG data [23], for example.

A variety of techniques and guidelines have been developed for the design and implementation of sonification [24–27]. Throughout sonification literature there are three main approaches recognised: earcons/event-based sonification (discrete sounds representing a defined event), parameter-mapping sonification (PMSon – in which changes in some data dimensions are represented by changes in acoustic dimensions), and model-based sonification (in which the user interacts with a model and receives some acoustic response derived from the data).

The current state of the art in sonification for network and server monitoring is summarised by Rinderle-Ma et al. [19], who identify systems for the sonification of computer-security data, in various stages of maturity. It is concluded that there is a lack of formal user and usability testing, even in those systems that are already fully developed [28–30]. Our survey work differs from that of Rinderle-Ma et al.: while that survey gives an overview of the design approaches taken in some existing sonification systems, our survey provides much greater detail on the sonification design of existing systems in terms of sonification techniques, sound mapping types, the network data and attack types represented and the network-monitoring scope. Furthermore, in this paper we propose an approach to designing and testing the utility of sonification systems for network monitoring, and we go on to actually report on the implementation of that research vision, namely our work on the development of a formalised model for designing sonifications for anomaly-based network monitoring.

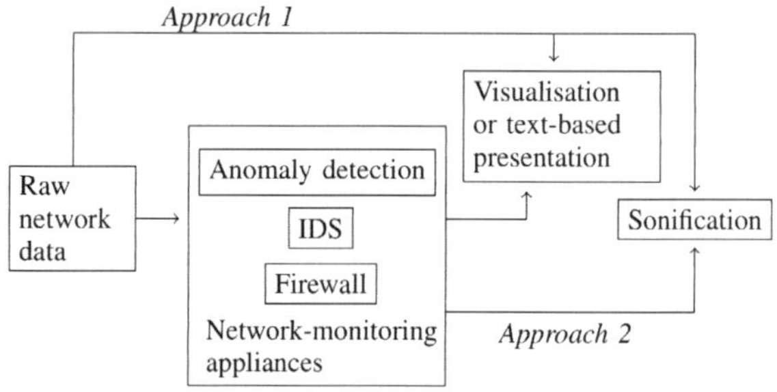

Figure 1. A summary of the existing relationship between traditional monitoring techniques and their potential relationship with sonification systems in SOCs.

Figure 1 shows the existing relationship between raw data, anomaly-detection techniques, network-monitoring appliances such as IDSs, and data-presentation techniques, and the position we envisage sonification might take in this setup. The figure shows two approaches to sonifying network-security monitoring data. In *Approach 1*, the raw network data is represented in the sonification – perhaps with some scaling or sampling methods applied. In *Approach 2*, the network data is not sonified in its raw form but is subject to some automated detection procedure prior to sonification. This either means that the output of some network-monitoring appliance – an IDS, for example – is sonified, or that there is some detection algorithm involved in the sonification method itself prior to the rendering of the data as sound.

TABLE I. EXAMPLES OF TYPES OF RAW NETWORK DATA

Data Type	**Description**
Packet header	The header information for individual packets on the network (including timestamp, source/destination IP/port, packet size, for example) from a network packet capture
Netflow	Data on collected network flows – sequences of packets sent over the same connection (including timestamp, flow duration, source/destination IP/port, for example)
Machine Logs	Data recorded at individual machines on the network. For example, network packets received and sent; processes running; central processing unit (CPU) usage

In Table I, we clarify the meaning of "raw network data" as it is used in Figure 1, by illustrating examples of types of data. The list is not exhaustive, but gives some indication of the network data to which we refer. These data are examples of the raw network data that is sonified directly in *Approach 1* of Figure 1.

B. *Applications of Sonification to Network Monitoring*

PEEP, a "network auralizer" for monitoring networks with sound, is presented in [28]. PEEP is designed to enable system administrators to detect network anomalies – both in security and general performance – by comparing sounds with the sound of the "normally functioning" network. The focus of PEEP is on the use of "natural" sounds – birdsong, for example – in sonifying network events. Recordings are mapped to network conditions (excessive traffic and email spam, for instance), and are played back to reflect these conditions. Abnormal events are presented through a change in the "natural" sounds. PEEP represents both network events (when an event occurs it is represented by a single natural sound) and network state (state is represented through sounds played continuously, which change when there is a change in some aspects of the state, such as average network load). There is no experimental validation of the performance of PEEP and its usefulness for monitoring networks, but the authors report the ability to hear common network problems such as excessive traffic using the sonification.

The Stetho network sonification system is given in [31]. Stetho sonifies network events by reading the output of the Linux tcpdump command, checking for matches using regular expressions, and generating corresponding Musical Instrument Digital Interface (MIDI) events, with the aim that the system creates sounds that are "comfortable as music". The aim of Stetho is to convey the status of network traffic, without a specific focus on anomaly detection. The research includes an experimental evaluation of the Stetho system – users' ability to interpret the traffic load from the sounds generated by Stetho is examined. The experiment shows that this monitoring information can be recognised by users from the sounds created by Stetho; however, only four users (subjects familiar with network administration) are involved in the evaluation experiment.

Network Monitoring with Sound (NeMoS) is a network sonification system in which the user defines network events, and the system then associates these events with MIDI tracks [32]. The system is designed to allow monitoring of different parts of a potentially large network system at once, with a single musical flow representing the whole state of the part of the system the system manager is interested in. The focus is not on network security but on monitoring network performance in general; printer status and system load, for example, can be represented through two different sound channels.

More recently, Ballora et al. look to create a soundscape representation of network state which aids anomaly detection by assigning sounds to signal certain types and levels of network activity such as unusual port requests [33] ("soundscape" definition given by Schafer [34]). The concept is a system capable of combining multiple network parameters through data fusion to create this soundscape. The fusion approach is based on the JDL Data Fusion Process Model [35], with characteristics of the data assigned to multiple parameters of the sound. The authors aim, firstly, to map anomalous events to sound and, secondly, to represent the Internet Protocol (IP) space as a soundscape in which patterns can emerge for experienced listeners. No user testing is carried out to establish the usefulness of the system for anomaly-detection tasks. However, the authors report being able to hear patterns associated with distributed denial-of-service (DDoS) and port-scanning attacks (see Table III).

Vickers et al. sonify meta properties of network traffic data [36] as a countryside soundscape. In that system, the log returns of successive values of network traffic properties (number of packets received and sent, number of bytes received and sent) are used to modulate the amplitude, pan, phase or spectral characteristics of four sound channels, including the sound of a running stream and rain. The aim of the system is to alert the system administrator to abnormal network behaviour with regard to both performance and security; it is suggested, for example, that a DDoS attack might be recognisable by the system's representation of an increase in certain types of traffic. There is, however, no evaluation of users' ability to recognise such information using the system. Vickers et al. then extend that work to further explore the potential for using sonification for network situational awareness [37]. For this context, i.e., continuous monitoring for network situational awareness – it is argued that solutions based on soundscape have an advantage over other sonification designs, and that there is a need for sonifications that are not annoying or fatiguing and that complement the user's existing sonic environment.

A soundscape approach is also adopted in the InteNtion system [29] for network sonification. Here, network traffic analysis output is converted to MIDI and sent to synthesisers for dynamic mixing; the output is a soundscape composed by the network activity generally rather than the detection of suspicious activity specifically. It is argued that the system could be used to help administrators detect attacks; however this is not validated through user testing. DeButts is a student project available online in which network data is sonified with the aim of aiding security analysts to detect anomalous incidents in network access logs [38].

García-Ruiz et al. investigate the application of sonification as a teaching and learning tool for network intrusion detection [39, 40]. This work includes an exploratory piece in which information is gathered regarding the subjects' preferred auditory representations of attacks. Sonification prototypes are given for the mapping of log-registered attacks into sound. The first uses animal sounds – auditory icons – for five different types of attack ("guess", "rcp", "rsh", "rlogin", "port-scan"); the second uses piano notes at five different frequencies as earcons to represent the five types of attack. Informal testing was carried out for these two prototypes, and suggested that the earcons were more easily identifiable, while the subjects could recall the attack types more easily using the auditory icons. While this is a useful start to comparing approaches to sonification design for network data, the mappings tested are limited, and further research is required into mappings involving other sound and data types.

Systems have been proposed to sonify the output of existing IDSs, and to act as additions to the function of these systems. Gopinath's thesis uses JListen to sonify a range of events in Snort Network Intrusion Detection System (a widely used open-source network IDS for UNIX derivatives and Windows) to signal malicious attacks [4]. The aim is to explore the usefulness of sonification in improving the *accuracy* of IDS alert interpretation by users; usability studies indicate that sonification may increase user awareness in intrusion detection. Experiments are carried out to test three hypotheses on the usability and efficacy of sonifying Snort. The findings are: musical knowledge has no significant effect on the ability of subjects to use the system to find intrusions; sonification decreases the time taken to detect false positives; immediate monitoring of hosts is possible with a sonified system. As noted by Rinderle-Ma et al. [19], however, the comparison is somewhat biased since the control group without auditory

TABLE II. REVIEW OF APPROACHES TO AND USER TESTING IN EXISTING SONIFICATION SYSTEMS FOR NETWORK MONITORING, ORDERED BY YEAR.

Author	**Year**	**Sonification approach description**	**User testing**	**Number of participants**	**Nature of participants**	**Network data type mapped**	**Sound type**	**Sonification technique**	**Monitoring scope**	**Evaluates utility for security monitoring?**	**Multimodal**
Gilfix [28]	2000	"Natural" sounds mapped to network conditions	✗			Raw data (network packet logs)	Natural (wildlife and nature) sounds	PMSon	Anomaly detection: conditions such as high traffic load and email spam are mapped to sound	✗	✗
Varner [41]	2002	Multimodal system: visualisation conveys status of network nodes; sonification conveys additional details on network nodes selected by the user	✗			Not specified	Not specified	Not specified	Network attack detection	✗	✓
Kimoto [31]	2002	Maps parameters of sound to raw network data	✓	4	Subjects familiar with network administration	Raw data (Linux tcpdump output)	Musical	PMSon	General network activity and network anomaly detection	✓	✓
Malandrino [32]	2003	Associates MIDI tracks to user-defined network events	✗			Raw data (printer status, server CPU, file server logs, network packet logs)	Musical	Event-based	Network performance	✗	✗
Gopinath [4]	2004	Instrument and pitch mapped to IDS alert type	✓	20	Computer Science students and staff	IDS alerts (Snort)	Real-world and musical	PMSon	Intrusion detection: IDS logs sonified to aid users monitoring intruders and vulnerable hosts	✓	✗
Papadopoulos [42]	2004	Combines network events rendered as spatial audio with 3D stereoscopic visuals to form a multimodal representation of network information. Sounds are created in response to changes in data patterns using Gaussian Mixture Modelling	✗			Raw data (incoming network flows)	Real-world and musical	PMSon	Anomaly detection: network data presented for pattern recognition	✗	✓
Qi [43]	2007	Maps traffic pattern (classified, queued and scheduled) to audio; bytes and packet rate are mapped to frequency and intensity of audio respectively	✗			Raw data (network packet logs)	Musical	PMSon	Network attack detection (DoS, port scanning)	✗	✓
El Seoud [40]	2008	Auditory icons (non-instrumental) and earcons (instrumental) mapped to attack type	✓	29	Telematics engineering students	Marked attacks from network log	Real-world and musical	Event-based	Network attack detection	✗	✗
Brown [44]	2009	Proposed system maps raw network traffic to sound to convey information on network status; current system maps properties of traffic classified as disruptive by an IDS to properties of piano notes	✗			Raw data (network packet logs) and IDS output	Musical	PMSon	Network anomaly detection (increase in traffic; HTTP error messages; number of TCP handshakes)	✗	✓
Ballora [33]	2011	Parameter-mapping soundscape for overall IP space; obvious sound signals for certain levels of activity	✗			Raw data (network packet logs)	Musical	PMSon	Anomaly detection: anomalous incidents sonified, and network state presented to human to enable pattern recognition	✗	✗
Giot [29]	2012	MIDI messages mapped to data output by SharpPCap library network traffic analysis; MIDI messages mixed to produce a soundscape	✗			Raw data (network packet logs)	Musical	PMSon	General network activity and attack detection	✗	✗
deButts [38]	2014	Maps distinct notification tones to anomalous network events; visualises network traffic activity (multimodal)	✗			Raw data (access logs)	Musical (single tones)	Event-based	Anomaly detection: defined anomalous incidents mapped to sounds	✗	✓
Vickers [36]	2014	Parameters of each sound generator (voice) mapped to the log return values for the network's self-organised criticality	✗			Raw data (network packet logs)	Natural	PMSon	Network performance and attack detection	✗	✗
Worrall [30]	2015	Multimodal system for real-time sonification of large-scale network data. Maps data parameters and events to sound; parameter-mapping sonification approach using melodic pitch structures to reduce fatigue	✗			Raw data (sampled network packet traffic)	Musical	PMSon	General network activity	✗	✓
Mancuso [45]	2015	Multimodal system for representing data on military networks, in which each source and destination IP is mapped to an instrument and pitch, and the loudness is increased when a packet size threshold is exceeded	✓	30	Local population and air force base personnel	Raw data (network packet logs)	Musical	PMSon	Network anomaly detection (packet size threshold, source and destination IPs sonified)	✓	✓

support had to conduct the tasks by reading log files, without access to the visualisation-based tools to which the group tested with auditory support had access.

Multimodal systems, that combine visualisation and sonification for network monitoring, have also been explored. Varner and Knight present such a system in [41]. Visualisation is used to convey the status of network nodes; sonification then conveys additional details on network nodes selected by the user. This multimodal approach is useful because it combines advantages of the two modalities – the spatial nature of visualisation, and the temporal nature of sonification – to produce an effective and usable system. García et al. describe the benefits and pitfalls of using multimodal human-computer interfaces for the forensic analysis of network logs for attacks. A sonification method is proposed for IDSs as part of a multimodal interface, to enable analysts to cope with the large amounts of information contained in network logs. The sonification design approach is not detailed, and the system is not tested with users.

The CyberSeer [42] system uses sound to aid the presentation of network-security information with the aim of improving network-monitoring capability. Sound is used as an additional variable to data-visualisation techniques to produce an audio-visual display that conveys information about network traffic log data and IDS events. The requirement for user testing to establish the most effective audio mappings is recognised, but no testing is carried out. García-Ruiz et al. describe the benefits and pitfalls of using multimodal human-computer interfaces for analysing intrusion detection [46]. A sonification method is proposed for IDSs as part of a multimodal interface, to enable analysts to cope with the large amounts of information contained in network logs.

Qi et al. present another multimodal system for detecting intrusions and attacks on networks in [43]; distinctive sounds are generated for a set of attack scenarios consisting of DoS and port scanning. The authors stipulate that the sounds generated could enable humans to recognise and distinguish between the two types of attack; however, user testing is needed to validate this conclusion and investigate the extent to which this approach is effective. A similar approach is adopted by Brown et al. [44]: the bit-rates and packet-rates of a delay queue are sonified in a system for intrusion detection.

NetSon [30] is a system for real time sonification and visualisation of network traffic, with a focus on large-scale organisations. In this work, there are no user studies, but the system is being used at Fraunhofer IIS, a research institution, who provide a live web stream of their installation [47]. Microsoft have a multimodal system, *Specimen Box*, for real-time retrospective detection and analysis of botnet activity. It has not yet been presented in a scientific publication, but a description and videos of the functioning system are presented online [48]. The system has not been subject to formal evaluation, but is used in operations at the Microsoft Cybercrime Centre.

Mancuso et al. conducted user testing to assess the usefulness of sonification of network data for military cyber operations [45]. Participants were tasked with detecting target packets matching specific signatures (see Table III), using either a visual display (a visual interface that emulated network packet analysis software such as Wireshark) only, or both visual and sonified displays. The aim of the testing was to assess the extent to which sonification can improve the performance and manage the workload of, and decrease the stress felt by, users conducting cyber-monitoring operations on military networks. The testing results show that the use of sonifications in the task did not improve participants' performance, workload or stress. However, only one method of sonifying the data was tested, in which each possible source and destination IP address was represented by a different instrument and note, and the loudness increased if a threshold packet size was exceeded. The results do not, therefore, show that using sonification does not improve performance, stress and workload in this context, but demonstrate only that this particular method of sonifying the data is ineffective.

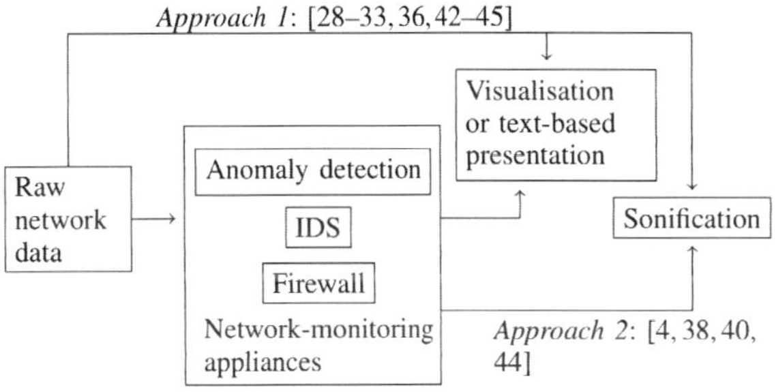

Figure 2. A summary of the data types used in previous network data sonification approaches.

In Figure 2 we show the approaches taken in previous work to designing network-data sonifications, in terms of the type of network data sonified. In this figure, we position the existing sonification systems surveyed onto the monitoring tool relationships diagram presented in Figure 1. Previously-proposed sonifications of network-security data can be divided into two sets: those that take *Approach 1* (in which the sonification system takes as input some raw network data, with scaling functions applied such that the sonification is a representation of the raw network data itself), and those that take *Approach 2* (in which the systems sonifies the output of some network monitoring tool such as an IDS, or sonifies the output of some inbuilt anomaly detection technique).

In Table II, we summarise the sonification design techniques used and user testing carried out in prior work. In Table III we examine in greater detail those existing sonification systems developed for enabling attack detection by sonifying raw network data specifically (*Approach 1* represented in Figure 2). For each system, we present the types of attacks targeted, and the network data features represented in the sonification. We summarise the reported effectiveness of these systems for "hearing" cyber attacks.

In summary, some prior work shows that sonification systems have promising potential to enable network-security monitoring capabilities. Previously-designed sonification systems have been reported to produce sonic patterns from which it is possible to "hear" cyber attacks [28, 33, 36, 43]. In particular, it is reported that DoS attacks and port-scanning attacks can be heard in previous systems sonifying raw network data. User testing has shown that other sonification design attempts were not useful for network-security monitoring tasks [45]; however, the sonification designs and applications tested in this work were limited, and this result is not comprehensive

TABLE III. ATTACK DETECTION AND NETWORK DATA FEATURE REPRESENTATION IN PREVIOUS SONIFICATION SYSTEMS.

Author	Network data features sonified	Can attacks be "heard"?	Attacks targeted
Gilfix [28]	Incoming and outgoing mail; average traffic load; number of concurrent users; bad DNS queries; telnetd traffic; others unspecified	Not assessed, but authors report ability to "easily detect common network problems such as high load, excessive traffic, and email spam"	Not specified
Varner [41]	Not specified	Not assessed	
Papado-poulos [42]	Packet rate; others not specified	Not assessed	
Qi [43]	Packet rate; byte rate	No experimental assessment, but authors report that the system produced sounds "notably" different enough that distinguishing between DoS and port scanning attacks is "relatively easy", while no sounds were produced under "normal" traffic conditions	DoS; port scanning
Brown [44]	Prolonged increase in traffic volume; number of TCP handshakes in progress; number of HTTP error messages	Not assessed	
Ballora [33]	Source IP address; destination IP address; frequency of packets in ongoing socket connections; packet rate; requests to unusual ports; geographic location of sender (suggested but not implemented)	Not assessed, but authors report finding "that patterns associated with intrusion attempts such as port scans and denials of service are readily audible"	Dataset used contains DoS and port-scanning attacks
Giot [29]	Packet size; Time-to-Live (TTL) of packet; bandpass of network; source IP address; destination IP address; protocol (type of service); number of useless packets (e.g. TCP ACK packet)	Not assessed	
Vickers [36]	Data sonified are log returns of successive instances of the following values: number of bytes sent; number of packets sent; number of bytes received; number of packets received	Changes in soundscape not noticeable under "normal" network conditions; noticeable change occurs when log returns large (large log return for number of packets received might indicate DDoS, for example)	Not specified
Mancuso [45]	Source IP address (of packet); destination IP address (of packet); packet size	Use of sonification alongside the visual interface did not improve participants' performance in detecting "target packets" compared with their performance using the visual interface alone	Not specific attacks – target packet characterised by "signatures": network transmissions originating from either of two particular source IP addresses, directed to either of two destination IP addresses, using either of two protocols, with packet size 500 bytes or more

enough to suggest that further research in this area is futile. It is clear that variations in sonification design approach may affect the usefulness of the system for network-security monitoring, and as such further research is required into appropriate sonification designs for the context.

C. Outstanding Challenges

Table II presents a summary of the sonification systems previously developed for network monitoring (solutions for which full systems or prototypes have been developed). From this, we have identified the key areas in which research is lacking: formalisation of a model for designing sonification systems for network monitoring, identification of data requirements, investigation of appropriate sonification aesthetics, and validation of the utility of the approach through user testing.

In general, a weakness in the articles is the amount of user testing carried out with the intended users – security analysts. Table II shows that little user testing has been carried out, and of that which has, little has specifically targeted security analysts – it is possible that some of the Air Force Base personnel who participated in the user testing by Mancuso et al. were security analysts, but this is not made clear in that paper [45]. Table II shows also that there has been little (and no comprehensive) evaluation of the usefulness of existing sonification systems for network anomaly detection. Gopinath evaluates the usefulness of a sonification with a focus on aiding users in monitoring the output of IDSs [4]. Mancuso et al. evaluate the effectiveness of their sonification system in enabling users to detect packets matching specific signatures, but test only one sonification design. There is therefore a clear need to assess and compare the use of a number of sonification designs for network anomaly detection. Extensive user testing is required to validate the usefulness of the approach and of proposed systems, and to refine the sonification design.

The systems listed vary in the data they represent. Some map raw network data to sound, some map the output of IDSs, while some aim to map attacks to sounds. However, there is no comparison of the efficacy of these approaches, or of the usefulness of sonic representations of different attack types. Identification of the network-data sources and features that should be sonified in order to represent network attacks is needed. The sonification design approaches used (event-based, parameter-mapping, and soundscape-based) also vary, as do the sound types (natural sounds, sounds that are musically informed) but there is as yet no comprehensive investigation into, or comparison of, the usefulness of these methods. Based on this, we propose that comparative research into the sonification aesthetics most appropriate for use in network monitoring is crucial, in order to inform sonification design. We further identify a requirement for the development of a formalised approach to designing sonifications in this field, to underpin developments and enable comparison. Next, we outline our proposed approach to sonification development and testing, with which we aim to address these issues.

IV. Proposed Approach

We propose an approach to developing sonification systems in this space. The approach involves formalising a model for designing sonifications for network monitoring, identifying the network data representation requirements, investigating appropriate design aesthetics for the context, and assessing the utility of the developed systems through comprehensive user testing. We believe that these elements combine to form a solution to the problem of designing and testing the utility of sonification systems for network-security monitoring.

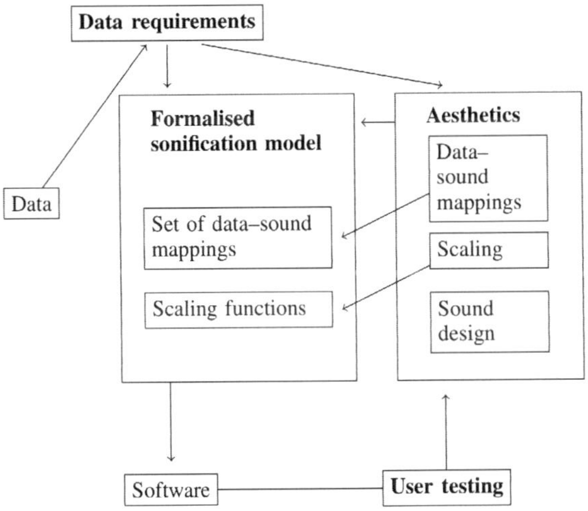

Figure 3. Proposed approach to designing sonification systems for network-security monitoring.

Figure 3 shows the parts of our approach, and their relationship with each other. The formalised network data sonification model takes as input aesthetic requirements and data requirements, and incorporates the results of iterative user testing. We now detail the research questions to be answered for each part of the approach.

A. Requirement for a Formalised Sonification Model

To enable us to architect and experiment with sonifications in a flexible way, we need an underpinning sonification model. This should enable us to utilise heterogeneous sonifications alongside each other in order to compare performance. No such model currently exists, and we therefore propose the development of a formalised model specifically for developing sonification systems for network monitoring. This model should describe a grammar for the representation of network data through parameter-mapping sonification that enables incorporation of and experimentation with appropriate design aesthetics, techniques of musical composition, and the science of auditory perception. It is important that the model encompasses prior art, and enables comparison with previous approaches to designing sonifications in this space.

A model for designing sonifications for use in the network-monitoring context should tailor aspects of sonification design such as cross-field interference to produce sonifications that are appropriate for network-monitoring tasks. A simple example is a simultaneous change in two network parameters: a statistically significant increase in traffic load, and messages received from an IP address that is known to be malicious (these two changes would generally be found by the statistical anomaly-based IDSs and signature-based IDSs, respectively, described in Section II). This could be the result of a DoS attack, and the sonification system should therefore attract the attention of the analyst. Cross-field interference could be leveraged through the choice of data-sound mappings used in this case (with a mapping to higher pitch and increased tempo – two sound parameters which interact such that each appears more increased that it really is – for the two data parameters respectively) to ensure that the attack is highlighted by the sonification.

In order to prevent sonification designs from causing listener fatigue, we propose that a rule-based approach to aesthetic sound generation may be appropriate. In particular, a sonification model should be non-prescriptive in terms of musical genre, and be applied to a variety of genres of music to generate a set of different-sounding sonifications of the same network data. We hypothesise that with this approach, users could be allowed to move between a set of musical genres at choice, each of which would sonify the network data according to the same grammar, and this could reduce the fatigue caused by the sounds. Below, we give the key questions to be addressed in building this model.

- **Which are the requirements specific to the network-security monitoring context for the mapping of data to sound?** In general, huge quantities of multivariate and highly complex data move through organisational computer networks. It is important that the model enables the sonification designer to reason about the parts of the data to be sonified, the key information about these parts that must be conveyed to the sonification user, and the most appropriate method of representing this information through sound. For example, an important task in SOCs is monitoring the security state of sensitive servers on the network – this could be those servers containing databases of customer records. Devising methods of mapping required information about selected aspects of the network to sound will be a key part of the model development process.
- **What are the inputs and outputs of the sonification model?** The sonification model should take as input both the data requirements for the representation, and the aesthetics derived: appropriate data-sound mappings and sound design, and methods of scaling the data to the sound domain. The model should provide a method for mapping the required data to sound, following the aesthetic requirements input. The model should itself then produce the input to some sonification software. Adaptability of the model according to differing aesthetic requirements is important, particularly as we aim to compare multiple aesthetic approaches, and refine the aesthetic requirement specification through iterative user testing.
- **How can we verify that the sonification model is capable of addressing prior art approaches?** In order to enable comparison of new sonification system designs with the approaches taken in prior work, it is important that prior approaches can be replicated through use of the sonification model developed. We

can verify the correctness of the model for this task by verifying that it has some representation of each relevant prior sonification approach.

B. Data Requirements

The data requirements include firstly the data sources used, since these produce different data types. For example packet capture header data might be represented – a different data type to machine log data (including machine CPU, for example) or file access log data. The data requirements must also include the data features addressed. These are the properties of the data that we choose to sonify, and may be low-level properties (such as a representation of source IP address from which each packet is received) or may be attack-detection features (such as packet rate thresholds against which data are compared).

The data requirements depend to a large part on the use-case. In developing sonification systems for anomaly detection by humans, data requirements should be derived from information about all data sources and features that enable network anomaly detection, and through which attacks are conveyed. On the other hand, for use in a multimodal system, which conveys part of the network data sonically while other data is conveyed visually, the sonification data requirements would depend on which data had been selected to convey visually, and which using the sonification. As another example, if the aim of sonification was to enable analysts to monitor network security as a non-primary task, the data requirements should be informed by the data sources that analysts may be frequently required to monitor while simultaneously conducting other tasks – these sources might include IDS alert logs, or the logs of critical servers on the network, for example.

- **Which data sources should be included in developing sonifications for network-security monitoring purposes?** It is important to identify those sources for which a sonified representation might add value in network monitoring; these might be raw network data sources such as packet captures, Netflow or Domain Name System (DNS) logs, or the sources might be monitoring systems such as IDSs or network firewalls. Buchanan et al. categorised the potential data sources used by security analysts in answering a number of different analytical questions (for example, in searching for the activities associated with a particular suspicious IP address) [49]. We hypothesise that raw network packet capture data is most suitable for network attack detection, because this constitutes a full representation of traffic on the network. However, it would be valuable to identify the network data sources security analysts consider most useful for network attack detection, and the methods by which those sources are currently monitored. For example, the information output of multiple such data sources are often integrated in Security Information and Event Management (SIEM) tools for monitoring by analysts.
- **Which data properties or features should be sonified to enable network anomaly detection by analysts?** In order to identify the data properties to be represented, attack characterisation can be used to extract the ways in which classes of network attacks (flooding attacks, for example) manifest in the network data sources selected for representation in the sonification. Some prior work identifies network data features for network anomaly detection, and for the detection of particular classes of threat such as Advanced Persistent Threats (APTs) and Botnets [50–52]. Some of this work involves interviews with security analysts to identify the properties of data analysts search for in network security monitoring to enable attack detection [49, 53]. The findings from attack characterisation and prior work can be bolstered through interviews with security analysts, to gather their views on the importance of particular network data features for network attack detection.

C. Sonification Aesthetics

While there has been some work in aesthetic sonification, as reported in Section III, it has not been heavily applied in the context of network monitoring. Prior work indicates that sonification aesthetic impacts on its effectiveness. In an experiment comparing sonifications of guidance systems, for example, it was shown that sonification strategies based on pitch and tempo enabled higher precision than strategies based on loudness and brightness [54]. It was also shown in [55] that particular sonification designs resulted in better participant performance in identifying features of Surface Electromyography data for a range of different tasks involved.

The aesthetics of the design are an important factor in producing sonifications that are suitable for continuous presentation in this context. In particular, the sounds should be unfatiguing [37, 56] and, if intended for use in non-primary task monitoring, should achieve a balance in which they are unobtrusive to the performance of other tasks while drawing sufficient attention when necessary to be suitable for SOC monitoring. While there are other techniques that may be useful, we propose an approach to this design that draws on techniques and theories of musical composition. We can draw on work in aesthetic sonification by Vickers [56], and on work in musification, i.e., the design of sonifications that are musical. Some key questions to be answered regarding sonification aesthetics for network-security monitoring are described below.

1) **Which are the most appropriate mappings from network-security data to sound?** Prior work has indicated preferred mappings from data to sound in certain contexts; for mapping physical quantities such as speed and size, for example [57]. Useful parallels can be drawn between these previous experiments and the network-monitoring context, and hypotheses can thus be made about appropriate data-sound mappings. However, it is important to perform a context-specific assessment of these mappings, in terms of their ability to convey the required network-monitoring information in a way that users can comprehend. Associations formed through the previous experiences of users may affect the ease with which they can use certain mappings; for example, based on prior work we might expect a mapping from packet rate to tempo of music to be intuitive. We propose that user experiments should be carried out as part of the sonification design process, to establish which mappings from data to sound are most appropriate. The results of these user experiments will form an input to the sets of data-sound mappings used in the sonification model, as shown in Figure 3.
2) **Which sonification aesthetics are suitable for use in**

network-security monitoring in SOCs? Comparison of a range of musical aesthetics (for example, a comparison between Classical Music and Jazz Music), should be carried out to identify those most suitable for the context. In particular, aesthetics that are unfatiguing, unobtrusive to other monitoring work, and able to attract the required level of attention from analysts, should be chosen. It may be that a suitable approach is to enable analysts to choose between a selection of musical aesthetics at will. It is important to assess the extent to which musical experience affects the ability of security analysts to use musically-informed sonification systems in network-monitoring tasks. The effect of users' musical experience on their ability to understand and make use of the sonification systems design will require investigation. Here, musical experience refers to the level of prior theoretical and aural musical training attained by the user. For this SOC monitoring context, analysts' use of the systems should not be impaired by a lack of musical experience.

3) **What granularity of network-security monitoring information can we represent usefully using sonification?** Given the huge volumes of network data observed on organisational networks, and the high speed of packet traffic on these networks, it should be assumed that some scaling or aggregation will be required in the sonic representation of certain data sources. The amount of information that can be conveyed through sound should be identified. This is both in the sense that sonification software is actually capable of rendering the information, and that humans can usefully interpret the information presented and hear the network data required for anomaly detection, i.e. that the sound is not overwhelming. Methods for producing network data inputs that can be usefully rendered as sound, such as aggregating packets over time intervals, or scaling quantities such as packet rate, should then be experimented with. Sampling packets is another possible approach; for example, Worrall uses sampled network packets as the input to his network data sonification using the *Sflow* tool, which takes packets from the traffic stream at a known sampling rate [30]. Comparative testing would be valuable at this stage to assess the levels of granularity of data sonification at which network anomalies can be heard. The results of this assessment of appropriate data granularity will form an input to the scaling functions of the sonification model, as shown in Figure 3.

Besides aesthetics, aspects of human perception must influence the design: the prior associations sounds may hold for users and the way in which this affects interpretation; the effect of musical experience on perception. It is important that the design takes into account factors in perception such as cross-field interference (in which different dimensions of sound – pitch and tempo, for example – interact in a way that affects perception of either) and does not induce cognitive overload for the user.

D. Comprehensive User Studies

As well as addressing sonification-aesthetic requirements through iterative user testing, we need to conduct user experiments to investigate the utility of sonification systems for network-security monitoring tasks. Section III indicates that of the proposals made for sonification systems for network monitoring, very few have conducted any user testing. None have conducted testing to the extent required for an appropriate understanding of the use of these systems and their suitability for actual deployment in security monitoring situations. As such, we identify a requirement for significantly more in-context user testing of sonifications for network-monitoring tasks, carried out with security analysts in SOCs, to inform the design and investigate the advantages and disadvantages of the approach. It is important that sonification systems are tested in the SOC environment, in order to investigate how well they incorporate with the particular characteristics of SOCs – a variety of systems running simultaneously, collaborative working practice, high levels of attention required from workers.

We will conduct user testing to investigate the hypothesis that sonification can improve the network-monitoring capabilities of security analysts. This hypothesis is proposed in light of prior work in other fields in which it is proven that certain capabilities can be improved by the presentation of sonified data, as outlined in Section III, and of the limited experimental evidence that shows that sonification can be useful for tasks involving network data specifically [4, 31].

For the validation of sonification as a solution to improving network-monitoring capabilities, there are certain key research questions that need to be answered through user testing.

1) **To what extent, and in what ways, can the use of sonification improve the monitoring capabilities of security analysts in a SOC environment?** User testing is required to establish the extent to which sonification can aid security analysts in their network-monitoring tasks. We theorise that there may be a number of use-cases for sonification of network data in SOCs. For example, investigation is needed to establish whether the presentation of network data through sonification can enable analysts to "hear" patterns and anomalies in the data, and in this way detect anomalies more accurately than systems in any cases. Given the strong human capability for pattern recognition in audio representations [56, 58, 59], and for contextualising information, it is plausible that a system that presents patterns in network data may enable the analyst to detect anomalies with greater accuracy than traditional rule-based systems. User testing should also establish whether presenting sonified network data can enable analysts to monitor the network as a non-primary task, maintaining awareness of the network-security state while carrying out other exploratory or incident-handling tasks. Finally, we propose user testing to assess whether multimodal systems, which fuse visualisations and sonifications of complex data – which might usually be presented visually across multiple monitors, for example – can aid analysts in their network-monitoring tasks.

2) **Are there certain types of attack and threat that sonify more effectively than others, and what implications does this have for the design of sonification systems for network monitoring?** It may be the case that certain types of attacks are better-represented through sonification than others, and that some attacks sound anomalous in a way that is particularly easy for analysts to use while others do not sonify well. Findings on this subject should inform sonification system design by distinguishing the attacks and threats in relation to which sonification performs best, and the areas in which the technique therefore

has the potential to be most effective.

3) **How does the performance of the developed sonification tools in enabling network attack detection compare with the performance of other network attack detection tools?** The performance of users in network attack detection using sonification alone, and using network monitoring setups incorporating sonification, should be compared to their performance using visualisation and text-based interfaces. Users' performances in detecting network attacks using the sonification should also be compared with the performance of automated systems such as IDSs. It is important to compare the attack detection performance (in terms of accuracy and efficiency) of humans using the sonification to that of automated systems, for particular classes of network attack.

Answers to these questions will provide a greater understanding of the role sonification can play in improving monitoring capabilities in SOCs, the limits of the approach, and the extent to which it can be reliable as a monitoring technique. In conducting this testing, we expect to draw from existing research on conducting user studies in general, and in a security context [60, 61].

V. Formalised Model for the Sonification of Network Security Data

In this section, we expand on our proposal in Section IV by presenting a formalised approach for the musical parameter-mapping sonification of network-security data. In particular, we focus on our formalised sonification model (as introduced in Section IV.A). We first identify requirements for sonifying network-security data, and from these requirements, construct a model for developing sonifications for network-security monitoring uses.

Some work in formalising the sonification of data has been presented previously. For parameter-mapping sonification, a formalised representation of the sonification mapping function is given by Hermann [23]. That representation was the basis of the parameter-mapping sonification model that we developed for network-security monitoring. In Hermann's representation, the parameter-mapping function $\mathbf{g} : \mathbb{R}^d \to \mathbb{R}^m$ describes the mapping from a d-dimensional dataset $\langle x_1, ..., x_d \rangle \in \mathbb{R}^d$ to an m-dimensional vector of acoustic attributes which are parameters of the signal generator. The q-channel sound signal $s(t)$ is computed as a function $\mathbf{f} : \mathbb{R}^{m+1} \to \mathbb{R}^q$ of the parameter-mapping function $\mathbf{g}$ applied to the dataset, and time t:

$$s(t) = \sum_{i=1}^{d} \mathbf{f}(\mathbf{g}(\mathbf{x}_i), t).$$

In developing our model, we draw on de Campo's Sonification Design Space Map (SDSM), which describes the questions to be addressed in any sonification design process [62]. The map presents, as axes, three key questions for reasoning about data aspects in sonification design. We also use the work of Hermann [23]; in particular, we extend Hermann's parameter-mapping sonification formalisation, by addressing the design questions indicated by the SDSM.

A. Requirements of the Model

In what follows, we describe the use of the SDSM design questions to extract requirements for the model. We present each question, then consider context-specific answers. We thus identify requirements particular to sonification for network-security monitoring.

- *Question 1: How many data points are required for patterns to emerge?*
  The presentation of network data at a range of different resolutions may be required for different monitoring applications – see Subsection IV.B:

  Requirement 1: the model should enable any number of data points to be represented.

- *Question 2: What properties of data dimensions should be represented?*
  The properties of data dimensions represented should be those through which indicators of attacks are shown. These may vary based on the network type and the source of the monitoring information:

  Requirement 2: the model should enable the inclusion of appropriate data dimensions for individual designs.

  Furthermore, these dimensions may be continuous (for example, packet rate), or discrete (for example, direction of packet flow – incoming/outgoing). Appropriate mapping of both continuous and discrete data dimensions should be enabled in order to prevent unnecessary loss of resolution in the data representation (for example, there would be a loss of resolution in a representation in which data with continuous values, such as packet rate, was mapped to a sound with a small number of discrete values, such as type of instrument):

  Requirement 3: the model should provide a systematic method of mapping continuous and discrete data dimensions to continuous and discrete sound dimensions.

- *Question 3: How many sound streams should be present in the design?*
  This depends on the network type, use-case and monitoring information source, but in general network data is multivariate, with many network elements, data sources, and packet flows that require monitoring. We require a method of communicating which of these streams is represented by particular sounds: we need to represent information about a number of different channels of the network data. This means, we need to know what is happening, and to which parts of the data:

  Requirement 4: the model should allow the inclusion of appropriate sound channels for individual designs, and provide a method for systematically identifying the channels and the dimensions required in the representation.

The formalised model should also meet certain other requirements, based on the observations that were made in Section IV. These can be summarised as follows:

- We argued that sonification aesthetics, and mappings, require testing for the context in which they are used. The model should therefore facilitate the insertion of those data-sound mappings selected, according to experimental results and user preferences:

  Requirement 5: the model should not prescribe data-sound mappings.

- We also argued that the problem of listening fatigue may be reduced, if users can select their own music and change it at will. Furthermore, experimentation with different musical aesthetics is required to determine those most suitable for the SOC environment. Therefore:

Requirement 6: the model should not prescribe musical genre, and should allow for choice in its selection.

B. Formalised Sonification Model

In Tables IV and V we present a formalised sonification model for designing musical parameter-mapping sonifications for use in network-security monitoring, developed to meet the requirements identified.

To construct the model, we divided Hermann's formalisation for the parameter-mapping sonification of a dataset [23] into individual mapping functions for *data channels* (corresponding to the channels identified in *Requirement 4*), *continuous data dimensions* and *discrete data dimensions* (corresponding to the dimensions identified in *Requirements 2* and 3). In Table IV, we define these *data channels* and *data dimensions*. Our approach is well-suited to this particular context because it allows us to reason about the channels of information to be presented for each particular use-case. Moreover, we can systematically identify continuous and discrete data, and their most appropriate mappings to sound. At the end of this section, we discuss how the model we develop meets the requirements identified.

The model comprises *components* (individual parts of the data and the sound to be mapped, which we present in Table IV), and *relations* (by which *components* are associated with one another, which we present in Table V). The *relations* are described by *mapping functions*.

A sonification is described by the tuple of its *components* and *relations* (the meaning of each of these is explained in Tables IV and V):

$$\langle CD_R, DD_R, VD_R, Rel_c, Rel_{d\alpha}, Rel_{d\beta}, Rel_v \rangle.$$

The *relations* presented in Table V are described by the *channel-mapping function* (which describes the *channel relation* Rel_c) and the *dimension-mapping function* (which describes both the *dimension relation* Rel_d and the *value relation* Rel_v). We also treat *sound dimensions* ds as functions of *sound channels* cs, which have values in the tuple of *sound values* of each *sound dimension*, vs.

The *channel-mapping function* $\boldsymbol{\psi}:\mathbb{R}^n \rightarrow \mathbb{R}^m$ describes the mapping from a tuple of n *data channels* $CD = \langle cd_1, ..., cd_n \rangle$ to a tuple of m *sound channels* $CS = \langle cs_1, ..., cs_m \rangle$. The q-dimensional sound signal $s(t)$ is computed as the sum over m *sound channels* cs of the *dimension-mapping function* $\boldsymbol{\Gamma}$: $\mathbb{R}^{m+1} \rightarrow \mathbb{R}^q$,

$$s(t) = \Sigma_{i=1}^{m} \boldsymbol{\Gamma}_i(cs_i, t),$$

where cs_i is the output of the *channel-mapping function* $\boldsymbol{\psi}$: $\mathbb{R}^n \rightarrow \mathbb{R}^m$ applied to the data channel cd_j and time t:

$$cs_i = \langle \boldsymbol{\psi}_i(cd_j, t) | j \in \{1, ..., n\} \rangle,$$

and $\boldsymbol{\Gamma}_i$ is the tuple of *dimension-mapping functions* $\boldsymbol{\gamma}_{ik}$, which are applied to the z data dimensions dd_{ik} of the data channels cd_j that were mapped by $\boldsymbol{\psi}_i$ to sound channel cs_i, and time t. The functions $\boldsymbol{\gamma}_{ik}$ describe the x continuous dimension mappings $\boldsymbol{\gamma}\alpha_1, ..., \boldsymbol{\gamma}\alpha_x$, and the y discrete dimension mappings $\boldsymbol{\gamma}\beta_1, ..., \boldsymbol{\gamma}\beta_y$, for each sound channel cs_i:

$$\boldsymbol{\Gamma}_i = \langle \boldsymbol{\gamma}_{i1}, ..., \boldsymbol{\gamma}_{iz} \rangle = \langle \boldsymbol{\gamma}\alpha_{i1}, ..., \boldsymbol{\gamma}\alpha_{ix}, \boldsymbol{\gamma}\beta_{i1}, ..., \boldsymbol{\gamma}\beta_{iy} \rangle.$$

We now explain how this model meets the requirements we identified. Since the *sound channels* and *sound dimensions* are left as an abstraction, *Requirements 5 and 6* are met. *Requirement 1* is also met through the use of abstract functions to describe the mappings themselves, meaning the resolution of the data presentation (number of data points presented) can be addressed through the choice of a function appropriate to any particular use of the model.

Requirement 4 is addressed by the division of the parameter-mapping into channels and dimensions; the *channel mapping function* addresses *Requirement 4*, while the *dimension mapping function* addresses *Requirement 2*. *Requirement 3* is met by the division of the *dimension mapping function* into a continuous and a discrete mapping function.

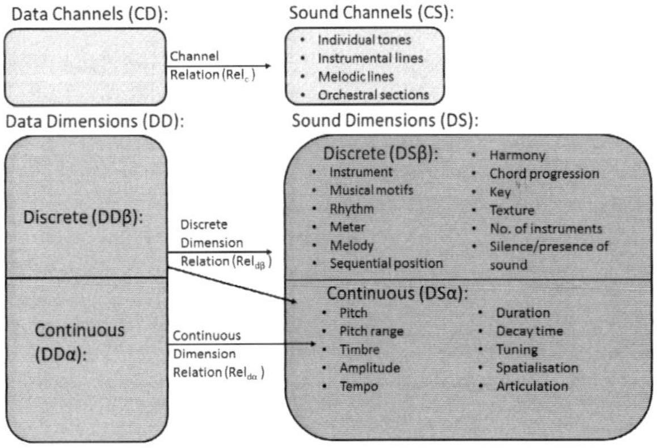

Figure 4. Data Sound Mappings Space of the Model

In Figure 4, we illustrate the space of data-sound parameter-mappings produced by the model. This shows the mappings from the sets of *data channels* and *data dimensions* (continuous and discrete) to possible *sound channels* and *sound dimensions*. We devised the list of *sound channels* and *sound dimensions* by drawing on sonification design literature such as a survey by Dubus et al. of sonification mappings used in prior work [57]; many of the items presented in Figure 4 are further described in that work. We also considered aspects of musical composition in creating these lists, which are not necessarily exhaustive, and can be added to.

VI. Application of the Model to Facilitate Prototype Design

To illustrate the application of the model, this section shows how we used it to design two prototype sonifications of network packet capture data, aimed at two different potential use-cases of sonification within network-security monitoring. We begin by presenting the two use-cases we considered. This is followed by an outline of the network attack characterisation that we used to derive the attack indicators to be represented for a defined network-monitoring scope. We demonstrate how the formalised model was applied, using these attack indicators, to generate prototype sonification systems for the two use-cases, and we describe the implementation of the prototypes.

TABLE IV. DESCRIPTION AND FORMAL NOTATION OF MODEL COMPONENTS

Component	Description	Formal Notation
Data channels	Parts of the network-security monitoring information, about which information should be presented, e.g., individual packets, IDS alerts, sensitive IP addresses on the network	The tuple CD of *data channels* cd
Data dimensions	Types of information we can present about *data channels*, e.g., amount of activity (at network IPs, for example), protocol used (in packet transmission), CPU usage (of network machines). These can have continuous or discrete values	The tuple DD of *data dimensions* dd. The tuple of data dimensions DD is the concatenation $DD\alpha ^\frown DD\beta$ of the tuple $DD\alpha$ of *continuous data dimensions* $dd\alpha$, and the tuple $DD\beta$ of *discrete data dimensions* $dd\beta$
Data values	The values *data dimensions* can take. These can be continuous or discrete, e.g. a continuous scale from low to high (for packet rate, for example); discrete names (of protocols)	The tuple VD_{dd} of *data values* vd_{dd} of the data dimension dd
Sound channels	Streams of sound which we can vary sonically, e.g., individual note events, or separate melodic/instrumental lines	The tuple CS of *sound channels* cs
Sound dimensions	Types of sonic variations we can make to sound channels, e.g. varying the tempo or loudness at which they are presented, or the harmonic structure they follow. These can have continuous or discrete values	The tuple DS of *sound dimensions* ds. The tuple of sound dimensions DS is the concatenation $DS\alpha ^\frown DS\beta$ of the tuple $DS\alpha$ of *continuous sound dimensions* $ds\alpha$, and the tuple $DS\beta$ of *discrete sound dimensions* $ds\beta$
Sound values	The values sound dimensions can take. These can be continuous or discrete, e.g. a continuous scale from slow to fast (tempo); discrete names of instruments	The tuple VS_{ds} of *sound values* vs_{ds} of the sound dimension ds

TABLE V. DESCRIPTION AND FORMAL NOTATION OF MODEL RELATIONS

Relation	Description	Formal Notation
Channel relation	*Data channels* are mapped to *sound channels*	*Channel relation* Rel_c: $CD \leftrightarrow CS$ is a total relation between the tuple of *data channels* and the tuple of *sound channels*
Dimension relation	*Data dimensions* are mapped to *sound dimensions* (which can be discrete or continuous) • *Continuous dimension relation*, in which *continuous data dimensions* are mapped to *continuous sound dimensions* • *Discrete dimension relation*, in which *discrete data dimensions* are mapped to *continuous* or *discrete sound dimensions*	*Dimension relation* Rel_d: $DD \leftrightarrow DS$ is a total relation between the tuple of *data dimensions* and the tuple of *sound dimensions* • *Continuous dimension relation* $Rel_{d\alpha}$: $DD\alpha \leftrightarrow DS\alpha$ is a total relation between the tuple of *continuous data dimensions* and the tuple of *continuous sound dimensions* • *Discrete dimension relation* $Rel_{d\beta}$: $DD\beta \leftrightarrow DS\beta$ is a total relation between the tuple of *discrete data dimensions* and the tuple of *discrete sound dimensions*
Value relation	Values of data dimensions are mapped to values of sound dimensions	For each *data dimension* dd, mapped to *sound dimension* ds, *value relation* Rel_{vdd}: $VD_{dd} \leftrightarrow VS_{ds}$ is a total relation between the tuple of *data values* of dd and the tuple of *sound values* of ds

Finally, we show how the model can be used to capture prior-art approaches to the sonification of network data.

A. Use-Cases

In Section II we highlighted potential advantages of using sonification for network monitoring. Here, we extend that discussion to create two different use-cases for sonification for network monitoring in SOCs. The first case focuses on enabling anomaly detection by security analysts deliberately listening to low-level network data, while the second case focuses on enabling peripheral monitoring of network-security information by security analysts as a non-primary task.

The two use-cases have different design requirements, since they target different modes of monitoring. Vickers differentiates between modes of auditory monitoring [56]. We associate *Use-Case 1* (as described below) with Vickers' description of the direct monitoring mode, in which the user deliberately listens to an audio interface as their main focus of attention, aiming to extract information or identify salient characteristics. *Use-Case 2* is associated with Vickers' peripheral monitoring mode, in which the user focuses attention on another primary task, while indirectly monitoring required information relating to another non-primary task, which is presented through a peripheral auditory display.

Use-Case 1: high-granularity sonification of network data to enable attack detection through pattern recognition by human security analysts: Humans have used sound in the past to detect anomalies with very high levels of resolution; an example is human sonar operators, who classify underwater sources by listening to the sound they make [63, 64]. Furthermore, sonification systems have been successfully designed for pattern recognition [58], and anomaly detection [59], for example, in prior work involving complex datasets.

The motivation for this use-case is that, as described in Section II, automated systems such as IDSs do not always detect attacks effectively or accurately, producing false-positives and false-negatives [2,3]. Presentation of data to humans in a visual form, using security visualisations, can enable detection of malicious network activity that is undetected by automated systems. Given the human ability for pattern recognition through listening, it should not be assumed that vision is the most effective medium for this in all cases without first comparing performances using vision and hearing experimentally [65].

To enable anomaly detection by humans, we aim to represent low-level network data with the highest granularity and resolution of information possible, such that patterns in the data may emerge naturally.

Use-Case 2: high-level sonification of network data for monitoring aspects of the network-security state as a non-

primary task: Analysts are required to carry out multiple tasks while monitoring the network for security breaches, maintaining an awareness of the security of the network [37]. This may mean, for example, continuing to monitor real-time network or IDS logs, while exploring or handling a potential security incident [66]. The aim of sonification in this use-case is to represent sonically the information that analysts need to maintain an appropriate awareness of the network-security state, in such a way that the information can be effectively monitored as a non-primary task. To produce a sonification suitable for use in peripheral monitoring tasks, we aim to present a higher level of information than in *Use-Case 1*: summaries of the data to enable comprehension of network-security state, rather than perception of anomalies and deviations from the normal.

Vickers argues that visual monitoring methods are not well suited to situations in which users are required to focus attention on a primary task, while monitoring other information directly, because of the demands this places on visual attention [56]. He summarises why sonification is well suited to monitoring peripheral information: "...the human auditory system does not need a directional fix on a sound source in order to perceive its presence". Experimental work has shown that sonification is an effective method of presenting information for monitoring as a secondary task. Hildebrandt et al. compared participants' performances in monitoring a simulated production process as a secondary task in three conditions – visual only, visual with auditory alerts, and visual with continuous sonification – while solving simple arithmetic problems as a primary task [67]. The results showed that participants performed significantly better in the secondary monitoring task using the continuous sonification than in the visual, or auditory alert, conditions. Furthermore, secondary monitoring using the continuous sonification had no significant effect on participants' performances in the primary task.

B. Data Requirements: Network Attack Characterisation

Despite the differences in the levels of information required for the two prototypes, the underlying data requirements are the same: for both cases, we require network data to be represented such that attacks are signalled by the sonification. We therefore used the same attack characterisation as the basis for both prototypes, enabling us to identify the network data that should be monitored to indicate the attacks within a defined network and monitoring information sources scope. We varied the treatment of the resulting data requirements in the application of the formalised model, taking into consideration the purpose of the prototype, and the required resolution of data presentation. In particular, for Prototype 1, we aimed to represent all attack indicators derived, while in Prototype 2 we focused on representing one particular attack indicator derived – the traffic rate at destination IP addresses on the monitored network, such that the amount of traffic received at each of these IPs may be monitored as a non-primary task.

We characterised the data requirements for representing indicators of attacks that can be detected within a network-monitoring scope; the scope was defined as follows:

1) The network is a local area network (LAN).
2) The network data monitored is packet header information, excluding packet contents.
3) Network data is monitored in real-time only (we, therefore, excluded aspects such as supply chain attacks on hardware components during manufacture and transportation).

With this scope in mind, we considered attacks in the Mitre Common Attack Pattern Enumeration and Classification (CAPEC) list (https://capec.mitre.org). This is a comprehensive listing and classification of computer attacks for use by, amongst others, security analysts. From this list, we selected attacks that fell within the defined scope. Excluding packet contents especially enabled us to narrow the scope of attacks considered initially to a list of around twenty types of attack, including reconnaissance such as port scanning, and threat realisation such as service flooding. This is because many of the attacks listed in CAPEC could not be detected by monitoring only packet header information without packet contents.

We characterised the attacks in terms of the way they are indicated through the network data monitored, i.e. packet header information. After completing this work, we were able to produce a summary of the data features needed to capture indicators of the attacks within the network monitoring scope. The data features we selected are defined as follows.

- *Packets*: the flow of packets into, out of or within the network.
    - *Rate*: the amount of traffic.
    - *Direction*: The direction in which network traffic is moving (entering network, leaving network, moving within network).
    - *Size*: the byte count of a packet.
    - *Protocol*: the protocol with which traffic is associated.
        - *Rate*: the amount of traffic transmitted using a particular protocol.
    - *Source IP*: the IP from which packets are sent, within or outside the network.
        - *Rate*: the amount of traffic associated with a source IP address.
        - *Range*: the number of source IP addresses as which traffic is observed.
    - *Destination IP/port*: the IP and port to which packets are sent, within or outside the network.
        - *Rate*: the amount of traffic associated with a destination IP address or port.
        - *Range*: the number of destination IP addresses or ports at which traffic is observed.

The derived data features are shown in Table VI. In the table, the leftmost three columns display the data features, while the rightmost three columns show the characterisation of three examples of attacks (TCP SYN scan, data exfiltration and DDoS) in terms of these features. The data features entered in each column are characteristics of those in the preceding column. For example, *rate* (third column) is a characteristic of *source IP*, (second column), which is itself a characteristic of *packet* (first column). The attack characterisation columns show how we used the data features to characterise three different network attacks. For example, given a data exfiltration attack, the data features listed in the second attack characterisation column of Table VI are required.

TABLE VI. NETWORK ATTACK CHARACTERISATION EXAMPLES AND DERIVED DATA PRESENTATION REQUIREMENTS

Required Data			Attack characterisation			
Features	**Features (Characteristics of First Column)**	**Features (Characteristics of Second Column)**	**Attack type:**	**TCP SYN scan**	**Data exfiltration**	**DDoS**
			Attack description:	TCP protocol, SYN packets sent to a range of destination ports on a host	Data exfiltrated from network to external address	Network is flooded by a high wide of traffic sent from multiple hosts
Packet						
	Rate					High
	Direction			Inbound	Outbound	Inbound
	Size					
	Protocol				FTP	
		Rate			High	
	Source IP			Single IP outside network	Single IP inside network	Multiple IPs outside network
		Rate		High	High	High
		Range				Wide
	Destination IP			Single IP inside network	Single IP outside network	One or more IPs inside network
		Rate		High	High	High
		Range				
	Destination port			Ports on single host IP inside network		
		Rate				
		Range		Wide (all ports targeted – scan)		

C. Prototype 1: Low-Level Network Data Sonification for Anomaly Detection by Humans

The aim of Prototype 1 is to sonically represent network data through which an attack might be signalled with as high a resolution as possible, in order to enable anomaly detection through emerging sound patterns. We show how we applied the model in the design of the sonification by considering appropriate data channels, dimensions and values. We develop a prototype design, and highlight challenges in the implementation.

Here we seek to present prototype designs. The purpose is not to develop final system designs, but to illustrate the use of the sonification model for designing sonifications for particular use-cases within network-security monitoring, and to demonstrate how the application of the model can be varied depending on the use for which the sonification is intended.

1) Applying the Sonification Model: We derived the *data channels*, *data dimensions* and *data values* for the prototype using the data requirements presented in Table IV. In this case, in order to achieve the highest possible resolution in the sonification of these data requirements, we aimed to present, as closely as possible, each packet captured, and to represent as much information about each packet as possible as dimensions of the packet channel. We therefore let the entries in the first column (a single entry: packets) of Table VI be the tuple of *data channels*, and all entries in the second column be the tuple of *data dimensions*. The entries in the third column are then conveyed naturally, through the mapping of the selected data channels and dimensions (for example, range of source IPs – third column – does not have a defined mapping, but is presented through the cumulation of the presentation of the source IP dimension for each individual packet).

For this prototype, the sonification is described by the tuple $\langle CD_R, DD_R, VD_R, Rel_c, Rel_{d\alpha}, Rel_{d\beta}, Rel_v\rangle$:

- $CD_R = \langle cd_{R1}\rangle = \langle packets\rangle$
- $DD_R = DD\alpha_R^\frown DD\beta_R = \langle dd\alpha_{R1}, dd\alpha_{R2}, dd\alpha_{R3}, dd\alpha_{R4}, dd\alpha_{R5}\rangle^\frown\langle d\beta_{dR1}, d\beta_{dR2}\rangle = \langle$Source IP, Destination IP, Destination Port, Rate, Size$\rangle^\frown\langle$Direction, Protocol$\rangle$
- $VD_{dR}=\langle vd_{dR1}, vd_{dR2}, vd_{dR3}, vd_{dR4}, vd_{dR5}, vd_{dR6}, vd_{dR7}\rangle = \langle\{1,...,2^{32}\},\{1,...,2^{32}\},\{1,...,2^{16}\},$ {low,normal,high},{small,normal,large}, {incoming,outgoing,internal},(the protocols present in the dataset)$\rangle$
- Rel_c is described by the function $\boldsymbol{\psi}_i : \mathbb{R}^1 \rightarrow \mathbb{R}^m$, $cs_i = \boldsymbol{\psi}_i(cd_1)$
- Rel_d and Rel_v are described by the function $\boldsymbol{\Gamma} : \mathbb{R}^{m+1} \rightarrow \mathbb{R}^q$, $\boldsymbol{\Gamma}_i=\langle\boldsymbol{\gamma}\alpha_{i1}, ..., \boldsymbol{\gamma}\alpha_{ix}, \boldsymbol{\gamma}\beta_{i1}, ..., \boldsymbol{\gamma}\beta_{iy}\rangle$ $\forall i \in \{1, ..., m\}$

We assume that the IP version is IPV4 in the above description of source and destination IP values. Although source and destination ports and IPs are not technically continuous they have such a high number of possible values (2^{32} for IPV4) that we treat them as such. In describing some data values, we used a notion of "normal". This is left as an abstraction in the model, and describes some *expectation* for the observed behaviour of the data dimensions. We discuss how this normal abstraction might be implemented in sonification designs in Section VI.E.

To simplify the design process, we describe data values for rate and size as discrete points of interest (for example, *low*, *high*, *narrow*, *wide*). This description does not exclude the possibility of mapping continuously in the representation, but allows indication of the polarity required in dimension mapping. In sonification, polarity is the direction of the mapping from data to sound. For example, *positive* mapping polarity from the data dimension *rate* to the sound dimension *amplitude* would be described:

- rate: high $\rightarrow$ amplitude: loud;
- rate: low $\rightarrow$ amplitude: soft.

In Figure 5, we present the sonification mapping space introduced in Figure 4, applied to Prototype 1. This shows the *data channels*, *continuous data dimensions* and *discrete data dimensions* with all possible mappings to *sound channels* and *sound dimensions*.

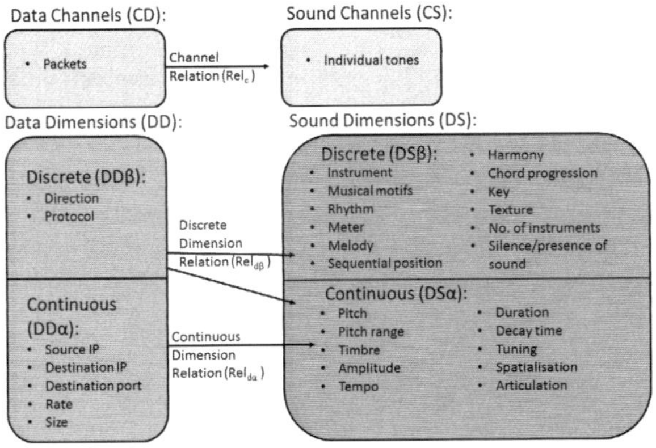

Figure 5. Data Sound Mappings Space: Prototype 1

To determine the mappings from data to sound for the prototype, we selected *sound channels*, *continuous sound dimensions* and *discrete sound dimensions* from the sets CS, $DS\alpha$ and $DS\beta$ respectively. We have not yet carried out testing of appropriate mappings for the data dimensions, as described in Section IV; this is left to future work. Instead, we made predictions about appropriate mappings at this stage, drawing on a survey of mappings used in the sonification of physical quantities in prior sonification work [57]. In that paper, prior work in which physical quantities are sonified is surveyed, and it is noted whether data-sound mappings were: assessed as good; assessed as poor; implemented but not assessed; or not implemented but mentioned as future work. We applied those assessed as good for quantities we considered representative of our data dimensions (for example, for the data dimension *rate*, we considered the physical quantities velocity, activity and event rate from [57]). From this, we derived the following information, which was then incorporated into the prototype design.

- **Rate.** Good mappings described for *velocity*: pitch, brightness, tempo, rhythmic duration. Good mappings described for *activity*: tempo, rhythmic duration [57].
- **Size.** Bad mappings described for *size*: pitch, tempo [57].

Applied to our sound mappings space, this generated the following rules.

- rate $\rightarrow$ pitch, tempo, rhythmic duration
- size NOT $\rightarrow$ pitch, tempo.

We thus arrived at the following set of *relations* for the prototype design.

- *Data channels*:
  - Packet $\rightarrow$ individual tone ($cs_1 = \psi_1(cd_1, t)$)
- *Data dimensions (continuous)*:
  - Rate $\rightarrow$ tempo (positive polarity) ($ds_{11} = \gamma\alpha_1(dd_{11}, t)$)
  - Destination IP $\rightarrow$ spatialisation (pan from left to right headphone) ($ds\alpha_{12} = \gamma\alpha_2(dd\alpha_{12}, t)$)
  - Source IP $\rightarrow$ pitch ($ds\alpha_{13} = \gamma\alpha_3(dd\alpha_{13}, t)$)
  - Destination port $\rightarrow$ articulation ($ds\alpha_{14} = \gamma\alpha_4(dd\alpha_{14}, t)$)
  - Size $\rightarrow$ amplitude (positive polarity) ($ds\alpha_{15} = \gamma\alpha_5(dd\alpha_{15}, t)$)
- *Data dimensions (discrete)*:
  - Protocol $\rightarrow$ instrument ($ds\beta_{11} = \gamma\beta_1(dd\beta_{11}, t)$)
  - Direction $\rightarrow$ register ($ds\beta_{12} = \gamma\beta_2(dd\beta_{12}, t)$)

Figure 6 shows the prototype design developed from these *relations*. In this sonification, each packet observed triggers an individual note event; these events shown as musical notes in Figure 6. The above dimension mappings are represented: the sonification maps data dimensions to the sound dimensions (including instrument, for example) of each note. The sound is panned on a continuous scale between left and right, corresponding to the continuous destination IP dimension. The rate of traffic at each destination IP is represented by the tempo of the notes played at that pan location; source IPs map continuously to frequency such that source IP range is represented by the range of frequencies played. As shown in Figure 6, destination ports map to articulation on a continuous scale. The instrument by which each note is played represents the protocol in which the packet is transmitted, and the direction of traffic is conveyed by differentiating between low, medium and high registers of music.

D. Prototype 2: High-Level Network-Data Sonification for Monitoring Network-Security Information as a Non-Primary Task

The aim of Prototype 2 is to enable security analysts to monitor network data for indicators of attacks as a non-primary task. The sonification must represent aspects of the network data that might signal an attack, in a way that is unobtrusive usually, but draws analysts' attention to aspects of the data when required (when a potential attack indicator arises). The use-case is different to an alert system: the goal here is to be informative about which data has changed, and how it has changed.

Our design approach for this use-case is to sonify a subset of the data through which attacks are indicated – the traffic rate at the destination IP addresses on the network. The rationale for this approach is that to be suitable for peripheral monitoring, the sonification should be uncomplicated to understand. We therefore elect not to sonify all indicators derived in our network-attack characterisation, as in Prototype 1, but to produce a simpler representation of a subset of these indicators. Our network-attack characterisation showed that high traffic rates at particular destination IP addresses on the network were frequently indicators of attacks (see Table VI).

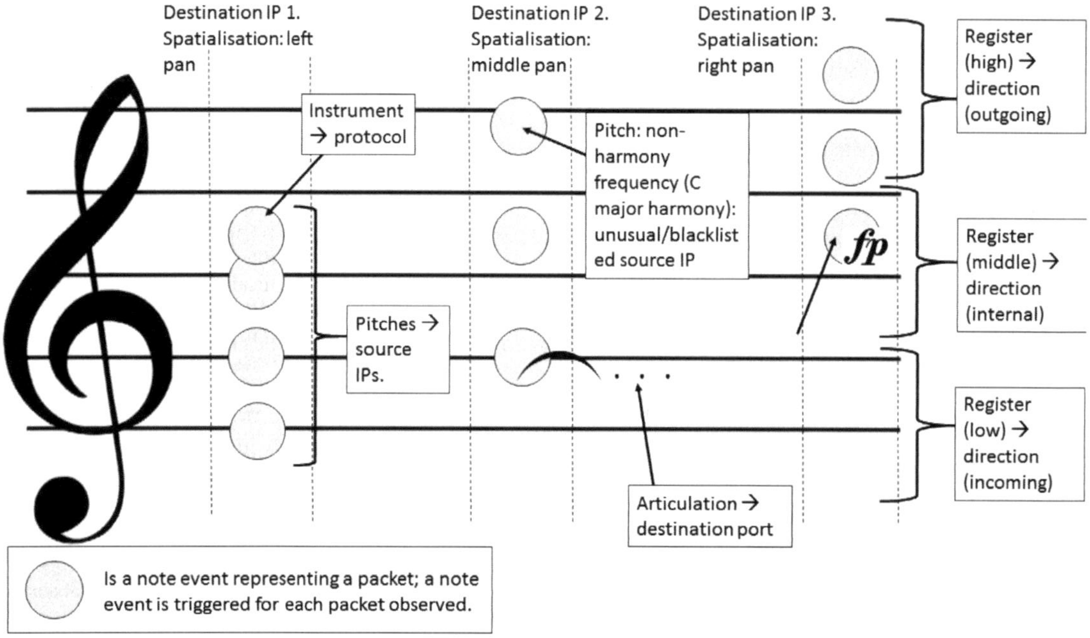

Figure 6. Prototype Diagram: Prototype 1

Monitoring the amount of activity at sensitive machines on the network such as those on which databases containing sensitive information are stored is important, and we selected this as the aim of this peripheral-monitoring sonification prototype. In the remainder of this section we show how this difference in approach influences the application of the model and leads to differing prototype designs.

1) Applying the Sonification Model: We derived the *data channels*, *data dimensions* and *data values* for the prototype by considering the data requirement: present the traffic rate at destination IP addresses on the network. Given the purpose of the sonification is to be suitable for use in peripheral monitoring, we aim to present sonified information such that data changes judged significant (in this case, large increases in traffic rate at any destination IP represented) draw attention, and the sonification is otherwise unobtrusive. We let 10 individual destination IP addresses be the data channels, and the packet rate be the data dimension.

For this prototype, the sonification is described by the tuple $\langle CD_R, DD_R, VD_R, Rel_c, Rel_{d\alpha}, Rel_{d\beta}, Rel_v \rangle$:

- $CD_R = \langle cd_{R1} \rangle = \langle \text{Destination IP addresses} \rangle$
- $DD_R = DD\alpha_R \frown DD\beta_R = \langle dd\alpha_{R1}, dd\alpha_{R2}, dd\alpha_{R3} \rangle \frown \langle d\beta_{dR1} \rangle = \langle \text{Rate} \rangle$
- $VD_{dR} = \langle vd_{dR1} \rangle = \langle \{\text{low,normal,high}\} \rangle$
- Rel_c is described by the functions $\psi_i : \mathbb{R}^{10} \rightarrow \mathbb{R}^m$, $cs_i = \langle \psi_i(cd_j) | j \in \{1,...,n\} \rangle$, where n is the number of network destination IP addresses represented
- Rel_d and Rel_v are described by the function $\mathbf{\Gamma} : \mathbb{R}^{m+1} \rightarrow \mathbb{R}^q$, $\mathbf{\Gamma}_i = \langle \gamma\alpha_{i1}, ..., \gamma\alpha_{ix}, \gamma\beta_{i1}, ..., \gamma\beta_{iy} \rangle$ $\forall i \in \{1,...,m\}$

The notes on the prescription of a "normal" value, and representations of polarity, following the presentation of the sonification for Prototype 1, hold for this case also: the "normal" packet rate for each IP could be prescribed by a human, set as an average calculated statistically, or calculated using Machine Learning.

In Figure 7, we present the sonification mapping space introduced in Figure 4, applied to Prototype 2. This shows the *data channels* and *continuous data dimensions* (there are no *discrete data dimensions* in this case) with all possible mappings to *sound channels* and *sound dimensions*.

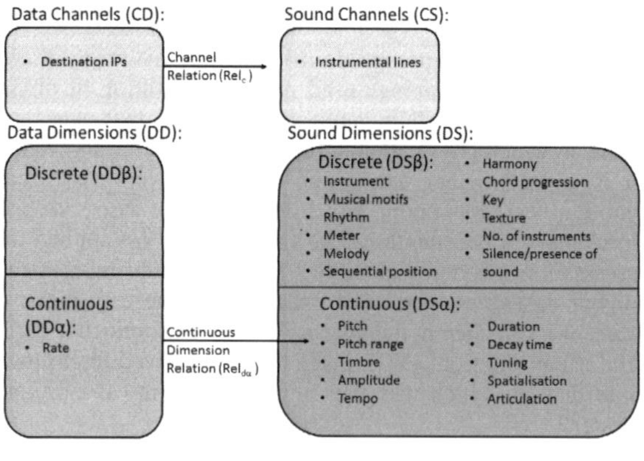

Figure 7. Data Sound Mappings Space: Prototype 2

As described for Prototype 1, we drew on prior work [57] to select from the set of *sound channels* and *continuous sound dimensions*. The **relations** we arrived at are as follows.

- *Data channels*
  - 10 destination IP addresses → 10

instrumental lines
$(cs_i = \psi_i(cd_i, t) \forall i \in \{1, ..., 10\})$

- *Data dimensions (continuous)*:
  - Rate → tempo (positive polarity)
    $(ds\alpha_{i1} = \gamma\alpha_1(dd\alpha_{i1}, t) \forall i \in \{1, ..., 10\})$

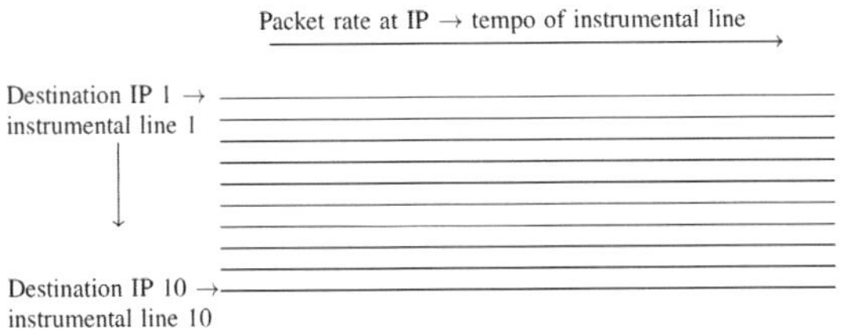

Figure 8. Prototype Diagram: Prototype 2

Figure 8 shows the prototype design developed from these relations. In this sonification, the individual instrumental lines that form the musical piece each present information about an individual destination IP address on the network (in the figure, we present an example in which 10 destination IP addresses are monitored). The lines each follow the base tempo of the musical piece when the packet rate at the destination IP addresses they represent is at its "normal" value. When the packet rate at an individual destination IP address exceeds its "normal" value, note repetition is introduced in the corresponding instrumental line, and the speed of note repetition is scaled to convey the size of the increase in packet rate. As such, a destination IP with a high traffic rate is represented in the sonification as an instrumental line with fast note repetition.

E. Implementation of Prototypes

We implemented both prototypes and used them to sonify the Centre for Applied Internet Data Analysis (CAIDA) "DDoS Attack 2007" dataset [68]. We describe our processes for, and the challenges that arose during, implementation of this dataset. The dataset contains a DDoS attack in which a large flood of incoming traffic is observed, sent from a wide range of source IP addresses to destination IP addresses on the network. We reflect on the sounds produced by the two sonifications of this dataset; in particular, the sounds produced at the time when the flooding begins compared with the sounds prior to the flooding.

We implemented the prototypes by reading the dataset in Python, and parsing the data values according to the mapping functions presented in Tables VII and VIII. These parsed values were then rendered as sound using Supercollider (http://supercollider.github.io/), a platform for audio programming and synthesis frequently used in prior sonification work. The sound rendering was controlled by Open Sound Control (OSC) messages sent from Python to Supercollider.

Although we have not yet conducted user testing for these prototypes, our initial assessment from listening to the sonifications ourselves is that there is a significant change in sound in both prototypes at the time that the dataset shows flooding from multiple source IPs. We invite the reader to listen to audio clips of each of the two network-security monitoring prototypes running on this dataset (https://soundcloud.com/user-71482294).

We encountered some challenges during the implementation phase; in the following, we reflect on possible solutions to these challenges, and hence identify directions for future development. The most significant challenge in the implementation of Prototype 1 arose as a result of the sheer number of packets logged in the dataset, and the small times between their arrival. Because of this, it was challenging to implement the *channel relation* ψ_1 – to render each packet observed as individual notes without overloading the sound engine, or creating sounds too complicated to be of use to human listeners.

We sampled randomly every 1 in 10 packets in the dataset to address this challenge; however, as future work it is important to investigate the most appropriate methods of aggregation, sampling and scaling. For example, a solution might be to aggregate the packets sent in each individual connection (between the same two IP addresses and ports, and using the same service) over time intervals (for example, every 0.1 seconds), and represent the aggregation over this time interval with a single note, whose amplitude varies depending on the number of packets aggregated in this time. This would be a potential way of addressing the problem of packet rates too fast to sonify, without losing the granularity of information provided by the representation of each individual packet. Grond and Berger write that sonification mapping functions may sometimes be linear, but other forms may be more suitable depending on the data [56]. Scaling exponentially, or using methods such as step-change analysis or Fourier Transforms, are examples of avenues worth exploring. Establishing the resolution with which we can represent each of the listed *data channels* and *data dimensions* will be a key part of the development and testing process.

The destination IP representation approach of Prototype 2 may become challenging on large networks. The aim of the prototype is to represent monitoring information in a relatively simple fashion suitable for peripheral monitoring. However, the number of instrumental lines required to represent the many destination IP addresses on a large organisational network would likely introduce complexity to the sonification and make extracting information about individual IP addresses difficult for the user. It is important to investigate experimentally how much information we can represent – in this case, how many destination IP addresses we can represent information about simultaneously in a way that is useful, and whether this can match the monitoring requirements of SOCs in large organisations.

F. Addressing Prior-Art Approaches Using the Sonification Model

We describe the use of our formalised sonification model in representing previously-published sonification system designs. In particular, we verify that our model can address all previous systems (those in which the sonification design is specified completely) that use a musical parameter-mapping sonification method to represent raw network data (these aspects of the systems are presented in Table II) [29, 33, 43–45]. Other relevant systems which use a musical parameter-mapping approach to represent raw network data are presented in [30, 31, 42], but the sonification designs for these works are not specified in enough detail to include.

In Table IX we present the relevant pre-existing sonification systems in terms of the *data channels* and *data dimensions*, and the *sound channels* and *sound dimensions* of our model. In Table X we present the *channel relations* and *dimension relations* for each prior sonification approach

TABLE VII. IMPLEMENTATION OF PROTOTYPE 1

Relation Addressed	Description of Implementation	Mapping Function
Channel relation: $cs_1 = \psi_1(cd_1, t)$	Individual packets observed are mapped to individual tones	The function ψ_1 can be described: for the pth packet cd_{1p} observed at time t, play a single tone cs_{1p} at time t
Dimension relation: $ds\alpha_{12} = \gamma\alpha_2(dd\alpha_{12}, t)$	Destination IP is mapped to spatialisation (pan from left to right headphone). Here, the possible destination IP addresses take values in the range $[0, 2^{32}]$, we converted destination IP addresses to values in this range using a function such that IP address 0.0.0.0 $\rightarrow$ 0, and 0.0.0.1 $\rightarrow$ 1. The pan value varies continuously in the range $[-1, 1]$	The function $\gamma\alpha_2$ can be described: for a note cs_{1p} played at time t, and IP conversion function *IPVal*, the pan value is $ds\alpha_{12p} = \frac{IPVal(dd\alpha_{12p}) \times 2}{2^{32}} - 1$
Dimension relation: $ds\alpha_{13} = \gamma\alpha_3(dd\alpha_{13}, t)$	Source IP is mapped to pitch. Here, the possible source IP addresses take values in the range $[0, 2^{32}]$ and the frequencies vary in the chosen range $[261.63, 2093]$. Frequency 261.63Hz corresponds to C4 – middle C – while frequency 2093Hz corresponds to C7, three octaves higher. We also use a hotlisting method: the top 50 source IPs we expect to observe are mapped to harmonic tones (the notes of a C major 7th chord), while source IPs outside this hotlist are mapped on a continuous scale to frequencies in the selected range	For a source IP hotlist tuple H_s, and tuple M_n of musical notes $\langle C, E, G, B \rangle$, the function $\gamma\alpha_3$ can be described: for note cs_{1p} at time t, and IP conversion function *IPVal*, the pitch value is $dd\alpha_{13p} \in H_s \implies ds\alpha_{13p} \in M_n$, $dd\alpha_{13p} \notin H_s \implies ds\alpha_{13p} = \frac{IPVal(dd\alpha_{13p}) \times (2093 - 261.63)}{2^{32}} + 261.63$
Dimension relation: $ds\alpha_{14} = \gamma\alpha_4(dd\alpha_{14}, t)$	Destination port is mapped to articulation. Here, the possible destination ports take values in the range $[0, 2^{16}]$, and the articulation takes values in the range $[0.1, 1]$. Many packets observed in this dataset did not have destination port values; in these cases we set the sound articulation value to be 0.5 in Supercollider.	The function $\gamma\alpha_4$ can be described: for a note cs_{1p} played at time t, the articulation value is $ds\alpha_{14p} = \frac{dd\alpha_{14p} \times 0.9}{2^{16}} + 0.1$
Dimension relation: $ds\alpha_{15} = \gamma\alpha_5(dd\alpha_{15}, t)$	Size is mapped to amplitude (positive polarity). Here, for the dataset we implemented the average packet size was 60 bytes, while occasional packet sizes were very large. We mapped the size values of the packets to the amplitude values of the sound using a logarithmic function, in which the average packet size, 60, mapped to an amplitude value we judged "comfortable" - the amplitude value 1 in Supercollider.	The function $\gamma\alpha_5$ can be described: for a note cs_{1p} played at time t, the amplitude value is $ds\alpha_{15p} = \frac{1}{2}(log_{10}(\frac{dd\alpha_{15p}}{60} \times 100))$
Dimension relation: $ds\beta_{11} = \gamma\beta_1(dd\beta_{11}, t)$	Protocol is mapped to instrument. Here, a hotlisting method is used again. The two protocols most frequently seen in this dataset are mapped onto two different instruments; the remaining protocols are mapped to another instrument. For this dataset, the tuple of hotlisted protocols is: $H_p = \langle$ICMP, TCP$\rangle$, and the tuple of instruments selected was: $M_i = \langle$strings, saxophone, piano$\rangle$	The function $\gamma\beta_1$ can be described: for a note cs_{1p} played at time t, the instrument value is $dd\beta_{11p} \in H_p \implies ds\beta \in \langle M_{i1}, M_{i2} \rangle$, $dd\beta_{11p} \notin H_p \implies ds\beta = M_{i3}$

TABLE VIII. IMPLEMENTATION OF PROTOTYPE 2

Relation Addressed	Description of Implementation	Mapping Function
Channel relation: $cs_i = \psi_i(cd_i, t) \forall i \in \{1, ..., 10\}$	Destination IP addresses within a hotlist of 10 addresses $H_d = \langle dst_1, ..., dst_{10} \rangle$ are mapped to 10 musical lines in the tuple $M = \langle m_1, ..., m_{10} \rangle$	The function ψ_i can be described: at any time t, play all musical lines $m_i \in M$
Dimension relation: $ds\alpha_{i1} = \gamma\alpha_1(dd\alpha_{i1}, t) \forall i \in \{1, ..., 10\}$	Rate is mapped to tempo (positive polarity), scaled such that the average rate for a particular destination IP is mapped to the base tempo of the music. The rate is measured by aggregating the number of packets observed at each IP per second, and comparing this with the average number to derive the tempo for the corresponding second of music	The function $\gamma\alpha_1$ can be described: for a musical instrumental line $m_i \in M$ played at time t, where the average rate for the corresponding destination IP address dst_i is $avrate_i$ and the base tempo of the music is $avtempo$, the tempo value is $ds\alpha_{i1} = \frac{dd\alpha_{i1}}{avrate_i} \times avtempo$

TABLE IX. APPLYING THE FORMALISATION TO CAPTURE PREVIOUS MUSICAL PARAMETER-MAPPING SYSTEMS FOR THE SONIFICATION OF RAW NETWORK DATA: COMPONENTS

Author	Data Channels	Data Dimensions	Sound Channels	Sound Dimensions
Qi [43] Mapping 1:	Traffic queue 16 (cd_1)	**Continuous**: byte rate ($dd\alpha_{11}$); packet rate ($dd\alpha_{12}$)	Piano notes (cs_1)	**Continuous**: frequency ($ds\alpha_{11}$); amplitude ($ds\alpha_{12}$)
Qi [43] Mapping 2:	Traffic queues 1–16 ($cd_1, ..., cd_{16}$)	**Continuous**: byte rate ($dd\alpha_{11}$); packet rate ($dd\alpha_{12}$)	16 groups of piano notes ($cs_1, ..., cs_{16}$)	**Continuous**: frequency ($ds\alpha_{11}$); amplitude ($ds\alpha_{12}$)
Brown [44]	Network traffic (cd_1)	**Continuous**: packet rate ($dd\alpha_{11}$; number of TCP handshakes ($dd\alpha_{12}$); number of HTTP error messages ($dd\alpha_{13}$)	Existing musical piece (cs_1)	**Continuous**: number of sharp notes ($ds\alpha_{11}$); pitch ($ds\alpha_{12}$); rhythm ($ds\alpha_{13}$)
Ballora [33]	Socket exchanges (cd_1); requests to unusual ports (cd_2); traffic in 5 different monitoring locations (within 2 subnets; between subnets; external traffic going to each subnet) (cd_3)	**Continuous**: source IP ($dd\alpha_{11}$); destination IP($dd\alpha_{12}$); frequency of packets in ongoing socket connections ($dd\alpha_{13}$); traffic rate ($dd\alpha_{34}$) **Discrete**: port number ($dd\beta_{21}$)	An individual strike of a gong (cs_1); humming sound (cs_2); 5 distinct whooshing sounds (cs_3)	**Continuous**: rumble's timbre ($ds\alpha_{11}$); sizzle's timbre ($ds\alpha_{12}$); stereo pan position ($ds\alpha_{13}$); force of strike ($ds\alpha_{14}$); timbre (of humming sound) ($ds\alpha_{25}$); amplitude (of whooshing sound) ($ds\alpha_{36}$)
Giot [29]	Packets (cd_1); useless packets (e.g. ACK packets) (cd_2)	**Continuous**: packet size ($dd\alpha_{11}$); time-to-live (TTL) ($dd\alpha_{12}$); rate/bandpass ($dd\alpha_{13}$); number of useless packets ($dd\alpha_{21}$) **Discrete**: Protocol ($dd\beta_{11}$)	Individual note events (MIDI) (cs_1); noise (cs_2)	**Continuous**: frequency ($ds\alpha_{11}$); note duration ($ds\alpha_{12}$); bandpass of resonant filter ($ds\alpha_{13}$); amount of noise ($ds\alpha_{24}$) **Discrete**: sound synthesiser ($ds\beta_{11}$);
Mancuso [45]	Individual packets (cd_1)	**Continuous**: source IP ($dd\alpha_{11}$); destination IP ($dd\alpha_{12}$) **Discrete**: packet size ($dd\beta_{11}$)	String note (cs_1); wind note (cs_2)	**Continuous**: pitch ($ds\alpha_{11}$, $ds\alpha_{21}$); amplitude ($ds\alpha_{12}, ds\alpha_{22}$)

TABLE X. APPLYING THE FORMALISATION TO CAPTURE PREVIOUS MUSICAL PARAMETER-MAPPING SYSTEMS FOR THE SONIFICATION OF RAW NETWORK DATA: RELATIONS

Author	Channel Relations	Dimension Relations
Qi [43] Mapping 1:	Single traffic queue → all piano notes ($cs_1 = \psi(cd_1)$)	Byte rate → frequency ($ds\alpha_{11} = \gamma\alpha_1(dd\alpha_{11}, t)$); packet rate → amplitude ($ds\alpha_{12} = \gamma\alpha_2(dd\alpha_{12}, t)$)
Qi [43] Mapping 2:	Traffic queue i → piano notes group i ($cs_i = \psi(cd_i) \forall i \in \{1, ..., 16\}$)	Byte rate → frequency ($ds\alpha_{i1} = \gamma\alpha_1(dd\alpha_{i1}, t) \forall i \in \{1, ..., 16\}$); packet rate → amplitude ($ds\alpha_{i2} = \gamma\alpha_2(dd\alpha_{i2}, t) \forall i \in \{1, ..., 16\}$)
Brown [44]	Network traffic → existing musical piece ($cs_1 = \psi(cd_1)$)	Traffic rate → number of sharp notes ($ds\alpha_{11} = \gamma\alpha_1(dd\alpha_{11}, t)$); number of TCP handshakes → pitch ($ds\alpha_{12} = \gamma\alpha_2(dd\alpha_{12}, t)$); number of HTTP error messages → rhythm ($ds\alpha_{13} = \gamma\alpha_2(dd\alpha_{13}, t)$)
Ballora [33]	Socket exchange → individual strike of gong ($cs_1 = \psi(cd_1)$); request to unusual port → humming sound; traffic in five different monitoring locations → five distinct whooshing sounds	Source IP → gong rumble's timbre ($ds\alpha_{11} = \gamma\alpha_1(dd\alpha_{11}, t)$); destination IP → gong sizzle's timbre ($ds\alpha_{12} = \gamma\alpha_2(dd\alpha_{12}, t)$); source IP, destination IP → stereo pan position ($ds\alpha_{13} = \gamma\alpha_3(dd\alpha_{11}, dd\alpha_{12}, t)$); frequency of packets → force of strike ($ds\alpha_{14} = \gamma\alpha_4(dd\alpha_{13})$); port number → timbre of humming sound ($ds\alpha_{25} = \gamma\beta_1(dd\beta_{21})$); traffic rate → amplitude of whooshing sound ($ds\alpha_{36} = \gamma\alpha_4(dd\alpha_{34})$)
Giot [29]	Packets → individual note events ($cs_1 = \psi(cd_1)$); useless packets → noise ($cs_2 = \psi(cd_2)$)	Packet size → frequency ($ds\alpha_{11} = \gamma\alpha_1(dd\alpha_{11}, t)$; TTL → note duration ($ds\alpha_{12} = \gamma\alpha_2(dd\alpha_{12})$); rate → bandpass of resonant filter ($ds\alpha_{13} = \gamma\alpha_3(dd\alpha_{13})$); protocol → sound synthesiser ($ds\beta_{11} = \gamma\beta_1(dd\beta_{11})$); number of useless packets → amount of noise ($ds\alpha_{24} = \gamma\alpha_4(dd\alpha_{21})$)
Mancuso [45]	Individual packets → string note, wind note ($cs_1 = \psi(cd_1)$, $cs_2 = \psi(cd_1)$)	Source IP → pitch of string note ($ds\alpha_{11} = \gamma\alpha_1(dd\alpha_{11}, t)$); destination IP → pitch of wind note ($ds\alpha_{21} = \gamma\alpha_2(dd\alpha_{12}, t)$); packet size → amplitude (of string note and wind note) ($ds\alpha_{12} = \gamma\beta_1(dd\beta_{11})$), ($ds\alpha_{22} = \gamma\beta_1(dd\beta_{11})$)

addressed. This shows that the systems addressed can all be represented in our model, which allows for comparative testing of newly-developed sonification systems against pre-existing approaches.

VII. Conclusion and Future Work

We conclude that there is a growing requirement for the validation of sonification as a means of improving certain monitoring capabilities in SOCs. The current state of the art provides evidence of the potential of sonification in advancing network-security monitoring capabilities. Systems proposed and in use have been shown to be as effective as, or more effective than, other network monitoring techniques insofar as a limited amount of testing has been performed [19].

As future work, we intend to perform proof-of-concept experiments for the sonification prototypes. For Prototype 1, we will sonify a number of network packet capture datasets containing instances of network attacks using the prototype, and assess whether "patterns" appear, or deviations from the "normal" sound of the sonification are heard, at the time of the attacks. For Prototype 2, we will assess experimentally whether the sonification conveys the packet rate at individual destination IP addresses on the network, in a way suitable for monitoring as a non-primary task.

As described in Section IV, a key stage in the sonification development is experimental identification of appropriate aesthetics: intuitive mappings from data to sound, for example. We have applied mappings in both presented prototypes based on our own intuition, and relevant aspects of prior work [57]. A direction for future work is conducting design experiments to determine the optimal mapping aesthetics, and incorporating these mappings into the formalised sonification model to generate final system designs. To assess the effectiveness of our sonification model and aesthetic approach, we need to contrast our approach with pre-existing approaches to parameter-mapping sonification for network-security monitoring [28, 33, 36, 43, 45], by comparing their performance in highlighting network attacks.

During the presentation of prototypes, we highlighted our use of a "normal" in describing the values of certain data dimensions. A challenge in the implementation of the prototypes lies in determining appropriate meanings of this "normal", which is left as an abstraction in the model. The normal might in practice be defined, or calculated using Statistics or Machine Learning for a particular network. The normal could also be defined not by the system itself, but discerned by the humans using the system, based on what they expect to be, or have become accustomed to, hearing. The former approach is likely to be more appropriate for enabling the peripheral monitoring capability targeted in *Use-Case 2*, while the latter (in which humans learn to "hear" some normal) may apply to *Use-Case 1*, given the aim to enable humans to detect anomalies.

Alternative methods of extracting the data requirements for network-attack detection should be explored. The attack characterisation approach taken here could be extended, and validated, through security analysts' input on their real network-data monitoring requirements. This should explore both how analysts detect anomalies indicating attacks through network data, and which aspects of network data they may realistically be required to monitor as a non-primary task (for addressing *Use-Case 2* in particular).

Also left to future work is the exploration of the potential interactions between sonification and visualisation, and of how multimodal system designs can be leveraged for the context. In Prototype 1, for example, we envisage that, while sonification is used here for the *perception* of anomalous events on the network – the recognition by humans that "something is wrong" – visualisation could complement the system by enabling *comprehension* of the nature of the events perceived, directed by the sonification. Similarly, Prototype 2 could be complemented by a visualisation that conveys exactly which destination IP address has experienced an increase in packet rate, following the event that the listening analyst's attention is drawn to some change in the sonification.

Further work should be carried out, as highlighted in Section IV, in user testing of the system, in order to assess whether users (in particular, the intended users: security analysts) can hear the patterns generated in the sonification at the time of the attacks. We intend to research the potential for sonification to match, or improve on, the performance of existing monitoring systems in the SOC environment such as security visualisations and IDSs. At this stage, usability aspects such as integration of sonification into the SOC environment should also be addressed.

REFERENCES

[1] L. Axon, S. Creese, M. Goldsmith, and J. R. C. Nurse, "Reflecting on the use of sonification for network monitoring," in Proceedings of the International Conference on Emerging Security Information, Systems and Technologies (IARIA), 2016, pp. 254–261.

[2] P. Garcia-Teodoro, J. Diaz-Verdejo, G. Maciá-Fernández, and E. Vázquez, "Anomaly-based network intrusion detection: Techniques, systems and challenges," computers & security, vol. 28, no. 1, 2009, pp. 18–28.

[3] S. Axelsson, "The base-rate fallacy and its implications for the difficulty of intrusion detection," in Proceedings of the 6th ACM Conference on Computer and Communications Security. ACM, 1999, pp. 1–7.

[4] M. Gopinath, "Auralization of intrusion detection system using Jlisten," Development, vol. 22, 2004, p. 3.

[5] Klahr, Rebecca and Amili, Sophie and Shah, Jayesh Navin and Button, Mark and Wang, Victoria, "Cyber Security Breaches Survey 2016," 2016.

[6] D. Denning, "An intrusion-detection model," IEEE Transactions on Software Engineering, no. 2, 1987, pp. 222–232.

[7] A. Lazarevic, L. Ertöz, V. Kumar, A. Ozgur, and J. Srivastava, "A comparative study of anomaly detection schemes in network intrusion detection." in Proceedings of SIAM International Conference on Data Mining, 2003, pp. 25–36.

[8] V. Chandola, A. Banerjee, and V. Kumar, "Anomaly detection: A survey," ACM Computing Surveys (CSUR), vol. 41, no. 3, 2009, p. 15.

[9] V. Kumar, J. Srivastava, and A. Lazarevic, Managing cyber threats: issues, approaches, and challenges. Springer Science & Business Media, 2006, vol. 5.

[10] D. E. Denning and P. G. Neumann, "Requirements and model for ides—a real-time intrusion detection expert system," Document A005, SRI International, vol. 333, 1985.

[11] N. Ye, S. Emran, Q. Chen, and S. Vilbert, "Multivariate statistical analysis of audit trails for host-based intrusion detection," IEEE Transactions on Computers, vol. 51, no. 7, 2002, pp. 810–820.

[12] D. Anderson, T. F. Lunt, H. Javitz, A. Tamaru, and A. Valdes, Detecting unusual program behavior using the statistical component of the Next-generation Intrusion Detection Expert System (NIDES). SRI International, Computer Science Laboratory, 1995.

[13] C. Tsai, Y. Hsu, C. Lin, and W. Lin, "Intrusion detection by machine learning: A review," Expert Systems with Applications, vol. 36, no. 10, 2009, pp. 11 994–12 000.

[14] Y. Zhang, Y. Xiao, M. Chen, J. Zhang, and H. Deng, "A survey of security visualization for computer network logs," Security and Communication Networks, vol. 5, no. 4, 2012, pp. 404–421.

[15] R. E. Etoty and R. F. Erbacher, "A survey of visualization tools assessed for anomaly-based intrusion detection analysis," DTIC Document, Tech. Rep., 2014.

[16] R. F. Erbacher, K. L. Walker, and D. A. Frincke, "Intrusion and misuse detection in large-scale systems," Computer Graphics and Applications, IEEE, vol. 22, no. 1, 2002, pp. 38–47.

[17] B. Shneiderman, "Dynamic queries for visual information seeking," IEEE Software, vol. 11, no. 6, 1994, pp. 70–77.

[18] J. Nicholls, D. Peters, A. Slawinski, T. Spoor, S. Vicol, J. Happa, M. Goldsmith, and S. Creese, "Netvis: a visualization tool enabling multiple perspectives of network traffic data," 2013.

[19] S. Rinderle-Ma and T. Hildebrandt, "Server sounds and network noises," in Cognitive Infocommunications (CogInfoCom), 2015 6th IEEE International Conference on. IEEE, 2015, pp. 45–50.

[20] Z. Halim, R. Baig, and S. Bashir, "Sonification: a novel approach towards data mining," in Proceedings of the International Conference on Emerging Technologies, 2006. IEEE, 2006, pp. 548–553.

[21] T. Hinterberger and G. Baier, "Parametric orchestral sonification of EEG in real time," IEEE MultiMedia, no. 2, 2005, pp. 70–79.

[22] P. Janata and E. Childs, "Marketbuzz: Sonification of real-time financial data," in Proceedings of the International Conference on Auditory Display, 2004.

[23] T. Hermann, "Sonification for Exploratory Data Analysis," Ph.D. dissertation, 2002, Bielefeld University.

[24] G. Kramer, Auditory display: Sonification, audification, and auditory interfaces. Perseus Publishing, 1993.

[25] A. de Campo, "Toward a data sonification design space map," in Proceedings of the International Conference on Auditory Display, 2007, pp. 342–347.

[26] S. Barrass and C. Frauenberger, "A communal map of design in auditory display," in Proceedings of the International Conference on Auditory Display, 2009, pp. 1–10.

[27] S. Barrass et al., "Auditory information design," Made available in DSpace on 2011-01-04T02: 37: 33Z (GMT), 1997.

[28] M. Gilfix and A. Couch, "Peep (the network auralizer): Monitoring your network with sound." in Proceedings of the Large Installation System Administration Conference, 2000, pp. 109–117.

[29] R. Giot and Y. Courbe, "Intention–interactive network sonification," in Proceedings of the International Conference on Auditory Display. Georgia Institute of Technology, 2012, pp. 235–236.

[30] D. Worrall, "Realtime sonification and visualisation of network metadata," in Proceedings of the International Conference on Auditory Display, 2015, pp. 337–339.

[31] M. Kimoto and H. Ohno, "Design and implementation of stetho—network sonification system," in Proceedings of the International Computer Music Conference, 2002, pp. 273–279.

[32] D. Malandrino, D. Mea, A. Negro, G. Palmieri, and V. Scarano, "Nemos: Network monitoring with sound," in Proceedings of the International Conference on Auditory Display, 2003, pp. 251–254.

[33] M. Ballora, N. Giacobe, and D. Hall, "Songs of cyberspace: an update on sonifications of network traffic to support situational awareness," in SPIE Defense, Security, and Sensing. International Society for Optics and Photonics, 2011, pp. 80 640P–80 640P.

[34] R. Schafer, The soundscape: Our sonic environment and the tuning of the world. Inner Traditions/Bear & Co, 1993.

[35] O. Kessler et al., "[functional description of the data fusion process]," 1991, Office of Naval Technology Naval Air Development Center, Warminster PA.

[36] P. Vickers, C. Laing, and T. Fairfax, "Sonification of a network's self-organized criticality," arXiv preprint arXiv:1407.4705, 2014.

[37] P. Vickers, C. Laing, M. Debashi, and T. Fairfax, "Sonification aesthetics and listening for network situational awareness," in Proceedings of the Conference on Sonification of Health and Environmental Data, 2014.

[38] B. deButts, "Network access log visualization & sonification," Master's thesis, Tufts University, Medford, MA, US, 2014.

[39] M. Garcia-Ruiz, M. Vargas Martin, B. Kapralos, J. Tashiro, and R. Acosta-Diaz, "Best practices for applying sonification to support teaching and learning of network intrusion detection," in Proceedings of the World Conference on Educational Multimedia, Hypermedia and Telecommunications, 2010, pp. 752–757.

[40] S. El Seoud, M. Garcia-Ruiz, A. Edwards, R. Aquino-Santos, and M. Martin, "Auditory display as a tool for teaching network intrusion detection," International Journal of Emerging Technologies in Learning (iJET), vol. 3, no. 2, 2008, pp. 59–62.

[41] P. Varner and J. Knight, "Monitoring and visualization of emergent behavior in large scale intrusion tolerant distributed systems," Technical report, Pennsylvania State University, 2002.

[42] C. Papadopoulos, C. Kyriakakis, A. Sawchuk, and X. He, "Cyberseer: 3d audio-visual immersion for network security and management," in Proceedings of the ACM workshop on Visualization and data mining for computer security. ACM, 2004, pp. 90–98.

[43] L. Qi, M. Martin, B. Kapralos, M. Green, and M. García-Ruiz, "Toward sound-assisted intrusion detection systems," in On the Move to Meaningful Internet Systems 2007: CoopIS, DOA, ODBASE, GADA, and IS. Springer, 2007, pp. 1634–1645.

[44] A. Brown, M. Martin, B. Kapralos, M. Green, and M. Garcia-Ruiz, "Poster: Towards music-assisted intrusion detection," 2009, poster presented at IEEE Workshop on Statistical Signal Processing.

[45] V. F. Mancuso et al., "Augmenting cyber defender performance and workload through sonified displays," Procedia Manufacturing, vol. 3, 2015, pp. 5214–5221.

[46] M. García-Ruiz, M. Martin, and M. Green, "Towards a multimodal human-computer interface to analyze intrusion detection in computer networks," in Proceedings of the First Human-Computer Interaction Workshop (MexIHC), Puebla, Mexico, 2006.

[47] "Fraunhofer IIS Netson," 2016, URL: http://www.iis.fraunhofer.de/en/muv/2015/netson.html [accessed: 24/02/2017].

[48] "Specimen Box, The Office for Creative Research," 2014, URL: http://ocr.nyc/user-focused-tools/2014/06/01/specimen-box/ [accessed: 24/02/2017].

[49] L. Buchanan, A. D'Amico, and D. Kirkpatrick, "Mixed method approach to identify analytic questions to be visualized for military cyber incident handlers," in Visualization for Cyber Security (VizSec), 2016 IEEE Symposium on. IEEE, 2016, pp. 1–8.

[50] T.-F. Yen, A. Oprea, K. Onarlioglu, T. Leetham, W. Robertson, A. Juels, and E. Kirda, "Beehive: Large-scale log analysis for detecting suspicious activity in enterprise networks," in Proceedings of the 29th Annual Computer Security Applications Conference. ACM, 2013, pp. 199–208.

[51] D. Zhao, I. Traore, B. Sayed, W. Lu, S. Saad, A. Ghorbani, and D. Garant, "Botnet detection based on traffic behavior analysis and flow intervals," Computers & Security, vol. 39, 2013, pp. 2–16.

[52] D. Acarali, M. Rajarajan, N. Komninos, and I. Herwono, "Survey of approaches and features for the identification of http-based botnet traffic," Journal of Network and Computer Applications, vol. 76, 2016, pp. 1–15.

[53] A. D'Amico, K. Whitley, D. Tesone, B. O'Brien, and E. Roth, "Achieving cyber defense situational awareness: A cognitive task analysis of information assurance analysts," in Proceedings of the human factors and ergonomics society annual meeting, vol. 49, no. 3. SAGE Publications, 2005, pp. 229–233.

[54] G. Parseihian, C. Gondre, M. Aramaki, S. Ystad, and R. K. Martinet, "Comparison and evaluation of sonification strategies for guidance tasks," IEEE Transactions on Multimedia, vol. 18, no. 4, 2016, pp. 674–686.

[55] S. C. Peres, D. Verona, T. Nisar, and P. Ritchey, "Towards a systematic approach to real-time sonification design for surface electromyography," Displays, 2016.

[56] T. Hermann, A. Hunt, and J. Neuhoff, The sonification handbook. Logos Verlag Berlin, GE, 2011.

[57] G. Dubus and R. Bresin, "A systematic review of mapping strategies for the sonification of physical quantities," PloS one, vol. 8, no. 12, 2013, p. e82491.

[58] E. Yeung, "Pattern recognition by audio representation of multivariate analytical data," Analytical Chemistry, vol. 52, no. 7, 1980, pp. 1120–1123.

[59] M. Ballora, R. Cole, H. Kruesi, H. Greene, G. Monahan, and D. Hall, "Use of sonification in the detection of anomalous events," in SPIE Defense, Security, and Sensing. International Society for Optics and Photonics, 2012, pp. 84 070S–84 070S.

[60] J. Rubin and D. Chisnell, Handbook of usability testing: how to plan, design and conduct effective tests. John Wiley & Sons, 2008.

[61] J. R. C. Nurse, S. Creese, M. Goldsmith, and K. Lamberts, "Guidelines for usable cybersecurity: Past and present," in Proceedings of the Third International Workshop on Cyberspace Safety and Security (CSS). IEEE, 2011, pp. 21–26.

[62] A. de Campo, "A data sonification design space map," in Proc. of the 2nd International Workshop on Interactive Sonification, York, UK, 2007.

[63] F. Briolle, "Detection and classification of the audiophonic sonar signal: perspectives of space simulation under headphones," Undersea Defense Technology, 1991.

[64] R. Mill and G. Brown, "Auditory-based time-frequency representations and feature extraction techniques for sonar processing," Speech and Hearing Research Group, Sheffield, England, 2005.

[65] M. Ballora and D. Hall, "Do you see what I hear: experiments in multichannel sound and 3D visualization for network monitoring?" in SPIE Defense, Security, and Sensing. International Society for Optics and Photonics, 2010, pp. 77 090J–77 090J.

[66] A. D'Amico and K. Whitley, "The real work of computer network defense analysts," in VizSEC 2007. Springer, 2008, pp. 19–37.

[67] T. Hildebrandt, T. Hermann, and S. Rinderle-Ma, "Continuous sonification enhances adequacy of interactions in peripheral process monitoring," International Journal of Human-Computer Studies, 2016.

[68] "The CAIDA UCSD DDoS Attack 2007 dataset," URL: https://www.caida.org/data/passive/ddos-20070804_dataset.xml [accessed 24/02/2017].

The Influence of the Human Factor on ICT Security: An Empirical Study within the Corporate Landscape in Austria

Christine Schuster
Institute for Empirical Social Studies
Vienna, Austria
e-mail: christine.schuster@ifes.at

Johannes Göllner, Christian Meurers, Andreas Peer, Peter Prah
Section Knowledge Management
Department of Central Documentation & Information
National Defence Academy of the Austrian Federal Ministry of Defence and Sports
Vienna, Austria
e-mail: {johannes.goellner | christian.meurers | andreas.peer | peter.prah}@bmlvs.gv.at

Martin Latzenhofer, Stefan Schauer
Digital Safety & Security
Austrian Institute of Technology
Vienna, Austria
e-mail: {martin.latzenhofer | stefan.schauer}@ait.ac.at

Gerald Quirchmayr[1], Thomas Benesch[2]
[1]Research Group Multimedia Information Systems
Faculty of Computer Science
[2]Institute for International Development
University of Vienna
Vienna, Austria
e-mail: {gerald.quirchmayr | thomas.benesch}@univie.ac.at

Abstract — **The human factor is a decisive risk factor in information security and is now on its way to be fully integrated into information security programs and risk management approaches. Due to this remaining lack of integration, we have designed a study on user attitudes towards information security issues in Austrian companies. This study included a comprehensive survey that was based on extensive desk research on risk, behavior and trust models. The second key part of the study reflects the results of two moderated focus groups that discussed information security issues derived from the analyzed literature. The third main component of our study is based on personal interviews with 891 respondents structured by the prepared survey. The analysis of the results from the focus groups and the personal interviews allowed the identification and confirmation of user perceptions and trustworthiness factors. Building upon the survey results, we propose a set of significant indicators that can help to identify ICT-related misuse and fraudulent behavior as a situation awareness instrument.**

Keywords— information security; user perceptions; attitude; human risk factor; work satisfaction; compliance.

I. Introduction

The trust employees have in their organization's information and communication technology (ICT) systems plays a crucial role when considering the organization's overall security situation. This has been emphasized by a comprehensive empirical study on ICT security in the corporate landscape in Austria carried out by the authors in 2015 and firstly presented at SECURWARE 2017 in [1], and is also amply discussed in the literature from various perspectives [2] [3]. Further, the attitude of employees as an indicator of emerging problems has also been described in recent publications [4] [5]. The key issue here is that the human behavior represents a major risk factor and is hard to control from an organization's perspective. Neither can these non-technical vulnerabilities be measured nor is there a real-time early warning system covering this aspect in a sufficiently reliable way. Repetitive awareness measures help to strengthen an organization's culture, but their effectiveness is hard to assess and those measures take a long time and many iterations. So far, there is no satisfying and reliable method that can be applied with reasonable effort to assess the human risk factor in an organization's environment [6] [7].

The afore mentioned empirical study was part of the project MetaRisk [8], which was supported and partially financed by the Austrian National Security Research Program KIRAS. The survey was conducted among employees with and without management functions. Based on the results of this survey, we investigated the situation regarding information security in Austrian companies in 2015. The key questions covered by this survey were the following:

1. How do individual staff members apply the safeguards that have been set up by their organization?
2. How do employees handle security-relevant incidents and, especially, which activities do they undertake to avoid or circumvent those incidents including activities that cause harm to the organization?
3. What is the general relationship between employer and employees?

By analyzing the employees' attitudes, tendency of activities and behavior patterns, we have identified possible indicators which can even point to insider fraud in extreme cases.

In the context of information security, the human aspects assume a decisive role as either an early warning of decaying information security awareness or as a careless attitude towards the issue. The continuously growing number of phishing, spear phishing and identity fraud attacks against normal and unexperienced users shows that these types of attacks have recently become even more attractive [9]. With more sophisticated forms of attacks, for example advanced persistent threats (APT) where perimeter controls substantially lose their protective effectiveness [10], the problem becomes more critical. These forms of attacks are trying to obtain an organization's most confidential business information, causing financial damage and in stealing trade secrets. On the other hand, economic pressure is growing in general and both employees and employers are trying to reduce cost, aim for leaner processes and at minimizing efforts, thus making the work environment less comfortable. This is one reason why the potential for misuse, business and cybercrime is rising [2] [7]. A small but significant set of indicators reflects the attitude of the employee towards the information security situation in an individual organization. Consequently, if we look at this set of indicators all together we can identify the principal vulnerabilities of an organization related to the human risk factor. If we link these indicators to particular types of attacks, e.g., social engineering, we can decide whether an organization is more vulnerable than another.

The present paper is structured into five sections. In Section II, we first present the scientific basis from the relevant literature and our motivation for the study. Section III describes the applied methodological approach of the survey performed for the study. In Section IV, we discuss the main results of the study compared to retrospectively documented attack stories from real life. Section V proposes aspects for further research and we present concrete indicators that can serve as basis for forming a radar chart and as input for a scorecard. This leads to a general overview of the influence of human risk on information security.

II. MOTIVATION AND BACKGROUND

As amply described in a large number of recent publications including textbooks, information security is an issue of continuously growing importance for organizations of all sizes. Recent trends in Austria [11, p. 8] [12] [13] and Germany [14] [15, p. 7] (the German situation is closely comparable to the Austrian one) have been a shift in attacks towards social engineering and fraud. An analysis of attack types performed in 2014 [16], shows which types of attacks were most successful in affected enterprises (Figure 1).

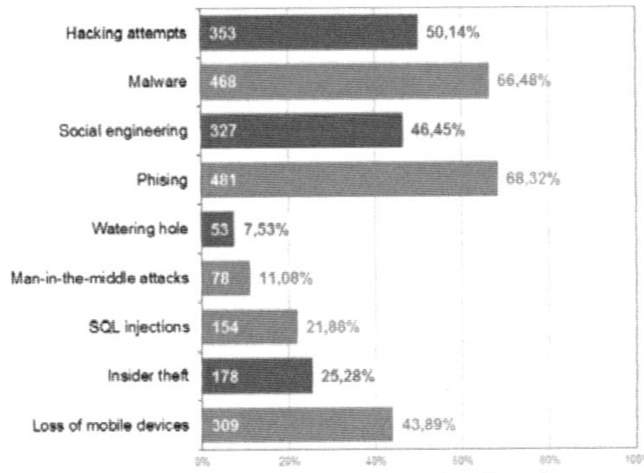

Figure 1. Successful attack types in affected respondent's enterprises in 2014, n=704 respondents [16, p. 6], edited

In this context, "phishing" attacks had the highest success rate, followed by the classic attack types "malware" and "hacking attempts" and by "social engineering". When looking at the latest, updated results of this study from 2015 [17], we can see that "social engineering" has surpassed the hacking attempts, now taking the third rank after "phishing" and "malware" in the list of the most successful attack types (Figure 2).

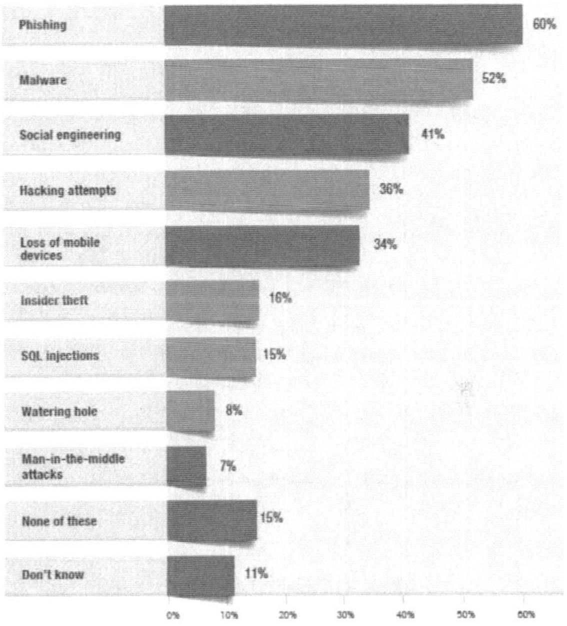

Figure 2. Successful attack types in affected respondent's enterprises in 2015, n=461 respondents [17]

The Austrian internet security report 2015 [12, p. 45] also explicitly states that social engineering methods are growing significantly in number and sophistication. This sort of attack can be seen as the currently most dangerous attack type. Therefore, the human factor has turned into the weakest link in the cyber defense chain of an organization.

As these attacks have a significant financial impact on affected companies [16], it is important to know the human vulnerabilities towards social engineering attacks and financial fraud that use information technology as a vehicle to commit crime. In one extreme case, such a financial fraud attack on an Austrian aerospace manufacturer recently caused an estimated damage of 50 million EUR [18]. Figure 3 illustrates this financial risk by pointing out that in 2014 almost half of US companies suffered financial damage from attacks at least annually [19, p. 28], while in 2016 the number of companies in the US which suffered damage of more than one million USD due to cybercrime doubled (i.e., from 7% in 2014 to 15% in 2016) [20]. At the same time, employees and managers are more and more ignorant of the impacts of cybercrime with just slightly more than half of the US companies having a cyber incident response plan that is "fully in operation" [20].

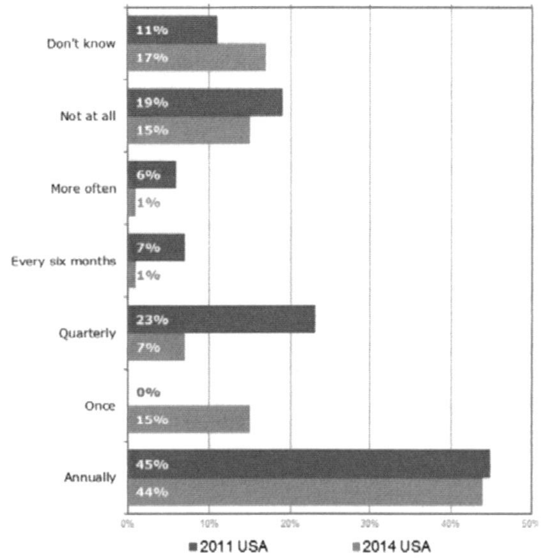

Figure 3. Relative financial impact of cybercrime on organizations [19, p. 28], edited

Figure 4 clearly shows that insiders – no matter whether they have malicious or non-malicious intents – contributed significantly to the damage that enterprises suffered in 2014 [16].

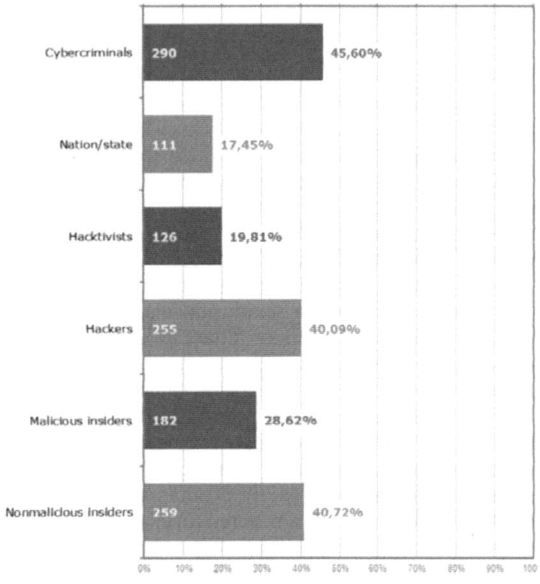

Figure 4. Threat actors 2014 [16, p. 5], edited

The risked posed by insiders has been confirmed in the 2015 report in [17] (Figure 5). This means that insiders will very likely continue to pose a high risk of security incidents also in the future.

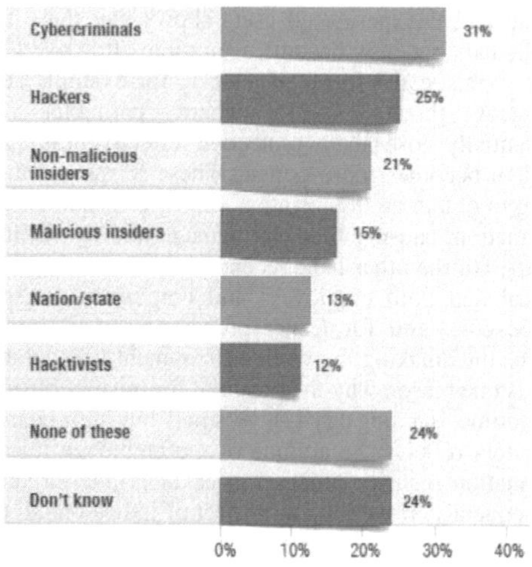

Figure 5. Threat actors 2015, n=461 respondents [16]

The list of threat actors consequently raises the question of how to ensure expected behavior of involved persons in an organization. The term compliance can be defined as the sum of all reasonable measures that address lawful and rule-consistent behavior of a company, its members and employees with regard to legal commands or prohibitions. The business integrity should also be consistent with social guidelines, moral concepts and ethical behavior [21]. In contrast, non-compliance entails all forms of non-observance of guidelines. It can be measured in terms of the seriousness of the infringement and can be categorized into violations that damage the company itself or employees. Three underlying motivational factors for divergent or non-ethical behavior of or within companies have been discussed in the literature: first, non-compliance can be justified by the personal benefit that employees gain by violating regulations. Second, the company as a whole can derive benefits from delinquent behavior. Third, non-compliance can be used to deliberately harm the company or external stakeholders [22, p. 225f]. Various factors might increase the likelihood of non-compliance: difficult working conditions; competitive pressures; unrealistic objectives and focus on simplistic success parameters; too much or too little control within a company's control system; management style; and corporate culture [22, p. 233ff].

In general, working conditions can be divided into three categories; macro, meso and micro level [23]. Raml [24, p. 87ff] allocates economic and social conditions, such as career perspective, economic situation, social status, balancing of family and working life to the macro and meso level. Similarly, work structures and resources (work organization, time models, work atmosphere, career opportunities, bonus payments, information related to work) belong to the macro and meso level [24]. On the other hand, resources and stress are located at the interface between employees and their own work, and are therefore assigned to the micro level [24]. This entails the scope of action, work contents, professional qualification, disturbances and interruptions in daily routine, too many regulations and restrictive surrounding conditions.

It is widely accepted that insiders pose a special form of threat to businesses, institutions and organizations [25] [26] [27]. Insiders are persons who have a legitimate access to components of the ICT infrastructure. In contrast to external hackers, they have always at least one access point to ICT systems, and thus they do not require time consuming efforts to obtain additional privileges. The predefined trust that insiders must be granted requires more sophisticated security measures. The insider threat is related to the level of their sophistication and depends on the users' breadth and depth of knowledge, as well as their finesse [27].

Insiders can trigger either an accidental or malicious threat, i.e., they can intentionally try to cause harm. Information security measures – e.g., encryption, access control, or least privileges principle – must be implemented regarding to human factors, e.g., with personnel checks or focused risk assessments regarding motivation, opportunity and capability [28]. While these insider threats cannot be eliminated, they can be assessed and managed. Users must understand the reasons for security controls in order to ensure their effectiveness. Hence, they may find ways to circumvent technical restrictions they are faced with [25].

A variety of models addresses the insider issue, either concentrating on certain aspects (e.g., end user sophistication [27]) or more holistic in nature [26] [29]. The latter approach incorporates characteristics of the organization, the actor including behavior and attitudes, and the attack itself; overall representing the interdependencies of the different influencing factors [26] [29].

Prior national and international studies on insider security threats [29] [30] [31] have been conducted in the last decade and show the increasing importance of this issue up till now. Despite a good coverage of security policies and measures, the users may obviously work around the controls fulfilling their job objectives in a timely manner. Key issues identified by these studies are data loss prevention, remote information access and the threat against the whole information life cycle. They identified awareness trainings and intensive monitoring measures as effective countermeasures [29] [30] [31].

Working conditions in Austria are regularly measured by the „Work Climate Index", which was first conducted in 1997 by the Institute for Empirical Social Studies in cooperation with the Upper Austrian Chamber of Labor. It has evolved into a longitudinal study since then and aims at capturing the perception of employees concerning their working conditions, and reveals long-term changes in the structure of employment (e.g., increases in precarious employment), evaluates the subjective situation of Austrian employees, and analyses specific subgroups of employees (e.g., women or older employees). Since 2008, the "Work Climate Index" is complemented with the "Austrian Occupational Health Monitor" focusing on questions of subjective work-related health. Both studies are based on 4.000 interviews conducted annually [32] [33] [34] [35]. Key finding of both studies is the relationship between time related stress and working conditions [32, p. 14]. The stress increasing factors are regulations exceeding the common working time hours Monday to Friday from 7 am to 5 pm (especially working on Saturdays or Sundays or at night) or working over-time regularly. Other factors are contributing to time-stress as well, for example permanent contact to customers, high responsibility, permanent surveillance or a lack of support from colleagues [36].

As a further step, our study follows a well-founded approach, combining qualitative question technique for discussion rounds and additionally contrasted by the results of a structured and rather restrictive predefined survey with a significant amount of participants. Despite the fact that human behavior can never be modeled accurately through surveys and the results may not be generalized as conclusive evidence for tactical changes in established organizations, the approach reflects a strongly required combination of work satisfaction with information security principles. Due to the extensive survey and the great random sample of respondents, this work might positively influences a proper methodology analyzing the human risk factor in organizations in future, e.g., heuristics, indicators, conditional relationships etc.

Based on attack types documented in recent publications [12] [14] [16], we have identified a series of major risk factors that contribute to the success of attacks and have consequently derived a targeted list of questions. Some of the most interesting questions that were asked in the study described in this paper are:

- What is the role of ICT security in your company?
- How are security and user guidelines handled?
- What is the current state of awareness among employees?
- Which measures are taken to increase the awareness for ICT security?
- Up to which extent is the private use of company equipment allowed?
- Are there currently any privacy or data loss problems?
- How does the company handle personal data?
- How does the company handle information security?
- Who is responsible for information security in the company?

It is expected that by analyzing the answers to these questions and linking them to attack types, a good assessment of an organization's preparedness for handling attacks can be performed based on organizational vulnerabilities and involving social engineering.

III. Study Design and Setting

The design of the empirical study is based on a well-proven approach that was developed by the Institute for Empirical Social Studies. We decided to use a mixed-method-approach developed by the Institute for Empirical Social Studies. We decided to use a mixed-method-approach [37] and combine quantitative and qualitative aspects of social research, starting with desk research and following up with two focus groups and personal interviews.

A. Desk Research

In the course of the desk research, we analyzed current studies on business crime [19] [38] [39], especially concerning (non-)compliance, fraud and personnel risk. Incidents of business cybercrime have generally been on the rise over the last years. Researchers assume that a large number of unreported incidents exist. Quite often, the perpetrators are among the organization's employees. Nevertheless, these incidents are due to employees' negligence and lack of awareness and not due to intentional or malicious acts. Our study showed that there are some conditions that influence non-compliant behavior: personal traits and moral awareness of an employee, the private situation of an employee; the working conditions, competitive pressure, excessive objective management, lack of internal control, leadership, and organizational culture. Based on these conditions, we derived the security level of the organization and the indicators which determine it. On this basis, we were able to develop suitable interview guidelines as well as questions and answers for the survey. These questions reflect the key aspects for non-compliance as identified in the desk research and based on the answers to these questions conclusions can be made how likely and organization will be affected by non-compliance.

B. Focus Groups

The second part of our study consisted of two focus groups, which took place on 23 and 29 April 2015. In general, a focus group is a moderated discourse method in which a small group of people is stimulated by information input to discuss a specific topic [40, p. 9ff].[41]. This input to get the group discussion started can be provided in form of a short presentation, an image or a website. The goal of a focus group is not to find consensus between the participants but to identify the different aspects of a specific topic.

Focus groups are often used for analyzing different opinions in the group and how participants accept other opinions and evaluate certain measures. A core goal of focus groups is to make use of group dynamics, e.g., to motivate the participants to provide information (the participants' contributions are used as reciprocal stimuli), to take advantage of the collective knowledge (which exceeds the individual intelligence of each participant) and to minimize interviewer or moderator effects by discussing with several participants in a focus group at the same time [42].

In general, and also in the course of our study, a facilitator structures the discussion among the participants of the focus group using an interview guideline. Such a guideline shall ensure that all aspects that are relevant to a topic are addressed during the discussions of the focus group. Additionally, the guideline also increases the comparability of the results of several focus groups that discuss a specific topic. The task of the facilitator is to ensure that all aspects of the interview guideline are covered, all participants are equally involved into the discussion, more quiet and reserved persons are encouraged to participate and not to animate dominant participants that use most of the air time [40, p. 15] [42].

There are no uniform ways to evaluate a focus group [40, p. 17]. In principle, the evaluation may focus either on the process of opinion formation (in this case, sequence and content analyses of the transcripts are used [43]), or on the group output on the content level (in this case, the central topics of the discussion are identified and a description and explanation of the different opinions is collected). For our study, we decided to focus on the content level and thus refrained from producing a verbatim transcription of the discussions, which initially were recorded on tape. Rather, we compiled minutes, which captured the participants' statements but partly already shortened them and in this way introduced our interpretation of these statements. The minutes were evaluated using deductive categories, which were also used to prepare the interview guideline, while remaining open towards any new categories that might result from the discussions [43, p. 91] [44, p. 258]. These categories also form the starting point for the presentation of the results given below.

The participants for the focus groups were selected through theoretical sampling based on the characteristics of individual members [44, p. 258] [45]. In this context, theoretical sampling means that the selection did not happen at random but in relation to characteristics which we considered to be significant in the respective framework [45]. The participants were recruited using the Computer Assisted Telephone Interview (CATI) system owned by the Institute for Empirical Social Studies. The scattering of the participants was improved using so-called "screeners", i.e., short questionnaires which record the characteristics that are relevant for the theoretical sampling. Before the start of the focus group, the participants completed a so-called "re-screener", which once again captured the main characteristics of all participants.

We invited both ordinary employees and persons with management functions to our focus groups. Since the selection was based on a theoretical sampling with characteristics like age, sex, and consumer behavior the aim was to form optimal focus groups with uniformly distributed characteristics. Accordingly, six ordinary employees (three men, three women) aged between 31 to 62 years took part in the first group. The second focus group consisted of eight persons in a management position (six men, two women) aged between 42 and 61 years. The group discussions were based on qualitative questioning techniques and facilitated by a trained person who used a structured interview guideline to guide the discussions, which allowed for an open exchange of opinions. The focus of the group discussions was on security measures, recent critical incidents in the area of information security, and on the relationship between employer and employees. All members described information and communication activities as a main part of their ordinary working routine. The participants received an incentive of 40 Euro to compensate for their expenses and motivate them.

C. Personal Interviews

In parallel to the focus groups, we conducted personal interviews with 891 employees of Austrian companies (53%

men, 47% women) including persons with management function in the period from January to March 2015. These face-to-face interviews were structured by a prepared survey consisting of 48 questions having either several predefined answer possibilities or offering a five-tier rating. The interviewer leads through the questionnaire, explains, discusses and finally documents the participant's answers. Participants were chosen by a multistage random sampling, where Austrian municipalities were grouped by the total number of inhabitants for each federal state and political district. Then, municipalities from each predetermined group were picked randomly. Within these municipalities, eligible households were picked randomly and were then used as samples for finding further addresses. Target persons were exclusively chosen based on their home addresses. Within each target household, members were assigned by random numbers, and only those were interviewed, whose number matched the one provided by the Kish selection grid [46]. Thus, each stage in the selection process of participants was guided by randomization.

The survey covered central issues of job satisfaction, general health situation, satisfaction with corporate management, security measures within the organization as well as ICT security in general. Twenty-five percent of the respondents were aged below 29 years, 34% between 30 and 44 years, and 41% older than 45 years. Each interview with workers (30%), employees (55%) and members of public administration affiliates (15%) took 25 minutes on average and was performed at the respondent's personal domicile. Most of the respondents had completed compulsory education (9%) or with apprenticeship as craftsmen (42%). 16% of respondents had gone to college and passed their school leaving examination, 16% went to college but did not finish it, and 17% had graduated from university. More than three fourths (76%) of respondents are employed full time, the rest worked less than 36 hours per week (24%). The results are shown separately between persons with a leading function (11%) and those without (89%). 39% of the respondents earn less than 1.500 EUR per month, 39% more than 1.500 EUR per month and 22% refused to indicate their salary.

The study design described above was geared both towards obtaining a better understanding of how information security works in companies and towards determining key indicators of non-compliance by indirectly gathering information of employees of Austrian companies. This benchmark approach aimed at obtaining an accurate and undistorted view of employees older than 16 years within Austria across various organizational sizes and business sectors. The research community could now start follow-up projects with the same or a similar study design, which would enable more detailed analysis of one business sector or company size.

IV. MAJOR RESULTS

A. *Focus Group Discussions*

The members of the focus groups reported on relevant information security incidents in their organizations, e.g., data loss of emails during archiving, loss of business data due to collapse of servers, stealing of material, sensitive information, and electronic equipment, physical damage by fire, perimeter control vulnerabilities, accounting errors due to account number conversion, and phishing. In general, the members of the focus groups point out the need for a balance between scope for development and restrictive measures. Both too much surveillance and the lack of it were considered as problematic. In the following paragraphs, we will discuss the results for the main five topics in further detail.

1) Topic 1: Infrastructure

Guidance for an employee's individual behavior is often replaced by external restrictions that are implemented through technical solutions, e.g., blocking of social media networks, automated logouts, frequently forced password changes, access and/or time cards. Such technical restriction might lead to a regulatory overkill and the employees will find ways to boycott or circumvent these restrictive systems. The majority of the focus group members took a liberal position on surfing the internet for private purposes during working hours. Due to the constantly increasing pressure on employees to fulfill their working objectives, the employer often leaves it up to the employees to decide how much of their time and breaks they spend on surfing the web. Page blocking mechanisms are seen as little effective, since employees can use their smartphones instead of a company desktop computer. Some respondents experience a total "computerization" of the daily work routines as a really threatening scenario. When people are only seen as 'operators' of computers (in the literal sense), this carries social risks. Generally, the members of the focus groups expressed a concern that artificial intelligence might soon dominate human intelligence and human labor might become obsolete.

2) Topic 2: Time Management

Work life balance is the most important prerequisite for healthy, hard-working and rule-abiding employees. Organizations increasingly perform health promotion measures and offer incentives to support work-life balance. Even though such measures make sense, there is also some skepticism towards them. Managers criticize these incentives if they are merely used as a ready-made argument in a (neo-) capitalistic system. The argument is that such incentives do not prevent job losses but disguise a "do more with less"-policy in the organizations. In this context, the technical progress in modern communication technologies can also have negative effects on employees' work life balance. The use of corporate smartphones and notebooks increases the availability of employees for work-related tasks and causes an "always online" feeling among employees, which removes the spatial and systematic barriers between work and personal life.

3) Topic 3: Awareness

Employees are often not familiar with the details of the ICT security policies and code of conduct in their company despite the fact that these form part of their contract. The companies do not offer any dedicated trainings but the ICT regulations are brought to the attention of the employees when they start their job. However, the published content is not any more up-to-date and thus the employees are not aware of the current regulations.

Data protection is seen in a broader and external context. The more benefits the rules and regulations bring for the employees or the society, they more likely will they follow them. A team operating with information, for example, might adhere to the protection of personal data because it wants that its own personal data is protected in the same way.

4) Topic 4: Surveillance

An excess of surveillance and regulations have a negative impact on the working atmosphere and productivity and creates a defiant attitude among employees. As in a self-fulfilling prophecy, employees provoke exactly those acts that they actually want to prevent. The focus group members agreed that regulations are necessary in sensitive areas and regarding sensitive processes, e.g., data of patients, clients, customers and handling of products or money. Employees and employers share the view that delivery on time is more important than the "objectively" monitored working speed, although employees often have the perception of being too much checked upon.

The loyalty of employees suffers when managers enforce strict time recordings or cancel home office agreements. It is demoralizing for employees if extra hours worked cannot be recorded in the time registration system due to system restrictions. Employees see break recording and break logging by computers as a form of "modern slavery".

5) Topic 5: Personal Interaction

Reactive behavior to handle security incidents is not an appropriate strategy. Punishing employees collectively for the misbehavior of single employees deteriorates morale of all staff. Concerning loyalty, there are synergies: employees trust others if others also trust and appreciate them. Hence, when managers foster team work, actively take over responsibility and select the right personnel, the sense of responsibility among employees grow. Happy employees are good employees. Favorable working conditions are an important precondition for motivated and loyal employees. Good relationships between employees and between employees and their managers, transparent information and communication structures, clear working organization and participation in decision making processes are needed to enhance employees' work and life satisfaction and to minimize psychological problems. It is important for the prevention of non-compliance to avoid unfavorable working conditions, e.g., unfair payment, unfair employment conditions, lack of appreciation by managers, lack of support or mobbing in teams or by managers, and lack of available resources. Against this background, it is important that organizations create a good working condition and a good working environment.

One of the most important tasks of human resource management for the future is to select the "right" employees for the "right" tasks in the organization. Consequently, managers focus on a professional personnel selection process. The integrity of the employees is of key importance and considered to be more important than the integrity of the technical systems, which will never function completely error-free. Selecting the right persons is especially important for management positions, because managers have influence on a company's success and working atmosphere. Bad managers can be a threat to the balance of an organization and thus managers should be selected and assessed carefully. Finally, the focus group discussed on whether more regulations and surveillance have the expected effect.

B. Interviews with prepared survey

The 48 answers of the questions discussed in the 891 personal interviews which were conducted by trained interviewers following a predefined survey can be contrasted to the outcome of the focus groups presented in the section before. Hence, the results are structured along the same five main topics.

1) Topic 1: Infrastructure

15% of the respondents answer to the question how many percent of the employees in the company do the major share of their work on a computer that the percentage is 100% – all employees predominantly use a computer for their work – whereas 12% answer that no one in the company uses a computer for the major share of their work. However, one quarter of the respondents cannot provide further details on this. On average, 56% of the employees predominantly use a computer for their work. There are significant differences between branches, size of the organization and number of sites that an organization has. Smartphone usage shows a similar pattern: 37% of the employees use a smartphone as business phone. In general, using smartphones for work is common in all branches. However, around one quarter of the respondents cannot answer the question and one third say that no smartphones were used as business phones in their company. Similar to the results for computer usage, the share of companies without smartphones is highest in companies with less than 10 employees (49%) and with only one site (39%).

30% of the employees (and 46% of the managers) indicate that the technical equipment provided by the employer may be used for private purposes. It is less common to use private devices for work. However, every fifth respondent indicates that this is allowed in his/her company. The use of private equipment, in particular, has negative implications both for the employees (the line between work and private life gets blurred) and for the companies ("bring your own disaster"). Overall, it can be concluded that, as expected, computers and smartphones form part of the basic equipment of any larger company and that employees (have to) work with them every day. This has led to the situation in the last decade that companies have to deal with the security implications of using these devices. Nowadays, this issue has to be addressed not only by large companies, but increasingly also by small and medium enterprises.

2) Topic 2: Time Management

As shown in Figure 6, one third of the employees answer company emails outside of working hours. Especially managers often can be reached outside of normal working hours: two thirds of them sometimes and 44% several times a week, whereas only 12% of normal employees work outside of normal working hours. The more the work depends on ICT services, the more the respondents communicate about work after working hours. Around 15% of employees are allowed to work at home. This proportion increases with the level of education: university graduates telework up to 35% of their working hours. The larger the company and the higher the employee's position in the hierarchy, the more likely is the employee to be allowed to work at home.

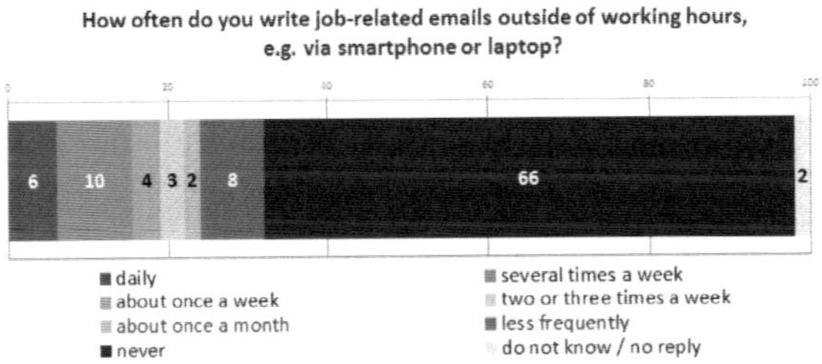

Figure 6. Employees' email communication outside of working hours (values in %; n=891)

35% of the respondents state that their jobs can be reconciled very well with their private interests and family commitments, and 46% think that they can reconcile these things rather well. On the other hand, only 3% of the respondents have the feeling that it is difficult to reconcile their private with their working life. Another 15% of the respondents are indifferent, but this shows that there is room for improvement for the concerned respondents. The group of persons aged 30 to 44 is less satisfied with their work-life balance. This is probably due to the fact that this group typically takes care of small children beside their work. Regarding the effects on human health, the survey shows that time pressure is the major stressor at the work place. Every fifth respondent feels very stressed by it, a quarter of the respondents states that they are moderately stressed by it. 7% feel very stressed and another 13% moderately stressed because work cuts into their leisure time. Both stressors affect managers slightly more than other respondents. The technological developments of the last years contribute to the fact that the line between work and personal life gets more and more blurred. Although these technologies also bring advantages e.g., flexible working arrangements and time management, they also carry risks for employees, e.g., for their health. For the key personnel of an organization these risks tend to be higher.

3) Topic 3: Awareness

More than half of the respondents and three fourths of the interviewed managers consider information security to be an important topic. The survey results indicate that the importance attached to information security grows in line with the size of the organization and has special relevance when the company has offices abroad. Almost 75% of the persons working in large-scale companies (more than 100 employees) assess information security's importance to be very high or high, as shown in Table I. The first row in Table I entitled with "Total" compares the corresponding percentage value without distinction of the organization sizes as reflected by row two to six. The survey also showed that the sensitivity regarding information security is low among employees of very small organizations and of organizations with a low ICT usage.

Table I. Importance of information security divided into company size (n=891)

Company Size (numeric values in %)	very high	high	medium	low	very low	don't know / not specified
Total	28,39	24,55	11,43	5,20	6,90	23,53
Below 10 employees	20,41	17,96	13,87	7,35	13,06	27,35
10 to 19 employees	24,42	26,27	12,44	5,53	5,53	25,81
20 to 49 employees	28,37	27,40	11,54	5,77	6,25	20,67
50 to 99 employees	34,07	30,77	7,69	3,30	3,30	20,87
100 or more employees	47,15	25,20	7,33	0,81	0,81	18,70

Information security was found to have an exceptional standing in companies in the finance and insurance sector (90%), in public administration (77%), and in the health and welfare sector (66%), presumably due to the awareness for processing sensitive data. Nevertheless, one third of the respondents indicate that they have no information security guideline for ICT usage. It is remarkable that especially employees with a lower level of education do not know about any regulations. The information security awareness is comparatively higher in the finance and insurance sector (93%) and in public administration (81%).

A similar picture appears when analyzing the existence of information security awareness measures. Only 28% of respondents report of (semi-)annual measures, 15% indicate that those measures are rarely performed, one third indicate that no such measures are performed, and one fourth of the respondents do not know whether such measures exist. These results indicate that for almost half of the respondent's organizations no awareness activities are in place. This is emphasized by the results about employee's awareness attitude in Figure 7; almost 60% of the respondents see information security awareness attitudes of their colleagues, but on the other hand 40% do not. The main topics addressed by these awareness measures concern the handling of passwords, behavior during information security incidents and using the internet, awareness concerning the sensitivity of the processed data, risks of mobile ICT devices and data storages, contracts with external personnel, and social engineering strategies.

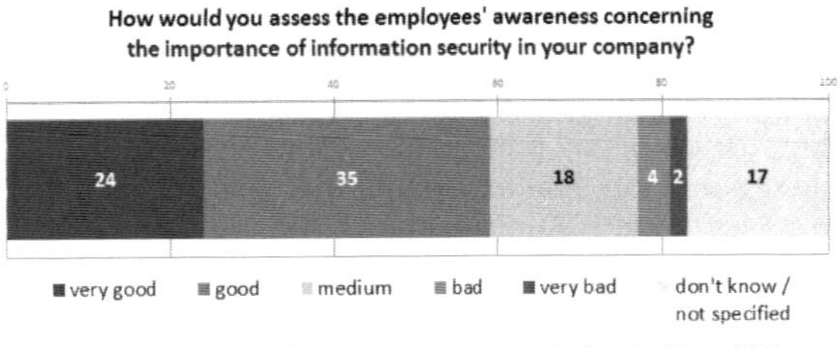

Figure 7. Employees' awareness assessment (values in %; n=891)

Furthermore, the employees are asked how specifically they handle sensitive information and security policies in their organizations. 8% say that employees talk (very) often about sensitive information, also outside the company; whereas 56% indicate that this basically never happens. 7% state that violations of security policies happen frequently, and 6% of the respondents indicate that they do not comply with ICT regulations. On the other hand, 63% and 59%, respectively, state that violations of security policies and violations of the ICT regulations virtually never happen. Figure 8 provides a summarizing sample of explicitly information security related questions and reflects the answers given in the 891 personal interviews. It shows not only the technical implementation of information security measures in the organizations, but in fact the degree of successfully enforcing them because the employees have obviously recognized the information security measures.

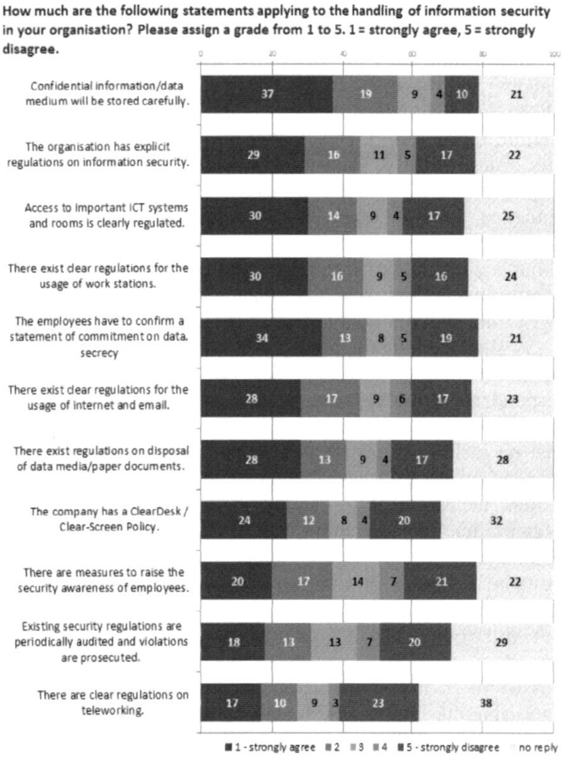

Figure 8. How employees handle information security (values in %; n=891)

4) Topic 4: Surveillance

Almost half of the respondents answer that internet and ICT services cannot be used for private purposes, whereas the rest of the respondents are not sure about it. Only 17% of the respondents report that they have an explicit permission to privately use the internet and ICT services provided by their organization. The smaller the organization, the more likely it is that the organization enforces no rules concerning this private use. Companies with offices abroad are more likely to have some rules concerning the private usage of ICT services. Almost three fourths of respondents indicate that there have been no data loss and data protection incidents in their organizations, whereas the rest cannot answer the questions. 86% of the respondents trust their employers concerning the processing of their sensitive data, only 8% do not. The proportion of those who do not trust their employers in this regard is higher in public administration: 18% have doubts whether their organization protects data appropriately. 46% of the respondents know which data his or her employer stores, whereas 45% do not know.

The main proportion of the employees uses working time recording systems, either manual recordings (33%) or an electronic badge (41%). In particular, large-scale enterprises use working time recording and access systems, have special visitor regulations, accounting systems for services or telephone cost monitoring. Video surveillance is more common in the finance and insurance sector, whereas Global Positioning System (GPS) locating is more common in transport services. As illustrated by Figure 9, around 68% of the respondents have no impression that their work place is monitored electronically – this is especially evident for employees from large-scale enterprises. On the other hand, 27% think that they are under surveillance at work.

In companies in Austria, a whistleblower hotline is rather unusual: 72% of respondents report that their organizations have no anonymous hotline, whereas 20% of respondents indicate that they do not know whether such a hotline exists. To conclude, performing a detailed evaluation of a company's information security is rather difficult, since employees are often not allowed to openly speak about security incidents, which results in a considerable number of unrecorded incidents.

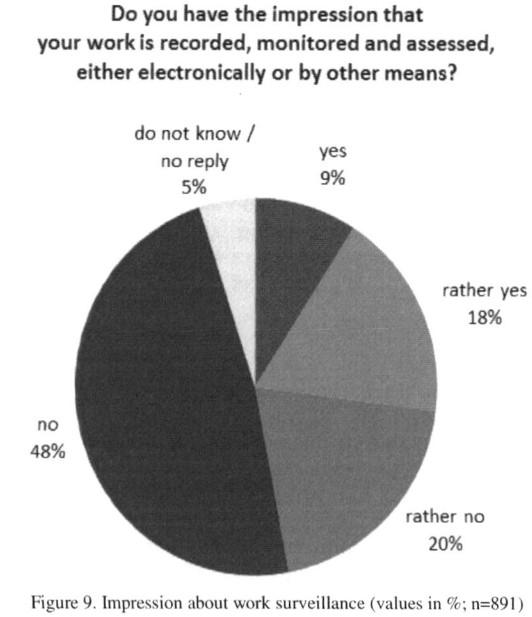

Figure 9. Impression about work surveillance (values in %; n=891)

1) Topic 5: Personal Interaction

The personal interviews with employees generally show that the respondents are most satisfied with the collaboration with their colleagues, the company`s image, the content of their work and the appreciation of their work by colleagues. More than 78% of the respondents and 63% of respondents with only compulsory education as highest education level stated their satisfactions with these aspects. This group indicated comparatively lower satisfaction levels in all categories than the rest of the respondents. Therefore, the satisfaction level of this specific group is explicitly indicated as a second percentage in the following results. Respondents indicated medium satisfaction with their line managers, their individual autonomy to take decisions on their working processes, their working time, and the social policies of the company (more than 66% and 45%, respectively). The respondents were least satisfied with training options, workload, employee participation and potential career possibilities (more than 48% and 33%, respectively).

As depicted in Figure 10, loyalty of employees to their organization is relatively high. If they were to choose again, 72% of the respondents would like to have a job in the same organization. On the other side, 9% would not strive for this. It has to be noted that women show a stronger tendency of choosing the same company again (75%) than men (69%). The results clearly show that with rising age the share of those employees who would strive for a job in the same company decreases. The share of managers that would choose a job in this organization again was above the average share (80%). Two thirds (66%) of the respondents would recommend a job in the organization for which they work. Among mangers the share is 78%. This share of 66% of respondents who would recommend their organization to relatives or friends is relatively high. On the other hand, only almost one out of ten employees would not recommend their organization. The most skeptical groups concerning these questions are persons with compulsory education (14%), persons with a net income less than 1.050 Euro (14%), and employees in companies with offices abroad in other EU countries (13%) and outside the European Union (19%).

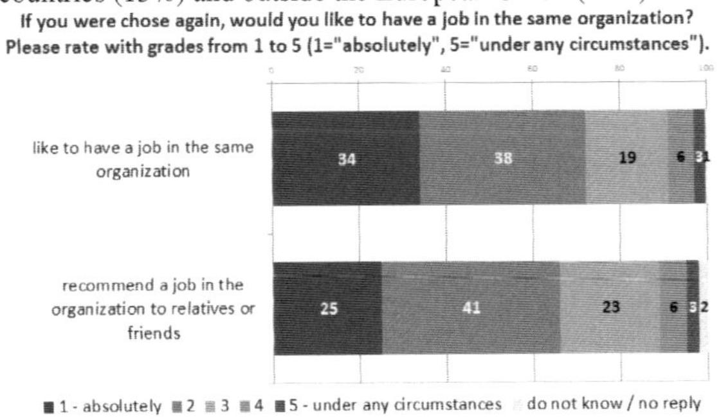

Figure 10. Loyalty of employees to their organization (values in %; n=891)

Furthermore, the interviews showed that seven to eight out of ten employees comply with ICT policies, do not cheat the organization, do not take home data or steal anything, do not harm the enterprise intentionally or unintentionally, do not print private documents and do not talk about sensitive information outside of the work. In contrast, up to 7% have committed at least one of those actions. 14% of employees and 19% of managers go to work when they are ill due to their sense of duty, workload and a lack of deputies. In general, one quarter of the employees states that they went to work at least one day in the past half year although they were having health problems. In contrast, 9% of the respondents indicated that they had stayed at home at least once in the past although they had not been ill.

Respondents considered ICT services to be a key issue in organizations, regardless of the business sector. Almost half of the respondents indicated that company smartphones are an important topic. The proportion of ICT and smartphone usage is considerably higher in organizations with less than ten employees and only one location. 30% of the employees and 46% of the managers are allowed to use the devices privately. Bring your own device (BYOD) is permitted only for one fifth of employees.

The overall handling of information security differs strongly between managers and employees. The knowledge on information security is substantially lower among employees. The probability, that an organization enforces regulations on information security, increases with the size of the organization or if the organization has offices abroad. Again, the finance and insurance sector, public administration and the health and welfare sector are those business sectors in which information security represents an integral part of organizational culture.

It is remarkable to note that only 15% of the respondents indicated that their organization has clearly defined who is responsible for information security, risk and compliance. On the contrary, 54% reported that their organization has not defined this responsibility and 31% did not know. In different organizations, the responsibility is defined in different ways and may lie with the ICT department, a dedicated person who is responsible for information security, an external company, an audit department or the top management. The likelihood, that appropriate responsibilities are established and enforced, increases with the size of the organization and whether the company has offices abroad.

V. Conclusions

Based on the findings described in Section IV above, we can draw the following top-5-conclusions:

- *High cyber security awareness.*
  The awareness concerning the importance of cyber security is exceptional in the highly sensitive areas, i.e., the Austrian financial and insurance sector (about 90%) and the public administration (about 77%).
- *Poor flow of information.*
  Although security awareness is high among employees, often the responsibilities are not clear. In more than eight out of ten companies it is indistinct who is responsible for information security. Further, one out of three companies does not have a security guideline employees are aware of and in almost 60% of the cases, security awareness measures are either non-existing or not visible for the employees.

- *Strong connection between employees and company.* Employee's loyalty to their company is rather high: roughly, less than one out of ten employees would strive for a job in another company and roughly two out of three managers would recommend a career in their companies to their relatives.
- *Loyal employees are honest employees.* Eight out of ten employees do not cheat the organization, take home important data or steal anything.
- *Sufficient work-life balance is crucial.* Less than one out of 20 employees think that their work-life balance is bad, but already one out of five feels heavily strained due to time pressure, identifying it as a health burden. Technological developments like mobile devices blur the line between work and personal life.

Considered in more detail, our findings show that non-compliance is more likely in an environment that is characterized by poor working conditions These include, among others, inadequate salary, job insecurity, insufficient appreciation of work, lacking support from team members or supervisors, mobbing, and lack of the resources that are necessary to get the work done. Further, competitive pressures, a focus on simplistic success parameters, problems in a company's control system, management style and corporate culture also panders to non-compliant behavior. Favorable working conditions are therefore important in order to enhance the motivation and loyalty of employees [47]. Thus, it is crucial for companies to ensure good working conditions. External regulations and technical solutions, e.g., automated logouts, frequent password changes, access and time badges, are replacing the individual behavioral orientation. Overregulation leads to employees boycotting or bypassing the control system. Excessive control and regulation has a negative impact on the work environment and hampers productivity. Employees often spend working hours with defiant attitudes.

Managers have great influence on the work environment of their employees [48]. Therefore, it is crucial that the managers are selected carefully because they contribute essentially to the company's success and working atmosphere. Good relationships between employees and managers, transparent information and communication structures, transparent work organization and participation in decision-making are necessary to enhance work-life satisfaction and reduce the occurrence of mental disorders. Work life balance in general is considered a requirement for healthy, hard-working, compliant behavior. At the same time, smartphones and laptops enable an integration of work and private life. Nevertheless, the result is that the line between work and leisure is becoming more and more blurred.

While Austrian companies, especially larger ones and also innovative small and medium-enterprises are generally well-prepared concerning information security, the average of small and medium-enterprises still needs substantial support due to a lack of available funding for cyber security measures in order to catch up. Besides the size of the organization, the business sector is decisive for whether information security measures are implemented or not. In sectors where employees are used to handle a lot of sensitive data, such as in the finance and insurance sector, the health sector or the public administration sector, advanced information security measures can be found. Our findings indicate that stronger regulations, monitoring and surveillance measures might not lead to the expected effects in all cases. Consequently, one of the main tasks for human resource management is the selection of loyal employees and the successful integration of employees into the organization.

Hence, the level of information security awareness in Austrian organizations is higher than reflected in the general studies we analyzed [16, p. 5] [17]. Employees are extensively honest. Future research might focus on a comparison of several countries in different cultural areas and within Europe because we expect differences [49]. Another approach we want to follow is to feed an appropriate risk management model with the data presented here. This more systematic research could lead to quantifiable key risk parameters and development of distinct thresholds for the human risk factor of information security. Due to the characteristics of behavior, attitude and perception a heuristic approach could generate input for a scorecard or radar chart with the suggested small set of most interesting questions.

ACKNOWLEDGMENT

This work was partly supported by the European Commission's Project No. 608090, HyRiM (Hybrid Risk Management for Utility Networks) under the 7th Framework Programme (FP7-SEC-2013-1).

REFERENCES

[1] C. Schuster, M. Latzenhofer, S. Schauer, J. Göllner, C. Meurers, A. Peer, P. Prah, G. Quirchmayr, and T. Benesch, "A Study on User Perceptions of ICT Security," presented at the SECURWARE 2016: The Tenth International Conference on Emerging Security Information, Systems and Technologies, Nice, 2016, pp. 281–288.

[2] M. Plischke, "Company's Prevention: Risk Management Competing with Technology [in German: Unternehmensprävention: Risikomanagement im Wettlauf mit der Technik]," *Inf. Manag. Consult.*, no. 3, pp. 57–60, 2009.

[3] C. Suchan and J. Frank, *Analysis and Design of Powerful IS Architectures: Model-based Methods from Research and Teaching in Practice [in German: Analyse und Gestaltung leistungsfähiger IS-Architekturen: Modellbasierte Methoden aus Forschung und Lehre in der Praxis].* Springer-Verlag, 2012.

[4] M. Baram and M. Schoebel, "Safety culture and behavioral change at the workplace," *Saf. Sci.*, vol. 45, no. 6, pp. 631–636, 2007.

[5] C. Buck and T. Eymann, "Human Risk Factor in Mobile Ecosystems [in German: Risikofaktor Mensch in mobilen Ökosystemen]," *HMD Prax. Wirtsch.*, vol. 51, no. 1, pp. 75–83, 2014.

[6] F. W. Guldenmund, "The use of questionnaires in safety culture research–an evaluation," *Saf. Sci.*, vol. 45, no. 6, pp. 723–743, 2007.

[7] B. Fahlbruch and M. Schöbel, "SOL–Safety through organizational learning: A method for event analysis," *Saf. Sci.*, vol. 49, no. 1, pp. 27–31, 2011.

[8] Federal Ministry for Transport, Innovation and Technology (BMVIT) and Austrian Research Promotion Agency (FFG), "KIRAS Security Research: MetaRisk," 2016. [Online]. Available: http://www.kiras.at/. [Accessed: 27-Dec-2016]

[9] M. Jakobsson and S. Myers, *Phishing and countermeasures: understanding the increasing problem of electronic identity theft*. John Wiley & Sons, 2006.

[10] S. Schiebeck, M. Latzenhofer, B. Palensky, S. Schauer, G. Quirchmayr, T. Benesch, J. Göllner, C. Meurers, and I. Mayr, "Practical Use Case Evaluation of a Generic ICT Meta-Risk Model Implemented with Graph Database Technology," *Int. J. Adv. Secur.*, vol. 9, no. 1 & 2, pp. 66–79, 2016.

[11] Federal Chancellery of Austria, Ed., "Cybersecurity in Austria [in German: Cybersicherheit in Österreich]." Mar-2015.

[12] nic.at and CERT Austria, "Report Internet Security Austria [in German: Bericht Internet-Sicherheit Österreich 2015]." Feb-2016.

[13] Ministry of Finance, Federal Chancellery of Austria, and A-SIT Center for Secure ICT, "ICT Security Portal – Cybermonitor [in German: IKT-Sicherheitsportal – Cybermonitor]," *Onlinesicherheit.at*, 16-Feb-2016. [Online]. Available: https://www.onlinesicherheit.gv.at. [Accessed: 16-Feb-2016]

[14] Bundesamt für Sicherheit in der Informationstechnik (BSI), "The Situation of IT Security in Germany 2015 [in German: Die Lage der IT-Sicherheit in Deutschland 2015]." Nov-2015.

[15] Bundeskriminalamt Wiesbaden, "Cybercrime Federal Overview 2014 [in German: Cybercrime Bundeslagebild 2014]." Bundeskriminalamt Wiesbaden, 2014.

[16] Information Systems Audit and Control Association (ISACA), Ed., "State of Cybersecurity: Implications for 2015 - An ISACA and RSA Conference Survey." 2014.

[17] Information Systems Audit and Control Association (ISACA), Ed., "State of Cybersecurity: Implications for 2016 - An ISACA and RSA Conference Survey." 2016 [Online]. Available: https://www.isaca.org/cyber/Documents/state-of-cybersecurity_res_eng_0316.pdf. [Accessed: 03-Jan-2017]

[18] G. Cluley, "Hackers Steal $55 million From Boeing Supplier," 21-Jan-2016. [Online]. Available: http://www.tripwire.com/state-of-security/security-data-protection/boeing-supplier-hacked-claims-55-million-worth-of-damage-as-stock-price-falls/. [Accessed: 16-Feb-2016]

[19] Pricewaterhouse Coopers, "Economic crime: A threat to business processes - PWC's 2014 Global Economic Crime Survey - US Supplement." 2014.

[20] Pricewaterhouse Coopers, "Adjusting the Lens on Economic Crime: Preparation brings opportunity back into focus - Global Economic Crime Survey 2016: US Results." 2016 [Online]. Available: https://www.pwc.com/us/en/forensic-services/assets/gecs-us-report-2016.pdf. [Accessed: 03-Jan-2017]

[21] H. Quentmeier, *Practice Manual Compliance: Fundamentals, Objectives, and Practical Advice for Non-lawyers [in German: Praxishandbuch Compliance: Grundlagen, Ziele und Praxistipps für Nicht-Juristen]*, 1. Aufl. Wiesbaden: Gabler, 2012 [Online]. Available: B:DE-101 application/pdf http://d-nb.info/1018131469/04 DNB-TOC Inhaltsverzeichnis 2

[22] W. Schettgen-Sarcher, S. Bachmann, and P. Schettgen, *Compliance Officer*. Wiesbaden: Springer Fachmedien Wiesbaden, 2014 [Online]. Available: http://dx.doi.org/10.1007/978-3-658-01270-0 Resolving-System Volltext

[23] Semmer, N., "Stress," in *Handwörterbuch Arbeitswissenschaft*, H. Luczak and W. Volpert, Eds. Stuttgart: Schäffer-Poeschl, 1997, pp. 332–339.

[24] R. Raml, "Positive indicators for health in context of work: an interdisciplinary extension of the term health and its consequences for the differentiation of health situations for employees [in German: Positive Indikatoren der Gesundheit im Kontext Arbeit: eine interdisziplinäre Erweiterung des Gesundheitsbegriffs und dessen Folgen für die Differenzierung gesundheitlicher Lagen bei unselbständig Beschäftigten]," Medizinische Universität, 2009.

[25] C. Colwill, "Human factors in information security: The insider threat–Who can you trust these days?," *Inf. Secur. Tech. Rep.*, vol. 14, no. 4, pp. 186–196, 2009.

[26] J. R. Nurse, O. Buckley, P. A. Legg, M. Goldsmith, S. Creese, G. R. Wright, and M. Whitty, "Understanding insider threat: A framework for characterising attacks," in *Security and Privacy Workshops (SPW), 2014 IEEE*, 2014, pp. 214–228.

[27] G. B. Magklaras and S. M. Furnell, "A preliminary model of end user sophistication for insider threat prediction in IT systems," *Comput. Secur.*, vol. 24, no. 5, pp. 371–380, 2005.

[28] J. Hunker and C. W. Probst, "Insiders and Insider Threats-An Overview of Definitions and Mitigation Techniques.," *JoWUA*, vol. 2, no. 1, pp. 4–27, 2011.

[29] A. M. Munshi, "A study of insider threat behaviour: developing a holistic insider threat model," 2013.

[30] RSA, "The Insider Security Threat in I.T. and Financial Services: Survey Shows Employees' Everyday Behavior Puts Sensitive Business Information at Risk." RSA, 2008.

[31] L. Tan, *Asia worried about insider threat. ZDNet Asia*. 2008.

[32] R. Raml, Ed., "Working conditions and stress: findings of the Austrian Work Climate Index [in German: Arbeitsbedingungen und Stress: Erkenntnisse aus dem österreichischen Arbeitsklima Index]," *Schriftenreihe Österr. Arbeitsklima Index - Austrian Work Clim. Index*, vol. Arbeitsbedingungen und Stress, no. 3, pp. 12–17, 2015.

[33] R. Raml, "Scientific fundamentals of the Austrian Occupational Health Monitor [in German: Wissenschaftliche Grundlagen des Österreichischen Arbeitsgesundheitsmonitors]," *Schriftenreihe Österr. Arbeitsklima Index - Austrian Work Clim. Index*, no. 2, pp. 12–19, 2012.

[34] R. Raml, "A theoretical evaluation of the Work Climate Index [in German: Eine theoretische Evaluierung des Arbeitsklima Index]," *Schriftenreihe Österr. Arbeitsklima Index - Austrian Work Clim. Index*, no. 1, 2009.

[35] R. Raml and A. Schiff, "The localization of the Work Climate Index in a sociologic, psychologic and economic

theory spectrum [in German: Die Verortung des Arbeitsklima Index im soziologischen, psychologischen und ökonomischen Theorienspektrum]." 2016.

[36] M. Tarafdar, Q. Tu, B. S. Ragu-Nathan, and T. S. Ragu-Nathan, "The impact of technostress on role stress and productivity," *J. Manag. Inf. Syst.*, vol. 24, no. 1, pp. 301–328, 2007.

[37] R. B. Johnson, A. J. Onwuegbuzie, and L. A. Turner, "Toward a definition of mixed methods research," *J. Mix. Methods Res.*, vol. 1, no. 2, pp. 112–133, 2007.

[38] A. V. Heerden, F. Weller, and G. Weidinger, "Business Crime. Gemrany, Austria, Switzerland in comparison. Business Crime in large-sized organizations and medium-sized business [in German: Wirtschaftskriminalität. Deutschland, Österreich, Schweiz im Vergleich. Wirtschaftskriminalität in Großunternehmen und dem Mittelstand]." KPMG, 2013.

[39] Pricewaterhouse Coopers, "Business Crime 2011. Security Situation in Austrian companies [in German: Wirtschaftskriminalität 2011. Sicherheitslage in österreichischen Unternehmen]." PWC, 2011.

[40] M. Schulz, "Quick and easy!? Fokusgruppen in der angewandten Sozialwissenschaft," in *Fokusgruppen in der empirischen Sozialwissenschaft*, Springer, 2012, pp. 9–22.

[41] D. Morgan, *Focus Groups as Qualitative Research*. 2455 Teller Road, Thousand Oaks California 91320 United States of America: SAGE Publications, Inc., 1997 [Online]. Available: http://methods.sagepub.com/book/focus-groups-as-qualitative-research. [Accessed: 03-Jan-2017]

[42] D. W. Stewart and P. N. Shamdasani, *Focus groups: Theory and practice*, vol. 20. Sage publications, 2014.

[43] U. Flick, *The SAGE handbook of qualitative data analysis*. Sage, 2013.

[44] U. Flick, "Qualitative Social Research-An Introduction [in German: Qualitative Sozialforschung–Eine Einführung]," *Reinbek Bei Hambg. Rowohlt*, no. 5th edition, Nov. 2012.

[45] C. Auerbach and L. B. Silverstein, *Qualitative data: An introduction to coding and analysis*. NYU press, 2003.

[46] L. Kish, "A procedure for objective respondent selection within the household," *J. Am. Stat. Assoc.*, vol. 44, no. 247, pp. 380–387, 1949.

[47] B. Aziri, "Job satisfaction: A literature review," *Manag. Res. Pract.*, vol. 3, no. 4, pp. 77–86, 2011.

[48] J. P. De Jong and D. N. Den Hartog, "How leaders influence employees' innovative behaviour," *Eur. J. Innov. Manag.*, vol. 10, no. 1, pp. 41–64, 2007.

[49] Z. Aycan, R. Kanungo, M. Mendonca, K. Yu, J. Deller, G. Stahl, and A. Kurshid, "Impact of culture on human resource management practices: A 10-country comparison," *Appl. Psychol.*, vol. 49, no. 1, pp. 192–221, 2000.

Verifying the Adherence to Security Policies for Secure Communication in Critical Infrastructures

Steffen Fries and Rainer Falk
Corporate Technology
Siemens AG
Munich, Germany
e-mail: {steffen.fries|rainer.falk}@siemens.com

Abstract—**Critical infrastructures (CI) as backbone of the society and economy are increasingly the target of cyber attacks. These infrastructures have been isolated in the past, but are connected more and more also with CI-external systems to allow for new and combined services. This immediately requires the protection of the communication connections to CI-external sites but also internally. Legislation and operation have taken this into account and provide the necessary framework for posing specific communication security requirements. From the technical side, different security counter measures exist to cope with the given requirements, but it has to be ensured that these technical means are not only provided, but in fact applied in operation. This paper describes a new approach to ensure that during the setup of a secure communication connection the appropriate security is effectively negotiated with respect to permissible cipher suites for authentication, message integrity, and confidentiality. The application within a Digital Grid is used as example application domain.**

Keywords–security; critical infrastructure; smart energy grid; industrial automation; Internet of Things; Digital Grid secure communication; security policy; security protocol; Transport Layer Security

I. INTRODUCTION

Critical Infrastructures (CI) and specifically cyber security in critical infrastructures have gained more momentum over the last years. The term "critical infrastructure" in the context of this paper is used to describe technical installations, which are essential for the functioning of the society and economy of a country, but also globally. Typical critical infrastructures in this context are the digital energy grid (including central or distributed energy generation, transmission, and distribution), water supply, healthcare, transportation, telecommunication services, just to state a few. The increased threat level becomes visible, e.g., through reported attacks on critical infrastructure, but also through legislation, which meanwhile explicitly requires the protection of critical infrastructures and reporting about serious attacks.

Information Technology (IT) security in the past was addressed mostly in common enterprise IT environments, but there is a clear trend to provide more connectivity to operational sites, which are quite often part of the critical infrastructure. Examples for operational sites are industrial automation or energy automation. This increased connectivity leads to a tighter integration of IT and Operational Technology (OT). IT security in this context evolves to cyber security to underline the mutual relation between the IT security and physical effects to the system or environment.

The digital energy grid consists of several interworking parts depending on data exchange in a secure and reliable way. These parts are given through the classical power system elements like a centralized power generation, power transmission (typically high voltage and wide area connections), power distribution (low and medium voltage) and the consumer at the end of the supply chain. In the last years, the usage of renewable energy, e.g., through solar cells or wind power, became increasingly important to generate environmentally sustainable energy and thus to reduce greenhouse gases leading to global warming. Utilizing renewable energy in the power grid can be achieved in basically two ways: replacing classical power plants with renewable power plants likewise connected to the transmission grid. Alternatively, Decentralized Energy Resources (DER) are connected to the distribution network. In both cases, the energy generation through a grid of renewables needs to be monitored and controlled to a similar level as in today's centralized energy generation by power plants, while utilizing widely distributed communication networks. DER may also be aggregated virtually on a higher level to build a virtual power plant (VPP). A VPP may be viewed from the outside in a similar way as a common power plant with respect to energy generation. But due to its decentralized nature, the demands on communication necessary to control the VPP are much more challenging.

This paper bases on the contribution to IARIA ENERGY 2016 [1] and enhances the base version with more background and technical details. It continues to focus on the digital energy grid as example for a critical infrastructure. The target architecture is depicted on abstract level in Figure 1 below. The paper investigates into cyber security requirements from different sources (like legislation, standardization and guidelines) providing specifics for secure communication and utilized technical security measures. Based on the analysis of security requirements, technical means are proposed to ensure the desired strength of security mechanisms (given through a security policy) specifically targeting the communication in the operation environment.

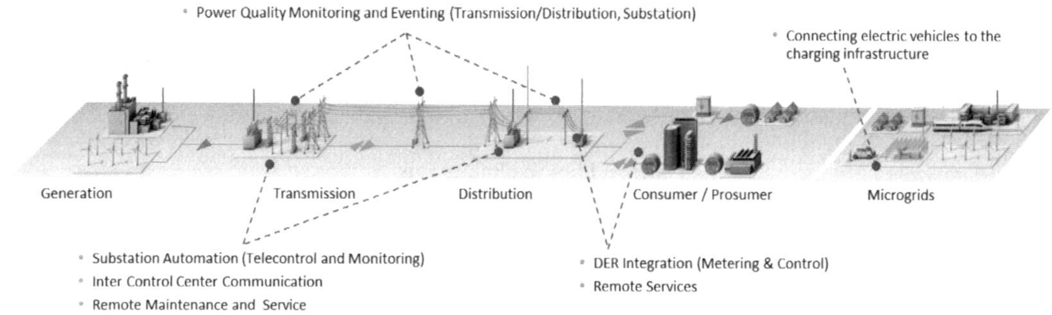

Figure 1. Overview Smart Energy Grid as Example for Critical Infrastructures

The remainder of the paper is structured as follows. Section II investigates in cyber security requirements given through regulation, standards and guidelines. Section III investigates into Transport Layer Security (TLS) [2] and IP Security (IPSec) as two common security protocols utilized in power systems. Section IV concentrates on the assurance that this security protocol is used with settings according to a given security policy. The technical proposal to achieve compliance to a given security policy for the communication between different entities of critical infrastructures using passive monitoring is the main contribution of this paper. Note that this concept has not been implemented, yet. Section V provides a short overview about existing techniques, concentrating on TLS inspection. The conclusion in section VI discusses applicability to further security protocols and the necessity for an evaluation to determine the impact of the proposed solution to the overall system.

II. SMART ENERGY GRID SECURITY REQUIREMENTS

As stated in the introduction, the operational environment of critical infrastructures, as in this paper the smart energy grid, differs from office environments or telecommunication environments in significant aspects. This leads to a different weight of general security requirements, like shown in the following Figure 2.

	Critical Infrastructures	Office IT
Anti-virus / mobile code	Uncommon / hard to deploy	Common / widely used
Component Lifetime	Up to 30 years	3-5 years
Outsourcing	Rarely used	Common
Application of patches	Use case specific	Regular / scheduled
Real time requirement	Critical due to safety	Delays accepted
Security testing / audit	Rarely (operational networks)	Scheduled and mandated
Physical Security	Very much varying	High (IT Service Center)
Security Awareness	Increasing	High
Confidentiality (Data)	Low – Medium	High
Integrity (Data)	High	Medium
Availability / Reliability	24 x 365 x ...	Medium, delays accepted
Non-Repudiation	High	Medium

Figure 2. Comparison CI and Office environment

As visible, integrity and availability have a much higher impact in the critical infrastructure. Moreover, the immediate impact of information security to safety is also more prevalent as in Office IT.

The comparison of general requirements in Figure 2 is used here to underline that solutions, which are typically used in Office IT networks, may not be directly applicable in CI networks. Differences can be explained through the different operating environments and operating conditions. These general security requirements are addressed in a variety of regulation, standards, guidelines and further customer specific or operator requirements. Figure 3 depicts example sources for such security requirements.

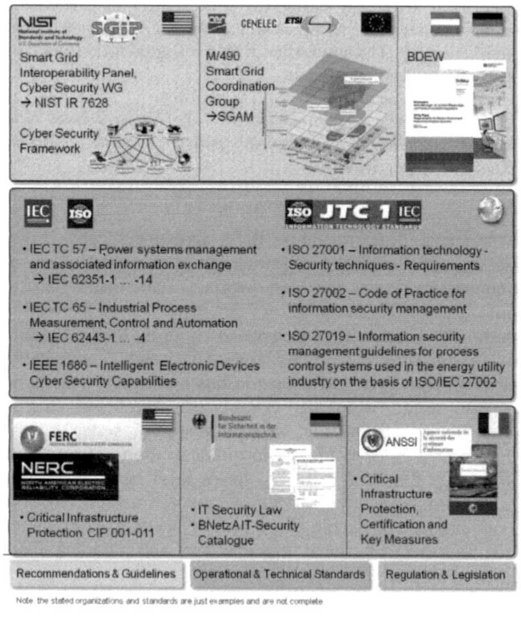

Figure 3. Sources for Security Requirements

As this paper focuses on communication security, the following subsections investigate into specific requirements targeting secure communication in the example requirement documents of different sources as stated in Figure 3. The overview about these activities is used to underline the ongoing definition of specific security requirements, which will result in specific technical solutions. To ensure the final technical solution copes with given security requirements, a technical solution for security policy verification is proposed in section IV, focusing on communication security. Specifically, passively monitoring is used here to not interfere with the original control communication.

A. Regulative requirements

The regulative requirements taken here as example, focus on the operation of critical infrastructures from a process point of view. To support the security processes technical security controls need to be supported by either the system or the deployment environment. Hence, procedural and technical security requirements cannot be seen independent.

- The North American Electric Reliability Council (NERC) has established the Critical Infrastructure Protection (CIP) Cyber Security Standards CIP–002 through CIP–011 [3], which are designed as foundation of sound security practices across bulk power systems. They provide a consistent framework for security control perimeters and access management with incident reporting and recovery for critical cyber assets and cover functional, as well as non-functional requirements. NERC CIP applies to asset owners and power system operators and consists of a mixture of organizational, process, and technical requirements. NERC-CIP version 3 is formally controlled and enforced in the U.S. and in Canada. The first version originated in 2006 and has been continuously enhanced. Meanwhile work is ongoing on version 6.

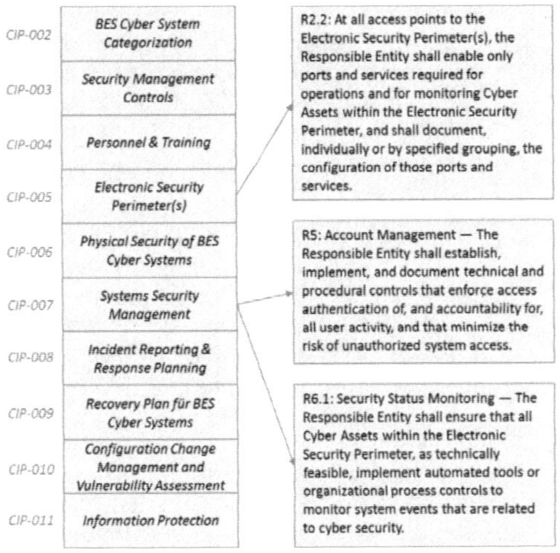

Figure 4. NERC-CIP Example Security Requirements

- A further example can be given by the legislation in Germany. Here, the IT security act has been finalized in 2015 requiring appropriate protection and monitoring, as well as reporting about security breaches for the operator of CI [4]. A specific regulation is the German Energy Act [5], which regulates in §21 the application of smart meters in facilities depending on the energy consumption/generation rate. The German "Bundesamt für Sicherheit in der Informationstechnik" (BSI) provides the technical guideline TR 03109 [6] to fulfill the requirements from the Energy Act and explicitly, how to ensure secure communication utilizing TLS to protect the communication. This targets specifically the data exchange of smart meters, either for control or for billing purposes. The protection means for secure communication are specifically defined and comprise the algorithms to be used for authentication, integrity protection, and confidentiality for TLS.
- In France, the "Agence nationale de la sécurité des systèmes d'information" (ANSSI) regulates cyber security. Specifically, for secure communication a technical note has been published providing appropriate protection [7]. This guideline provides recommendations of specific sets of algorithms (cipher suites) to be used for TLS as well as operational modes and extensions of the protocol to address discovered weaknesses.

The common approach of these regulations is that they cover organizational requirements, process requirements and also technical requirements. The examples show that the security of communication is one part of the requirements for which specific technical means are stated.

B. Standards

Besides legislation, there exists a variety of standards, formulating security requirements or provide specific solutions to secure communication in an interoperable way. Standards specify solutions like specific features or protocols in an interoperable way to support the interworking of different vendor's products. The motivation for this investigation is to show that specific security requirements and security counter measures can be directly derived from standards. These security countermeasures in turn can be evaluated in the deployments of critical infrastructures like the digital grid. This motivates the solution, later on described in section IV.

The following bullet list builds on the standards stated in Figure 3 and gives a more detailed overview about the content of the different standards.

- IEC 62443, especially IEC 62443-3-3 [8]

  IEC 62443 is a security requirements framework defined in the IEC (International Electrotechnical Commission) and can be applied to different automation domains, including energy automation, process automation, building automation, and others. In the set of corresponding documents security requirements are defined, which target the solution operator and the integrator but also the product vendor.

As shown in Figure 5, different parts of the standard are grouped into four clusters covering

- common definitions and metrics
- requirements on setup of a security organization (ISMS related), as well as solution supplier and service provider processes
- technical requirements and methodology for security on system-wide level and
- requirements to the secure development lifecycle of system components, and security requirements to such components at a technical level.

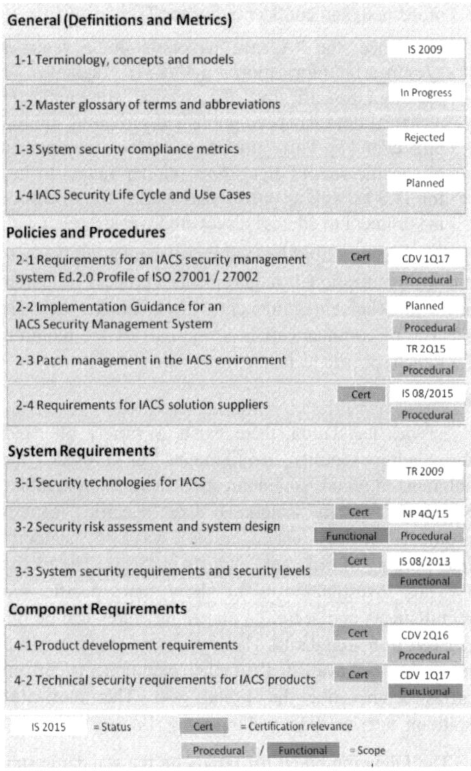

Figure 5. IEC 62443 Overview and Status

According to the methodology described in IEC 62443-3-2, a complex automation system is structured into zones that are connected by and communicate through so-called "conduits" that map for example to the logical network protocol communication between two zones. Moreover, this document defines Security Levels (SL) that correlate with the strength of a potential adversary as shown in Figure 6 below. To reach a dedicated SL, dedicated requirements have to be met.

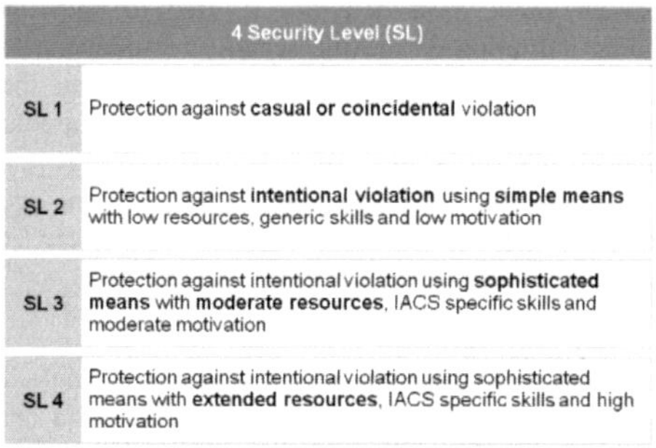

Figure 6. IEC 62443 defined Security Level

For each security level, IEC 62443 part 3-3 defines a set of requirements. Seven foundational requirements group specific requirements of a certain category:

- FR 1 Identification and authentication control
- FR 2 Use control
- FR 3 System integrity
- FR 4 Data confidentiality
- FR 5 Restricted data flow
- FR 6 Timely response to events
- FR 7 Resource availability

For each of the foundational requirements there exist several concrete technical security requirements (SR) to address a specific security level. In the context of communication security, these security levels are specifically interesting for the conduits connecting different zones. The following examples are taken from IEC 62443-3-3 [8] to illustrate some of the foundational requirements:

- FR3, SR3.1 Communication integrity: "The control system shall provide the capability to protect the integrity of transmitted information".
- FR4, SR4.1 Communication confidentiality: "The control system shall provide the capability to protect the confidentiality of information at rest and remote access sessions traversing an untrusted network."
- FR5, SR 5.2 Zone boundary protection: "The control system shall provide the capability to monitor and control communications at zone boundaries to enforce the compartmentalization defined in the risk -based zones and conduits model."

These requirements are used here as an example that IEC 62443 requires the support of certain functionality. Also, as seen especially by the last example in the list, the monitoring of the connections is required.

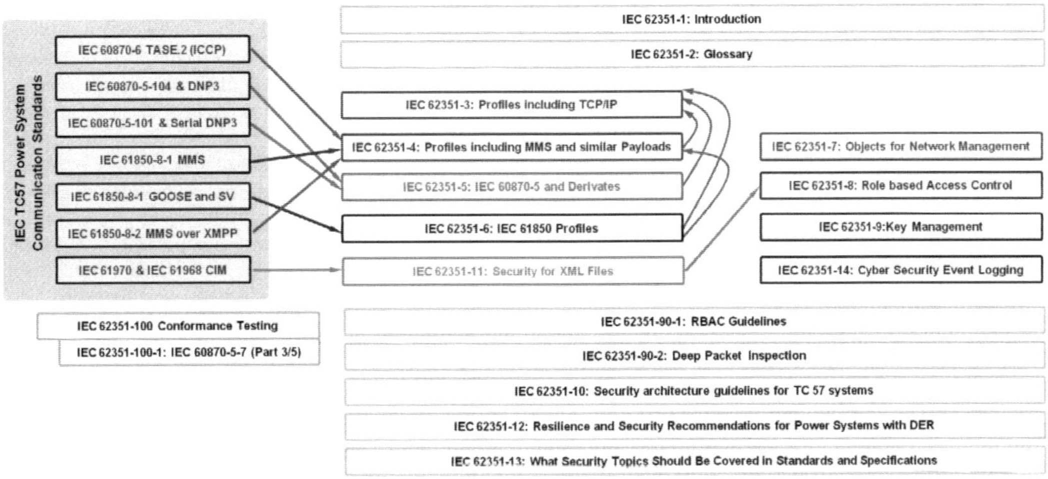

Figure 7. IEC 62351 Overview [9]

- IEC 62351, especially IEC 62351-3 [9]

  IEC 62351, which is also defined in the IEC, targets security mechanisms applicable to the power systems domain specifically. As IEC 62443, the standard is split into different parts addressing specific security topics, as shown in Figure 7.

  Different to IEC 62443, IEC 62351 describes security controls on a very detailed level to achieve interoperability in the utilized security means. Hence, it can be seen as a set of security controls to address some of the security requirements posed by IEC 62443. Specifically, IEC 62351-3 targets to secure TCP based communication by profiling the use of TLS and is referenced from other IEC 62351 parts. Profiling of TLS relates to narrowing available options in TLS like the requirement to utilize mutual authentication reducing the number of allowed algorithms or the disallowance of utilizing certain cipher suites, not providing sufficient protection. Moreover, this part also provides guidelines for utilizing options, which depend on the embedding environment. An example is the relation of using session renegotiation and session resumption in conjunction with the update interval of the certificate revocation information. As stated, IEC 62351-3 is always used in conjunction with other parts of IEC 62351 like part 4, addressing substation automation communication from a control center or communication between control center or part 5 for telecontrol.

- IEEE 1686 [10] specifies the expected security capabilities for Intelligent Electronic Devices (IED) regarding the access, operation, configuration, firmware revision and data retrieval from an IED. Also addressed is the encryption of communications with the IED. It serves as a procurement specification for new IEDs or analysis of existing IEDs.

  Beyond others, there are specific requirements for communication security. These address for instance:

  - File transfer is only allowed using Secure File Transfer Protocol
  - Network management shall be provided with SNMPv3.
  - Secure tunneling using cryptographic VPNs.

  Specific cryptographic algorithms are not required, but the support of the stated functionality.

C. Guidelines

Besides regulations and standards, there also exist guidelines on how to address secure communication in specific application environments.

- The "Bundesverband für Energie- und Wasserwirtschaft" (BDEW) introduced a white paper defining basic security measures and requirements for IT-based control, automation and telecommunication systems for energy and water systems, taking into account general technical and operational conditions [10]. It can be seen as a further national approach targeting similar goals as NERC-CIP, but at a less detailed level. The white paper addresses requirements for vendors and manufacturers of power system management systems by directly relating to ISO 27002 [11]. Section 2.3 of this white paper focuses on communication and formulates specific requirements for integrity and confidentiality of connections.
- NISTIR 7628 [12] originates from the Smart Grid Interoperability Panel (Cyber Security WG) of the National Institute for Standards and Technology (NIST).

It targets the development of a comprehensive set of cyber security requirements. The document consists of three subdocuments targeting strategy, security architecture, and requirements, and supportive analyses and references. It specifically formulates requirements for smart grid information system and communication protection.

- SGIS Report: The security subgroup of the European Smart Grid Coordination Group (SG-CG) targeted the European Commission mandate M/490 [13] and addressed cyber security in the (European) smart grid. Smart Grid services shall be enabled through a Smart Grid information and communication system that is inherently secure by design within the critical infrastructure of transmission and distribution networks, down to connected properties. The report describes an analysis framework applied to different use cases and mapped to standards work to address identified security requirements. The investigation into security was closely connected to Smart Grid Architectural Model (SGAM) developed by a different working group. The final report of the security subgroup (see [14]) provides recommendations of security means, to be applied in the different zones and domains of SGAM. Secure communication has been specifically referenced through the IEC 62351 series and general security protocols like TLS, which will be investigated in the next subsection.

III. SECURE COMMUNICATION PROTOCOLS

As shown in the previous section, there are numerous examples of requirements to secure communication, which leads to the necessity to be able to verify that the appropriate communication security is applied in fact in operational use. This section investigates example protocols to ensure secure communication by taking TLS and IPSec as example, as they are widely used, also in substation automation. The goal is to analyze the protocol session establishment phase and specifically into options to monitor the negotiation of security parameters to ensure the compliance to a given security policy. This information shall be used afterwards to discuss options to monitor the session establishment passively. As it will be shown in the following subsections, only in case of TLS passive monitoring of the security parameter establishment can be performed. Therefore, for the discussion of a technical solution, TLS is used further on as example.

A. TLS to Secure TCP Communication

TLS is widely used in power automation systems (see IEC 62351 in section II.B), to protect the communication for automation control and monitoring, but also for remote management.

TLS in its current version 1.2 defines protection means for TCP-based communication and is defined by the Internet Engineering Task Force (IETF) in RFC 5246 [2]. Protection here relates to different security services like unilateral or mutual authentication, message integrity, or message confidentiality, which can be negotiated during the initial handshake. Note, that the standard has a long history and is constantly being evolved to cope with new advances in cryptography and communication security. Currently there is work ongoing on version TLS 1.3, which will provide more radical changes compared to the enhancements in the previous version iteration. TLS supports a variety of authentication options for the communicating peers and allows the negotiation of the protection of the preceding communication in terms of integrity and confidentiality and also key management related options like key updates, etc. The combination of cryptographic algorithms for authentication, integrity, and confidentiality protection is called cipher suite.

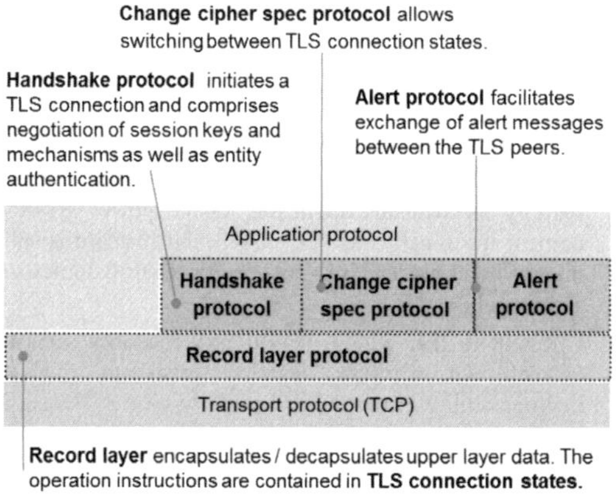

Figure 8. TLS Protocol Structure

TLS is built upon several sub protocols that encapsulate the protocol operation in the different phases as shown in Figure 8. For the discussion in this paper the most interesting phase is the TLS v1.2 handshake, as it is performed in clear and allows the monitoring of the negotiated security options for the following communication session. Figure 9 shows the message exchange during the TLS v1.2 handshake.

Especially, the first phase of the handshake is in focus here, as it conveys the information for the cipher suite negotiation and the authentication of the communicating peers. In the *ClientHello* message, the client passes a list of cipher suites to the server containing the combinations of cryptographic algorithms supported in order of the client's preference. The server will then select a cipher suite and respond with a *ServerHello* message if a matching proposal was found. If no matching proposal was found, the server will issue a failure alert. Assumed that the server will authenticate towards the client, it will send its certificate as part other response. This allows the client to identify the server, validate the server certificate, as well as to utilize the server certificate during the further session key establishment. If the server additionally requires a client authentication as part of the TLS handshake, it will send a *CertificateRequest* message.

The second phase of the handshake targets the client identification (if requested) and the session key establishment and the authentication of both sides. In this step, the client will provide its certificate if requested in the *Certificate* message. The *Finished* message from the server to the client concludes the handshake and is the first message encrypted using the negotiated session key. It also contains a hash over the previously exchanged handshake messages to have a delayed verification of the integrity of the performed handshake.

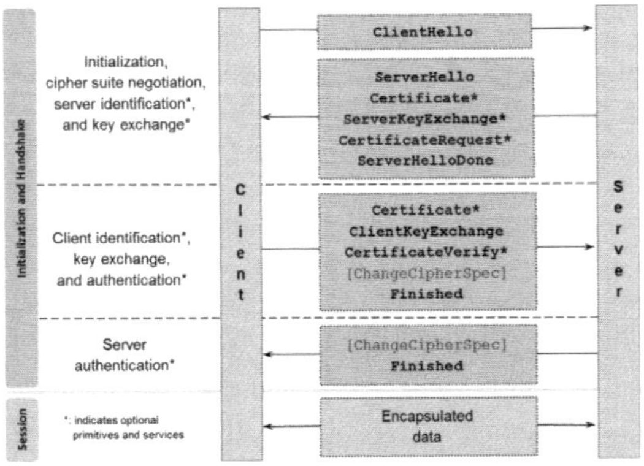

Figure 9. TLSv1.2 Handshake for TLS Session Setup

Based on the provided TLS overview the handshake phase can be used to monitor the establishment of a secure communication, which can be audited by an independent component. This can be used additionally to the server security policy configuration to ensure that the negotiated security settings for a communication channel provide a strength required by the security policy. The independent audit option will reveal failures in the configuration of the client or server side or both.

Besides TLS protection of TCP based communication there exists also a derivation of TLS for UDP based communication. This security protocol is called Datagram Transport Layer Security – DTLS and is defined in RFC 6347 [15]. The handshake is similar to TLS, but is enhanced with a cookie mechanism to cope with the missing reliability of TLS. Hence, the message context during the handshake of DTLS can be analyzed in the same way as for TLS.

Besides the initial handshake, TLS supports further session management operations to support session key renegotiation or the resumption of previously closed sessions. Session renegotiation is essentially the performance of a complete handshake during an ongoing TLS session. It is performed to establish a new session key and also to verify the credentials used for authentication. Especially the latter is becoming necessary for long lasting connections between devices. This is due to the fact, that the certificates used during the handshake have a limited validity period. Additionally, they may be revoked if the corresponding private key has been compromised. To ensure that this is detected, the certificates used for authentication are re-evaluated during session renegotiation. Session resumption is different as it reuses the already established pre-master secret from a previous session to either negotiate a new session key during the still ongoing session or to resume the previous session, if it was closed before. This enables a much faster session startup as the asymmetric operation is omitted. Note that session resumption is at maximum allowed 24 hours after the original session has been closed. Session renegotiation and session resumption during a still running session are both performed over the already existing TLS session. This makes a passive monitoring of the handshake impossible, if encrypting cipher suites have been negotiated during the initial handshake. Session resumption of a session that has been closed before will perform the TLS handshake on a "fresh" TCP connection. In this case, the handshake is performed in clear text, as the TLS connection needs to be reestablished. Hence, the resumption can be passively monitored for security policy compliance.

As stated before, TLS is a protocol that is under constant development. Over the years it has become more versatile also due to its extensibility. This extensibility has been used to enhance the feature set but also to address discovered weaknesses. Currently TLS v1.3 is under development with the goal to redesign the handshake to offload some of its complexity and also to be able to have a more performant session setup. This version is currently in draft status [16] but expected to be released as RFC during 2017.

In contrast to TLS v1.2 the new handshake can be performed in one message less, resulting in a 1.5 roundtrip handshake as shown in Figure 10. Also new is the option to already encrypt part of the information in the TLS server response message. The *Client.Hello and the Server.Hello* messages are till sent in clear text, allowing the inspection regarding compliance to a given security policy regarding the utilized cipher suites. Also, the server certificate is visible. A different approach has been taken for the client side authentication. In TLS v1.3, the *Certificate.Request* message from the server and the *Certificate* message from the client are sent encrypted. This hinders the inspection of the certificate by simply monitoring the TLS handshake. On the other hand, it increases the privacy of the client side, as eavesdropping by an adversary on path may not expose the client identity.

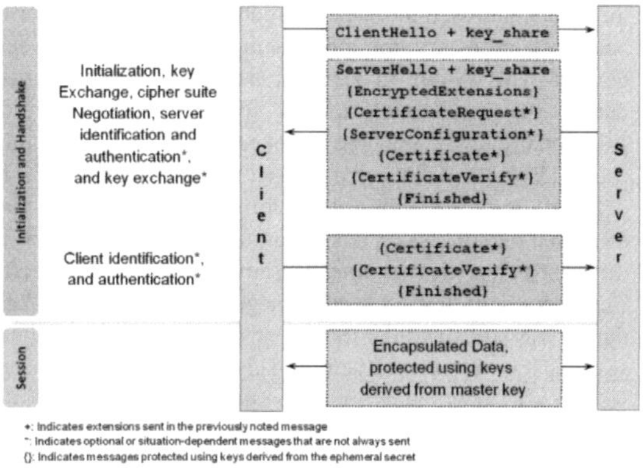

Figure 10. TLSv1.3 Handshake for TLS Session Setup

Based on the session establishment analysis, the initial handshakes of a TLS connection can be passively monitored to verify the adherence to a given security policy.

B. *IPSec and IKE to to support secure tunneling*

IPSec is a protocol typically being used to build secure communication tunnel, so-called Virtual Private Networks (VPN). The advantage of an IPSec based VPN is the option to tunnel different protocols either TCP-based or UDP-based. Therefore, this approach is often used to connect two distinct zones or sites. An example is the application to connect a substation and a control center, for which the IPSec VPN is used to protect IEC 61850 control communication or IEC 60870-5-104 telecontrol communication and additionally voice-over-IP (VoIP) communication to enable a direct interaction from the control center with a service technician located in the substation.

In contrast to TLS, IPSec describes the protocol protecting the bulk communication without an integrated key management. The key management for IPSec can be done manually or automated. For an automated key management the Internet Key Exchange (IKE) is available in version 1 and version 2. In both versions, IKE distinguishes two phases:

- In phase one, a secure key management channel between the involved IKE peers is established.
- In phase two, Security Associations for security protocols (e.g. IPSec) are established on request via the secure key management channel.

While IKEv1 supports a variety of authentication modes and also different modes for the phase one key exchange, IKEv2 has been specified to reduce this complexity. IKEv2 is defined by the IETF in RFC 4306 [17]. Figure 11 below shows the message exchanges for both phases including the different parameter contained in these messages. It becomes immediately visible, that within phase 1, after the first roundtrip the remaining communication is encrypted. Therefore, only the first handshake of the phase 1 key exchange can be passively monitored.

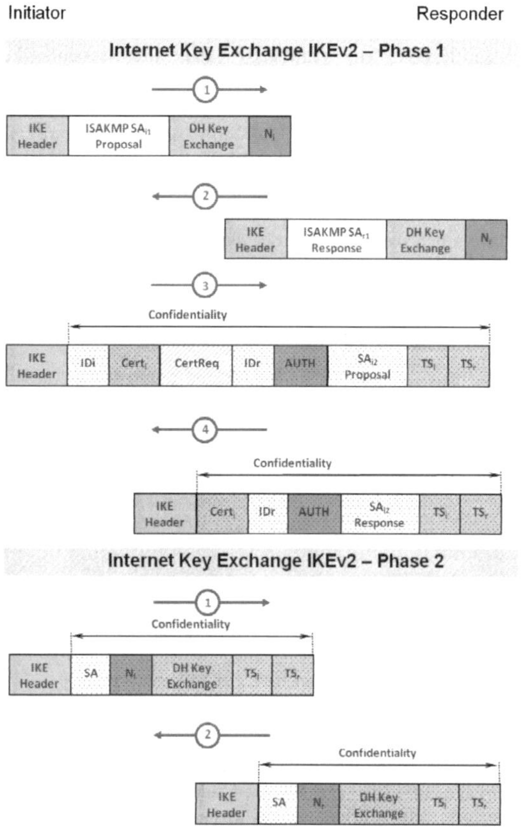

Figure 11. IKEv2 Phase 1 and Phase 2 Key Exchange

These messages negotiate cryptographic algorithms (contained in the security association payload SA), exchange nonces (N), and perform a Diffie-Hellman key agreement (DH) for the second phase of IKE. The security association parameters for the actual IPSec session are negotiated in IKE phase 2, which is encrypted using the negotiated parameter from IKE phase 1. As shown, this key management cannot be monitored passively to verify the negotiation of IPSec parameter according to a security policy. Here, an investigation at either side of the VPN tunnel would be necessary, e.g., by verifying the negotiation of the security association based on the settings and the system security log.

IV. Ensuring Secure TCP Communication

As depicted in the previous section by taking TLS as example, it is possible to monitor the security negotiation of secure communication protocols in a passive way, without interfering with the protocol and by a component not involved in the actual communication. To utilize this property, an additional component – a crypto option filter – in a network is defined. This crypto filter may be realized as separate component or may be part of an already existing component of the message exchange (not the actual data processing), e.g., a switch. This allows for inpath and also for offpath monitoring. Offpath monitoring specifically enables monitoring options without an influence to the control communication in terms of delay. The task of the crypto filter is essentially the monitoring of clear text session establishment phases of cryptographic protocols to evaluate the adherence of a given security policy. The crypto filter is defined as part of this paper; an evaluation of the approach has not been done, yet.

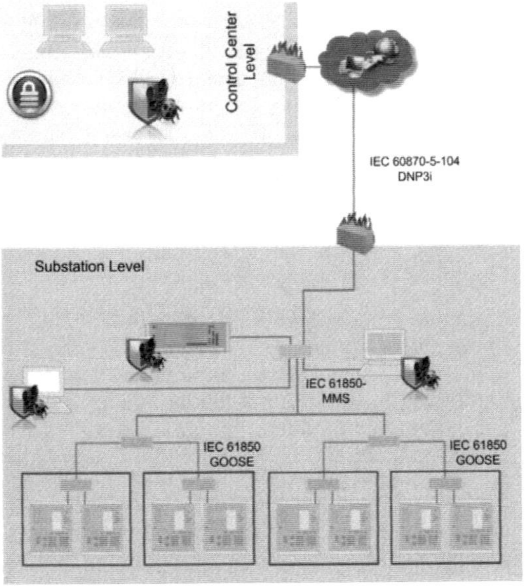

Figure 12. Substation to Control Center Communication

Figure 12 shows the underlying use case targeting the communication between a substation and a control center connected over a public network using a dedicated protocol (here: IEC 60870-5-104) for telecontrol, which is secured by TLS. Both sides are required to authenticate within TLS on the base of X.509 certificates and to provide support for one of the following cipher suites:

- TLS_RSA_WITH_AES_128_CBC_SHA
- TLS_DH_ DSS_WITH_AES_128_SHA
- TLS_DH_DSS_WITH_AES_256_SHA
- TLS_ECDHE_ECDSA_WITH_ AES_128_SHA

The following cipher suites are explicitly forbidden, as they do not provide confidentiality of the data exchange or not even integrity protection (first bullet)

- TLS_RSA_WITH_NULL_NULL
- TLS_RSA_WITH_NULL_SHA256
- TLS_ECDHE_ECDSA_WITH_NULL_SHA

This data is typically contained in a policy configuration data base together with connection specific information to identify the associated security policy.

In the following, two approaches for the realization of a crypto option filter from a network design perspective are described. This also comprises a functionality to utilize the information for ensuring a match to a given security policy, which may then lead to the interruption of communication establishment, if the security policy is not met.

Figure 13 shows a variant, in which the crypto option filter is placed directly into the communication path. This realization may be based on existing network components in the communication path. The data analysis component monitors the connection establishment and the TLS handshake without interrupting the communication channel establishment. The handshake messages *ClientHello* and *ServerHello* carry the specific information about the cipher suite negotiation, which is monitored and compared with the data from security policy database. Additionally the exchange of the server and client side certificate is monitored. As an additional service, the crypto filter may validate the exchanged certificates to ensure that they are not outdated or revoked. Depending on the match of the security negotiation parameter with the security policy, the communication establishment may be terminated through the policy enforcement component.

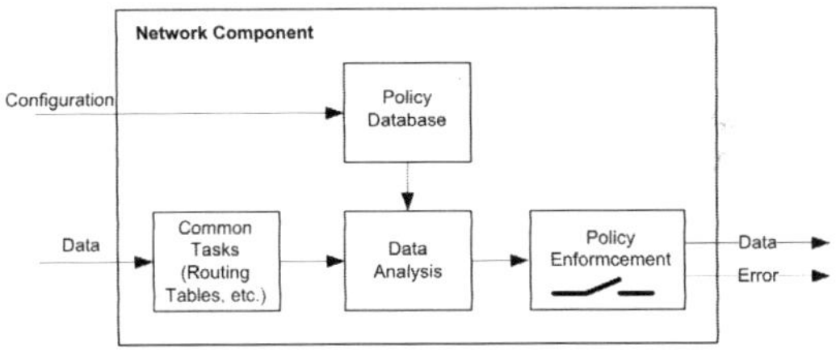

Figure 13. In-path Crypto Option Filter

In contrast to the in-path crypto option filter, Figure 14 shows an off-path filter. The general evaluation is similar to the in-path filter, with the exception of the data access. As the filter is not directly placed in the communication path, a probe on the network duplicates the traffic and forwards it to the off-path crypto option filter. This probe may be a separate component or a monitoring port on the existing infrastructure component as shown in Figure 14. If it is a separate component, the probe may already preprocess the handshake and extract the information, which can then be provided to the crypto option filter. If the functionality is included in an existing infrastructure component, the complete TLS handshake may be forwarded to the crypto option filter for inspection. Alternatively, the policy enforcement component may integrate the traffic duplication.

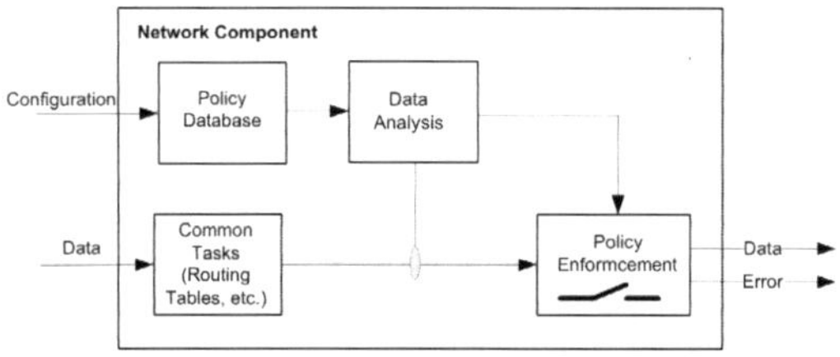

Figure 14. Off-path Crypto Option Filter

The off-path variant has the clear advantage that the policy checking component can be centralized, independent from the actual communication path to be checked.

Note that the description for the crypto option filter focused on the TLS 1.2 version as discussed in Section III.A. TLS 1.3 will result in simplifications of the current more complex handshake and will reduce the available options and also shorten the handshake phase to three messages. Most importantly, TLS 1.3 will utilize the established key already in the handshake phase to protect messages. The monitoring approach as described is not completely possible. While the negotiation of cipher suites can still be followed as it proceeds in clear, the client certificate exchange is encrypted. Hence, the certificate may not be checked anymore.

V. EXAMPLES FOR EXISITING SOLUTIONS

Monitoring of communication protocols for specific content can be done on-path (as part of the immediate communication path) or off-path as also stated in the previous section. Off-path techniques may involve for instance the monitoring port of switches, which allow direct access to the routed data and thus to analyze these data. This is only possible for communication protocols, which perform the data exchange in clear, without applying encryption. If encryption is applied, access to the utilized session key would be necessary. On-Path techniques insert a new component (middlebox) into the communication path, which terminates the communication connection to both sides and allows for the inspection of the data exchange. Examples are deep packet inspection modules, which can be operated on Firewalls to inspect the data for viruses, malware or also malformed protocol messages. Utilizing these components to ensure adherence to a session security policy are not know. The described solution in section IV for TLS can be seen as enhancement to packet inspection. In the specific case, the clear text handshake of TLS is leveraged to allow for the application of both techniques, on-path and off-path.

Alternatively to the described solution for TLS, there is ongoing research on changing the handshake of TLS to allow middleboxes to inspect traffic on-path as described in [18] without breaking end-to-end security called mcTLS (Multi Context-TLS). The basic principle here is to perform an enhanced handshake involving middleboxes into the handshake phase of TLS. Specifically, the middleboxes are authenticated during the handshake and thus know to both communicating ends. Moreover, each side is involved in the generation of the session key, which is also provided to the middlebox. There is also additional keying performed for the exchange of pure end-to-end keys, allowing the application of key material known to the middlebox to encrypt the traffic and for integrity protection, while the end-to-end based keys are used to provide an end-to-end integrity. The latter approach ensures that the middlebox can read and analyze the content of the communication in the TLS record layer, but any change done by the middlebox is detected by a violation of the end-to-end integrity check value. This approach has the advantage that it provides an option to check the associated security policy during the session setup and at the same time monitor traffic as an authorized component. The drawback is that the solution focuses solely on TLS and cannot be applied to other protocols without changes. Also, it is always included as an in-path component, which may result in unwanted performance influences. This shows another approach, which requires also requires more effort for the realization as it requires changing the utilized security protocol.

VI. CONCLUSIONS AND OUTLOOK

This paper described a solution to ensure that communication between different components of a system is in fact protected according to a dedicated security strength as defined by a given security policy. It ensures that the required level of security is indeed utilized during operation. As shown, requirements for secure communication exist through different guidelines, standards, and also legislation. The proposed solution was shown in the context of substation to control center communication, to ensure mutual authentication and an appropriate protection of the communicated information. As the smart energy grid does increasingly integrate DER systems, the chance of communicating privacy related data increases. And so do the requirements for protected communication.

The example shown related to the protocol TLS, which is used in power system automation to secure the communication. Besides that, it has been shown, that the approach has its limits on the example of IPSec as here, the main information about the bulk data exchange protection are already negotiated in an encrypted manner and therefore not visible to a passive monitoring component.

In the investigated case of TLS, the proposed crypto filter verifies the establishment of secure communication channels according to a given security policy, it can also be used to offload further validation tasks from the communication peers, like the validation of the peer certificates utilized during connection establishment. Also shown have been limitations for TLS, in the context of renegotiations of the session parameter. As in the case of IPSec, the renegotiation of session parameter is performed over an encrypted connection and can therefore not be monitored passively. If there is a requirement to also monitor these exchanges, classical proxy solutions terminating the secure channel can be used, with the influence on session setup and potential additional components.

As stated in the beginning, this paper describes the concept for ensuring the establishment of secure communication channels in a nonintrusive manner. The consequent next step is the integration of the proposed approach in a prototype, to validate the effectiveness.

REFERENCES

[1] S. Fries and R. Falk, "Ensuring Secure Communication in Critical Infrastructures," Proceeding IARIA ENERGY 2016, pg. 15-20, June 2016, ISBN: 978-1-61208-484-8,

[2] T. Dierks and E. Rescorla, "The Transport Layer Security (TLS) Protocol Version 1.2", RFC 5246, Aug. 2008, http://tools.ietf.org/html/rfc5246 [retrieved: Jan. 2016].

[3] NERC-CIP, North American Electric Reliability Corporation, "CIP Critical Infrastructure Protection Standards", Version 5, http://www.nerc.com/pa/Stand/Pages/CIPStandards.aspx, [retrieved: Jan.2016]

[4] German IT Security Law, July 2015, http://www.bgbl.de/xaver/bgbl/start.xav?startbk=Bundesanzeiger_BGBl&jumpTo=bgbl115s1324.pdf (German) [retrieved: Jan. 2016]

[5] German Energy Act, EnWG, July 2012, http://www.gesetze-im-internet.de/bundesrecht/enwg_2005/gesamt.pdf (German) [retrieved: Jan. 2016]

[6] Technical Guideline TR 03109, Technische Vorgaben für intelligente Messsysteme, 2015, https://www.bsi.bund.de/DE/Publikationen/TechnischeRichtlinien/tr03109/index_htm.html (German) [retrieved: Jan. 2016]

[7] ANSSI Technical Note, Security Recommendations for TLS, February 2017, https://www.ssi.gouv.fr/uploads/2017/02/security-recommendations-for-tls_v1.1.pdf [retrieved: Mar. 2017]

[8] IEC62443-3-3:2013, "Industrial communication networks – Network and system security – Part 3-3: System security requirements and security levels", Edition 1.0, August 2013.

[9] IEC 62351-x Power systems management and associated information exchange – Data and communication security, http://www.iec.ch/smartgrid/standards/ [retrieved: Jan. 2016].

[10] IEEE 1686, "IEEE Standard for Intelligent Electronic Devices Cyber Security Capabilities," Mai 2013Bundesverband der Energie- und Wasserwirtschaft, Datensicherheit, BDEW "Whitepaper Requirements for Secure Control and Telecommunication Systems," Version 1.1, 03/2015., http://ldew.de/bdew.nsf/id/52929DBC7CEEED1EC125766C000588AD/$file/Whitepaper_Secure_Systems_Vedis_1.0final.pdf [retrieved: Jan. 2016]

[11] ISO 27002, "Information technology - Security techniques - Code of practice for information security controls," 2013

[12] NIST IR 7628 Guidelines for Smart Grid Cybersecurity: Vol. 1 - Smart Grid Cybersecurity Strategy, Architecture, and High-Level Requirements, Vol. 2 - Privacy and the Smart Grid, Vol. 3 - Supportive Analyses and References, NISTIR 7628 Rev. 1, (Volumes 1-3), http://nvlpubs.nist.gov/nistpubs/ir/2014/NIST.IR.7628r1.pdf [retrieved: Jan 2017]

[13] Mandate M490, http://ec.europa.eu/growth/tools-databases/mandates/index.cfm?fuseaction=search.detail&id=475# [retrieved: Jan 2017]

[14] CEN/CENELEC/ETSI Smart Grid Reports: www.cencenelec.eu/go/SmartGrids/ [retrieved: Jan. 2017]

[15] E. Rescorla and N. Modadugu, "Datagram Transport Layer Security Version 1.2," RFC 6347, January 2012, https://tools.ietf.org/html/rfc6347, [retrieved: Jan. 2017]

[16] E. Rescorla, "The Transport Layer Security (TLS) Protocol Version 1.3," Draft, https://tools.ietf.org/html/draft-ietf-tls-tls13-18, October 2016, [retrieved: Jan. 2017]

[17] C. Kaufman, "Internet Key Exchange (IKEv2) Protocol," RFC 4306, December 2005, https://tools.ietf.org/html/rfc4306, [retrieved: Jan. 2017]

[18] D. Naylor et al., "Multi-Context TLS (mcTLS), Enabling Secure In-Network Functionality in TLS," http://mctls.org/, [retrieved: Jan. 2017]

Modeling User-Based Modifications to Information Quality to Address Privacy and Trust Related Concerns in Online Social Networks

Brian P. Blake and Nitin Agarwal
University of Arkansas at Little Rock
Little Rock, Arkansas, USA
e-mail: bpblake@ualr.edu and nxagarwal@ualr.edu

Abstract—**This research seeks to understand user-based modifications to information quality due to data privacy and trust related concerns within online social networks. It explores the interrelationships and trade-offs between data privacy, trust, and information quality. To this end, we present an extensive literature review to frame our research. The greatest implications of this research come through development of integrated research matrix frameworks, a privacy/trust/information quality modeling syntax, and forthcoming structural equation scoring measures that will be applicable to future research efforts. In application, the relationship matrices can be applied to the conceptual modeling syntax. Further, the results of the structural equation model will show the strength and directionality of the effects of related matrix aspects on one another. The research will enhance methods of modeling and measuring data privacy, trust, and information quality within online social networks. Regarding online social networks, it lends itself to a better understanding of the quality of shared information in given data privacy and trust scenarios. It provides future researchers with a formal framework for relating privacy, trust, and information quality as well as a formal way to understand information quality modification.**

Keywords-information quality; privacy; trust; online social networks.

I. INTRODUCTION

This work is an extended version of a paper [1] previously presented at the Sixth International Conference on Social Media Technologies, Communication, and Informatics (SOTICS) in Rome, Italy on August 25, 2016.

Social media as communication media have surged in popularity over the past decade. Social networking websites such Facebook, MySpace, and Twitter have been the champions of this social phenomenon [2]. As the use of social media networks increases there are growing concerns about data privacy. Borcea-Pfitzmann, Pfitzmann, and Berg [3] noted in 2011 that as information technology evolves it greatly influences perceptions and demands regarding privacy. Because of this, developments in social computing are driving a new wave of privacy discussions. Government and corporate database privacy issues are often discussed and remain highly important, but per Zittrain [4] these are "dwarfed by threats to privacy that do not fit the standard analytical template for addressing privacy issues". He used the term Privacy 2.0 to refer to this non-standard view. Zittrain argued that governments or corporations are not always the ones managing surveillance and that control of the transfer of personal information can be eliminated by peer-to-peer technologies.

Frederick Lane, when discussing privacy in a webbed world as part of American Privacy, declared that "information wants to be free" [5]. He continued that social network sites succeed because individuals crave community and will share personal information to build it. "Online social networks," he stated, "thrive because they enable us to share personal information more quickly and easily than ever before, creating the impression that we are all newsworthy now". Lane further noted that individuals make seemingly rational decisions to post information online to receive perceived benefits, but fully rational decisions require complete information and most individuals do not understand what little control they hold over information posted on social networking sites or personal websites. In a similar vein, Zittrain stated that "people might make rational decisions about sharing their personal information in the short term, but underestimate what might happen to information as it is indexed, reused, and repurposed by strangers" [4].

A. *Research Focus*

In research related to the general concepts of privacy, trust, and information quality (IQ) each is often addressed in a multi-faceted manner focusing on dimensions, aspects, and properties. To further this, trust, privacy, and information quality as areas of study are interrelated and overlapping in relation to online information disclosure, but how they interact with each other is not fully defined. This is especially true in relation to online social networks (OSNs). Previous research, such as Bertini [6], has noted that there is a direct relationship between privacy, trust, and an individual's willingness to share information of increasing quantity and quality. This creates an opportunity for research. From a practitioners' perspective, there is a need to model, measure, and understand social network information exchanges regarding privacy, trust, and information quality trade-offs and modifications. From a users' perspective, there is a need to understand both the trust aspects and the visibility of information shared online more fully as well as implications from future use of that data. The goal of this research therefore is to apply an information quality perspective to the modeling of data privacy within social media networks to enable the exploration of the interrelationships and tradeoffs between data privacy, trust, and information quality.

This research will address two problem areas. First, a standard way to frame, model, and measure the relationship of the sub-aspects of data privacy, trust, and information quality to facilitate understanding does not exist. This limits research in relation to a comprehensive understanding and restricts cross-discipline communication. Second, a specific understanding of how information quality modification is used by members of online social networks as a reaction to privacy and trust related concerns has not been fully addressed by the information quality research field. This limits the understanding of outcomes based on existing research models regarding both antecedent influence and behavioral intentions vs. actual behavior within online social networks from an information quality perspective. A greater understanding of these factors can facilitate online social network organization changes to encourage greater sharing while simultaneously giving a deeper insight into how information is shared from an information quality point of view.

B. *Research Implications*

The greatest implications of this research will come through development of integrated matrix frameworks, a privacy/trust/information quality modeling syntax, and structural equation scoring measures that will be applicable to future research efforts. Through these efforts, we hope to provide statistical models for advancing the understanding of privacy, trust, and information quality. The research can enhance methods of modeling and measuring data privacy at both the data element and entity levels. In application to online social networks, it may lend itself to raised awareness of data visibility in social media as well as a better understanding of the quality of shared information in given data privacy and trust scenarios.

C. *Structure*

The remainder of this paper is organized as follows. Section II describes background literature regarding privacy, trust, information quality, and online social networks. Section III presents a further review of literature as it bears on the interrelated aspects of this research. Section IV presents research methodologies and discusses initial results of the research. Section V summaries research, discusses challenges, and looks at future research opportunities.

II. BACKGROUND

For better understanding, this section will highlight background literature regarding privacy, trust, information quality, and online social networks.

A. *Privacy*

According to Daniel Solove in Understanding Privacy [7], nearly 120 years after "The Right to Privacy" by Warren and Brandeis was first published in the Harvard Law Review, current views in the field of privacy form a "sweeping concept" that includes "freedom of thought, control over one's body, solitude in one's home, control over personal information, freedom from surveillance, protection of one's reputation, and protection from searches and interrogations". He highlighted others who describe privacy as "exasperatingly vague", "infected with pernicious ambiguities", and "entangled in competing and contradictory dimensions". Helen Nissenbaum [8] noted that privacy is commonly characterized in literature as either a constraint on access or a form of control. As theorists conceptualize privacy, they are typically searching for a core common denominator that forms the essence of privacy, but Solove argued that privacy is not easily conceptualized in this manner. He stated that a common denominator approach broad enough to include the varied aspects of privacy is likely to be vague and overly inclusive, while narrower approaches risk being too exclusive and restrictive. Privacy conceptualizations in existing literature can therefore be grouped into targeted common core definitions and broader privacy frameworks.

1) *Privacy Common Core Conceptualizations*

The six major common core conceptualizations reviewed by Solove [7] can be found in Table I and are presented in the following section. Privacy as the right to be let alone is closely tied to Warren and Brandeis as detailed above. Another common view is privacy as limited access to the self. According to Solove, this view is highlighted by Godkin, Bok, Gross, Van Den Haag, O'Brien, and Allan. As noted above, Godkin believed in privacy as the right to decide how much knowledge of personal thoughts and private doings the public at large should be allowed. Bok formulated privacy as protection from unwanted access by others. Van Den Haag, in turn, argued for exclusive access to a realm of one's own. A third common core conceptualization is privacy as secrecy. Posner presented privacy as the right to conceal information or facts about oneself. Similarly, Jourard defined privacy as an outcome of withholding certain knowledge from others. This sets up a dichotomy in which information is either hidden (private) or known (public) and once it is known it can no longer be considered private. Solove noted that this "fails to recognize that individuals may want to keep things private from some people but not others" [7], which is a truth highly relevant to information disclosure in online social network. The fourth conceptualization is privacy as control over personal information. Westin argued that privacy involves determining for oneself when, how, and to what extent information is shared. Miller viewed privacy as control of the circulation of information about oneself. Fried defined privacy not as the absence of information about us, but through the control of that information. This conceptualization is often the focus of privacy systems within online social media networks. Personhood and the right of individuality is the fifth conceptualization. Freund noted that certain attributes that are "irreductible" from self-identity. Protection of individuality and personal dignity is the core of privacy according to Bloustein. Likewise, Benn framed privacy as respect for individuals as choosers. A final common core conceptualization is privacy as intimacy. Gerstein argued that privacy is essential for the formation of intimate relationships. Privacy is extended beyond simple rational autonomy according to Farber. Finally, according to Inness, privacy deals with intimate information, access, and decisions.

TABLE I. PRIVACY COMMON CORE CONCEPTUALIZATIONS [7]

Common Core Conceptualizations		
Who	**What**	**Details**
Warren and Brandeis	The Right to be Let Alone	• The right of each individual to determine to what extent thoughts, sentiments, and emotions can be communicated to others. A general immunity of the person and the right to one's personality.
Godkin, Bok, Gross, Van Den Haag, O'Brien, Allan	Limited Access to the Self	• Right to decide how much knowledge of personal thoughts and private doings the public at large should be allowed (Godkin). • Protection from unwanted access by others (Bok). • Exclusive access to a realm of one's own (Van Den Haag).
Posner, Jourard	Secrecy	• The right to conceal information or facts about oneself (Posner). • Privacy as an outcome of withholding certain knowledge from others (Jourard).
Westin, Miller, Fried	Control over Personal Information	• Determining for oneself when, how, and to what extent information is shared (Westin). • Control of the circulation of information about oneself (Miller). • Not the absence of information about ourselves, but the control of that information (Fried).
Freund, Bloustein, Reiman, Benn	Personhood	• Attributes that are irreductible from oneself (Freund). • Protection of individuality and personal dignity (Bloustein). • Respect for individuals as choosers (Benn).
Farber, Gerstein, Inness	Intimacy	• Privacy as essential for intimate relationships (Gerstein). • Extends privacy beyond simple rational autonomy (Farber). • Privacy deals with intimate information, access, and decisions (Inness).

2) Privacy Framework Conceptualizations

Major privacy frameworks have been offered by Solove [7], Nissenbaum [8][9], Holtzman [10], and Rössler [11] (see Table II). From a research perspective, these broader privacy frameworks have a strong structural relationship to the predominant multi-dimensional framework of information quality. Commonalities can be found across most of these privacy frameworks. The sub-components of the Solove and Rössler frameworks have a strong relationship to each other. Generally, sub-components of these frameworks, as Nissenbaum contended, focus around the twin concepts of access and control. In addition, varied determinations and combinations of these framework sub-components will form key aspects of the contextual norms on which Nissenbaum's contextual integrity framework is based.

TABLE II. PRIVACY FRAMEWORK CONCEPTUALIZATIONS

Privacy Frameworks Conceptualizations	
Daniel Solove [7] Multi-Dimensional Taxonomy of Privacy	• Privacy as "a cluster of many distinct yet related things." • Information Collection: Surveillance and Interrogation • Information Processing: Aggregation, Identification, Insecurity, Secondary Use, and Exclusion • Information Dissemination: Breach of confidentiality, Disclosure, Exposure, Increased accessibility, Blackmail, Appropriation, and Distortion • Invasions: Intrusion and Decisional interference
David Holtzman [10] The Seven Sins Against Privacy	• Basic Privacy Meanings: Seclusion (right to be hidden), Solitude (right to be left alone), self-determination (right to control information about oneself) • Seven Privacy Sins: intrusion, latency, deception, profiling, identity theft, outing, and loss of dignity • Privacy Torts: Appropriation, Intrusion, Private Facts, False Light
Helen Nissenbaum [8][9] Contextual Integrity	• "Contextual integrity ties adequate protection for privacy to norms of specific contexts, demanding that information gathering and dissemination be appropriate to that context and obey the governing norms of distribution within it." • "A right to live in a world in which our expectations about the flow of personal information are, for the most part, met; expectations that are shaped not only by force of habit and convention, but a general confidence in the mutual support these flows accord to key organizing principles of social life, including moral and political ones."
Beate Rössler [11] Characterization of Different Types of Privacy	• Informational Privacy: Limited access to information, confidentiality, secrecy, anonymity, and data protection • Physical Privacy: Limited access to persons, possessions, and personal property • Decisional Privacy: Decision-making about sex, families, religion, and health-care • Proprietary Privacy: Control over the attributes of personal identity

Daniel Solove is recognized as a global privacy expert with an extensive body of work on the subject. Solove [7] presented privacy as "a cluster of many distinct yet related things". His privacy framework conceptualization presented in Understanding Privacy organizes privacy into four areas containing related sub-aspects in which privacy concerns have been be historically raised. These privacy areas include information collection, information processing, information dissemination, and invasions. Information collection encompasses surveillance and interrogation issues. Information processing encompasses aggregation, identification, insecurity, secondary use, and exclusion issues. Information dissemination encompasses breach of confidentiality, disclosure, exposure, increased accessibility, blackmail, appropriation, and distortion issues. Finally, Invasions encompasses intrusion and decisional interference issues. Further definition details for Solove's privacy sub-areas can be found in Table III.

His framework has a strong focus on the collection, processing, and dissemination of information. This aligns well with online social networks and standard information product flows. Solove's framework also aligns well with common multi-dimensional information quality concepts. Because of this, as well as his recognition as a privacy expert, Solove's privacy conceptualization is used as a basis for the privacy aspects of this research.

TABLE III. A TAXONOMY OF PRIVACY [7]

A Taxonomy of Privacy	
Information Collection	
Surveillance	The watching, listening to, or recording of an individual's activities
Interrogation	Various forms of questioning or probing for information
Information Processing	
Aggregation	The combination of various pieces of data about and individual
Identification	The linking of information to a particular individual
Insecurity	Carelessness in protecting stored information from leaks and improper access
Secondary Use	The use of collected information for a purpose different from the use for which it was collected without the data subject's consent
Exclusion	The failure to allow data subjects to know about the data that others have about them and participate in its handling and use
Information Dissemination	
Breach of confidentiality	Breaking a promise to keep a person's information confidential
Disclosure	The revelation of truthful information about a person that affects the way others judge his or her reputation
Exposure	Revealing another's nudity, grief, or bodily functions
Increased accessibility	Amplifying the accessibility of information
Blackmail	The threat to disclose personal information
Appropriation	The use of the data subject's identity to serve another's aims and interests
Distortion	Disseminating false or misleading information about individuals
Invasions	
Intrusion	Invasive acts that disturb one's tranquility or solitude
Decisional interference	Incursions into the data subject's decisions regarding her private affairs

B. *Social Media Networks*

Social media is media designed to be disseminated through social interactions created using highly accessible and scalable publishing techniques. It uses internet and web-based technologies to transform broadcast media monologues (one to many) into social media dialogues (many to many). It supports the democratization of knowledge and information, transforming people from content consumers to content producers [12]. Social media networks have been growing in popularity in part due to the increased affordability and proliferation of internet-enabled devices that bring social connectivity through personal computers, mobile devices, and internet tablets [13]. In general, social media networks can be grouped into categories based on the nature of their social interactions (See Table IV). Examples of popular social network sites include Facebook, LinkedIn, Twitter, YouTube, Flickr, Instagram, and Pinterest. Apps, such as WhatsApp, could also fall under social signaling. With Facebook acquiring WhatsApp, it becomes quite non-trivial for users to understand the privacy aspects of the data sharing policies between WhatsApp and Facebook. More broadly speaking, the constant emergence of new social media apps and their acquisitions or mergers create a highly complex environment for users' awareness of the privacy policies that govern data capturing and sharing.

Boyd and Ellison [14] describe online social networks as services that enable individuals to "construct a public or semi-public profile within a bounded system", to "articulate a list of other users with whom they share a connection", and to "view and traverse their list of connections and those made by others within the system". Aggarwal [13] states that social networks can be generalized as "information networks, in which the nodes could compromise either actors or entities, and the edges denote the relationship between them". Online social networks are rich in data and provide unprecedented opportunities for knowledge discovery and data mining. From this perspective, there are two primary social network data types. The first type is linkage-based structural data and the second is content-based data. In relation to privacy, Aggarwal highlights three types of disclosure:

> [S]ocial networks contain tremendous information about the individual in terms of their interests, demographic information, friendship link information, and other attributes. This can lead to disclosure of different kinds of information in the social network, such as identity disclosure, attribute disclosure, and linkage information disclosure. [13]

This research focuses primarily on attribute disclosure, but it may be possible in future research to extend it to the other two areas as well.

Several other classifications of social media data have also been published. Jeremiah Owyang [37] highlights seven types of social media data from a customer marketing perspective. These include demographic, product, psychographic, behavioral, referrals, location, and intention data. From a more structural perspective, Bruce Schneier [15] proposed that social network data can be divided into six categories (see Table IV). Hart and Johnson [16] noted that Schneier's taxonomy highlights three primary sources through which information can be disseminated: through the users themselves, through other individuals, or through inference. Regarding privacy, all three of these sources can lead to privacy compromises. Facebook [17] also shares a similarly structured view of data in its published data use policy.

TABLE IV. TYPES OF SOCIAL NETWORK DATA [15]

Types of Social Network Data	
Service Data	Data users give to a social networking site in order to use it
Disclosed Data	What users post on their own pages
Entrusted Data	What users post on other people's pages
Incidental Data	What other people post about a user
Behavioral Data	Data the site collects about user habits by recording what users do and who users do it with
Derived Data	Information about users that is derived from all the other data

Because of the benefit of its structural divisions, Schneier's framework is used in this research as the foundation for social media network data classification. In addition, from a social media classification perspective, this research will focus on the friendship network aspects of the Social Signaling as illustrated in Table V. To further define the research scope, the modeling aspects of this research will focus on information shared by online social media users via disclosed data, entrusted data, and incidental data per Schneier's framework.

TABLE V. SOCIAL MEDIA CATEGORIES [12]

Social Media Categories	
Social Signaling	Blogs (Wordpress, Blogger), Microblogs (Twitter), Friendship networks (Facebook, MySpace, LinkedIn, Orkut), Snapchat
Social Bookmarking	Del.icio.us, StumbleUpon, Pocket
Media Sharing	Instagram, Flickr, Pinterest, Photobucket, YouTube, Megavideo, Justin.tv, Ustream
Social News	Digg, Reddit
Social Health	PatientsLikeMe, DailyStrength, CureTogether
Social Collaboration	Wikipedia, Wikiversity, Scholarpedia, AskDrWiki
Social Games	Pokémon Go, Foursquare, FarmVille, Second Life, EverQuest (Virtual Worlds)
Q & A	Quora, Yahoo! Answers

C. *Information Quality*

Information quality (also known as data quality) is a multidisciplinary field with research spanning a wide range of topics, but existing researchers are primarily operating in the disciplines of Management Information Systems and Computer Science [18]. Within quality literature, the concept of "fitness for use" has been widely adopted as a definition for data quality [6][18]-[21]. But to be applicable, this definition of fitness for use must be contextualized [6]. In this regard, previous writings and research have presented data quality as a multi-dimensional concept [18]-[22].

In 1996, Wang and Strong published an empirical framework to capture the multi-dimensional aspects of information quality that are most important to data consumers [20]. This research was presented in application by Strong, Lee and Wang in "Data Quality in Context" the following year [21]. Since that time, their framework has been widely cited in information quality literature. The Wang Strong Quality Framework [20] contains four categories of data quality: Intrinsic DQ, Contextual DQ, Representational DQ, and Accessibility DQ. These four categories contain fifteen data quality dimensions (see Table VI).

TABLE VI. WANG STRONG QUALITY FRAMEWORK [20]

DQ Category	DQ Dimensions
Intrinsic DQ	Accuracy, Objectivity, Believability, Reputation
Accessibility DQ	Accessibility, Access Security
Contextual DQ	Relevancy, Value-Added, Timeliness, Completeness, Amount of Data
Representational DQ	Interpretability, Ease of Understanding, Concise Representation, Consistent Representation

Intrinsic data quality includes the dimensions of Accuracy, Believability, Objectivity, and Reputation. Intrinsic dimensions "have quality in their own right" [20]. Fisher, Lauria, Chengalur-Smith, and Wang [19] describe these as non-contextual self-contained quality aspects.

Contextual data quality includes the dimensions of Value-Added, Relevancy, Timeliness, Completeness, and Amount of Data. Contextual dimensions "must be considered within the context of the task at hand" [20] and are "specifically tied to the particular use or user in order to determine quality" [19].

Representational data quality includes the dimensions of Interpretability, Ease of Understanding, Representational Consistency, Conciseness of Representation, and Manipulability. Representational dimensions relate to the format and meaning of the data [20] and focus on the importance of the presentation and usability of data [19].

Finally, Accessibility data quality includes the dimensions of Access and Security [20] and deal with the availability and protection of data [19]. Definitions of these data quality dimensions from Pipino, Lee, and Wang [22] can be found in Table VII.

TABLE VII. DATA QUALITY DIMENSIONS [22]

Dimensions	Definitions
Accessibility	The extent to which data are available, or easily and quickly retrievable
Appropriate Amount of Data	The extent to which the quantity and volume of available data is appropriate
Believability	The extent to which data are accepted or regarded as true, real and credible
Completeness	The extent to which data are of sufficient depth, breadth, and scope for the task at hand
Concise Representation	The extent to which data are compactly represented
Consistent Representation	The extent to which data is presented in the same format
Ease of Manipulation	The extent to which data is easy to manipulate and apply to different tasks
Free-of-Error	The extent to which data is correct and reliable
Interpretability	The extent to which data is in appropriate languages, symbols, and units, and the definitions are clear
Objectivity	The extent to which data is unbiased, unprejudiced, and impartial
Relevancy	The extent to which data is is applicable and helpful for the task at hand
Reputation	The extent to which data is highly regarded in terms of its sources or content
Security	The extent to which access to data is restricted appropriately to maintain its security
Timeliness	The extent to which the data is sufficiently up-to-date for the task at hand
Understandability	The extent to which data is easily comprehended
Value-Added	The extent to which data is beneficial and provides advantages from its use

More recent research by Dan Myers [54][55] reviewed the major IQ dimension frameworks found in current literature and worked to conform them into a unified standard. This conformed standard is shown in Table VIII. Myers' efforts are beneficial and as his conformed standard is further validated and accepted, our proposed framework matrices will likely be updated in future research to align with this standard. Initially, however, the Wang Strong Quality Framework will continue to be the information quality basis for our research framework.

TABLE VIII. CONFORMED DIMENSIONS OF DATA QUALITY [54]

List of Conformed Dimensions of Data Quality		
Conformed Dimension	**Underlying Concepts**	**Non Standard Terminology for Dimension**
Completeness	Record Population, Attribute Population, Truncation, Comprehensiveness, Existence	Fill Rate, Coverage, Usability, Scope
Accuracy	Agree with Real-world, Match to Agreed Source	Consistency
Consistency	Equivalence of Redundant or Distributed Data, Consistency in Representation	Integrity, Concurrence, Coherence
Validity	Values in Specified Range, Values Conform to Business Rule, Domain of Predefined Values, Values Conform to Data Type, Values Conform to Format	Accuracy, Integrity, Reasonableness
Timeliness	Time Expectation for Availability, Concurrence of Distributed Data	Currency, Lag Time, Latency, Information Float
Currency	Current with World it Models	Timeliness
Integrity	Referential Integrity, Unique Identifier of Entity, Cardinality	Validity, Duplication
Accessibility	Ease of Obtaining Data, Access Control, Retention, Fact Captured as Data	Availability
Precision	Precision of Data Value, Granularity	Coverage
Lineage	Source Documentation, Segment Documentation, Target Documentation, End-to-End Graphical Documentation	
Representation	Easy to Read & Interpret, Presentation Language, Media Appropriate, Metadata Availability	Presentation

D. *Trust*

Trust, like privacy and quality, is a widely-studied concept across multiple disciplines. This has led to the development of a broad array of definitions and understandings of trust over time [23]-[27]. Marsh [23] highlighted that trust values have no units, but can still be measured by such notions as 'worthwhileness' and 'intrinsic value'. At the same time, trust is an absolute medium in which one either trusts or does not trust. This implies that trust in application is based on threshold values above which or below which an entity is either trusted or not trusted as seen in Fig. 1. These thresholds will also vary with different entities and in different circumstances. In a similar manner, Kosa [28] noted that "[t]rust can be examined as a continuous measure, as in evaluation or reliability assessments, or a binary decision point when referring to a decision".

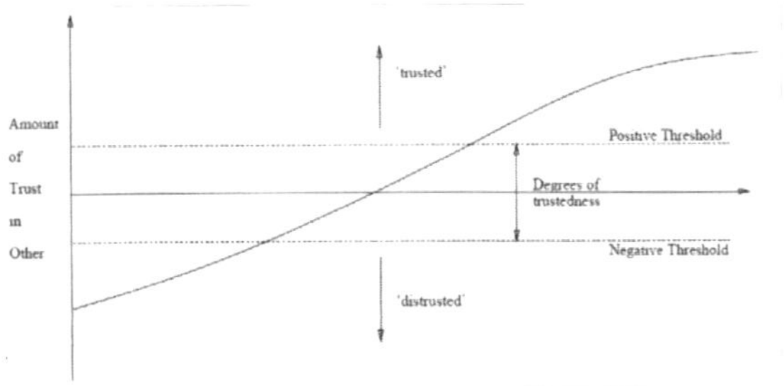

Figure 1. Positive and Negative Thresholds for Trust [23]

Gefen [27], citing Mayer, Davis, and Schoorman [29] defined trust as "a willingness to be vulnerable to the actions of another person or people". Continuing his review of trust literature, Gefen noted that trust is "an important component of many social and business relationships, determining the nature of the interactions and people's expectations of it". Highly relevant to the research being proposed is the role that trust plays in both online social and e-commerce interactions. In specific regard to trust in an online or data driven environment, Bertini [6], defined trust as "the willingness to assume the risks of disclosing data when benefits overcome concerns on the assumption that commitments undertaken by another part will be fulfilled".

Prior research has attempted to unify the disparate definitions and views of trust into various frameworks or models that show the multi-dimensionality of trust. Among these, McKnight and Chervany [25] defined four constructs of trust as well as ten measurable sub-constructs in an interdisciplinary conceptual typology of trust. Their four constructs include: Disposition to Trust meaning "the extent to which one displays a consistent tendency to be willing to depend on general others across a broad spectrum of situations and persons"; Institution Based Trust meaning "one believes the needed conditions are in place to enable one to anticipate a successful outcome in an endeavor or aspect of one's life"; Trusting Beliefs meaning "one believes (and feels confident in believing) that the other person has one or more traits desirable to one in a situation in which negative consequences are possible"; and Trusting Intention meaning "one is willing to depend on, or intends to depend on, the other person in a given task or situation with a feeling of relative security, even though negative consequences are possible."

Carsten D. Schultz [24] in his research presented a situational trust model. He related his work to the trust constructs of McKnight and Chervany [25] and built upon a communication model by Shannon and Weaver published in 1949. Schultz's situational trust model allows for trust to be stated as: "Specific trust is trust placed by a trustor in a trustee concerning a trust object in a trust environment" [24]. Subsequently, Schultz detailed the concept of trust transactions that show the progression cycle from initial trust to resulting trust as it passes through trustworthiness regarding intended behavior, trust in expectation of behavior, and evaluation of actual behavior. Finally, Schultz presents a trust equation that can supplement a given instance of his situational trust model with a reference to previous trust experiences.

Mayer, Davis, and Schoorman [29] strove to differentiate trust from other related constructs. They presented an integrative model of organizational trust. Within this research, they expanded upon the characteristics of a trustee and presented a concept of perceived trustworthiness. The identified characteristics, or primary factors, of perceived trustworthiness they presented are Ability, Benevolence, and Integrity. In this, Ability relates to the skills, characteristics, and competencies that enable someone to have influence with a specific domain. Benevolence is related to the level of goodwill a trustee is believed to have toward a trustor. Integrity relates to how a trustee is perceived to adhere to an acceptable set of principles. The authors proposed that "trust for a trustee will be a function of the trustee's perceived ability, benevolence, and integrity and of the trustor's propensity to trust". They further noted that, while related, these three attributes are separable and may vary independently of one another.

Gefen [27] drew on concept of trustworthiness presented by Mayer, Davis, and Schoorman to develop a validated scale specifically related to online consumer trust. The results of his research showed that each of the aspects of trustworthiness as tested against online behavioral intentions is different. This may suggest that each of the three aspects of trustworthiness "affect different behavioral intentions because different beliefs affect different types of vulnerability" [27]. Gefen's research also illustrated the measurability of aspects such as trust regarding interactions in an online domain. This is important to the research at hand.

In specific regard to social networks, Adali et al. [30] highlighted that trust also has a major role in the formation of social network communities, in assessing information quality and credibility, and in following how information moves within a network. They further noted the social mechanisms of trust formation in online communities are a new research area and there are many unknowns. In their research, they referenced the concept of embeddedness and highlighted that trust may grow out of increased interactions between individuals. In this regard, they focused on behavioral trust, which they defined as "observed communication behavior in social networks". They further divide behavioral trust into the measurable components of conversational trust based on the communication between two nodes and propagation trust based on the sharing of received information. Other research by Zuo, Hu, & O-Keefe [36] focused on the transferability of trust in social networks through evaluation first of recommendation trust, which is a topical trust based on honest recommendations and second of attribute trust, which is an absolute trust based on general trustworthiness without regard to a specific topic.

E. Interdependencies

Prior research presented by Bertini [6] begins to highlight the interdependencies between data privacy, trust, and information quality. If quality is defined as fitness for use and accuracy, reliability, and trustworthiness are key aspects of high quality data, then "high quality data require data subjects to disclose personal information raising some threat to their own privacy". Bertini, citing Rose [51], Hoffman, Novak, and Peralta [31], Neus [52], and Hui, Tan, and Goh [53], noted that "studies reveal that data subjects often provide incorrect information or withdraw from interaction when they consider the risks of disclosing personal data higher than the reward they can get from it". As stated previously, control is a key aspect in several conceptualizations and definitions of privacy. Bertini emphasized that lack of control leads to increased concern over "unauthorized secondary use, excessive collection of data, improper access and processing or storing errors". Citing research by Gefen [27], Paine et al. [60], and Hoffman, Novak, and Peralta [31], Bertini built on the concept that "[d]ata subjects' level of trust determine both the quantity and the quality of information they disclose" [6] by presenting the relationship between privacy and data quality as a trust mediated process. Bertini noted that the concept of benevolence as presented by Mayer, Davis, and Schoorman is a central trust factor in that both trustee and trustors should believe that the other is sincere, otherwise data sharing processes breakdown or become cumbersome. He believed that giving users control and allowing them to interact with their data, especially dynamic data, will both increase trust and spontaneously improve data quality. Conversely, when privacy or control is threatened, it causes a loss of trust, which leads to an immediate decrease in the quality of data being disclosed.

Kosa [28] stated that "research on privacy and trust as linked phenomena remains scarce". She noted that the formalization of trust is much more mature than the formalization of privacy and proposed that because of their conceptual similarities formalization concepts developed in relation to trust could be utilized in the formalization of privacy. Kosa highlights that both trust and privacy are highly information type and sensitivity specific, relationship dependent, purpose driven, and measured on a continuous scale. In example of the application of trust formalizations to privacy, she diagramed, as seen in Fig. 2, proposed thresholds for privacy based on the trust threshold detailed by Marsh [23].

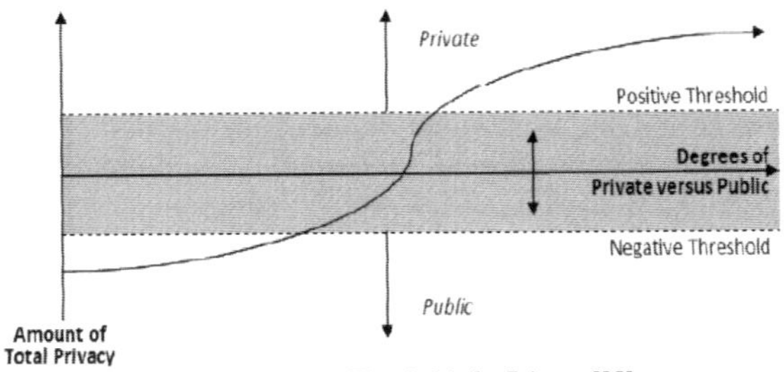

Figure 2. Proposed Thresholds for Privacy [28]

Further, Kosa presented trust as positively correlated to privacy, but privacy as negatively related to trust. She stated that "Perceptions of trustworthiness may increase the tendency of people to share information willingly, thus giving up their privacy" but the "exercise of privacy may impede trust; if [one chooses] to withhold information, about for example, [his] identity the second party is less likely to trust [him] in the given exchange". This seems counter to the privacy/trust view presented by Bertini [6] above, but it is really a reflection on the relationship of different dimensions between trust and privacy.

For this research, the interdependency between trust, privacy, and information quality as well as the multi-dimensional nature of these concepts highlighted in this section are key foundations. These concepts will be extended in specific relation to online social network sites with a focus on modeling data privacy and measuring the corresponding trade-offs in information quality and/or trust.

III. LITERATURE REVIEW

Literature has previously been highlighted in background overview of the four components related to this research: privacy, information quality, online social networks, and trust. This section will focus on the review of literature as it bears on the interrelated aspects of this research. Prior research focusing on online social media as it relates to privacy, trust, and quality can be grouped by topic area to include: analysis of user behaviors; privacy related application development; privacy scoring and privacy leakage; and privacy awareness, user control, and privacy visualization.

A. *Analysis of User Behaviors*

In many cases, prior research involved surveys of online social network users. Typically, these surveys focused on attitudes toward privacy, awareness of privacy issues, use of privacy controls, and disconnects between stated beliefs and actual online. Fogel and Nehmad [38] surveyed risking taking, trust, and privacy concerns in a small set of college students. Gross and Acquisti [39] analyzed patterns of information revelation and related privacy implications in a survey of more than 4,000 Carnegie Mellon University students. In further research, Acquisti and Gross [40] analyzed the impact of privacy concerns on behavior, compared stated and actual behavior, and documented behavior changes following exposure to privacy-related information. Hoadley, Xu, Lee, and Rosson [41] surveyed Facebook users soon after the introduction of Facebook's News Feed. This allowed them to explore how easier access to information and "illusory" loss of control can trigger privacy concerns in users. Madejski, Johnson, and Bellovin [42] presented an empirical evaluation based on a small subset of participants measuring privacy attitudes and intentions against actual privacy setting on Facebook. Dwyer, Hiltz, and Passerini [43] surveyed users of both Facebook and MySpace regarding perceptions of trust and privacy concerns as well as willingness to share information and develop new relationships. Andrew Boyd [44] presented a two-year longitudinal study of social media users to examine privacy attitudes and self-reported behaviors over time. He extended the Internet Users' Information Privacy Concern model (IUIPC) model for applicability within Social Networking sites to investigate influences on online attitudes and behaviors regarding privacy. Boyd found that with time privacy concerns and distrust increased while willingness to disclose personal information decreased. Another longitudinal study conducted by Dey, Jelveh, and Ross [45], used web crawling rather than user surveys to explore privacy trends for personal attributes available on public Facebook profile pages. They found that users had become dramatically more private between March 2010 and June 2011. They cited media attention and Facebook's redesigned privacy page as key factors in this trend. Wisniewski, Knijnenburg, and Lipford [59] analyzed online social network users against 36 privacy behaviors and 20 feature awareness items to categorize users into six distinct privacy management strategies. Aspects of these strategies parallel our research well. This prior research generally focused on how privacy awareness affected the use of privacy controls and the overall disclosure of information. These aspects will be incorporated in the conceptual and structural models for this research, but this research will also expand on this by looking more fully at modification to the quality of information in the face of privacy awareness.

B. *Privacy Related Application Development*

Several types of privacy related applications are also presents in current literature. These include user interface concepts, APIs for controlling and/or visualizing privacy settings, and stand-alone privacy driven social network concepts. Concepts from this research may be extended into application development in the future, but it is beyond the scope of this current proposal.

C. *Privacy Awareness, User Control, and Visualization*

Current literature shows a strong focus on increasing awareness and understanding of privacy issues through visualization and user controls. Kolter and Pernul [46] presented a method for generating privacy preferences. They focused their research on awareness of what information websites and online services are seeking and the corresponding ability of users to minimize the amount of data they release as well as control and restrict how their disclosed data is used by the collecting service or passed on to third-party services. Krishnamurthy and Willis [47] highlighted the need for bit or data element level privacy controls noting that "[l]imiting access to just friends or those in a network is not fine-grained enough". They proposed that each set of interactions in an online social network should indicate the bare minimum of private information required. This would allow users to set automated interaction thresholds based on their personal privacy thresholds as well as directly control access when additional information is requested. Acquisti and Gross [40] summarized that "the majority of [Facebook] members claim to know about ways to control visibility and searchability of their profiles, but a significant minority of members are unaware of those tools and options". Hart and Johnson [16] noted that while users often disclose data directly, personal information can also be revealed accidently through aggregation of information, shared by service providers, or published by others. They further noted that users are often unaware of the impacts of their information disclosure or even when understood they do not want to expend the effort needed to utilize access control systems. Hart and Johnson proposed that a well-designed privacy preference system must achieve multiple goals: a) Allow users to specify viewers, b) Allow succinct polices to apply to large content collections, c) Utilize flexible access control policies, and d) Infer restricted privacy policies on new content. Offenhuber and Donath [48] developed ways to represent the individuality of nodes and links that comprise social networks. They focused on representing the actual activity and message exchanges between nodes to give context to generic high-level connections within a social network. Borcea-Pfitzmann, Pfitzmann, and Berg [3] proposed that privacy could only be preserved or regained through a combination of data minimization, user control, and contextual integrity. Finally, in more recent literature, Mármol, Pérez, and Pérez [56] discussed the user awareness and control aspect of reporting offensive content in social networks. They presented a reputation-based assessment approach to the flagging of content by users.

In extension of this prior research, the development of relationship matrices for data privacy, online social network data, trust, and information quality in this research will allow for more targeted awareness of privacy issues and specific focus areas for privacy controls. The development of syntax for conceptual modeling in turn lends itself, as Krishnamurthy and Willis highlighted, to better understanding a data element level view of information disclosure. Understanding gained through the development of a structured equation model will lend itself to measuring aspects of data minimization and user control in application within online social networks.

D. *Privacy Scoring and Privacy Leakage*

Becker and Chen [49] state that the prevention of information from going beyond its intended privacy boundaries is basic principle in computer science and that information escaping these boundaries is known as information leakage. Their research sought to measure and limit privacy risk attributed to friend connections within an online social network. The concept of risk attributed to online social network connections will be addressed in this research through the components of users' privacy and trust in the conceptual model syntax. Irani, Webb, Pu, and Li [50] focused on the aggregation of information leakage across multiple networks, which they defined as the social footprint of an online identity. Through this, they developed measures of attribute leakage. In this research, information leakage through aggregation will be noted as a privacy concern in the overall relationship matrices, but it will lie outside the scope on the final stages of the research. Lui and Terzi [33] proposed a framework for computing user privacy scores that indicate the potential privacy risk due to social network participation. Their research utilizes concepts from Item Response Theory and their methodology incorporates both the sensitivity and visibility of individual data elements into the calculation of an aggregated privacy score. The concepts of Liu and Terzi strongly influenced the development of the conceptual syntax for this proposed research. Ros, Canelles, Pérez, Mármol, and Pérez [57] presented a method for optimized, delay-based posting in online social networks as a privacy protection against observed activity that may reveal time-sensitive details. Their paper can be related to this current research in that delay-based posted is a modification to the timeliness dimension of information quality as a method of privacy protection. Finally, Parra-Arnau, Rebollo-Monedero, and Forné [58] addressed privacy risks and proposed quantitative privacy measures of users' profiles.

IV. Methodology and Results

The research will contain three interconnected components. The first is the development and validation of select relationship matrices for data privacy, online social network data, trust, and information quality as a research framework. The second is the development of a syntax and conceptual model as a standard way to document the trust, privacy, and information quality aspects within online social networks. Finally, a structural equation model will be developed to measure and validate expected information quality modifications as a reaction to calculated privacy risks based on data elements of different data types, content sensitivity, and data visibility. In application, the overlapping aspects of privacy, information quality, and trust in the relationship matrices can be applied to the expanded modeling syntax as illustrated in Fig. 6. Further, the results of the structural equation model will show the strength and directionality of the related matrix aspects' effects on one another. While these components can be generalized across multiple online social networks, for this research, when analyzing online social networks, Facebook will be used as the primary point of reference when talking about social media structures because of the size and activity levels of its user base.

A. *Framework Matrices*

This research focuses on the general overlap of the multi-faceted dimensions, aspects, and properties of trust, privacy, information quality, and online social networks. It seeks to identify where these areas overlap regarding both online social networks and each other. This phase of the research hypothesizes that:

H1: The multi-faceted dimensions, aspects, and properties of trust, privacy, and information quality can be effectively overlaid within a series of related matrices.

H2: An understanding of intersections of these sub-aspects lends itself to a broader understanding of the relationship of these concepts.

H3: An understanding of intersections of these sub-aspects lends itself to specific target areas for future research.

As a starting point for this research, a framework matrix has been developed to map the points of intersection between Solove's [7] taxonomy of privacy, Schneier's [15] divisions of social network data, Wang and Strong's [20] multiple dimensions of information quality, and the trustworthiness characteristics of Ability, Benevolence, and Integrity as presented by Mayer, Davis, and Schoorman [29] and Gefen [27]. As noted above, the development and validation of select relationship matrices for data privacy, online social networks, information quality, and trust as a research framework will be the first deliverable from this research. This will be accomplished in part through a validation in current literature. Hogben [32], for example, highlighted specific online social network privacy threats that include digital dossier aggregation, secondary data collection, recognition and identification, data permanence, infiltration of networks, profile squatting and ID theft related reputation slander, and cyberstalking/cyberbullying. These can be shown to align neatly with the proposed privacy components within the framework matrix. In addition, a select survey of information quality, online social network, and privacy related professionals and experts will be undertaken. Their opinions in relation to the framework matrices will be gathered and reconciled. The framework matrix will be further validated in the proposed structured equation modeling phase of this research as the trade-offs between framework relationships are measured.

B. *Syntax and Conceptual Modeling*

Regarding modeling privacy in social networks, one general approach is the mapping of entity level social graph connections of the network. This high-level node and edge view is the most common social graph view. This approach visualizes the issue, but focuses on privacy at the level of overall connections. A second approach presented by Lui and Terzi [33] and others is the calculation of mathematical data element level and entity level privacy scores. This is a more detailed approach focused on the numeric scoring of data privacy. The concepts of Lui and Terzi were an early influence on the development of this syntax. This research gives the opportunity to blend previous research into an expanded approach. This is done by developing a method to model the data privacy of specific data elements that can then be incorporated in the future into trade-off scoring research. This method may also lend itself in future research to the creation of elemental data privacy social graphs, which will allow for the visualization of actual data sharing, not just entity level connections.

The second key aspect of this research is to develop a syntax and conceptual model as a standard way to document the trust, privacy, and information quality aspects within online social networks. In support of this effort, the finalized syntax and conceptual model will be presented in an ontology language, such as OWL2, rather than in the simplified form presented here. This phase of the research hypothesizes that:

H4: Instances of trust, privacy, and information quality interactions can be expressed at the data element level in notation sets expressing element, users, privacy, trust, and quality components.

H5: Instances of trust, privacy, and information quality interactions can be expressed at the data element level as a conceptual model.

A further research question, if these hypotheses hold true, is whether this can be implemented in a way that will aggregate to an overall user level notation and conceptualization. This research will seek to validate these hypotheses through illustration of the conceptual model using synthetic and real world examples as well as validation by extension through structural equation modeling. To control for scope, this research will focus on the user-controlled social sharing aspects of online social network information such as Disclosed, Entrusted, and Incidental data rather than organizational (system and third party) aspects such as Behavioral, Derived, and Service data. In this regard, the following syntax structures are being presented as a concept to be further developed in future research.

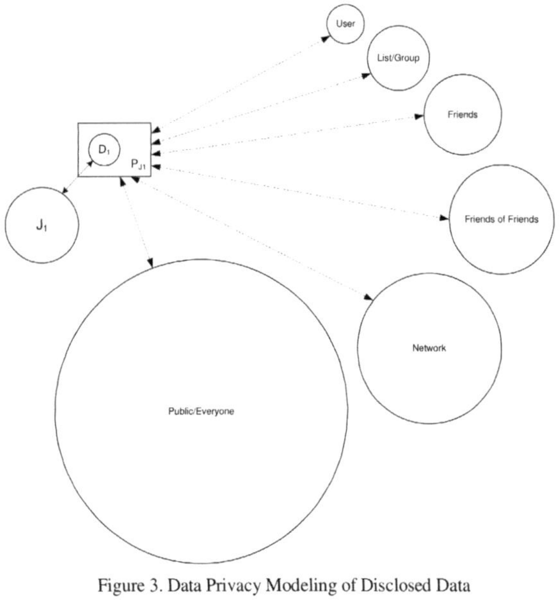

Figure 3. Data Privacy Modeling of Disclosed Data

For disclosed data elements that users post on their own pages, the most apparent privacy aspect is the visibility level of the data element set by the users' privacy settings. Visibility levels are typically set by users' overall privacy settings or by specific selection when posting a data element. One research question related to this is how trust and information quality are related to a user's determination of visibility related privacy settings. Disclosed data syntax follows the form of Disclosed Data as D1(J1, PJ1) where D1 = Disclosed Data Element with a descriptive set of J1 = Posting Entity and PJ1 = User Privacy Factors. This is shown in Fig. 3 with possible user and group related visibility settings illustrated.

For entrusted data elements that users post on other people's pages, there are two main privacy considerations related to the visibility level of the data element. The first is the posting entity's own privacy settings. The second is the receiving entity's privacy settings. Generally, the posting entity's privacy settings are the controlling factor in terms of data visibility. Entrusted data syntax follows the form of Entrusted Data as E1(J1, J2, PJ1, PJ2) where E1 = Entrusted Data Element with a descriptive set of J1 = Posting Entity, J2 = Receiving Entity, PJ1 = Privacy Factors of the Posting Entity, and PJ2 = Privacy Factors of the Receiving Entity. This is shown in Fig. 4 with possible user and group related visibility settings illustrated.

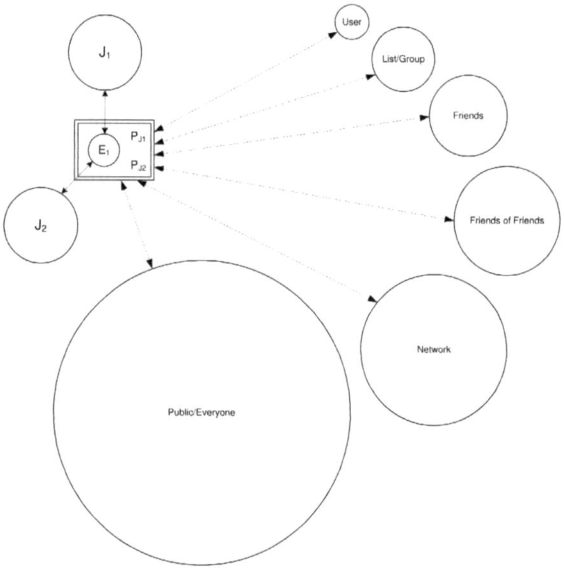

Figure 4. Data Privacy Modeling of Entrusted Data

For incidental data elements that users post about others, there are also two main privacy considerations. As with entrusted data, the first consideration is the Posting Entity's own privacy settings. This most typically relates to the visibility of the data element. The second consideration is the exclusion factor of the Topic Entity. A Topic Entity is the person, group, or thing that is the subject of a posted data element. Exclusion relates to the level of control and involvement a user has regarding information that is shared about or actions taken that affect him or her. Within online social networks, this relates to whether the incidental data element is directly linked, often through tagging, to the Topic Entity. Topic Entities can often reduce visibility of shared data by preventing tagging or removing tags on incidental data elements, but preventing tagging will increase a user's exclusion factor because the user will be less likely to be directly linked and therefore will not be notified when incidental data is posted. In addition, while a user can reduce visibility by blocking or removing user tags, he or she usually cannot prevent the comments or references themselves from being made by other users. Because of this lack of control, the trustworthiness characteristic of benevolence plays an important role in incidental data.

Incidental data syntax follows the form of Incidental Data as I1(J1, J3, PJ1, EJ3) where I1 = Incidental Data Element with a descriptive set of J1 = Posting Entity, J3 = Topic Entity, PJ1 = Privacy Factors for the Posting Entity, and EJ3 = Exclusion factor of Topic Entity. This is shown in Fig. 5 with possible user and group related visibility settings illustrated.

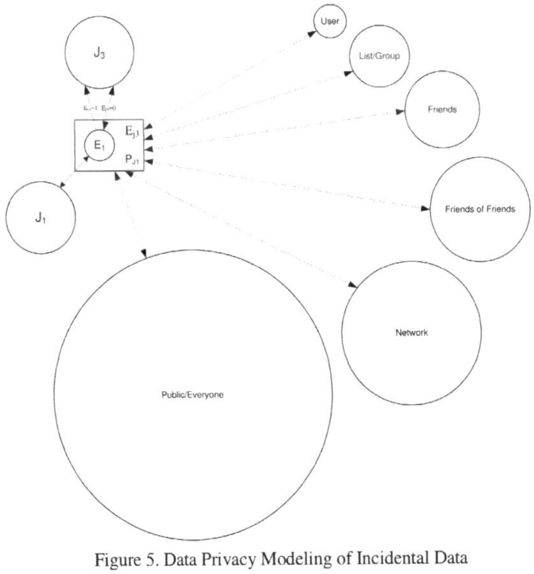

Figure 5. Data Privacy Modeling of Incidental Data

In expansion of this syntax, an important question to be addressed in this research is whether and how quality and trust components such as Q1 as Data Element Quality, TJ1J2/TJ1Jx as Relational Trust between Entities, and TS as System Trust can be incorporated directly into this model syntax. This will need to be developed to facilitate comparative measurement of trade-offs between data privacy, information quality, and trust. This expanded syntax could follow the form of Entrusted Data with Trust and Quality as E1(J1, J2, PJ1, PJ2, TS, TJ1J2, TJ1Jx, QE1) where E1 = Entrusted Data Element with a descriptive set of J1 = Posting Entity, J2 = Receiving Entity, PJ1 = Privacy Factors for the Posting Entity, PJ2 = Privacy Factors for the Receiving Entity, TS = System Trust, TJ1J2 = Relational Trust between Posting and Receiving Entities (subset of TJ1Jx), TJ1Jx = Relational Trust between Connected Entities, and QE1 = Set of Data Element Information Quality Factors. This expanded syntax is shown in Fig. 6.

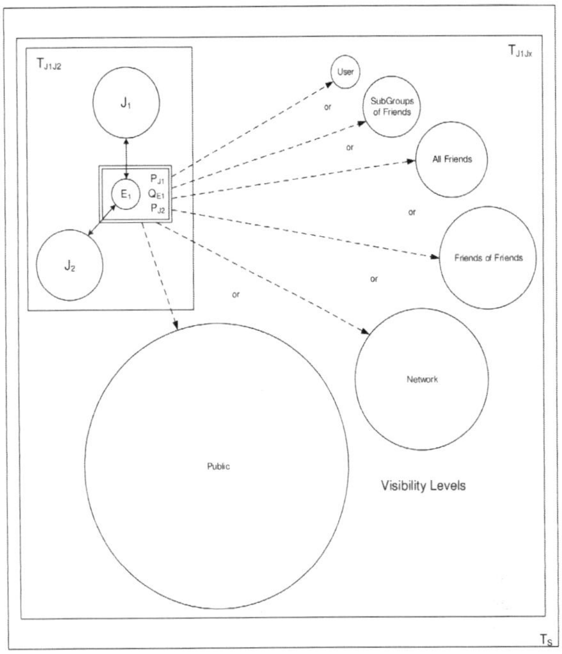

Figure 6. Data Privacy Modeling of Entrusted Data with Trust and Quality

C. *Structural Equation Modeling*

The goal of the comparative scoring component of this research is to tie the conceptual modeling syntax back to information quality, trust, and data privacy relationships identified in the framework matrices in the first research component. This will have a strong research impact through the creation of a comparative mathematical model of data privacy attributes, information quality dimensions, and trust characteristics. This research phase will develop a structural equation model to measure and validate expected information quality modifications as a reaction to calculated risks based on data elements of different data types, content sensitivity, and data visibility. Previous research has shown the benefit of structural equation models in the development and validation of the Internet Users' Information Privacy Concerns [34] and User Privacy Concerns and Identity in OSNs [35] constructs. This research will also use structural equation modeling to extend and build upon those concepts.

As seen in Fig. 7, Malhotra, Kim, and Agarwal [34] developed the Internet Users' Information Privacy Concerns (IUIPC) construct based on the extension of personal dispositions to data collection, privacy control, and privacy awareness to beliefs regarding trust and risk and how those beliefs affected behavioral intention regarding Internet usage. This research will extend the IUIPC casual model to online social network specific contextual variables of varied data element type and data sensitivity. It will also incorporate aspects of information quality modification rather than utilize the direct share/not share behavioral intention utilized by Malhotra, Kim, and Agarwal.

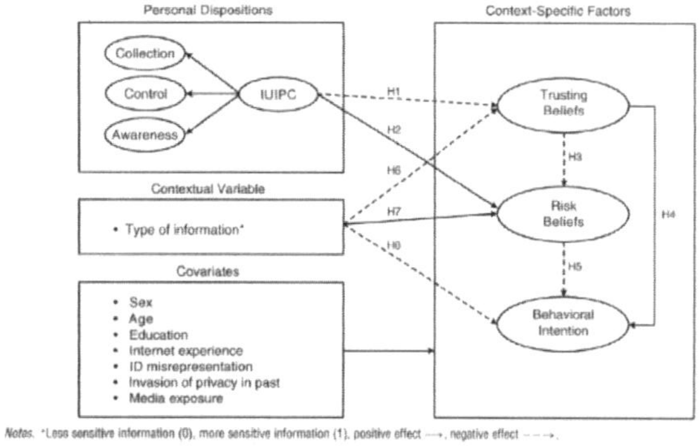

Figure 7. Proposed Model by Malhotra, Kim, and Agarwal [34]

Krasnova, Günther, Spiekermann, and Koroleva [35] developed a model for Privacy Concerns and Identity in Online Social Networks (PCIOSN). This cross-discipline research comes more from the social sciences and is developed through a social identity disclosure perspective. They argue that while IUIPC has been widely utilized these applications are lacking because "OSN members are subject to the specific privacy-related risks rooted in the public and social nature of OSNs". They further noted that in terms of primary privacy concerns individuals differentiate between online social network users and provider or third-party organizations. Their high-level research model (see Fig. 8) has a degree of overlap with the proposed framework matrix found in this research. It is based on specific privacy concerns affecting the amount, accuracy, and control aspects of shared information.

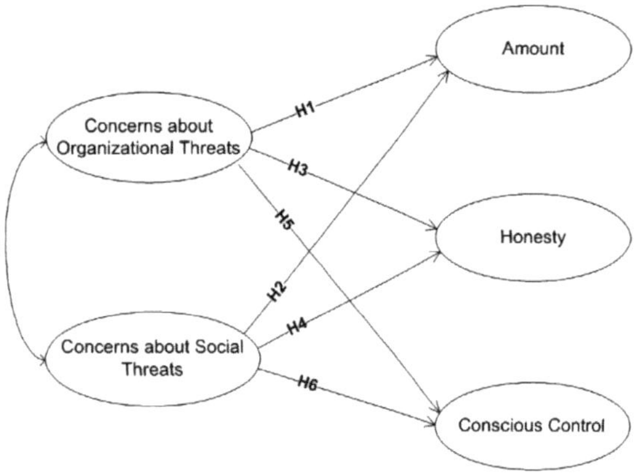

Figure 8. PCIOSN Research Model [35]

This research will extend their model to directly map specific privacy and trust aspects from the framework matrix into the threat components of the PCIOSN model. The proposed research will also specifically map dimensions of individual self-disclosure [35] to specific IQ dimensions, as well as incorporate other relevant IQ dimensions from the proposed framework matrix. Of additional research interest is whether the IUIPC and PCIOSN models can be incorporated into a single view through the modeling aspects of this research. This research hypothesizes that:

H6: Behavioral intent to share information is not a simple binary response. Instead it is a degree based response that uses information quality modification to mitigate privacy and trust concerns between the thresholds of open disclosure and full non-disclosure (see Fig. 9).

H7: Data element types (wall posts, photos, comments, shares, likes, check-ins, etc.) have measurably different thresholds for content sensitivity.

H8: Completeness, Accuracy, Accessibility, Amount, Understandability, and similar quality dimensions of shared information are negatively related to calculated privacy and trust concerns as a modification control.

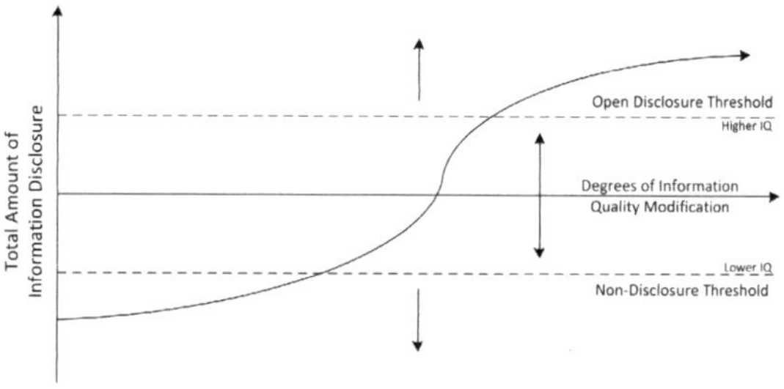

Figure 9. Initial Information Quality Modification Concept

Hypothesis 6 is an extension of Marsh's Positive and Negative Thresholds for Trust [23] and Kosa's Proposed Thresholds for Privacy [28] as applied to information quality. It should also be noted that any modification of Accessibility IQ dimension mitigates privacy and trust concerns by changing the visibility of a given piece of information rather than changing the shared information itself. As with the second research component, this research will be confined to specific data elements within selected social network data types to control for scope. It will focus first on the user-controlled social sharing aspect of Disclosed data, but may easily extend to Incidental and Entrusted data in future research. Specific trust characteristics, information quality dimensions and data privacy aspects will be selected. For these selected attributes, measurable indicators within online social networks will be identified and corresponding variables and questions for metrics and measurement will be determined. Structural equation modeling (SEM) will be utilized as a method for measuring the balance trade-offs present between specific trust characteristics, information quality dimensions and data privacy aspects. Structural Equation Modeling validation typically includes confirmatory factor analysis, as well as assessment of the internal consistency, convergent validity, and discriminant validity of the measured constructs. Multiple aspects of the research survey instrument needed to perform the SEM analysis will be based on results of the first two components of this research. As the framework matrix is validated and the syntax and conceptual model are designed, the survey instrument for SEM analysis will be finalized.

V. Conclusions, Challenges, and Opportunities

This paper presents an ongoing research effort. To this point, the relationship matrices for data privacy, online social networks, information quality, and trust as a research framework have been developed and a corresponding validation survey has been created and is being implemented. Furthermore, an initial syntax for conceptual modeling has been presented. Currently, elements of the proposed structural equation model and its required survey as a validation instrument are under development.

TABLE IX. FRAMEWORK MATRIX SUBSET

	Types of Social Networking Data		
	Disclosed Data	**Entrusted Data**	**Incidental Data**
	What you post on your own pages	What you post on other people's pages	What other people post about you
Data Privacy Issues	Increased Accessibility	Increased Accessibility	Identification
	Insecurity	Secondary use	Exclusion
	Appropriation	Identification	Breach of Confidentiality
	Secondary Use	Exclusion	Disclosure
		Breach of Confidentiality	Exposure
		Disclosure	Distortion
		Exposure	Intrusion (onto your pages)
		Distortion	Increased Accessibility
		Intrusion (onto their pages)	Secondary use
Information Quality Dimensions	Accuracy	Accuracy	Accuracy
	Appropriate Amount	Appropriate Amount	Appropriate Amount
	Relevancy	Relevancy	Relevancy
	Security	Security	Security
	Believability	Believability	Believability
	Reputation	Reputation	Reputation
	Understandability	Understandability	Understandability
	Accessibility	Accessibility	Accessibility
	Objectivity	Objectivity	Objectivity
	Ease of Operation	Ease of Operation	Ease of Operation
Trust	Benevolence	Benevolence	Benevolence
	Integrity	Integrity	Integrity

The developed framework matrices are presented in full in Appendices A-D, but as noted in the Section III, only syntax for conceptual modeling of Disclosed, Entrusted, and Incidental data has been developed. This framework matrix subset is presented in Table IX. This table illustrates several key factors. First, intersection points of the matrix may highlight different or similar aspects of privacy, trust, and information quality. Differentiations are shown for only data privacy issues in this subset, but they can be seen more readily in the full framework matrix presented in Appendix A. Second, related social sharing aspects of online social network information, such as the user-controlled areas of Disclosed, Entrusted, and Incidental data, will be more similar to each other than to organizational (system and third party) aspects such as Behavioral, Derived, and Service data. It should also be noted that aspects as initially presented in the matrix intersection points are not in any specific rank order. Even when similar aspects are presented, those aspects may have different levels of importance based on the social networking data type being researched. Finally, the dotted lines found in the data privacy grids for Entrusted and Incidental data are there to indicate distinctions between data privacy violations that may happen to a user and data privacy violations that a user may cause to happen to others.

A. Research Contributions and Implications

To date, relationship matrices for data privacy, online social networks, information quality, and trust as a research framework has been developed and presented here. The framework is currently being validated via a survey of experts. We fully intended to include the results of our validation survey here, but those results have been delayed and will instead be presented in a forthcoming paper. An initial conceptual model and syntax for data privacy, trust, and information quality in online social networks has also been developed and shared. Furthermore, an Initial Information Quality Modification Concept has been presented in extension of Marsh's Positive and Negative Thresholds for Trust and Kosa's Proposed Thresholds for Privacy.

The greatest implication of this research is its applicability to future research efforts. This research could enhance methods of modeling and measuring privacy, trust, and information quality within online social networks. It will lend itself to a better understanding of the quality of shared information in given data privacy and trust scenarios. Finally, it will provide future researchers with a formal framework for relating privacy, information quality, and trust in online social networks as well as a method for understanding information quality modification.

B. Limitations and Challenges

First, while a broad framework matrix can be presented, the scope for validation and deeper research is limited to social network data types that relate to user specific aspects of the framework matrix. The role of provider and third-party related online social network data types are highly noteworthy, but they will be addressed in only a limited manner, if at all, in this research. Second, to limit scope during the development of a syntax and conceptual model, not all variations of data element types and entity interactions will be addressed. Once again, to control research scope, the focus will be on select user specific aspects of the framework matrix as well as a targeted set of matrix overlays. This series of scope limitations is detailed more specifically within the Methodology section of this paper.

Challenges for this research may include determining and attracting a diverse set of respondents to create a representative population in phase three of this study. For measurements within structural equation modeling to be considered valid certain minimum respondent thresholds must be met based on the number of components within the model. In addition, structural equation modeling analysis requires the identification of alternate models. Because of the dynamics of social networks, identifying all alternative models may be difficult.

C. Future Research Opportunities

For the next phase of this research, a structural equation model for understanding the trade-offs and influences between data privacy, trust, and information quality in online social networks is being developed. A survey will be undertaken to validate the model. Results from these efforts will then be expressed in application via the presented conceptual model and syntax after it is formalized in an ontology language such as OWL2.

Future research is likely to include expanded validation of different areas of overlap within framework matrices. It would be of interest to explore application of this research beyond the user-controlled aspects such as Disclosed, Entrusted, and Incidental data to include Service, Behavioral, and Derived data within online social networks. Finally, updating the presented research framework matrices to fit new research as it develops, such as the Conformed Dimension of Data Quality, will keep this research applicable.

REFERENCES

[1] B. Blake and N. Agarwal, "Understanding User-Based Modifications to Information Quality in Response to Privacy and Trust Related Concerns in Online Social Networks," The Sixth International Conference on Social Media Technologies, Communication, and Informatics (SOTICS), pp. 18-28, 2016.

[2] B. Blake, N. Agarwal, R. Wigand, and J. Wood, "Twitter Quo Vadis: Is Twitter Bitter or are Tweets Sweet?" The Seventh International Conference on Information Technology: New Generations (ITNG), pp. 1257-1260, 2010.

[3] K. Borcea-Pfitzmann, A. Pfitzmann, and M. Berg, "Privacy 3.0 := Data Minimization + User Control + Contextual Integrity," it - Information Technology, vol. 53, no. 1, pp. 34-40, 2011. [Online]. Available from: https://tu-dresden.de/ing/informatik/sya/ps/die-professur/beschaeftigte/kbo_de. 2017.05.29.

[4] J. Zittrain, The Future of the Internet - And How to Stop it, New Haven, CT: Yale University Press, 2008.

[5] F. S. Lane, American Privacy: The 400-Year History of our Most Contested Right, Boston, MA: Beacon Press, 2009.

[6] P. Bertini, "Trust Me! Explaining the Relationship Between Privacy and Data Quality," Information Technology and Innovation Trend in Organization, 2010. [Online]. Available from: http://www.cersi.it/itais2010/. 2017.05.29.

[7] D. J. Solove, Understanding Privacy. Cambridge, MA: Harvard University Press, 2008.

[8] H. F. Nissenbaum, Privacy in Context: Technology, Policy, and the Integrity of Social Life. Stanford, CA: Stanford University Press, 2010.

[9] H. Nissenbaum, Privacy as contextual integrity. *Washington Law Review*, vol. *79*, no. 1, pp. 101-139, 2004. Available from http://www.nyu.edu/projects/nissenbaum/main_cv.html#pub. 2017.05.29.

[10] D. H. Holtzman, Privacy Lost: How Technology is Endangering Your Privacy, San Francisco: Jossey-Bass, 2006.

[11] B. Rössler (Ed.), Privacies: Philosophical Evaluations, Stanford, Calif: Stanford University Press, 2004.

[12] N. Agarwal, Types of Social Media, lecture presented for Social Media Mining and Analytics course at the University of Arkansas at Little Rock, 2016.

[13] C. C. Aggarwal, Social Network Data Analytics, New York: Springer, 2011.

[14] D. M. boyd and N. B. Ellison, "Social Network Sites: Definition, History, and Scholarship," Journal of Computer-Mediated Communication, vol. 13, no. 1, pp. 210-230, 2008.

[15] B. Schneier, "A Taxonomy of Social Networking Data," IEEE Security & Privacy Magazine, vol. 8, no. 4, p. 88, 2010, doi: 10.1109/MSP.2010.118

[16] M. Hart and R. Johnson, "Prevention and Reaction: Defending Privacy in the Web 2.0," 2010. [Online]. Available from: http://www.w3.org/2010/policy-ws/papers/04-Hart-stonybrook.pdf 2017.05.29.

[17] Facebook, Data Policy, [Online]. Available from: https://www.facebook.com/about/privacy/your-info 2016.07.16

[18] S. E. Madnick, R. Y. Wang, Y. W. Lee, and H. Zhu, "Overview and Framework for Data and Information Quality Research," Journal of Data and Information Quality, vol. 1, pp. 2:1-2:22, 2009.

[19] C. Fisher, E. Lauria, S. Chengalur-Smith, R. Wang, Introduction to Information Quality, M.I.T. Information Quality Program, 2006.

[20] R. Y. Wang and D. M. Strong, "Beyond Accuracy: What Data Quality Means to Data Consumers," Journal of Management Information Systems, vol. 12, no. 4, pp. 5-33, 1996.

[21] D. M. Strong, Y. W. Lee, and R. Y. Wang, "Data Quality in Context," Commun. ACM, vol. 40, pp. 103-110, May 1997.

[22] L. L. Pipino, Y. W. Lee, and R. Y. Wang, "Data Quality Assessment," Commun. ACM, vol. 45, pp. 211-218, Apr. 2002.

[23] S. P. Marsh, Formalising Trust as a Computational Concept, unpublished doctoral dissertation, University of Stirling, 1994. [Online]. Available from: https://dspace.stir.ac.uk/ 2017.05.29.

[24] C. D. Schultz, "A Trust Framework Model for Situational Contexts," Proceedings of the 2006 International Conference on Privacy, Security and Trust: Bridge the Gap between PST Technologies and Business Services (PST '06), New York, NY, USA: ACM, pp. 50:1-50:7, 2006.

[25] D. McKnight and N. Chervany, "Conceptualizing Trust: A Typology and E-commerce Customer Relationships Model," Proceedings of the 34th Annual Hawaii International Conference on System Sciences, p. 10, 2001.

[26] A. Gutowska, Research in Online Trust: Trust Taxonomy as a Multi-Dimensional Model, Technical Report, School of Computing and Information Technology, University of Wolverhampton, 2007.

[27] D. Gefen, "Reflections on the Dimensions of Trust and Trustworthiness Among Online Consumers," SIGMIS Database, vol. 33, pp. 38-53, 2002.

[28] T. Kosa, "Vampire Bats: Trust in Privacy," Eighth Annual International Conference on Privacy Security and Trust (PST), 2010, pp. 96-102, doi: 10.1109/PST.2010.5593227.

[29] R. C. Mayer, J. H. Davis, and F. D. Schoorman, "An Integrative Model of Organizational Trust," The Academy of Management Review, vol. 20, no. 3, pp. 709-734, 1995.

[30] S. Adali, R. Escriva, M. K. Goldberg, M. Hayvanovych, M. Magdon-Ismail, B. K. Szymanski, and G. Williams, "Measuring Behavioral Trust in Social Networks," 2010 IEEE International Conference on Intelligence and Security Informatics (ISI), 2010, pp. 150-152.

[31] D. L. Hoffman, T. P. Novak, and M. Peralta, "Building Consumer Trust Online," Commun. ACM, vol. 42, pp. 80-85, Apr. 1999.

[32] G. Hogben (Ed.), ENISA Position Paper No. 1: Security Issues and Recommendations for Online Social Networks, European Network and Information Security Agency, Nov. 2007. [Online]. Available from: https://www.enisa.europa.eu/publications/archive/security-issues-and-recommendations-for-online-social-networks 2017.05.29

[33] K. Liu and E. Terzi, "A Framework for Computing the Privacy Scores of Users in Online Social Networks," Ninth IEEE International Conference on Data Mining (ICDM '09), 2009, pp. 288-297, doi: 10.1109/ICDM.2009.21.

[34] N. K. Malhotra, S. S. Kim, and J. Agarwal, "Internet Users' Information Privacy Concerns (IUIPC): The Construct, the Scale, and a Causal Model," Information Systems Research, vol. 15, no. 4, pp. 336-355, 2004. doi: 10.1287/isre.1040.0032.

[35] H. Krasnova, O. Günther, S. Spiekermann, S., and K. Koroleva, "Privacy Concerns and Identity in Online Social Networks," Identity in the Information Society, vol. 2, no. 1, pp. 39-63, 2009, doi: DOI 10.1007/s12394-009.

[36] Y. Zuo, W. Hu, & T. O'Keefe. "Trust Computing for Social Networking," Sixth International Conference on Information Technology: New Generations (ITNG '09), pp. 1534-1539, 2009, doi: 10.1109/ITNG.2009.278

[37] J. Owyang, "7 Types of Social Data that Help You Understand Consumers," Lecture presented at Eleven Social Media Tips for 2011, Feb. 2011. [Online]. Available from: http://netbase11for11.com/

[38] J. Fogel and E. Nehmad, "Internet social network communities: Risk taking, trust, and privacy concerns," Computers in Human Behavior, 25(1), pp. 153-160, 2009.

[39] R. Gross and A. Acquisti, "Information revelation and privacy in online social networks," ACM Workshop on Privacy in the Electronic Society (WPES '05), pp. 71-80, 2005.

[40] A. Acquisti and R. Gross, "Imagined Communities: Awareness, Information Sharing and Privacy on The Facebook," The 6th Workshop on Privacy Enhancing Technologies, pp. 1-22, 2006.

[41] C.M. Hoadley, H. Xu, J.J. Lee, and M.B. Rosson, "Privacy as Information Access and Illusory Control: The Case of the Facebook News Feed Privacy Outcry," Electronic Commerce Research and Applications, 9(1), pp. 50-60, 2010.

[42] M. Madejski, M. Johnson, and S.M. Bellovin, The Failure of Online Social Network Privacy Settings, Available from: https://mice.cs.columbia.edu/getTechreport.php?techreportID=1459

[43] C. Dwyer, S. Hiltz, and K. Passerini, "Trust and Privacy Concern Within Social Networking Sites: A Comparison of Facebook and MySpace," The Thirteenth Americas Conference on Information Systems, 2007. [Online]. Available from: csis.pace.edu/~dwyer/research/. 2017.05.29.

[44] A.W. Boyd, "A Longitudinal Study of Social Media Privacy Behavior," ArXiv E-prints, pp. 1-10. [Online]. Available from http://arxiv.org/abs/1103.3174. 2017.05.29.

[45] R. Dey, Z. Jelveh, and K. Ross, "Facebook Users Have become Much More Private: A Large-Scale Study," The 4th IEEE International Workshop on Security and Social Networking (SESOC), pp. 1-7, 2012. [Online]. Available from http://cis.poly.edu/~ratan/ 2017.05.29

[46] J. Kolter and G. Pernul, G. (2009). "Generating User-Understandable Privacy Preferences," International Conference on Availability, Reliability and Security (AES '09), pp. 299-306, 2009. doi: 10.1109/ARES.2009.89

[47] B. Krishnamurthy and C.E. Wills, "Characterizing Privacy in Online Social Networks," The First Workshop on Online Social Networks (WOSN '08), pp. 37-42, 2008.

[48] D. Offenhuber and J. Donath, "Comment Flow: Visualizing Communication Along Network Path," Interface Cultures: Artistic Aspects of Interaction, 2008. [Online]. Available from: medialab-prado.es/mmedia/1094 2017.05.29

[49] J. Becker and H. Chen, "Measuring Privacy Risk in Online Social Networks," Web 2.0 Security and Privacy (W2SP 2009), 2009. [Online]. Available from http://w2spconf.com/ 2017.05.29

[50] D. Irani, S. Webb, C. Pu, and K. Li, "Modeling Unintended Personal-Information Leakage from Multiple Online Social Networks," Internet Computing, 15(3), pp. 13-19, 2011. doi: 10.1109/MIC.2011.25

[51] E. Rose, "Balancing Internet Marketing Needs with Consumer Concerns: A Property Rights Framework," ACM SIGCAS Computers and Society, 31(1), pp. 17-21, 2001.

[52] A. Neus, "The Quality of Online Registration Information: Factors Influencing User Decisions to Reveal Authentic Personal Information to Online Marketers as Part of a Perceived Barter," MIT Conference on Information Quality (IQ 2000), 2000.

[53] K.L. Hui, B.C.Y. Tan, and C.Y. Goh, "Online Information Disclosure: Motivators and Measurements," ACM Transactions on Internet Technology, 6(4), pp. 415-441, 2006.

[54] D. Myers, "Conformed Dimensions of Data Quality," DQMatters, 2017. [Online]. Available from: http://dimensionsofdataquality.com 2017.05.29

[55] D. Myers, "The Value of Using the Dimensions of Data Quality." Information Management, Aug. 2013. [Online]. Available from: https://www.information-management.com/news/the-value-of-using-the-dimensions-of-data-quality 2017.05.29

[56] F.G. Marmol, M.G. Perez, and G.M. Perez, "Reporting Offensive Content in Social Networks: Toward a Reputation-Based Assessment Approach," IEEE Internet Computing, 18(2), 32-40, 2014. doi:10.1109/mic.2013.132

[57] S.P. Ros, A.P. Canelles, M.G. Pérez, F.G. Mármol, and G.M. Pérez, "Chasing Offensive Conduct in Social Networks," ACM Transactions on Internet Technology, 15(4), 1-20, 2015. doi:10.1145/2797139

[58] J. Parra-Arnau, D. Rebollo-Monedero, and J. Forné, "Measuring the privacy of user profiles in personalized information systems," Future Generation Computer Systems, 33, 53-63, 2014. doi:10.1016/j.future.2013.01.001

[59] P.J. Wisniewski, B.P. Knijnenburg, and H.R. Lipford, "Making privacy personal: Profiling social network users to inform privacy education and nudging," International Journal of Human-Computer Studies, 98, 95-108, 2017. doi:10.1016/j.ijhcs. 2016.09.006

[60] C.B. Paine Schofield, A.N. Joinson, T. Buchanan, and U.-D. Reips, "Privacy and self-disclosure online," Conference on Human Factors in Computing Systems, 2006.

APPENDIX A - FRAMEWORK MATRIX: INFORMATION QUALITY, DATA PRIVACY, AND TRUST IN SOCIAL MEDIA NETWORKS

	Types of Social Networking Data					
	Service Data	**Disclosed Data**	**Entrusted Data**	**Incidental Data**	**Behavioral Data**	**Derived Data**
	Data you give the social network site in order to use it	What you post on your own pages	What you post on other people's pages	What other people post about you	Data the site collection about your habits by recording what you do and who you do it with	Data about you that is derived from all other data
Data Privacy Issues	Insecurity Secondary use Breach of Confidentiality	Increased Accessibility Insecurity Appropriation Secondary Use	Increased Accessibility Secondary use Identification Exclusion Breach of Confidentiality Disclosure Exposure Distortion Intrusion (onto their pages)	Identification Exclusion Breach of Confidentiality Disclosure Exposure Distortion Intrusion (onto your pages) Increased Accessibility Secondary use	Aggregation Insecurity Secondary Use Breach of Confidentiality Identification Exclusion	Aggregation Insecurity Secondary Use Breach of Confidentiality Identification Exclusion
Information Quality Dimensions	Accuracy Appropriate Amount Relevancy Security Accessibility Concise Representation Consistent Representation	Accuracy Appropriate Amount Relevancy Security Believability Reputation Understandability Accessibility Objectivity Ease of Operation	Accuracy Appropriate Amount Relevancy Security Believability Reputation Understandability Accessibility Objectivity Ease of Operation	Accuracy Appropriate Amount Relevancy Security Believability Reputation Understandability Accessibility Objectivity Ease of Operation	Accuracy Appropriate Amount Relevancy Security Timeliness Concise Representation Completeness Consistent Representation Accessibility Understandability Interpretability	Accuracy Appropriate Amount Relevancy Security Accessibility Understandability Interpretability Consistent Representation Concise Representation
Trust	Ability Benevolence Integrity	Benevolence Integrity	Benevolence Integrity	Benevolence Integrity	Ability Benevolence Integrity	Ability Benevolence Integrity

APPENDIX B - FRAMEWORK MATRIX: DATA PRIVACY AND INFORMATION QUALITY

	Types of Data Privacy Issues				
	Information Processing				
	Aggregation	Identification	Insecurity	Secondary use	Exclusion
Information Quality Dimensions	Accuracy Appropriate Amount Relevancy Believability Timeliness	Accuracy Believability Reputation	Security Accessibility	Appropriate Amount Accessibility Security Relevancy Accuracy	Security Accessibility Understandability Interpretability Timeliness

	Information Dissemination					
	Breach of Confidentiality	Disclosure	Exposure	Increased Accessibility	Appropriation	Distortion
Information Quality Dimensions	Reputation Accuracy Believability Accessibility	Reputation Believability Accuracy Accessibility Appropriate Amount Relevancy	Reputation Believability Accuracy Accessibility Appropriate Amount	Accessibility Security Appropriate Amount	Security Reputation Believability Accuracy	Reputation Believability Accuracy Accessibility

	Invasions	
	Intrustion	Decisional Interference
Information Quality Dimensions	Security Accessibility Appropriate Amount	Security Accessibility Appropriate Amount

APPENDIX C - FRAMEWORK MATRIX: DATA PRIVACY AND TRUST

	Types of Data Privacy Issues					
	Information Processing					
	Aggregation	Identification	Insecurity	Secondary use	Exclusion	
Trust	Ability Benevolence Integrity	Ability Benevolence Integrity	Ability Benevolence Integrity	Benevolence Integrity	Benevolence Integrity	
	Information Dissemination					
	Breach of Confideniality	Disclosure	Exposure	Increased accessibility	Appropriation	Distortion
Trust	Benevolence Integrity	Benevolence Integrity	Benevolence Integrity	Ability Benevolence Integrity	Benevolence Integrity	Benevolence Integrity
	Invasions					
	Intrustion	Decisional Interference				
Trust	Ability Benevolence Integrity	Ability Benevolence Integrity				

APPENDIX D - FRAMEWORK MATRIX: TRUST AND INFORMATION QUALITY

	Characteristics of Trust		
	Ability	Benevolence	Integrity
Information Quality Dimensions	Accessibility Timeliness Ease of Operation	Objectivity Reputation Appropriate Amount Relevancy Accuracy Completeness	Believability Reputation Objectivity

Protecting Data Generated in Medical Research: Aspects of Data Protection and Intellectual Property Rights

Iryna Lishchuk, Marc Stauch
Institut für Rechtsinformatik
Leibniz Universität Hannover
Hannover, Germany
e-mail: lishchuk@iri.uni-hannover.de, stauch@iri.uni-hannover.de

Abstract—**This paper investigates legal approaches towards protecting the data generated in medical research. One of the core features of the rules for the processing and sharing of data generated in medical research is their complexity. Thus, data containing personally identifiable information would qualify as personal data and the processing of such data would be subject to the law on data protection. Equally, the generation of data in the course of medical research may involve considerable investment or effort and have an economic or scientific value for the researcher or right holder, including through use in publications, and may well be considered as Intellectual Property (IP). Contractual approaches may also define the rules how the data may be used and shared.**

Keywords-IP rights; data rights; medical data; data curation; personal data; data protection.

I. INTRODUCTION

IT developments in the field of bioinformatics have opened new ways of data procession. The creation of new data, as well as new knowledge, derived out of existing datasets as a result of medical research, may well be considered as an IP and qualify as an object of protection by IP rights [1]. Equally, data generated in medical research, which by one or another parameter may be related to an identifiable natural person, also have the quality of personal data with the resulting protection by the law on data protection.

Innovative genome sequencing techniques are able to process 4 PB data per year (11 TBytes per day), thus reaching the level of Twitter with the processing power of 12 Terabytes per day [2]. Mathematical and computational modeling is used to integrate and interpret the massive amount of data, uncovered in molecular and cell biology [3]. Cancer system biology, which studies how individual components interact to give rise to the function and behavior of the cancerous system as a whole [4], produces a number of data types: molecular data, epigenetic data, clinical data, imaging data, pathology data and other laboratory data.

In the process, the availability of a large amount of data collected in the clinical trials combined with modern data processing techniques have allowed the discovery of new data correlations. For instance, the SIOP 2001/GPOH trial of patients with Nephroblastoma (a malignant tumor arising from the embryonic kidney that occurs in young children, especially in the age range 3–8 years [5]) revealed that whereas 90 % of patients respond to preoperative chemotherapy with tumor shrinkage, in about 10 % the tumor does not shrink, but increases in return, thus making the situation worse [6]. Such discoveries necessitate in-depth research and application of powerful data analytics techniques to identify correlations between negative tumor response and specific characteristics of the non-responding patients.

Thus, advances in data-mining and analytics have made it possible to generate new data and derive new knowledge from existing datasets. This, as well as new methods of differentiating and capturing biological phenomena (including at the micro-level) has led to an exponential growth in available medical data. In principle, such data, recorded in patient or research databases can be of tremendous value when analyzed, in revealing linkages, e.g., between environmental and/or genetic factors and diseases, as well as for comparing patient responses to different treatment therapies. A major advantage too is that such connections can often be identified straight from the records, without the need for further invasive and potentially risky research.

At the same time, as the potential value of health data becomes better understood, efforts to monopolize clinical data by exclusive IP or proprietary rights are also expanding. Copyrights, patent rights, sui generis database rights and the legal regime of undisclosed information may come into consideration, depending, however, on the data – the subject matter of protection. For instance, there are cases when the commercial use of health related data has been asserted under the coverage of database rights [7]. Patentable inventions have also been derived out of the biological material and associated data of the patients and successfully commercialized [8]. The property rights in medical research data may also be claimed under contractual schemes [9]. At some point copyrights may also come to consideration for monopolizing data in medical domain [10].

However, as a precondition for allowing a significant amount of clinical data to be usefully exploited, there is an important initial step required in the form of data curation. In this regard, as we analyze below, most types of IP protection are tailored to protect specific objects that have already passed a certain threshold of maturity (data repositories, confidential information with assignable commercial value, etc.); but, as we discuss, none as such guarantees adequate protection to protect the prior investment made in curating the data.

In what follows, we begin by describing the data curation process in medical research in Section II, explore the complex nature of medical data in terms of law in Section III, proceed to the requirements of data protection for the processing of personal data in Section IV. In Section V, we investigate the potential options of protecting the medical research data by IP rights and in Section VI then consider their application in the context of a concrete research initiative, namely the EU FP7 project 'CHIC'. Thereafter, contractual approaches towards the government of rights in data are examined in Section VII, before Section VIII concludes by suggesting a potentially more effective approach to protecting researcher investment in curation.

II. Data Curation

The clinical data provided for e-health research usually comprises a large mass of data of multiple data types, formats, words, figures, numerical parameters, abbreviations, etc. Furthermore, even where data is of the same underlying type, this will often have been recorded in different ways – using different clinical concepts and/or measuring systems. This reflects the decentralized, autonomous nature of health care delivery, with different institutions and clinicians often employing different classificatory descriptions and/or record systems.

Data integration is key here, but the format, scope, parameter, structure, context, terminology, completeness, etc., of the individual and heterogeneous data are not standardized, which may affect their quality, and ultimately their interoperability and integration [11]. This could also potentially affect collaboration of the different researchers in this field if they use different semantics and techniques to describe, format, submit, and exchange data.

From a technical standpoint, data integration is still a significant challenge. The curation required to ensure the data relates to and measures the same phenomena with sufficient accuracy to be usable is a large and painstaking task. It includes the problem of dealing with incomplete data fields and cross-checking that various indices were measured and recorded in a similar way (e.g., images were taken using similar equipment, co-morbidities were classified using the same terminology, etc.). In the process the curator may often wish to add metadata to alert the data user to such issues. It is evident too that considerable expertise and skill is required for the task to be performed well: the curator needs to have a real feel and understanding for the subject matter in order to make sensible judgments in resolving various gaps and uncertainties.

In this regard, a starting point in the context of curation may be to see raw data in terms of the 'given', which as yet lacks semantic meaning, with the latter only emerging through the addition of an interpretive context (which also marks the change in state from data into information). It is suggested that the technological development and transformation of raw or incompletely processed data into information (or the uncovering of additional semantic meaning), brought about by the curative process represents a suitable object for IP protection.

At this point a legal challenge arises. On the one hand, an intellectual and/or technical investment made in curating the data and generating new data outcomes may justify an interest of the investors in monopolizing the resulting data as their IP. On the other hand, the data used in medical research originally comes from the patient, which renders such data a potential candidate for protection as personal data. That is so, if the medical data contain personally identifiable information, i.e., it may by some or the other characteristics be linked to the data subject.

Against this background, both the economic value of the derived data and the tentative quality of the data as personal data make the data generated in medical research a complex object of legal protection and dictate the type of protection applicable.

III. Complexity of Medical Data in terms of Law

The legal complexity of the data generated in medical research is one of the major factors, which determine the type of protection applicable and the rules governing the use of such data. The medical research data may qualify both as personal data and intellectual property.

Indeed, out of scientific disciplines, medical research (both as sociological research) tends to share significantly less data than others (65% in comparison to 90% in biology or 85% in climatology) [12]. Frequently, this "*low data sharing culture*" is justified by the legal and ethical requirement to protect the privacy of individuals, that is to say data protection [12].

On the other hand, as noted, even where medical data is void of indices, which would render such data personal data in the meaning of data protection law, the aspects of intellectual property also need to be taken into account. If the researcher or research institution, who holds such data in its legitimate possession, considers such data as its "intellectual property" and has an economic interest in exploiting such data for individual gain (e.g., reputation, scientific publication), such qualification of the data may also affect data sharing and determine the circumstances for such data to be shared. It is common in the scientific world that "*Data that a researcher feels could still be exploited for future publications are usually not shared*" [13]. Another practice usual for medical sciences is that the data is no longer protected after the appearance of publications [14]. The legitimate interests of the data holder may also affect the terms and circumstances for such data to be shared. For instance, such data may only be made available to the circles, which may prove a justified scientific interest in the data (e.g., data sharing upon certain conditions inside a research consortium or a limited medical community) [14].

What may also play a role is whether a medical project relates to Big Science, such as physics, Earth and climate science, or Small Science, in particular, small experiments, narrow disciplines [15]. For Big Science data there are "government controlled repositories", which normally govern the use of data as a "public good" [15]. An example is Clinical Trials Registries and Databases, such as registries operated by the National Library of Medicine in the USA [16], the UK Current Controlled Trials [17] and the Japan Pharmaceutical Information Center [18]. However, for Small Science projects, which comprise the majority of data repositories, such pre-determined regulatory frameworks for the handling of data do not exist. The protection practices applied vary from discipline to discipline and have rather an informal character [15].

In the light of these considerations, for the purposes of choosing and applying adequate protection measures, it is relevant first to ascertain whether the data has a quality of personal data (and is subject to the requirements of the law on data protection); the next questions are whether it has an economic value for the data holder and may be treated as intellectual property (subject to the rules of IP law), or whether such data is considered as a "public good" and must be treated as such.

IV. Data Protection

For legal purposes, the first important question to decide is whether the medical research data contain personally identifiable information. In the meaning of European data protection law, it would be the case if by some or the other characteristics the data may be linked to the data subject. If so, the processing and sharing of such data would be subject to the law on data protection.

Article 2 (a) of the EU Data Protection Directive 95/46/EC (DPD) [19] (which is to be superseded by the General Data Protection Regulation [20] by 25 of May 2018) defines personal data as follows:

"*'personal data ' shall mean any information relating to an identified or identifiable natural person ('data subject'); an identifiable person is one who can be identified, directly or indirectly, in particular by reference to an identification number or to one or more factors specific to his physical, physiological, mental, economic, cultural or social identity;*".

As is apparent, this is a wide definition, and in principle it may certainly cover some medical data. An example may be a brain image that also shows some of the patient's face; indeed, in the light of modern software, a set of cross-sectional brain images may also qualify – this is if it would be possible with the software to put such images together to reconstruct the face of the patient based on the image parameters. Since health data qualifies as sensitive data [21], the processing of such data is subject to stringent requirements of procession (Article 8 DPD) and must be explicitly legitimized, e.g., by informed consent of the patient (Article 8 (2) (a) DPD) or the national laws that also provide for adequate privacy safeguards (Article 8 (4) DPD) [19].

Medical research is usually conducted on the human body or with the use of clinical data. Blood samples, serum, tissue samples, cells usually constitute material for laboratory examinations, from which the data, used in medical research, is derived. When the laboratory tests are taken in course of medical treatment and/or diagnosis, the patient normally consents to the use of the excised material and data for the purposes of clinical care [9]. However, as a rule such consent does not extend and does not entitle the physician to use such clinical data for research [8]. The use of clinical data for research requires legal justification, which as a rule may be obtained either by informed consent of the data subject or by compatible use of data.

The use of previously collected data for research constitutes secondary use of data. In principle, Article 6 (b) DPD allows secondary use of data subject to specific conditions: "*personal data must be collected for 'specified, explicit and legitimate' purposes (purpose specification) and not be 'further processed in a way incompatible' with those purposes (compatible use).*" [19].

By implication, the compatibility assessment is to be made on a case-by-case basis and in consideration of all relevant circumstances. In particular, the following key factors shall be taken into account:

- "*the relationship between the purposes for which the personal data have been collected and the purposes of further processing;*
- *the context in which the personal data have been collected and the reasonable expectations of the data subjects as to their further use;*
- *the nature of the personal data and the impact of the further processing on the data subjects;*
- *the safeguards adopted by the controller to ensure fair processing and to prevent any undue impact on the data subjects.*" [22].

The use of data for scientific research withstands the compatibility assessment as long as the controller implements "appropriate safeguards" and by that ensures "*that the data will not be used to support measures or decisions regarding any particular individuals*" [22]. Such safeguards may be taken in the form of technical and/or organizational measures aimed to ensure functional separation (such as partial or full anonymisation, pseudonymisation, and aggregation of data), privacy enhancing technologies, as well as other measures to prevent the use of data to take decisions or other actions with respect to individuals [22].

From these legal observations it follows that - in simple terms - the use of health data for research must be legitimized: either by the patient´s informed consent or by the law, allowing compatible use of data subject to compatibility assessment and application of appropriate de-identification and security measures. This is also likely to remain the position after the General Data Protection Regulation (replacing the DPD) comes into effect in May 2018 [20]. In such cases, the research conducted subject to adoption of appropriate de-identification and security measures should not cause privacy implications.

It is apparent that by imposing these requirements, the law on data protection aims to protect and safeguard privacy of the individual. "*Data protection rules may be seen as embodying and safeguarding core ethical principles of autonomy, dignity and privacy; they are about making sure that persons remain able to decide how their data will be used and are not exploited or instrumentalised through opaque data processing practices;*" [23]. These matters are essential in order for patients to have trust in medical research and innovative eHealth applications [23].

However, when talking about protecting medical research data it is essential to distinguish the primary goal of such protection. In this respect it must be noted that the purpose and meaning of the law on data protection is to protect privacy of the individual, and not to do with the economic or exploitation interests in the data itself. Therefore, when legal protection is sought to protect economic interests of the data holder, the law on data protection would not fulfill that objective. The requirements of the law on data protection must rather be taken into account as a necessary means of protecting privacy and rights of the data subjects.

V. POTENTIAL IP PROTECTION

In contrast to the law on data protection, which serves to protect privacy rights of the individuals, the IP law aims to reward and protect the creators - either authors or inventors – for their intellectual or economic input into society.

A. Data as Protectable Subject Matter

When we consider the data produced in medical research, such as measurements, experiments, outcomes of data analytics, etc., in the context of IP law, we can observe that, as a rule, such data do not automatically fall into the category of IP protected objects. In the absence of legal protection applicable directly, alternative protection mechanisms are frequently sought, such as: copyrights, sui generis database rights under IP law; or through the application of the legal regime of undisclosed information, an aspect of competition law. In addition, contractual mechanisms may be used to address proprietary interests in data. However, the application of these forms of protection may often be problematic. For instance, copyright may not arise in the absence of creative input or proprietary claims in data may be challenged due to the questionable legal nature of property rights in data [24]. More generally, IP law would normally not protect the data as such. Instead, a requirement for IP protection is that added value produced from the data. Examples may be a creative scientific work covered by copyright, an industrially applicable invention in the patent law or commercial value of the information protectable as know-how by competition laws.

This also fits with the underlying motivation for IP protection, which is to motivate an author or inventor, by rewarding them for their intellectual activity (here, in extracting value from the data). In contrast, raw data, which is void of such intellectual input does not constitute a protectable IP and as a matter of policy should be kept free for public use.

The applicability of the IP laws in relation to medical research data is considered in more detail below.

B. Copyright and Related Rights

Clinical data comes for the most part from clinical trials, laboratory results, medical examinations, etc. An example of the clinical research data is shown in Figure 1 [25]. Such data is usually expressed in some numeric parameters, figures, words, combinations of such items. The representation of clinical data in this format is suitable and useful for digital data processing. However, the isolated items, be they words, keywords, syntax, figures or mathematical concepts as such, will not attract copyright. According to the Court of Justice of European Union (CJEU), items, *"considered in isolation, are not as such an intellectual creation of the author who employs them."* [26]. In order to be protected by copyright, the data must constitute the expression of the original author´s creativity, which is only present when *"through the choice, sequence and combination of those words that the author may express his creativity in an original manner and achieve a result which is an intellectual creation"* [26].

The protection of clinical data by copyright may under circumstances be acceptable for the medical reports, written by the physician or the patient, insofar as the expression of original creativity is achieved [10]. However, for isolated datasets, especially where (as is desirable) the curator follows a standardized procedure, it seems much less likely that sufficient originality exists for copyright purposes.

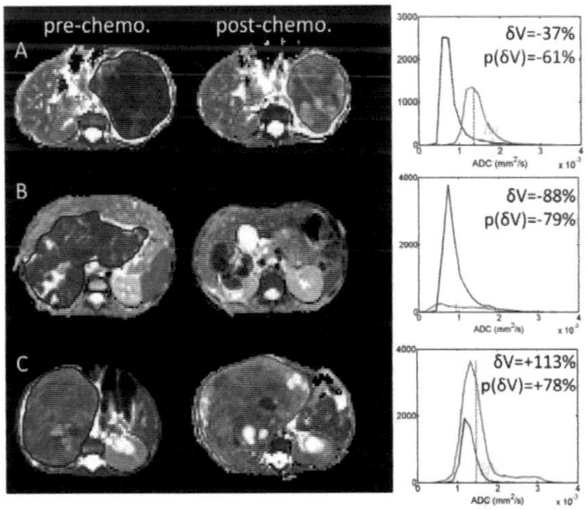

Figure 1. DWI and ADC mapping of nephroblastoma from different patients before and after pre-operative chemotherapy. Presented at the annual meeting of the British Chapter of the ISMRM, September 2012, provided by Prof. Kathy Pritchard-Jones from UCL. Copied from CHIC Deliverable D2-2 "Scenario based user needs and requirements" [25].

As may be seen from the image, some data is presented in visual form and is represented by images. However, medical images are normally produced by technical means (such as X-Ray, Ultrasound, etc.) and lack the creativity – an indispensable pre-requisite for copyright. A similar standard of copyright and requirement of original creativity applies to photographic works as well. According to Recital 16 Directive 2006/116/EC [27], a photographic work is protected by copyright, if it is original. A work *"is to be considered original if it is the author's own intellectual creation reflecting his personality"*. Other criteria such as merit or purpose are not relevant for copyright. According to the CJEU decision in the case C 145/10 REC of Eva-Maria Painer [28], copyright protects pictures taken by an individual, exercising free and creative choices, thus stamping a picture with his personal touch. It follows that only pictures taken by an individual expressing some level of the author´s personality and creativity may be protected by copyright. On the other hand, images, generated automatically, will lack the necessary creativity. Since the images, produced in medical domain, are normally taken automatically and the process of recording is mostly completely managed by technical means, such images normally do not express creativity and do not attract the protection by copyright, respectively.

Apart from the rights considered so far, in the field of copyright *senso strictu*, there are a number of other emerging rights granted as a response to relevant investment. These rights are normally provided to the person, who invests in producing the protectable information. Such rights are referred to as related rights. Protection by related rights does not necessarily link to the intellectual creation (as the case is with traditional copyright), but rather to the economic investment.

The major rationale for protection by related rights tends to shift between intellectual creation and the investment of resources required [29]. A mixture of artistic creation and investment attracts exclusive rights to performers in fixations of their performances. The economic investment constitutes a major factor, which renders exclusive rights to phonogram producers in their phonograms, to the film producers in respect of first fixations of their films, to broadcasting organizations in fixations of their broadcasts [30].

However, the number of related rights as of now is rather limited (mostly to those, indicated above). Therefore, attaching added value to the data enriching, post-processing, modification, etc., does not constitute the kind of investment protectable by related rights.

C. Sui Generis Database Right

As a rule, clinical institutions, participating in medical research, manage and maintain their clinical data in clinical data repositories. Some clinical institutions manage their clinical information and store the results of clinical trials using project-tailored data management systems. For example, the CHIC project utilises an Ontology-based Clinical Trial Management Application (ObTiMA) [31]. Other institutions prefer data management systems specific to their medical activities. Against this background, an option of protecting the clinical data under the umbrella of sui generis database rights comes into consideration first.

The legal protection of databases is provided for by the Directive 96/9/EC of 11 March 1996 on the legal protection of databases (the Database Directive) [32]. Such protection is granted in recognition of the fact that constructing a database requires "*investment of considerable human, technical and financial resources*" [32]. The Directive 96/9/EC aims to reward and protect such investment by providing the maker of a database with a sui generis data base right that places him in a position to prevent unauthorized access and copying of the database contents, which he compiled. In this regard, Article 7 Database Directive states:

"*Member States shall provide for a right for the maker of a database which shows that there has been qualitatively and/or quantitatively a substantial investment in either the obtaining, verification or presentation of the contents to prevent extraction and/or re-utilization of the whole or of a substantial part, evaluated qualitatively and/or quantitatively, of the contents of that database.*" The object of protection in terms of the Database Directive is a 'database' meaning "*a collection of independent works, data or other materials arranged in a systematic or methodical way and individually accessible by electronic or other means*" [32].

Databases are given their own *sui generis* right of protection for the *"blood, sweat and tears that go into producing a database"* [33]. Consequently, as we have just seen, the Database Directive demands that *"there has been qualitatively and/or quantitatively a substantial investment in either the obtaining, verification or presentation of the contents"* [32]. The type of investment required can be time, financial resources, personnel, or technical means invested, or indeed any other "sweat of the brow"-type resource, as distinct from creative, intellectual efforts.

The CJEU is very strict in its understanding that the investment must be made to *obtain* the contents. A database that is a mere spinoff/by-product from another investment/activity (such as scientific data resulting from research) does not typically qualify for protection under the Database Directive's *sui generis* regime. There must additionally be a further substantial investment in obtaining, verifying or presenting the data [34].

In other words, the CJEU demands that the investment be made specifically to *"seek out existing independent materials and collect them in the database"* [35]. An investment in *"the creation of materials which make up the contents of a database"* [35] is deemed insufficient. As a result, creators of data rarely enjoy a sui generis right of protection for any non-original database constructed out of that data – so-called "single source databases" [36] – unless there is also a substantial investment in the verification or presentation of the contents.

"*Verification*" is understood to mean steps taken to ensure the information is reliable. As with the requirement of "obtaining" data, an investment in verifying information during the information's creation is excluded [34].

"*Presentation*" is defined as the way data is structured and made accessible to others, so that the creation of an index or the design of a user interface can all be seen to fulfill the requirements of an investment in the presentation of the contents [34].

Finally, the investment must also be of a "*qualitatively and/or quantitatively*" substantial nature [32]. The Database Directive does not define "*substantial*" and neither has the ECJ ruled on the matter. However, the Preamble of the Directive indicates that, "*as a rule, the compilation of several recordings of musical performances on a CD (...) does not represent a substantial enough investment to be eligible under the sui generis right*" [32]. Member States generally adopt a low level approach to the requirement, and the Advocate General has taken the same stance [34].

As regards the quantitative and/or qualitative qualification, these are understood to mean investments quantifiable and not-quantifiable, respectively, such as money on the one hand and intellectual effort on the other [37].

In fact, additional substantial investment is often present in the case of data resulting from clinical trials. Such data must first undergo an extensive verification process before it can be used in research and entered into a database. Importantly, the data verification process is subsequent and separate from the obtaining/creation of the original data, as otherwise it would be excluded from protection.

Accordingly, protection by the sui generis right can be considered as a plausible option for clinical data repositories, provided the given repository satisfies the above criteria. As regards the scope of the database right, it would protect the collected data from being copied as a whole or in substantial part, evaluated "*qualitatively and/or quantitatively*" and either copied in one action or step by step [32].

Provided the clinical data repository qualifies as a database in the meaning of Database Directive and the clinical institution holds the sui generis database rights, the institution may stipulate the terms of using the repository contents as a whole, grant the rights of use under contractual license, prevent and enforce the unauthorized extraction/reutilization of the repository contents as a whole or in substantial part. The rights holder may thereby leverage how the contents of its repository may be used, whether the data items may be extracted (downloaded) and in what form or quantity, whether the data may be transferred to external parties or whether the data processing may only be done on its premises.

At the same time, this sui generis protection applies to the contents of the repository as a whole or in substantial part and may apply separately and irrespective of protectability of data items by other rights, such as copyrights. Article 7 (4) makes this explicit, saying that the database right: "*shall apply irrespective of eligibility of the contents of that database for protection by copyright or by other rights. Protection of databases [....] shall be without prejudice to rights existing in respect of their contents*".

Thus, the holder of the repository may manage the use of the repository contents as a whole. However, the use of separate data items in the repository may remain governed by the terms, stipulated by the data providers and/or holders of rights in such items. For instance, the access rights to the datasets, handled as confidential, may require signing of non-disclosure agreement (NDA) and the use of such data may be limited and be subject to technical protection measures, etc.

In this regard, we consider further the options of protection, which potentially may apply to separate datasets, next.

D. Know-how

Because of the high sensitivity of health related data (and the potential harm to the patient's interests in privacy, dignity and autonomy from disclosure), clinical data in the medical treatment domain is managed under the rules of professional medical secrecy and subject to fiduciary duties. Similarly, as was discussed in Section IV, the data, so far as individual patients may be identified from it, will be subject to data protection rules. In this regard, a plausible option (fitting well with such privacy-based considerations) for protecting the research investment made in collecting or curating clinical data may be to invoke the legal regime of know-how (or undisclosed information). This is, especially so after such data leaves the medical domain and enters the domain of clinical research (where not necessarily all parties are bound by the rules of professional secrecy).

Protection of undisclosed information is provided by Section 7, Article 39 et seq. TRIPS Agreement [38] and the Directive 2016/943 on the protection of undisclosed know-how (the Trade Secret Directive) [39]. The legal regime of know-how enables natural and legal persons, who are in legitimate possession of valuable information, to prevent such information "*from being disclosed to, acquired by, or used by others without their consent in a manner contrary to honest commercial practices.*" [38]. Unfair practices for these purposes would include the acquisition of information via "*unauthorised access to, appropriation of, or copying of any documents, objects, materials, substances or electronic files.... containing the trade secret or from which the trade secret can be deduced*" [39]; violation of contractual duties, breach of confidentiality obligations, inducement to breach, etc. [38].

In order to be protectable, the relevant information should have the quality of protectable subject matter. The Trade Secret Directive, both as Article 39 TRIPS Agreement accord protection to information, which:

"*(a) is secret in the sense that it is not, as a body or in the precise configuration and assembly of its components, generally known among or readily accessible to persons within the circles that normally deal with the kind of information in question;*

(b) has commercial value because it is secret; and

(c) has been subject to reasonable steps under the circumstances, by the person lawfully in control of the information, to keep it secret." [39].

At the same time, one weak point of protecting clinical data as know-how is that the know-how protection across Europe is not that well harmonized with varying data objects considered as protectable know-how and the laws, which accord such protection, ranging from IP laws to competition laws [40].

The newly adopted Trade Secret Directive is intended to harmonize the national laws in relation to know-how protection and in many aspects repeats the provisions of the TRIPS Agreement: in particular, it relates to the protectable subject matter and requirements for protection (Article 2), acts of unlawful acquisition, use and disclosure of information (Article 4), availability of legal remedies against the unlawful acquisition, use and disclosure of trade secrets (Article 6 et seq), etc. With respect to protection of medical research data as know-how, it may also be queried how far the Trade Secret Directive would improve the protection for data, the preparation of which consumed much effort, but which for one or another reason may not reach the level of protectable know-how. Here the key obstacles in applying know-how protection to the clinical data, processed for research, relate to the need (in order to be protected) for such data to be secret, subject to confidentiality measures and have economic value.

First, to satisfy the criterion of secrecy, the information, sought to be protected, must be accessible to a limited number of persons only. The use of such information must be subject to confidentiality measures. The application of confidentiality measures means that the data must be stamped as "Confidential" and the sharing of such data must be contingent upon non-disclosure obligation and observation of the confidentiality measures. Disclosure of such datasets without due confidentiality measures might compromise the regime of secrecy so that protection would be forfeited. As regards the requirement of economic value of know-how, this will be considered to be present if through publication, the research investment and competitive standing of the entity doing the work would be undermined [41].

In relation to the volumes of clinical data made available for research, this requirement, besides being at odds with the underlying data sharing culture of academic research, would create further workload. The data, subject to the regime of confidentiality, must first be strictly identified. The confidentiality mark would need to be attached to individual data items and any use and disclosure of such data to any third party must be subject to the latter signing a non-disclosure agreement (NDA). This preservation of the confidentiality mark, conclusion of NDA and control over handling such data as confidential would present another challenge.

Against these considerations, the protection of clinical data under the legal regime of know-how might, in principle, be possible in relation to some defined amount of data, but hardly offers a feasible solution, when protection of large amounts of data, processed in medical research is sought. It also may operate against the ethos of openness, if optimal use is to be made of the data by the research community, exploiting the full potential of available datasets.

VI. Application of IP Regimes to Data Curation in CHIC

A. Background

The research project "Computational Horizons In Cancer (CHIC): Developing Meta- and Hyper-Multiscale Models and Repositories for In Silico Oncology", is an ICT research project in the clinical domain [42]. CHIC develops clinical trial driven tools and services within a secure infrastructure, which facilitate the creation of multiscale cancer hyper-models (integrative models) by technical means. These composite multiscale constructs of models (hyper-models or integrative models) are intended to synthesize and imitate the biological processes, which occur in course of tumor progression, at several temporal and spatial levels (molecular, cellular, etc.) at once.

In this context too, the study of how individual cancer components interact with each other has led to the generation of different types of data, such as: molecular data, epigenetic data, clinical data, imaging data, pathology data and other laboratory data [43]. These different data types are assembled in order to systematically explore and formalize them in mathematical models.

Subsequently, the models are developed and validated against clinical data either taken from the literature or provided by the clinical partners [44]. The data management systems, used by the clinical partners, differ. Whereas the integration of data from data management system ObTiMA is harmonized, the data from individual clinical data repositories need to be adapted to the requirements of the project. The use of divergent data management systems by the clinical institutions leads to the situation that the data, collected from different sources, is not inter-operable with each other and mostly cannot be used for research as such. The clinical data also needs to be post-processed by the modelers so that it fits into the set of parameters, which the models recognize and can utilize as an input for running the simulations. Such data curation is a very important step because the inputs, outputs and descriptions of processes, simulated by the models, need to be standardized into the set of parameters, acceptable and usable by all cancer models.

B. Applicability of IP Regimes to Project Data Curation

The clinical data, which after the necessary de-identification enters the domain of CHIC, is placed and stored in the CHIC clinical data repository. The CHIC data repository hosts data categorized per data type: imaging data (DICOM etc.), descriptive/structural data (age, sex, etc.), other files (histological reports), links (to other data repositories) etc. The datasets for each type are accessible individually so that the data corresponding to the model parameters may be chosen. The fact that the repository is built "based on the experience already accumulated during the implementation of other data repositories" should be sufficient to prove the requisite investment in "either the obtaining, verification or presentation" of its contents [32]. Against this background, the database right in the CHIC clinical data repository is likely to be granted.

Protection of the CHIC data repository by the sui generis database rights would be accorded to the maker of the database. In the meaning of the Database Directive, the maker of a database is seen as "the person who takes the initiative and the risk of investing", but excluding subcontractors [32]. Thus, the party, who constructed the CHIC repository, would be in a position to manage the use of the repository, such as by allocating the access rights to the project parties or external parties, to define the rights of use (access only, modification, download, etc.), to divide the repository into sections and define different regimes of uses depending on the data stored therein, etc. Grant of the sui generis protection would also entitle the right holder to enforce his rights, once unauthorized copying of the repository contents on the large scale has occurred.

Apart from the protection of the repository contents as a whole by sui generis database rights, the items in the repository may also enjoy protection in their own right. Since the clinical data repository deals with highly sensitive information (meaning that already for that reason, access to the data is strictly limited), application of the legal regime of know-how to some data items at least may be an option. As we saw above, for this, the data items selected for know-how protection, must be identified, the access and use of such data be limited to a defined number of people only, and the management of such data be subject to confidentiality measures. In the case of CHIC, the regime of secrecy may be applied to the data by marking it as "Confidential" and making the disclosure of such data subject to the non-disclosure obligation. From the technical perspective, the confidentiality mark would then need to be placed and borne by the data throughout the whole research process so that the data marked as "confidential" at the time of input comes out marked "confidential" at output. This would present an additional workload, but is implementable. Also, disclosure of such data items to the CHIC parties subject to the non-disclosure obligation would not present a significant obstacle, because the project parties are bound by the contractual relations within the project. The factual use of data within the project may also be managed by technical measures, such as granting or denying access rights, rights of use and extraction, and limiting the data processing to within the technical infrastructure of CHIC. Whereas the application of such contractual and technical confidentiality measures to the clinical data in CHIC may be feasible, in how far such technical and confidentiality measures may be implemented in other medical research projects may be questionable.

By contrast, copyrights and related rights offer less plausible options for protecting the clinical data in CHIC. As noted above, the clinical data in CHIC is represented by technical data from clinical trials, which is composed from different parameters. As observed in Section III, isolated items are not protectable by copyright. Copyright will fail for lack of creativity expressed in such data. Equally, the investment, deployed in curating the data for CHIC, does not qualify as investment protectable by related rights.

However, in the case of CHIC, the exploitability of clinical data under the umbrella of IP rights is limited by the restraints of data protection and research ethics. Whereas for the lifetime of the CHIC project, the de-identification of clinical data was ensured and clinical research ethically approved, the exploitation of the data beyond the scope of the project might be possible, if the adequate legal and security framework would be set up.

C. Related Studies

Indeed, the legal mechanisms offered by IP rights are widely used now by the players in the healthcare sector to support the claims and protect the investment they might have in the data. The database rights and the legal regime of know-how are the tools that suit these interests best and are used by the holders of clinical data most.

One example is deCODE. In the case of deCODE, a Health Sector Database, initially built to hold centralized health records of the population of Iceland [45], migrated into the genetics research database. By application of modern genomics techniques to the data (120,000 research participants), it allowed to find genetic sequences associated with diseases [7]. In consideration of the relatively small population of Iceland, access to a large amount of data allowed deCODE to find itself in a position to be able to predict the genetic dispositions to diseases of about 200,000 living and 80,000 deceased Icelanders, who have not consented to participate in the research [7]. Apart from the privacy considerations (which go beyond the scope of legal analysis presented in this paper), the case of deCODE allows us to infer that centralization of a large amount of clinical data in one database combined with modern IT solutions allows to retrieve new correlations and exploit the added value under the coverage of database rights (which may not always be in compliance with the principles of data protection law).

A similar example is the case of NIVEL. NIVEL, the Netherlands institute or health services research, has built a primary care database, which "*uses routinely recorded data from health care providers to monitor health and utilisation of health services in a representative sample of the Dutch population.*" [46]. NIVEL obtains the data under contractual arrangements with general practitioners. Under the application of double de-identification measures [47] and giving the patients the possibility to opt-out, NIVEL uses itself and allows the use of data for clinical research.

The legal regime of confidentiality is another legal measure, which is often applied to preserve the secrecy of clinical data. Where the use of data in the domain of healthcare services is subject to the obligation of professional secrecy [19] [20]), the secrecy of data, or certain datasets, may be maintained by contractual mechanisms for the data to leave the healthcare sector (and enter the research domain). The application of confidentiality measures is typical for the data derived in clinical trials. Article 39 (3) TRIPS calls for protecting the data collected in clinical trials for the pharmaceutical products "*which utilize new chemical entities, the submission of undisclosed test or other data, the origination of which involves a considerable effort*" [38]. For the purposes of making the results of clinical trials public (either in scientific literature or clinical trial registries and databases), the legal regime of undisclosed information and contractual arrangements are often applied to preserve the secrecy of certain datasets against undesirable disclosure [48]. This approach is often used by the pharmaceutical industry.

VII. CONTRACTUAL APPROACHES

A. Contractual Approaches

Insofar as the IP regimes for protecting the data, produced in medical research projects fail, one further method for regulating rights in data may be by contractual relations.

Such relations exist at different levels. Thus, research projects are normally conducted by educational or research institutions and the research is typically done by research associates. Usually, the researchers do their work on the materials of the institution and achievement of scientific results in dependent position belongs to their employment obligations. In such circumstances, the researcher receives remuneration for the work he does, the institution acquires the ownership and also the exploitation rights over the achieved results, provided the agreement does not foresee otherwise [9].

Students or PhD students, who produce some research results under a membership relation to the university, do not have an obligation to create scientific works and are not obliged to pass ownership in their results to the university. In this constellation, the respective student owns the results of his work. In contrast, the PhD students, who are bound to the university by employment relations and do the research by order of the university, fall under the regulation of ownership in employment, considered above. Thus, the ownership over research results, achieved by a PhD student in an employee position, would normally pass to the institution [9].

In other cases, where the researchers perform some work as freelancers or sub-contractors, the question who acquires what rights in the results of the performed work depends on the contract [49].

Secondly, at an institutional level, third party funded projects and the rights in research results are typically governed by a contract between the sponsor and relevant project partner institution(s). The sponsor is typically interested to exploit the project results and grants the funding in exchange for acquisition of the ownership and exploitation rights over the research results. This model normally does not cause problems in practice [9]. The research institutions are bound by these contractual relations and it is their obligation to procure the ownership over the research results from the personnel, whom they engage into the project, and to ensure that the rights in research results are passed to the sponsor free from third party claims.

However, some research agreements are formulated in another way. For example, an agreement may provide that research results shall be the ownership of the party "*carrying out the work generating such results*". The like provision may cause legal problems in practice. Let us consider the application of this rule in relation to the results of simulations done in a research project such as CHIC.

As we saw, in the context of that project, the simulations, which produce the data outputs, are executed by the models, developed by the modeling parties. Based on this provision, (a) the modeling parties, who developed the simulation software and (b) the clinical parties, who provided the clinical data for running the simulations may each claim rights in data outputs.

a) Modeling parties: by interpreting the above contract rule broadly, the modeling parties, who have developed the simulation software, may argue that they carried out the work generating the model, which produces the data, and shall own the rights in data, generated by the model, respectively. However, on a narrow interpretation, the modelers carried out the work generating the model, and not the data, calculated by the model, and shall own copyrights in the model code, and not in the data outputs from the model, respectively.

b) Clinical parties: may also claim rights in the results of simulations, since they provided the data, which the models used as an input to compute the data outputs. The counter-argument of the clinical parties may be that software models are used as a tool for data processing and do not give the modelers any rights in the data outputs themselves. An analogy with the use of Microsoft word for writing a PhD thesis, which does not confer on Microsoft any rights in the PhD thesis itself may support this argument.

This example shows that such contractual formulation may create legal uncertainty: first, with respect to qualifying simulation outputs as research results and, second, with respect to identifying the project party, who owns or holds the exploitation rights over such results. Unclear contractual formulations may give rise to potential legal disputes if the one or the other party would like to appropriate the data, achieved in the result of simulations for itself, and would seek to interpret the agreement in its favor.

A successful example showing how the contractual mechanism can be used to balance the rights of research participants against researchers´ rights is the case of PXE International (Pseudoxanthoma Elasticum (PXE)). PXE International is a research foundation, which represents the interests of individuals and families living with PXE, promotes and invests into PXE research [50]. When engaged into genetics research and the gene associated with the PXE disease was discovered and patented, PXE International managed to negotiate economic rights in the patent (i.e., deciding on the licensing strategy, sharing royalties, co-defining the prices) in exchange for the contribution of tissue and data that it made into the research [7] [51].

VIII. CONCLUSIONS

As we have seen, there are various ways in which the activity of curating clinical datasets could benefit from IP protection. Thus, collecting, arranging the data into a repository and making it suitable for use may render the investment, deployed in collecting and presenting the data, protectable by sui generis database rights. Similarly, the generation of research data and adoption of additional confidentiality and security measures to keep this data secret to the broader community may render such data protectable as know-how.

However, the present approach that seeks to maintain (commercial) data confidentiality by keeping data secret leads to a fragmented research environment, and reduces the chances for greater data interoperability to be achieved. Here the law - aided by technology should aim to encourage greater openness, while assuring appropriate incentives and rewards for skilled curation. This could, e.g., take the form of an officially endorsed mechanism or system for measuring and tagging changes produced in a given data set (or the merging of several data sets) resulting from curation efforts, as the reward-trigger. At the same time, as another crucial policy element, the law needs – especially in the case of the curation of sensitive health data – to ensure that privacy and other interests of patients and research subjects are and remain adequately protected.

In particular, it will here be necessary to take account of (and compensate for) the knock-on effects of IP changes, where data-holders are no longer (also) motivated by commercial considerations to keep their data secure and confidential. This concern is all the greater here since the activities of data sharing and curation being encouraged, also by their nature present enhanced risks to personal privacy. The point of curation is precisely to uncover new connections and patterns in data that help generate robust inferences (usable – for good or ill) about the relevant data subjects. Accordingly, it is submitted that any system for rewarding investment in data curation should also require (as a condition for such rewards) that the data curator takes every appropriate measure to counterbalance the associated enhanced risks to privacy.

ACKNOWLEDGMENT

The research leading to these results has received funding from the European Union Seventh Framework Programme FP7/2007-2013 under grant agreement No 600841.

REFERENCES

[1] I. Lishchuk and M. Stauch, "Options for Protecting Medical Data by IP Rights," in Proc. GLOBAL HEALTH 2016, The Fifth International Conference on Global Health Challenges, Venice, 2016, pp. 29-34.

[2] J. Eils, "Strategy of sequencing the whole genome in clinical practice," presented at The Eighth International Conference on eHealth, Telemedicine, and Social Medicine eTELEMED 2016, April 24 - 28, 2016 - Venice, Italy.

[3] A. Popel and P. Hunter, "Systems biology and physiome projects," Wiley Interdiscip. Rev. Syst. Biol. Med.1:153–58, 2009.

[4] T. Deisboeck, M. Berens, A. Kansal, S. Torquato, A. Stemmer-Rachamimov, and E. Chiocca, "Pattern of self-organization in tumour systems: complex growth dynamics in a novel brain tumour spheroid model. Cell Prolif." 34:115–34, 2001.

[5] Children's Cancer Research Fund, Types of Childhood Cancer, Nephroblastoma <http://www.childrenscancer.org/main/wilms_tumor_nephroblastoma/> 02.05.2017.

[6] CHIC Deliverable No. D2.2 Scenario based user needs and requirements <http://chic-vph.eu/uploads/media/D2-2_Scenario-based_user_needs_and_requirements.pdf> 02.05.2017.

[7] D. M. Gitter, "Informed Consent and Privacy of De-Identified Information and Estimated Data, Lessons from Iceland and the United States in an Era of Computational Genomics," (Published Conference Proceedings style), in Proc. ALLDATA 2016, The Second International Conference on Big Data, Small Data, Linked Data and Open Data (includes KESA 2016), Lissabon, 2016, pp. 7-12.

[8] Moore v. Regents of University of California, Supreme Court of California, July 9, 1990, 51 Cal. 3d 120.

[9] H.-D. Lippert, „Wem gehören Daten, die im Rahmen von Forschungsprojekten gewonnen werden?"/"To whom belongs the data generated in research projects?" in: Geistiges Eigentum: Schutzrecht oder Ausbeutungstitel?/in: Intellectual Property: Protection right or title to exploit, Springer, Volume 5, 2008, pp. 359-369.

[10] Haimo Schack, "Zur Rechtfertigung des Urheberrechts als Ausschliesslichkeitsrecht"/"On justification of copyright as exclusive right," in: Geistiges Eigentum: Schutzrecht oder Ausbeutungstitel?/in: Intellectual Property: Protection right or title to exploit, Springer, Volume 5, 2008, pp. 124-140.

[11] European Commission, "E-Health Task Force Report – Redesigning health in Europe for 2020," Luxembourg 2012, ISBN 978-92-79-23542-9

[12] C. Tenopir, et al, "Data Sharing by Scientists: Practices and Perceptions," 2001, in: PLoS ONE, Vol. 6, No. 6, S. 1-21.

[13] KE (Knowledge Exchange), "Sowing the Seed: Incentives and Motivations for Sharing Research Data," a Researcher's Perspective, 2014<www.knowledge-exchange.info/Default.aspx?ID=733> 02.05.2017.

[14] J. Ludwig, „Zusammenfassung und Interpretation/Summary and Interpretation," Publ. in: Heike Neuroth, Stefan Strathmann, Achim Oßwald, Regine Scheffel, Jens Klump, Jens Ludwig (Hg.): Langzeitarchivierung von Forschungsdaten. Eine Bestandsaufnahme. Boizenburg: Werner Hülsbusch, 2012, pp.295-310.

[15] J. Reichman and P.F. Uhlir, "A Contractually Reconstructed Research Commons for Scientific Data in a Highly Protectionist Intellectual Property Environment," 2013 <http://scholarship.law.duke.edu/cgi/viewcontent.cgi?article=1283&context=lcp> 02.05.2017.

[16] U.S. National Institutes of Health, registry and results database of publicly and privately supported clinical studies of human participants conducted around the world <www.clinicaltrials.gov> 03.05.2017.

[17] BioMed Central Ltd, ISRCTN registry: a primary clinical trial registry recognised by WHO and ICMJE that accepts all clinical research studies <www.controlled-trials.com> 03.05.2017.

[18] JAPIC Clinical Trials Information <www.clinicaltrials.jp> 03.05.2017.

[19] Directive 95/46/EC of 24 October 1995 on the protection of individuals with regard to the processing of personal data and on the free movement of such data, OJEU No L 281 /31, 23.11.95.

[20] Regulation (EU) 2016/679 of the European Parliament and of the Council of 27 April 2016 on the protection of natural persons with regard to the processing of personal data and on the free movement of such data, and repealing Directive 95/46/EC (General Data Protection Regulation), OJEU, Volume 59 4 May 2016.

[21] Article 29 Data Protection Working Party, Advice paper on special categories of data ("sensitive data"), Ref. Ares(2011)444105 - 20/04/2011.

[22] Article 29 Data Protection Working Party, Opinion 03/2013 on purpose limitation, adopted on 2 April 2013, 00569/13/EN WP 203.

[23] CHIC Deliverable No. D4.4 Whitepaper - Recommendations for an amended European legal framework on patients' and researchers' rights and duties in E-health related research.

[24] B. J. Evans, "Much Ado about Data Ownership", Harvard Journal of Law & Technology, Vol.25, Number 1 Fall 2011.

[25] CHIC, Deliverable D2-2 "Scenario based user needs and requirements", <http://chic-vph.eu/uploads/media/D2-2_Scenario-based_user_needs_and_requirements.pdf> 03.05.2017.

[26] CJEU, Judgment of 16 July 2009, Case C 5/08, Infopaq International A/S v Danske Dagblades Forening, Ref. 45.

[27] Directive 2006/116/EC on the term of protection of copyright and certain related rights (codified version), OJEU, L 372/12, 27 December 2006.

[28] CJEU, Judgment of 7 March 2013, Case C 145/10 REC, Eva-Maria Painer v. Standard VerlagsGmbH, Axel Springer AG, Süddeutsche Zeitung GmbH, Spiegel-Verlag Rudolf Augstein GmbH & Co. KG, Verlag M. DuMont Schauberg Expedition der Kölnischen Zeitung GmbH & Co. KG.

[29] H. Zech, "Information als Schutzgegenstand,“ Tübingen, 2012, ISSN: 0940-9610 (Jus Privatum).

[30] Directive 2001/29/EC of 22 May 2001 on the harmonisation of certain aspects of copyright and related rights in the information society, OJEU L 167/10 - L 167/19, 22.6.2001.

[31] H. Stenzhorn, et al, "The ObTiMA system - ontology-based managing of clinical trials," Stud Health Technol Inform. 2010;160(Pt 2):1090-4.

[32] Directive 96/9/EC of the European Parliament and of the Council of 11 March 1996 on the legal protection of databases, OJEU, L 77/20 - L 77/28, 27.3.96.

[33] J. A. Bovenberg, "Property Rights in Blood, Genes & Data: Naturally Yours?" p. 159, 2006.

[34] E. Derclaye, "The Legal Protection of Databases," pp. 92 et seq, 2008.

[35] CJEU, Case C-203/02 The British Horseracing Board Ltd and Others v William Hill Organization Ltd., para 42.

[36] European Commission, DG Internal Market and Services Working Paper – First evaluation of Directive 96/9/EC on the legal protection of databases, 2005, p. 14<http://ec.europa.eu/internal_market/copyright/docs/databases/evaluation_report_en.pdf> 03.02.2017.

[37] CJEU, Case C-338/02 Fixtures Marketing Ltd v Svenska Spel AB, para 28.

[38] Agreement on Trade-Related Aspects of Intellectual Property Rights, the TRIPS Agreement, Annex 1C of the Marrakesh Agreement Establishing the World Trade Organization, Marrakesh, Morocco, 15 April 1994.

[39] Directrive (EU) 2016/943 of 8 June 2016 on the protection of undisclosed know-how and business information (trade secrets) against their unlawful acquisition, use and disclosure, OJEU L157/1, 15.06.2016.

[40] Hogan Lovells International LLP, "Report on Trade Secrets for the European Commission – Study on Trade Secrets and Parasitic Copying (Look-alikes), MARKT/2010/20/D," 2011.

[41] K. Lodigkeit, Intellectual Property Rights in Computer Programs in the USA and Germany, Peter Lang GmbH, 2006, pp. 98-101.

[42] Computational Horizons In Cancer (CHIC): Developing Meta- and Hyper-Multiscale Models and Repositories for In Silico Oncology <http://chic-vph.eu/project/> 03.02.2017.

[43] C. Coveney, J. Gabe, and S. Williams, "The sociology of cognitive enhancement: medicalisation and beyond," Health Sociol. Rev., 20 (2011), pp. 381–393.

[44] J. Dejaegher, L. Solie, S. De Vleeschouwer, and S. W. Van Gool, "Dendritic Cell Vaccination for Glioblastoma Multiforme: Clinical Experience and Future Directions," In G. Stamatakos and D. Dionysiou (Eds): Proc. 2014 6th Int. Adv. Res. Workshop on In Silico Oncology and Cancer Investigation – The CHIC Project Workshop (IARWISOCI), Athens, Greece, Nov.3-4, 2014 (www.6thiarwisoci.iccs.ntua.gr), pp.14-18. (open-access version), ISBN: 978-618-80348-1-5.

[45] A. Abbott, "Icelandic database shelved as court judges privacy in peril," Nature, vol. 429, p. 118, May 13, 2004, doi:10.1038/429118b.

[46] NIVEL, databases and panels <https://www.nivel.nl/en/databases-and-panels> 30.05.2017.

[47] S. Gutwirth, R. Leenes, P. De Hert, „Data Protection on the Move. Current Development in ICT and Privacy/Data Protection," 2016, p.101 et seq.

[48] Joint Position on the Disclosure of Clinical Trial Information via Clinical Trial Registries and Databases <www.ifpma.org/clinicaltrials> 30.05.2017.

[49] C. Reed and J. Angel, "Computer Law: The Law and Regulation of Information Technology," 6th ed, 2007, p. 352 et seq.

[50] PXE International <https://www.pxe.org/about-pxe-international> 30.05.2017.

[51] P. Smaglik, "Tissue donors use their influence in deal over gene patent terms," NATURE, Vol. 407, 19,10, 2000, p. 821.

Tree Based Distributed Privacy in Ubiquitous Computing

Malika Yaici
Laboratoire LTII
University of Bejaia
Bejaia, 06000, Algeria
yaici_m@hotmail.com

Samia Ameza*, Ryma Houari† and Sabrina Hammachi‡
Computer Department, University of Bejaia
Bejaia, 06000, Algeria
*ameza_samia@yahoo.fr †ri.houari@hotmail.fr
‡hassiba_rima@yahoo.fr

Abstract—**Ubiquitous computing aims to integrate computer technology in man's everyday life in various fields. To improve interactivity, it offers the user the ability to access various features and services of its environment and from any mobile lightweight autonomous device while adapting them to the user's context. Cloud computing allowed ubiquitous systems to be more efficient at a more reduced cost. This accentuates security problems and particulary privacy preserving. The existing mechanisms and solutions are inadequate to address new challenges. In this paper, a new security architecture called Tree Based distributed Privacy Protection System is proposed. It supports protection of users private data and addresses the shortcomings of existing systems. Furthermore, it takes into account the domain dissociation property, in order to achieve decentralized data protection.**

Keywords–Ubiquitous Computing; Cloud computing; Security; Private Data Protection; Privacy; Integrity.

I. INTRODUCTION

The growing number of Internet users and the integration of mobile clients has changed distributed computer science, by allowing the creation of smart and communicating environments, thus offering to the user the opportunity to make interactions with its environment and its equipments easily and transparently leading to the concept of ubiquitous computing.

The importance of security and privacy in ubiquitous and pervasive systems is universally agreed. This paper is an extension of initial work in this area that was presented in [1] (UBICOMM 2016). The scope has been broadened and significant extensions has been made. In particular, we have added new material to Section III, Section V, and Section VI. Other amendments have been made throughout the paper.

The origins of ubiquitous systems date back to 1991, when Mark Weiser [2] presented his futuristic vision of the 21st century computing by establishing the foundations of pervasive computing. It aims to integrate computer technology in man's everyday life in various fields (Health, Public services, etc.). To improve interactivity, it offers the user the ability to access various features and services of his environment and from any mobile device (personal digital assistant PDA, tablet computer, smartphone, etc.).

The most important feature of pervasive computing is context awareness. The user context affects the available services as the surrounding networking environment adapts to the needs of the user. Various pieces of information are made available to the networks in order to provide a concise user experience, thus leading to privacy issues.

Cloud computing is another emerging technology that is still unclear to many security problems [3]. Cloud Computing is a model of computing, in which the users can rent infrastructure, platform or software services from other vendors without requiring the physical access to the rented service. There are three main types of cloud offerings: Infrastructure as a Service (IaaS), Platform as a Service (PaaS) and Software as a Service (SaaS).

IaaS offers virtualized instances of bare machines leaving the installation and customization of softwares including the Operating System to cloud computing customers. In PaaS, an application framework is provided to the customers for developing their software with. A SaaS provider offers a particular application as a web service, which customers can customize to their needs.

The Cloud Service Provider (CSP) focuses on infrastructure and software expertise, and aims to optimize their utility by providing centralized services for one or many clients. The benefit to the cloud service client (CSC) is that the cost associated with the underlying infrastructure and software services, needed to support the CSCs application, is reduced. In spite of the widespread adoption, organizations are still wary of storing their sensitive data with a CSP. Privacy risk remains a major concern in the cloud computing environment.

The emergence of these technologies has created new security problems, for which solutions and existing mechanisms are inadequate, especially concerning the problems of authentication and users' private data protection. In such a system, the existence of a centralized and homogeneous security policy is in fact not desirable. Centralized approaches are suitable for systems with fewer number of (web) services and limited number of client requests, since it is always prone to bottleneck delays and single point failure. It is therefore necessary to give more autonomy to security systems, mainly by providing them with mechanisms establishing dynamic and flexible cooperation and collaboration.

Privacy is one feature that must be accounted for in all systems that include human users or any kind of data pertaining to humans. This must be planned for, from the design phase, and handled in all phases of system deployment. Privacy is, however, also a difficult concept and largely a culturally dependent trait. What can be expect to keep private, and not the least, from whom do we keep information private. Nevertheless, whatever privacy level we decide on, one should ensure that it is credibly maintained [4].

The objective of our work is to develop an architecture that meets the security constraints of the ubiquitous systems that support the protection of user's private data. The idea is to consider the separation of different user data on separate domains, so that an intruder never reaches all of the user's private information and protect them against unauthorized and unwanted access and limit the transmission of such sensitive data. Even though the study has been done for ubiquitous systems, the proposed method can be applied to cloud computing as well.

The paper is organized as follows: after this introduction, some existing research works on the domain are presented in Section II (Ubiquitous environment security requirements) and Section III with a comparison between them. Then, in Section IV, the proposed system is given with an illustrative example. An improved solution based on a tree structure is presented in Section V, with some algorithms, and a comparison with the pre-cited existing solutions. A conclusion and some perspectives finish this paper.

II. Security in Ubiquitous Systems and Cloud Computing

Ubiquitous systems are mainly distributed, reactive to context, and deal with user personal data. It is therefore necessary to give more autonomy to their security systems, mainly by providing them with mechanisms through dynamic and flexible cooperation and collaboration to ensure the smooth flow of data in this system. We must develop robust protocols that ensure high confidence in the services and minimize the vulnerabilities of such systems.

A. *Ubiquitous features*

Different kinds of terms, such as ambient intelligence, ambient networking and ubiquitous computing, have been introduced to portray the visions of enhanced interaction between the users and the surrounding technology. The main features of ubiquitous environment are the user mobility and the proliferation of light devices, communicating through light and wireless infrastructure. Thus, the convergence of terrestrial infrastructure (Local Area Network LAN, fiber optic, etc.) and mobility (Global system for mobile GSM, 4G and WIFI) enables users to have access to a vast and limitless network of information and services regardless of place and time.

One vision, preached by [5], lists the following as key requirements:

- Unobtrusive hardware
- Seamless communication
- Dynamic and distributed device networks
- Natural feeling human interfaces
- Dependability and security

All these features create complex security problems. This requires the introduction of advanced authentication methods, the management and distribution of security keys between the various entities on the network, while respecting the constraints of wireless networks, such as the radio interface capacity and mobile devices, resources that represent the bottleneck of such networks.

B. *Cloud computing*

There are a variety of ways that the privacy of data can be compromised in a cloud service environment [6]. This includes the following:

1) Sharing of data with an unauthorized party: The Cloud provider could compromise the confidentiality of the data by sharing the data that it stores with unauthorized parties.
2) Corruption of data stored: The Cloud Computing providers root access to physical machines allows them to have access capacity for data modification or deletion.
3) Malicious Internal Users: The employee of a Cloud Computing Provider who has root access to these physical machines, could access the data and use it for their own advantage.
4) Data Loss or Leakage: When a virtual machine is used in an infrastructure, it poses a variety of security issues, which could lead to a compromise of the data.
5) Account or Service Hijacking: If the service is hijacked, or the computer is hacked into by an intruder, the hacker will have access to data.

Storing the data in the cloud, can increase the privacy risks for not only the cloud client (simple or organization) but also for the cloud implementers, the services providers and the data subject. Privacy Enhancing Technologies (PET) can be used by the developers of the application to enhance the individuals privacy in an application development environment. PET technologies include:

- Privacy management tools that enable inspection of server-side policies that specify the permissible accesses to data
- Secure online access mechanisms to enable individuals to check and update the accuracy of their personal data
- Anonymizer tools, which will help users from revealing their true identity by not revealing the privately identifiable information to the cloud service provider.

A state of the art of Privacy solutions in the cloud is given in [3] and [6].

C. *Security Requirements*

The main issues that must be addressed in terms of security are [7]:

1) Authentication mechanisms and credential management,
2) Authorization and access control management,
3) Shared data security and integrity,
4) Secure one-to-one and group communication,
5) Heterogeneous security/environment requirements support,
6) Secure mobility management,
7) Capability to operate in devices with low resources,
8) Automatic configuration and management of these facilities.

To guarantee the security of ubiquitous systems and the cloud, they must meet the following requirements as defined in [8]:

- Decentralization: Ubiquitous environment is designed to allow the user and all its resources to be accessible anywhere and anytime. The mobile user must have access to his attributes, and prove his identity in this environment without claiming all the time the centralized server of his organization. The security policy implementation should be as decentralized as possible. A decentralized approach is always desired whenever dealing with a consequent number of spread data and clients.
- Interoperability: The heterogeneity is a feature of ubiquitous applications. The proposed solution involves the implementation of a decentralized system for collaboration and interaction between heterogeneous organizations.
- Traceability and non-repudiation: The design of a completely secure ubiquitous system is impossible. But, the implementation of mechanisms to quickly identify threats or attacks (such as non-repudiation / tracking) provides an acceptable issue.
- Transparency: Ubiquitous computing aims to simplify the use of its resources. In ubiquitous applications and environments, the problems of authentication are more complex because of the lack of unified authentication mechanism. Several techniques have been designed to make user authentication easy and done in a transparent manner (Single Sign On).
- Flexibility: New authentication techniques have emerged such as biometrics, Radio frequency identification (RFID), etc. Thus, a security system for ubiquitous environment must be able to integrate these different means of identification and adapt authentication mechanisms to the context of the user, the capacity and the type of used devices.
- Protection of Privacy: The identity and attributes of a person are confidential information that is imperative to protect. To secure these data we must implement protocols that protect and ensure confidentiality.

III. Privacy in Ubiquitous systems

The implementation of security solutions in ubiquitous environments has many constraints, like limited capacity of batteries, device mobility and limited time response. Imposing Privacy in the cloud is still a challenge.

Mobile devices and the Internet of Things (IoT) present some problems such as incorrect location information, privacy violation, and difficulty of end-user control. A conceptual model is presented in [9], to satisfy requirements, which include a privacy-preserving location supporting protocol using wireless sensor networks for privacy-preserving childcare and safety, where the end-user has authorized credentials anonymity.

In [10], the author uses the framework of contextual integrity related to privacy, developed by Nissenbaum in 2010 [11], as a tool to understand citizen's response to the implementation of IoT related technology in a supermarket. The purpose was to identify and understand specific changes in information practices brought about by the IoT that may be perceived as privacy violations. Issues identified included the mining of medical data, invasive targeted advertising, and loss of autonomy through marketing profiles or personal affect monitoring.

Information availability is already evident in the emergence of social networking and the way people freely give out information about themselves and the people they know, providing avenues for identity theft. Thus, in the advent of ambient computing environment, user has to trust the system in order to agree to disclose information about themselves, i.e., adjust their privacy settings accordingly. However, the trust evaluation made by a person can be affected and it is not always a rational thing.

Trust is a concept that may involve and justify the disclosure of personally identifiable sensitive information. Trading privacy for trust is thus a way for balancing the subjective value of what is revealed in exchange of what is obtained. A flexible privacy-preserving mechanism trading privacy for trust-based and cost-based incentives is given in [12]. In a classical view of privacy, a user exposes (part of) personal information in order to be trusted enough to get access to the service of interest. In other words, privacy disclosure is traded for the amount of reputation that the user may need to be considered as a trustworthy partner in some kind of negotiation.

Mobile terminals are usually personal items, so privacy is to be considered when virtualization in cloud computing is used and data processed remotely. In [13], a mobile terminal virtualization framework is proposed to meet issues such as security, privacy and quality of service by encrypting data communications by the cloud server usign an asymmetric cryptography scheme.

The author of [14] presents a study of privacy implications of location-based information provision and collection on user awareness and behaviour, in the particular case when using GeoSNs (Geo-Social Networking applications). The first result is the extent of potential personal information that is derived from location information, and the second result is the need to improve users knowledge, access and visibility of their data and to be able to control and manage their location data.

Middleware is an essential layer in the architecture of ubiquitous systems, and recently, more emphasis has been put on security middleware as an enabling component for ubiquitous applications. This is due to the high levels of personal and private data sharing in these systems. In [7], some representative security middleware approaches are reviewed and their various properties, characteristics, and challenges are highlighted.

Privacy by Design concept integrates respect for users privacy into systems managing user data from the early stage. Mobile applications do not suit this concept and lack transparency, consent and security. In [15], a new permission model suitable for mobile applications is given. It is integrated into mobile operating systems; well designed, it makes a proactive privacy-respecting tool embedded in the system. The authors focus permissions on data and the action that can be carried out on this data, rather than on the technology used.

A. Literature Review

Several security systems providing protection of sensitive data have been proposed and we chose to detail some of them:

1) Hybrid Hash-based Authentication (HHA): Dhasarathan et al. [16] present an intelligent model to protect user's valuable personal data based on multi-agents. A hybrid hash-based authentication technique as an end point lock is proposed. It is a composite model coupled with an anomaly detection interface algorithm for cloud user's privacy preserving (intrusion detection, unexpected activities in normal behavior).

2) Privacy-enhanced Operating Systems (POS): In [17], the authors focus on information privacy protection in a post-release phase. Without entirely depending on the information collector, an information owner is provided with powerful means to control and audit how his/her released information will be used, by whom, and when. A set of innovative owner-controlled privacy protection and violation detection techniques have been proposed: Self-destroying File, Mutation Engine System, Automatic Receipt Collection, and Honey Token-based Privacy Violation Detection. A next generation privacy-enhanced operating system, which supports the proposed mechanisms, is introduced. Such a privacy-enhanced operating system stands for a technical breakthrough, which offers new features to existing operating systems.

3) Private Information Retrieval (PIR): This protocol allows users to learn data items stored on a server, which is not fully trusted, without disclosing to the server the particular data element retrieved. In [18], the author investigates the amount of data disclosed by the the most prominent PIR protocols during a single run. From this investigation, mechanisms that limit the PIR disclosure to a single data item are devised.

4) Private Set Intersection (PSI): Efficiency and scalability become critical criteria for privacy preserving protocols in the age of Big Data. In [19], a new Private Set Intersection protocol, based on a novel approach called oblivious Bloom intersection is presented. The PSI problem consists of two parties, a client and a server, which want to jointly compute the intersection of their private input sets in a manner that at the end the client learns the intersection and the server learns nothing. The proposed protocol uses a two-party computation approach, which makes use of a new variant of Bloom filters called by the author Garbled Bloom filters, and the new approach is referred to as Oblivious Bloom Intersection.

5) Differential Privacy: Releasing sensitive data while preserving privacy is a problem that has attracted considerable attention in recent years. One existing solution for addressing the problem is differential privacy, which requires that the data released reveals little information about whether any particular individual is present or absent from the data. To fulfill such a requirement, a typical approach adopted by the existing solutions is to publish a noisy version of the data instead of the original one. The author of [20] considers a fundamental problem that is frequently encountered in differentially private data publishing: Given a set D of tuples defined over a domain Ω, the aim is to decompose Ω into a set S of sub-domains and publish a noisy count of the tuples contained in each sub-domain, such that S and the noisy counts approximate the tuple distribution in D as accurately as possible. To remedy the deficiency of existing solutions, the author presents PrivTree, a histogram construction algorithm that adopts hierarchical decomposition but completely eliminates the dependency on a predefined limit h on the recursion depth in the splitting of Ω.

6) Paillier scheme: Nowadays, biometric data are more and more used within authentication processes. Such data are usually stored in databases and underlie inherent privacy concerns. Therefore, special attention should be paid to their handling. The most currently available biometric systems lack sufficient privacy protection. The authors of [21] propose a privacy preserving similarity verification system based on the Paillier scheme. This scheme, being an asymmetric as well as additive homomorphic cryptography approach, enables signal processing in the encrypted domain operations. They also introduce a padding approach to increase entropy for better filling the co-domain, combine the benefits of signal processing in the encrypted domain with the advantages of salting. The concept of verification of encrypted biometric data comes at the cost of increased computational effort. The proposed scheme in [21] lowers the error rates and reduces the amount of data disclosed in an authentication attempt using a privacy-preserving biometric authentication scheme.

7) Pseudonymization: Pseudonymization as a data privacy concept is not new and in general it is about who creates the pseudonyms, who has access to them and who has access to data. In [22], the author presents a unified view on pseudonyms and an in-house pseudonymization solution. A pseudonym is a local identifier with no relation with the demographics of a person. Persistent identifiers are introduced to maintain the updates and internal matching considerations. Then an algorithm, to create a pseudonym from a person identifiers, is given, with a national pseudonymization service to resist update problems and wrong matching decisions.

8) Chaavi: A privacy preserving architecture as a solution for webmail systems is given in [6], in which users can retain their mail in the servers of their service providers in a cloud, without compromising functionality (searchability of mails) or privacy. The authors proposed *Chaavi*, a webmail infrastructure, based on the public/private key model, to encrypt email with a custom implementation of encrypted indices for keyword searches, using the servers infrastructure. Chaavi consists of the following components:

- A browser: The browser is responsible for rendering the pages created by the web application.
- Browser extensions: They are used to encrypt the secure message sent to the server, to decrypt the messages that are sent from the server and, additionally, they have key generation and key management functionality.
- A Web application: The webmail application provides graphical user interfaces for the users to read, send and search messages.
- A data base: This database is looked up when the user performs a keyword search.

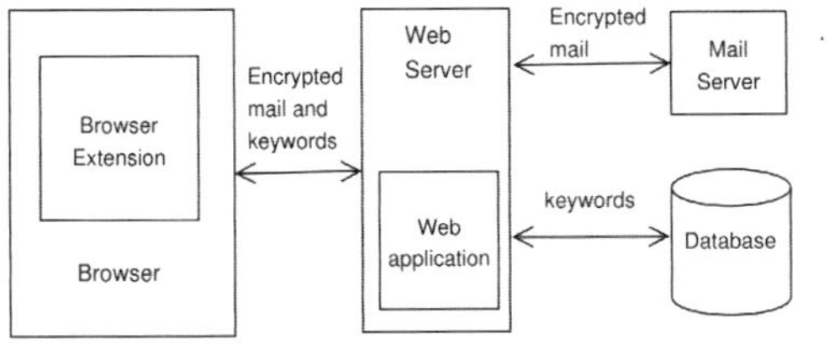

Figure 1: Chaavi - Architecture [6].

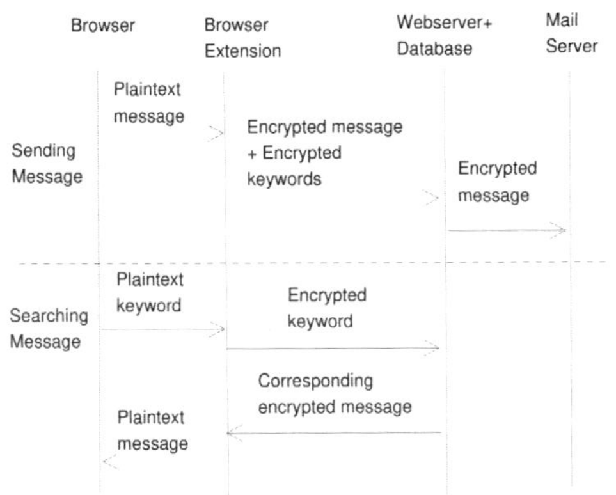

Figure 2: Sending and Searching for a Message in Chaavi [6].

- A mail server: The mail server sends and receives email communicated to it through the Internet.

Figure 1 gives the overall architecture of the system.

When a user sends a message from the web application (Figure 2), the Encryption module encrypts the message and extracts and encrypts the keywords. The web application sends the encrypted message and keywords to the web server. On receiving the encrypted message and the keywords, at the server-side, the application saves the encrypted message alongside with the encrypted keywords in a database for future retrieval. The application then transfers the mail to the Mail Server (SMTP server) to be be delivered to recipient.

9) TREMA: Trust of a peer is based on its prior transactions with other peers. The main challenge is how to collect and distribute reputation scores of peers efficiently. TREMA [23] is a tree-based reputation management solution where nodes are organized at different positions in a tree, based on their reputation, with peers of higher reputation at higher levels. A peer always trusts his ancestors while he is answerable for his descendants. When two peers execute a transaction, a trust route is formed between them. If the transaction succeeds a reward is given to all nodes in the route, but if the transaction fails all the nodes in the route are penalized. If a child becomes trustee than his parent, a swap of their positions is done. One inconvenient in using a tree structure is the possibility to obtain a weakly connected tree, which may cause a partition. the authors proposed adding extra-links. The implementation proposed is based on the following APIs:

- NodeFind: finding and connecting a new node to an existing one in the system.
- NodeJoin: a new node that wishes to join the network, NodeFind must be executed first then a message "JOIN" is sent to the contact node. If the contact node is not the correct one, it forwards the message to the nodes in its subtree. This opertaion may take $O(logn)$ steps.
- NodeLeave: If a node wishes to leave the network, then the system will establish new tree links and close old ones.
- NodeFailureDiscovery: In case a node discovers one of its neighbors is not responding, then the node will be considered as a "leave node" and NodeLeave will be called.

10)iPrivacy: Users wish to preserve full control over their sensitive data and cannot accept that is accessible by the service provider. Previous research was made on techniques to protect data stored on un-trusted servers. An approach where confidential data is stored in a highly distributed data base, partly located on the cloud and partly on the clients, is given in [24]. To ensure data protection three major techniques on managing sensitive data exist:

- Data encryption
- Data fragmentation and encryption
- Data fragmentation with owner involvement.

These approaches suppose that the data is stored uniquely on cloud servers. The author of [24], proposes that the user gets a copy of data and a local agent maintains authorized data replicated and accessed by other authorized users in the cloud. The solution consists of two parts: a trusted client and a remote untrusted synchronizer (see Figure 3). The client maintains local data storage where:

- The files that she owns are (or at least can be) stored as plain-text;
- The others, instead, are encrypted each with a different key.

The Synchronizer stores the keys to decrypt the shared dossiers owned by the local client and the modified dossiers to synchronize. When another client needs to decrypt a dossier, she connects to the Synchronizer and obtains the corresponding decryption key. The data and the keys are stored in two separate entities, none of which can access information without the collaboration of the other part.

B. Synthesis

The different approaches have been evaluated based on the requirements of ubiquitous computing security (see Table I where ✓ stands for requirement guaranteed by the method, X otherwise, and – means that the requirement is not relevant).

- Hybrid Hash-based Authentication: The solution is based on multi-agents in cloud environment so decentralization and interoperability is evident. Transparency and Flexibility are not guaranteed because

TABLE I: COMPARISON BETWEEN EXISTING PRIVACY SOLUTIONS.

	Decentralization	Inter-operability	Traceability	Autonomy	Flexibility	Privacy
HAA	✓	✓	–	X	X	X
POS	✓	–	✓	X	X	X
PIR	–	–	–	X	X	✓
PSI	✓	✓	–	X	X	✓
Differential Privacy	✓	–	–	–	X	✓
Pallier Scheme	X	X	✓	X	X	✓
Pseudonymisation	✓	✓	✓	X	X	X
Chaavi	X	X	✓	X	X	X
TREMA	✓	✓	✓	X	X	X
iPrivacy	✓	X	✓	X	X	✓

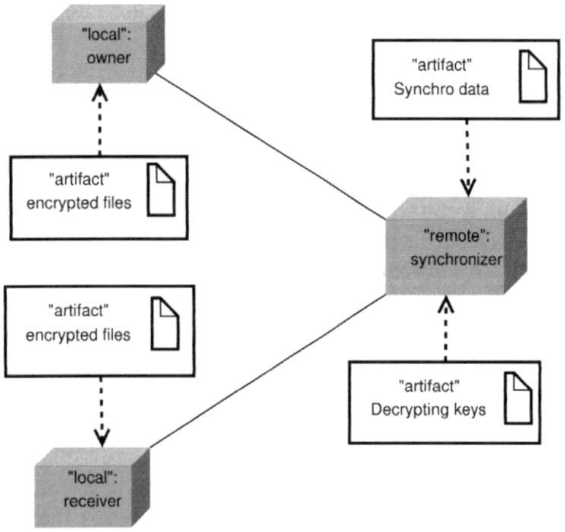

Figure 3: Proposed data management in iPrivacy [24].

the solution is an end-point solution and computations are needed. So we considered that privacy is not guaranteed because intrusion is always possible.

- Privacy-enhanced Operating Systems: The proposed Operating System offers decentralization and inter-operability because it is an OS. But no autonomy or flexibility is offered because the user executes the privacy protection mechanisms. We deduce that privacy is not guaranteed because it is a post-release solution.
- Private Information Retrieval: In this case we cannot talk about interoperability, traceability, or decentralization. But the protocol is not transparent or flexible because the client system takes part in the computations but in the same time this guarantees privacy, because only one item is treated in PIR.
- Private Set Intersection: The protocol treats the case of big data (cloud) so many servers are considered (decentralization and interoperability). Like for PIR protocol, the client takes part in the computations, so it is not transparent or flexible. Privacy is supposed guaranteed.
- Differential Privacy: It deals with data decomposition so decentralization is possible, but the proposed system is not a protocol so interoperability, traceability, or autonomy cannot be evaluated. Because the computations are complex, flexibility is not considered, but this guarantees privacy.
- Pallier scheme: Dealing with biometric authentication mechanism means centralization and homogeneity. The proposed solution is complex, which makes it not flexible but privacy is assured.
- Pseudonymization: Multiple virtual identities means a decentralized supposed inter-operable system. The pseudos are generated by the client application, which makes it not autonomous and non flexible. Traceability is a requirement, for matching considerations, but this also makes privacy not guaranteed.
- Chaavi: It consists of a homogeneous webmail infrastructure with a centralized mail server. The contribution is in the encryption module added to the client browser, which makes it non flexible. Of course, traceability is guaranteed, but not privacy because it is based on a simple messages encryption approach.
- TREMA: The solution is proposed for a Peer to Peer (P2P) system organized as a tree, this implies decentralization and inter-operability. It is based on trust relation between the nodes, so traceability is also supposed. But the trust management and the possible change of position in the tree, makes it not flexible and lacks autonomy. We supposed that privacy is not guaranteed because it is a trade-off between trust and privacy.
- iPrivacy: The system supposes a highly distributed database, which means decentralization but no inter-operability. This database is partly located on the cloud and partly on the client, which means no flexibility and no autonomy. Privacy and traceability are of course guaranteed because of the structure of a database.

IV. PROPOSITION OF A NEW MANAGEMENT SYSTEM OF PRIVATE DATA

A. *Problem Positioning*

The development of Web services, the vast heterogeneity of the connection techniques and conditions of communication (including bandwidth), the proliferation of mobile devices, and the heterogeneity of protocols and their deployment in mobile and ubiquitous computing increase significantly the risks related to the protection of user's privacy. Implemented security policies impose protocols that enable the conservation and management of personal data, and limit their transmissions from mobile devices as well as their movement within the network. This is a good approach to avoid some attacks like sniffing.

The security solutions presented previously are typically based on backing up data on a single server. The private data of the user are stored on a single server, the invocation (request) to a secure service by a user, will acquire its data from the server after an authentication procedure. However, these solutions suffer from two deficiencies: the first is the inability to access the data without a reliable connection, secure, permanent and fast server, a set of conditions difficult to meet in any environment. The second is the centralization of data on a single server, which represents a vulnerability because if the server is compromised the entire system will be.

As part of our project, we will mainly deal with the following two issues:

- How to protect private data of the mobile user in a transparent way, easily and without being intrusive?
- How to decentralize the data and the user's personal information in a fast and secure manner?

B. *The Proposed Architecture*

To satisfy ubiquitous environmental security requirements such as decentralization, flexibility and protection of private data, we opted for a hierarchical architecture. The principle of this solution is the distribution of the user data on a set of servers so that each of them contains only the information needed for user authentication, and the servers (nodes) are distributed randomly over a virtual structure. This data is scattered in the system as follows:

- Personal data is not on a single server, but on multiple different servers.
- No server owns the totality of a particular client personal data.

The entities involved in this architecture are as follows:

- The user: a human being (client), who is the consumer of the service.
- Generator of identifier (GenID): a node that is responsible for generating a unique identifier for users during their registration in the system.
- Domains: A domain represents a business, a service provider (music, videos, bank, etc.).

The architecture is based on the following hypothesis:

- The architecture is ephemeral and only the request message and the transmission of personal information uses the links.
- No node knows the entire structure.
- A node knows only its successors and its predecessor.
- A pre-authentication of the domains of the environment is performed using a third party authentication.
- Each user has at least one certificate (issued by his domain of affiliation) and can acquire others in other domains.

Each user has a universal identifier, distributed among all domains at its first registration in the system, which allows gathering its data. Some user data can be replicated on some servers, but each of them stores the personal information necessary to it and the additional information obtained from other nodes are deleted.

C. *Illustrative Example*

Suppose Alice has an identity certificate containing her name, photograph, date of birth, address, Social Security number, fingerprint, account number, her public key and her profession.

Alice's complete identity certificate → {
Alice
Professor
Birth date
Security ID
Photo
Fingerprint
Public key
Address
Bank account ID
}

If she wants to rent a car, Alice must present a document (certificate) confirming the user name and some personal information such as her photo and address. However, the same document may contain other information that Alice does not wish to divulge, such as age or job.

Car rental→ {
Alice
~~Professor~~
~~Birth date~~
~~Security ID~~
Photo
~~Fingerprint~~
~~Public key~~
Address
~~Bank account ID~~
}

This case is not unique. During a consultation with a doctor, Alice must be able to present a document showing only the name, date of birth and social security number. This illustrates the need for mechanisms for the decentralization of personal information in order to protect the private data of users.

Doctor→ {
Alice
Birth date
Security ID
Photo
}

$$\text{Bank} \rightarrow \begin{cases} \text{Alice} \\ \text{Professor} \\ \text{Fingerprint} \\ \text{Bank account ID} \end{cases}$$

D. The Broadcast Distributed Privacy Protection System Architecture

To achieve decentralization of private data, we proposed a distributed architecture named Broadcast distributed privacy protection system (BDPPS) based on the decentralization of private data, so a hierarchical architecture is needed. To reflect structural relationships and hierarchies, we used a binary tree. The advantages of binary trees are well known: flexibility, easy construction and management (searching, insertion), etc.

Fragmentation and distribution of sensitive data has always been the best solution to protect these data (with encryption) in any domain. In [25], a multi-dimensional binary search tree is adopted to adapt geometrical constraints, thus reducing amount of computations in trying to improve the data-mining k-means algorithm for cluster analysis. A binary partition tree is used in [26] as a region-based to process multi-dimensional Synthetic Aperture Radar (SAR) data. In [27], an m-branch tree ($m > 3$) is preferred than binary or ternary trees, to implement a scalable authenticated dynamic group key exchange protocol.

The basics of this architecture are as follows:

- Private user data is distributed on a set of servers so that each one contains only the information necessary for its operation.
- The domains are distributed over the nodes of the tree in a random manner.
- If a domain needs the private data of a user who depends on another domain, a search request will be broadcasted on all system nodes.
- Upon receipt of the response, there is a deadline for the additional data to be deleted.

The major drawback of this architecture is the large number of requests sent through the tree when searching private information. To remedy this problem we decided to improve this proposal, based on how to divide the domains in the system.

V. IMPROVED SOLUTION

To minimize the number of messages circulating in the tree and increase the quality of service, we proposed an improved architecture named Tree Based distributed privacy protection system (TBDPPS). The idea is to increase the probability of finding the sought data by "parallel" depth-first traversal of the tree, and to arrange these data in a complementary manner between two close nodes (servers).

The organization of services is done in a manner allowing the users data to be structured in a complementary and easy way. The sent request follows a tree structure in depth in order to increase the probability of finding the searched data. If a server needs more information, instead of asking the user, it retrieves them from the nearest server in the tree. Each node server is supposed to receive a request from a parent node or a child node for some specific information that it has but they do not.

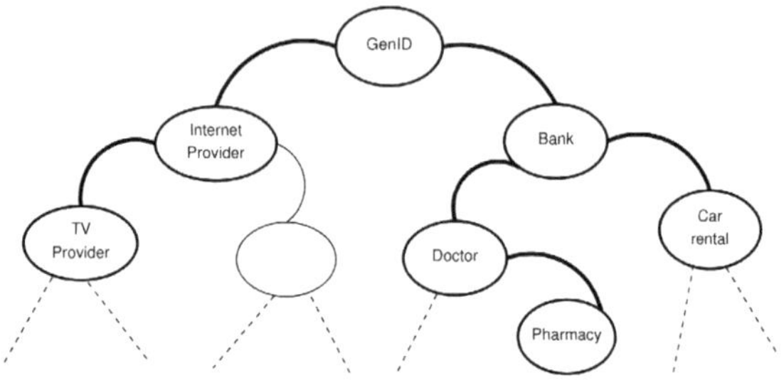

Figure 4: The tree broadcast distributed privacy protection system principle.

For example, a service that has an activity like downloading videos, music, etc., it would be better to have the bank node as a closest neighbour, in order to complete the transaction process as quickly as possible (Figure 4).

This distribution of domains offers various advantages:

- Message number Reduction flowing in the tree.
- Increase in the quality of service.
- Simplicity and ease of personal data management.

A. Example

Following the previous example, by using her PDA, Alice was authenticated with a car rental service to rent a car. According to the proposed architecture, it is the car rental server that will retrieve data about the payment (account Identifier).

The server prepares a query that contains the necessary parameters such as domain code, the user ID and the needed data (Bank account ID), and then sends them to his child nodes on the tree. The latter seeks the ID of the user and the account number, if they have the desired data they send the response request containing the necessary information, if not they send the request to their child nodes and so on. If no child node exist then the request is sent to its parent node. The car rental service node and the bank node belong to the same subtree, as shown in Figure 4.

B. Decentralized system structure

The system consists of a set of nodes, which are distributed in a decentralized manner; each node in the system does not have a global knowledge about other nodes except direct neighbours. A tree structure is good for storing and retrieving data.

Definition 1: The decentralized system can be formalized as $T = \{N, L\}$, such that $N = \{n_1, n_2, ..n_m\}$ represents the list of nodes in the network, n_i represents the ith node in the system and m is the total number of nodes, and $L =$

$\{n_i, n_j\}, (1 \leq i \leq m$ and $1 \leq j \leq m$ where $i \neq j)$ is a set of links between different nodes in the system.

Definition 2: Each node n_i in the set N can be formalized as a tuple of $\{S_i, Ln_i, Rn_i\}$ where:

- S_i is the list of services in the ith node
- Ln_i is the node connected to n_i on the left
- Rn_i is the node connected to n_i on the right.

Remark: The GenID node (root) is a particular node and maintains another parameter Ds, a set of all nodes data descriptions Ds_i, which contains the data categories of each node.

The following definition sets the parameters needed to construct the virtual tree based on the user's personal data placed on each node and their level of importance.

Definition3: $D_i = \{d_1, d_2, ...d_k\}$ is a list of user's information affiliated to ith node, for each data, a sensitivity level s_i is associated.

C. Community construction

Each node that is part of the system is considered as an entry point. Each node n_i is connected, at least, to one node n_j that is already present in the system. The establishment of connection between both n_i and n_j is based on the intersection of the sets of sensitive data (same level) needed by both nodes.

The GenID node is created first with the implementation for the system, then each new domain is added to the tree through the root at the request of the service. Joining or leaving the tree will be done by executing the following APIs:

-FindPosition: Finding a node to connect a new one. The best node position will depend on the number of common sensitive items needed by the new node with the existing node. For example, node Pharmacy have much more common items with node Doctor rather than Bank node. Let a new node has Ds_{new} as a data description set of its sensitive data, then the best node to which to connect the new node is the node n_i with Ds_i such that $Ds_i \bigcap Ds_{new}$ is the largest and Ln_i or Rn_i is null. If many nodes satisfy this equation then the node, which will generate a less set of transformations of the tree, will be chosen.

-JoinTree: When a new node wants to join the system, a request is sent to GenID (root), which will execute FindNode to find the best position, then the joining operation is executed (updating tree links).

-LeaveTree: When a node wants to leave the system, a request is sent to the root, and the leaving operation is executed. A node leaves the system if the business or service associated to the domain/node exits no more for example. This operation is critical because some needed data items shared with other nodes may disappear.

- NodeFailure: When a node detects a failed node (non-responding) it sends a request to the GenID node, which will execute the leaving process.

If the tree is skewed and unbalanced the search cost may increase. In a weakly connected tree structure partitions may appear, so extra-links, with non-affected nodes, may be added to reserve places for eventual servers joining the tree.

D. Algorithms

In the following section, the different algorithms executed by the tree's nodes when receiving user's requests are described and they use the following defined variables:

`codD`: The domain code, which sends the research request.

`reqID` : Request identifier.

`userID` : User identifier.

`privateData` : The set of private data belonging to a domain.

`Ldata` : The set of needed data to satisfy the user's request.

`data` : The set of data conveyed by requests/responses.

`found` : A Boolean variable (initially `FALSE`).

1) User registration: When a user submits a registration request to a domain in the system for the first time, this domain sends a request to the GenID node. This node first verifies the validity of the request (a real new user), if it is valid it generates a unique identifier (a numeric or alphanumeric string), then broadcasts it on the tree. The registration of the new user on the requested service domain will concern only the partial needed private data. If the user is known to GenID but not to the domain, thus a new domain, then it will be registered in this domain with the partially needed private data.

The algorithm implemented on the GenID node is given in Algorithm 1.

Algorithm 1 User registration

Require: Request by a new user
Ensure: User identifier `userID`.

```
if new user then
    if current node code = GenID code then
        generate a userID to user
    end if
    save userID
    send(codD, reqID, userID) to child nodes.
else
    register user to domain
end if
```

A user request for a service in a domain will, eventually, lead to its registration in other domains (if not already done), if the fulfillment of the service requires other data associated to these other domains.

2) Service request: When a user requests a service to a domain the latter searches its database to retrieve the user's private data. If there is a lack of information necessary for a proper operation of the service, the server propagates a request containing some parameters in its sub-tree to find the missing data simultaneously through both right and left child nodes. If the answer obtained from its sub-tree is negative then the request will be sent to the parent node.

The search stops when the initiator domain has recovered all the necessary data, or has received the request sent by a node (child for the root node or parent for other domain) and the variable found is false. The main steps are as follows:

Step1: The user submits a service request to a domain as given in Algorithm 2.

Algorithm 2 Service request Algorithm

```
Require: Request by a user affiliated to domain(Ldata)
Ensure: Satisfaction of a service
if Ldata ⊂ privateData then
    service satisfied
else
    send(codD, reqID, userID, Ldata, found) to
    child nodes
end if
```

Step2: The receipt of the request by another domain: Upon receipt of this request, the domain checks if the user ID and data exists, if yes it will formulate a response containing the found data (`private data'` is a part of `private data`) and sends to the issuer (`codD` of the request), otherwise it sends the request to his child nodes, if they exist, or to its parent node. The result is given in Algorithm 3.

Algorithm 3 Request reception Algorithm

```
Require: Request(codD, reqID, userID, data, found)
Ensure: Collect missing private data
if (userID ∈ domain) && (data ⊂ privateData)
then
    found ← TRUE
    data←privateData'
    send(codD, reqID, userID, data, found) to
    codD node
else
    if ∃ child nodes then
        send(codD, reqID, userID, data, found) to
        child node
    else
        send(codD, reqID, userID, data, found) to
        parent node
    end if
end if
```

The statement `data←privateData'` concerns only the wanted data from the set `privateData`.

Step3: The receipt of the request by the issuer: Upon receipt of the request, the issuer verifies the boolean variable `found` if it is true. Then it compares the data received with the data sought and if all the data are found then the service is executed, otherwise the issuer will make another request by omitting all the found data and sending it to another child if it exists or to the parent to explore another sub-tree. The service is unsatisfied when the issuer receives the request by one of its neighbors (child for the root and parent for other nodes) and the variable `found` is `FALSE`. The term "`card`" stands for the cardinal of a set. Algorithm 4 illustrates this step.

The statement `data ← Ldata-data` concerns the case when `data` contains more than one item, so the found items are retrieved from the set `data` to continue the search for the rest of items.

Algorithm 4 Issuer request reception Algorithm

```
Require: Request(codD, reqID, userID, data, found)
Ensure: Satisfaction of a service.
if found=TRUE then
    if card(Ldata) = card(data) then
        Service satisfied
    else
        data ← Ldata-data
        send(codD, reqID, userID, data, found) to
        child node
    end if
else
    if parent node not visited then
        send(codD, reqID, userID, data, found) to
        parent node
    else
        Service not satisfied
    end if
end if
```

If a service is satisfied the `Ldata` is deleted after a fixed delay, which is the time needed for the service to be satisfied. Each transmitted sensitive data d_i will be accompanied with a time to live (TTL) depending on its sensitivity level s_i.

If all the links of the tree exist, then all the needed data exist on the tree and it will be found. In this case, the searching time will be, at maximum, the time of parallel browsing of the tree (height size).

A service cannot be satisfied if the needed data is not found, and this is possible only if the concerned server node (which has the data) or the links are down. In this case, a request is repeated after a random delay.

VI. VALIDATION

We have proposed a solution that solves the problem of data privacy for mobile users. Our proposal is to define a new architecture that takes into account the separation of different domains in the system and corresponds to a tree. The user's personal data are distributed across a set of servers so that none will ever have all the user's private data except those required for its operation.

A. Simulation results

Figures 5 and 6 show the results of a small simulation (using Matlab) of the time response and the number of visited nodes of the proposed method depending on the size of tree and the number of missing items in the data. The time response depends on the number of visited nodes, which depends on the tree height ($log(m)$) and, even if the number of missing items increases, the parallel parsing of the tree is done at maximum once.

B. Synthesis

The proposed method is also evaluated based on the requirements of ubiquitous computing security as defined in Section II.C:

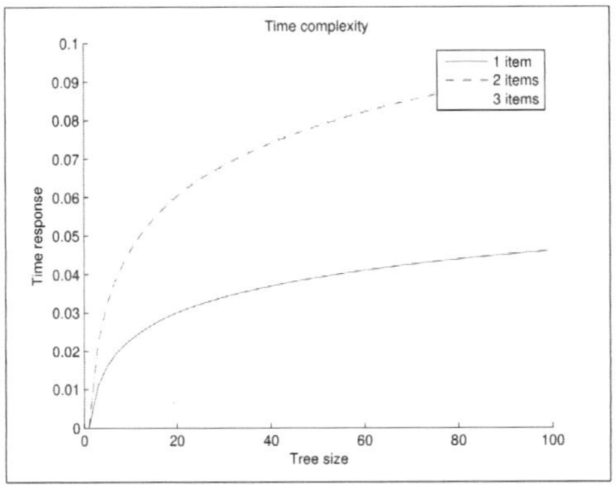

Figure 5: Time response for a single request.

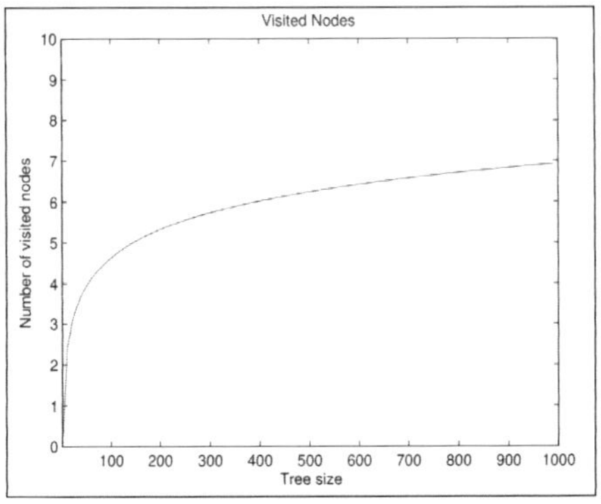

Figure 6: Number of visited nodes.

- Decentralization: In the proposed system, the different domains making up the ubiquitous environment do not share user's private data. Each domain maintains a subset of the user's necessary data.
- Interoperability: The collaboration between the nodes of the system is done to allow a collection of different private data that a domain needs. Each system node can communicate with other remote nodes across his neighbors, by sending the different requests.
- Transparency: The TBDPPS system reduces the interaction of the user during the authentication process and service request. Indeed, a user authenticates first to a service then can acquire other services in an easy and intuitive way, because it is the first server that will retrieve the rest of the user's private data.
- Traceability: Transactions in our system are made via certificates that guarantee non-repudiation of users (certificates owners) in order to identify any performed transactions.
- Flexibility: The system TBDPPS offers the user the possibility to be authenticated regardless of the capacity of the use device and the different identification methods.
- Privacy protection: Taking into account the separation of the different data on separate domains of the system, so that an intruder cannot have the totality of the user's private information, thus protecting these data against unwanted disclosure, the proposed architecture allows the protection of users private data and overcomes the problems of their storage on a vulnerable single server.
- Data distribution: The propositions given in [19] and [20] deal with distributed private data but the client is an actor, so transparency is not verified. For the latter, it even preconizes a tree architecture but noisy information are included. In our proposition only the private data is distributed, which means less data transmission.
- Autonomy: The proposed system operates without the client intervention. So a hacker cannot get a user's private data. Attacks like sniffing cannot succeed because only some of private data is circulating on the network. Finally, the only dangerous attack is a non-trusted or corrupted server (node), but we supposed that all the domains are authenticated using a trusted third-party protocol.
- Number of messages: Only one type of message will be used. A request is used to collect the missing private data, and the same request is used to send the response to the request issuer.
- Algorithmic complexity: the complexity of the proposed method is given depending on the type of trees (from the best to the worst), and on each situation.

Type of binary tree	Complexity
Complete tree	$O(\log m)$
Full tree	$O(\log m)$
One-branch tree	$O(m)$

Situation	Complexity
Registration	$O(\log m)$
Full private data present	$O(1)$
One missing item	$O(2 * \log m)$
More than one missing	$O(2 * \log m)$

The variable m is the number of domains/nodes in the system/tree.

C. *Threat analysis*

Threat analysis is an important part in security engineering and it forms the basis for the security design of a system. In our threat analysis, we consider following information items to be of special sensitivity: user identity, user contact information, and user bank information.

The main goal for attacks, which we assume in our analysis, is to obtain private information about the user. The threats are considered to be related to illegal combining of user records in different parts of the system, or to the threats introduced by direct external eavesdropping and active intrusion into system

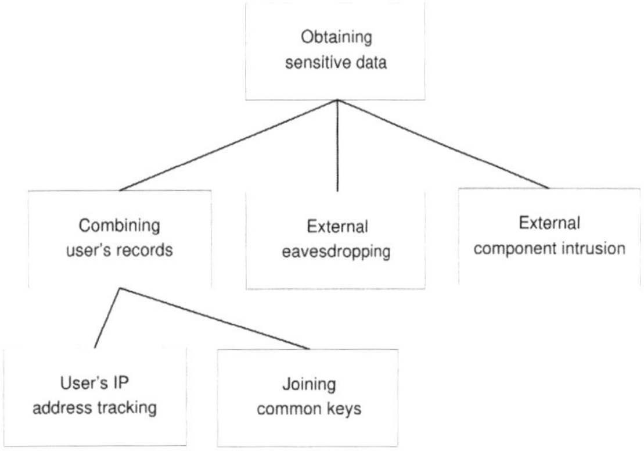

Figure 7: Attacks tree.

components. The attack tree used in our analysis is shown in Figure 7 [28].

The solutions to the different attacks are present in the proposed distributed solution.

- In some cases the IP address may be linkable to a specific device. The private data (not all) is transmitted from the user to a server only once during registration. Then the other transmissions are done between trusted encrypted communicating servers. That's why the second attack "Joining common keys" is also not present. A commonly used method to protect against the threat "user IP tracking" is the use of an anonymities proxy if needed.
- Distributing the user information in the system decreases the impact and the risk of the threat "combining user's records". The distribution may decrease the client privacy concerns, as no one in the system has information about users files, real identity and credit card information.
- As all communications between the user's device and the system and between the different servers of the system are supposed protected using encryption for example, then the probability of successful eavesdropping attacks is very low. The eavesdropping will not impact user's privacy perceptions so much, that it would have a negative impact on the adoption of the proposed solution.
- To avoid intrusion, each user is identified once and affiliated to the first domain (service) requested. This operation is supposed associated with guarantees as for a classical registry in a bank for example. So any intruder will be at least detected by the supposed affiliated domain.

VII. Conclusion

Ubiquitous environment allows performing the appropriate actions to the user while adapting to environmental conditions, preferences and user profile. Building such an environment is very difficult, given the user's everyday environments composed of heterogeneous devices, leading to a dynamic system.

The proposed solution considers a distribution of user's personal data on a set of servers (domains/nodes) linked in a binary tree-based virtual architecture. Examples of such tree are given, and algorithms implementing the registration of a new user and the propagation of a request and its response are proposed.

The proposed method overcomes the aforementioned deficiency, and takes into account decentralization and the method of domain dissociation to make communication easy and flexible. The number of domains is limited so the tree size is limited and, since it is a binary tree, its construction will be easier. The proposed approach is applicable to ubiquitous systems, but also to cloud computing. Indeed, the different cloud service providers are the domains/nodes of the tree and a user is the cloud service consumer. The communications between the servers are supposed encrypted.

Solutions for the recognized privacy threats leads to some complex security implementations, and a tradeoff between the two is advised, because if users find the system too complex to use, they might find it hard to trust and not adopting it. Distributed solution may require more privacy statements, service agreements, and other legal documents. Searching separated data means more complicated data storage system and data structures in the research analysis.

A dynamic construction of the virtual tree is preconized. Only the one-to-one links of the tree are to be built by identifying the parent-child link. This may be done at the first user's request by the Generator of identifiers node. To achieve this a method for domains dissociation in the system based on private data located in each node is proposed. The established communications at the request will be deleted after to obtain a virtual or ephemeral tree.

As future work, it would be interesting to consider a virtual identifier to guarantee confidentiality. Hiding user's identity, by protecting his personally identified information (PII) thus assuring confidentiality, is the first step to guarantee privacy. This approach is our current research work.

References

[1] M. Yaici, S. Ameza, R. Houari, and S. Hammachi, "Private data protection in ubiquitous computing ," in Proceedings of the 10th IARIA Conference on Mobile Ubiquitous Computing Systems, Services and Technology (UBICOMM), October 9-13, 2016, Venice, Italy. pp. 1–8, ISBN: 978-1-61208-065-9.

[2] M. Weiser, "The computer for the 21st century," Scientific American, Vol. 265, 1991, pp. 94–104, ISSN: 0036-8733.

[3] S. N. Kumar and A. Vajpayee, "A Survey on Secure Cloud: Security and Privacy in Cloud Computing," American Journal of Systems and Software, Vol. 4, No. 1, 2016, pp. 14–26, ISSN:1942-2636.

[4] G. H. Køien, "Reflections on Evolving Large-Scale Security Architectures," International Journal on Advances in Security, Vol. 8, No. 1 / 2, 2015, pp. 60–78, ISSN:1942-2636.

[5] K. Ducatel, M. Bogdanowicz, F. Scapolo, J. Leijten, and J-C. Burgelman, "Scenarios for ambient intelligence in 2010," ISTAG report, European Commission, 2001. https://cordis.europa.eu/pub/ist/docs/istagscenarios2010.pdf (last access 06/05/2017).

[6] K. Ramachandran, H. Lutfiyya, and M. Perry, "A Privacy Preserving Solution for Webmail Systems with Searchable Encryption," International Journal on Advances in Security, Vol. 5, No. 1 / 2, 2012, pp. 36–45, ISSN:1942-2636.

[7] J. Al-Jaroodi, I. Jawhar, A. Al-Dhaheri, F. Al-Abdouli, and N. Mohamed, "Security middleware approaches and issues for ubiquitous applications," Computers and Mathematics with Applications, Vol. 60, 2010, pp. 187–197, ISSN: 0898-1221.

[8] R. Saadi, The chameleon : A security system for nomadic users in collaborative and pervasive environments. PhD Thesis, Institut National des Sciences Appliques de Lyon, France, Jun. 2009.

[9] J. Kim, K. Kim, J. Park, and T. Shon, "A scalable and privacy-preserving child-care and safety service in a ubiquitous computing environment," Mathematical and Computer Modelling, Vol. 55, 2012, pp. 45-57, ISSN: 0895-7177.

[10] J. S. Winter, "Surveillance in ubiquitous network societies: normative conflicts related to the consumer in-store supermarket experience in the context of the Internet of Things," Ethics and Information Technology, Vol. 16, March 2014, pp. 27-41, ISSN: 1572-8439.

[11] H. Nissenbaum, Privacy in context: technology, policy, and the integrity of social life. Stanford University Press, Stanford, 2010, ISBN: 0804752370.

[12] A. Aldini, "A Framework Balancing Privacy and Cooperation Incentives in User-Centric Networks," International Journal on Advances in Security, Vol. 8, No. 1 / 2, 2015, pp. 16–27, ISSN:1942-2636.

[13] T. Zheng and S. Dong, "Terminal Virtualization Framework for Mobile Services," International Journal on Advances in Security, Vol. 8, No. 3 / 4, 2015, pp. 109–119, ISSN:1942-2636.

[14] F. S. Alrayes and A. I. Abdelmoty, "No Place to Hide: A Study of Privacy Concerns due to Location Sharing on Geo-Social Networks," International Journal on Advances in Security, Vol. 7, No. 3 / 4, 2014, pp. 62–75, ISSN:1942-2636.

[15] K. Sokolova, M. Lemercier, and J.-B. Boisseau, "Respecting user privacy in mobiles: privacy by design permission system for mobile applications," International Journal on Advances in Security, Vol. 7, No. 3 / 4, 2014, pp. 110–120, ISSN:1942-2636.

[16] C. Dhasarathan, S. Dananjayan, R. Dayalan, V. Thirumal, and D. Ponnurangam, "A multi-agent approach: To preserve user information privacy for a pervasive and ubiquitous environment," Egyptian Informatics Journal, Vol. 16, 2015, pp. 151-166, ISSN: 1110-8665.

[17] Y. Zuo and T. O'Keefe,"Post-release information privacy protection: A framework and next-generation privacy-enhanced operating system," Information Systems Frontiers, Vol. 9, 2007, pp. 451-467, ISSN: 1387-3326.

[18] N. Shang, G. Ghinita, Y. Zhou, and E. Bertino,"Controlling Data Disclosure in Computational PIR Protocols," in Proceedings of the 5th ACM Symposium on Information, Computer and Communications Security (ASIACCS) April 13-16, 2010, Beijing, China. ACM Communications, Apr. 2013, pp. 310–313, ISBN: 978-1-60558-936-7.

[19] C. Dong, L. Chen, and Z. Wen,"When Private Set Intersection Meets Big Data: An Efficient and Scalable Protocol," in Proceedings of the 20th ACM Conference on Computer and Communications Security (CCS), November 4-8, 2013, Berlin, Germany. ACM Communications, Nov. 2013, pp. 789–800, ISBN: 978-1-4503-2477-9.

[20] J. Zhang, X. Xiao, and X. Xie,"PrivTree: A Differentially Private Algorithm for Hierarchical Decompositions," in Proceedings of the International Conference on Management of Data (SIGMOD), June 26–July 01, 2016, San Francisco, CA, USA. ACM Communications, Jul. 2016, pp. 155–170, ISBN: 978-1-4503-3531-7.

[21] V. Köppen, C. Krätzer, J. Dittmann, G. Saake, and C. Vielhauer, "Impacts on Database Performance in a Privacy-Preserving Biometric Authentication Scenario," International Journal on Advances in Security, Vol. 8, No. 1 / 2, 2015, pp. 99–108, ISSN:1942-2636.

[22] U. Rothe, "A Generalized View on Pseudonyms and Domain Specific Local Identifiers," International Journal on Advances in Security, Vol. 7, No. 3 / 4, 2014, pp. 76–92, ISSN:1942-2636.

[23] Q. H. Vu, "TREMA: A Tree-based Reputation Management Solution for P2P Systems," International Journal on Advances in Security, Vol. 4, No. 3 / 4, 2011, pp. 163–172, ISSN:1942-2636.

[24] E. Damiani, F. Pagano, and D. Pagano, "iPrivacy: A Distributed Approach to Privacy on the Cloud," International Journal on Advances in Security, Vol. 4, No. 3 / 4, 2011, pp. 185–197, ISSN:1942-2636.

[25] G. Di Fatta and D. Pettinger, "Dynamic Load Balancing in Parallel KD-Tree k-Means," in Proceedings of 10th IEEE International Conference on Computer and Information Technology (CIT 2010), June 29-July 1, 2010, Bradford, West Yorkshire, UK.. IEEE Computer Society, 2010, pp. 2478–2485, ISBN: 978-0-7695-4108-2.

[26] A. Alonso-González, C. López-Martínez, P. Salembier, S. Valero, and J. Chanussot, "Multidimensional SAR Data Analysis Based on Binary Partition Trees and the Covariance Matrix Geometry," in Proceedings of 2014 International Radar Conference (Radar2014), October 13-17 2014, Lille, France.. pp. 1–6, ISBN: 978-1-4799-4195-7.

[27] Z. ZeQuan and X. QiuLiang, "Scalable Authenticated Dynamic Group Key Agreement Based on Multi-Tree," in Proceedings of third International Symposium on Electronic Commerce and Security, 29-31 July 2010 , Guangzhou, China. IEEE Computer Society, 2010, pp. 126–130, ISBN: 978-1-4244-8231-3.

[28] H. Kokkinen, M. V. J. Heikkinen, and M. Miettinen, "Post-Payment Copyright System versus Online Music Shop: Business Model and Privacy," International Journal on Advances in Security, Vol. 2, No. 2 / 3, 2009, pp. 112–128, ISSN:1942-2636.

Micro-CI: A Model Critical Infrastructure Testbed for Cyber-Security Training and Research

William Hurst, Nathan Shone, Qi Shi

Department of Computer Science
Liverpool John Moores Univerity
Liverpool, UK
Email: {w.hurst, n.shone, q.shi}@ljmu.ac.uk

Benham Bazli

School of Computing
Staffordshire University
Stafford, UK
Email: behnam.bazli@staffs.ac.uk

***Abstract*—Critical infrastructures encompass various sectors, such as energy resources and manufacturing, which tend to be dispersed over large geographic areas. With recent technological advancements over the last decade, they have developed to be dependent on Information and Communication Technology (ICT); where control systems and the use of sensor equipment facilitate operation. However, the persistently evolving global state of ICT has resulted in the emergence of sophisticated cyber-threats. As dependence upon critical infrastructure systems continues to increase, so too does the urgency with which these systems need to be adequately protected. Modelling and testbed development are now crucial for the study and analysis of security within critical infrastructures; particularly as testing within a live system can have far-reaching impacts, including potential loss of life. Existing testbed approaches are not replicable or involve the use of simulation, which impacts upon the realism of the datasets constructed. As such, the research presented in this paper discusses the novel development of a replicable and affordable critical infrastructure testbed for cyber-security training and research. The testbed can be used to anticipate cyber-security incidents and assist in the development of new and innovative cyber-security methods. The access to real-world data for training, research and testing new design methodologies is a challenge for security researchers; as such, the aim of this project is to provide an original methodology for the construction of accessible data for cyber-security research. The testbed data is evaluated through a comparison with a simulation comprised of the same components. By using neural network algorithms, it is demonstrated that physical generate datasets are more suitable for cyber-security experimentation.**

Keywords–critical infrastructure; cyber-security; modelling; testbed; data analysis; teaching.

I. Introduction

Critical infrastructures are comprised of a network of interdependent man-made systems [1]. They interoperate to provide a continuous flow of services, which are essential for economic development and social well-being. Food and water distribution, energy supply, finance, military defence, manufacturing, transport, governmental services and healthcare are all notable examples of services provided by critical infrastructures [2]. One of their key defining factors is society's dependence on their amenities and the potential loss encountered if a successful physical or cyber-attack takes place. For example, Reichenbach *et al.* detail that public life within Germany would reach civil war levels if power supply breaks down [3]; optimistic worst-case scenarios had this occurring within a 10-day period. This illustrates the emphasis placed on critical infrastructure safeguarding practices.

All critical infrastructure areas are becoming substantial Information and Communication Technology (ICT) users; making use of automation to facilitate production and expand their services. ICT has also increased in areas such as agriculture and water [4], where control systems and the use of sensor equipment increases the efficiency of production to satisfy growing demands. For example, the use of robotics in farming to assist with labour-intensive work is revolutionising the way in which crops are grown and maintained [4]. However, the challenge of low-power operation, means that almost no update, encryption or debugging capabilities are possible for the sensors in place.

Infrastructure interdependencies have developed as ICT usage has increased. Many companies accept that IC systems' communication is not encrypted and try to hide them within internal networks. Many network protocols have now been replaced by normal TCP and HTTP. The challenge is, many systems that were not accessible before, are now within the public internet. In addition, a critical failure in one infrastructure can directly lead to disruptions in others, exacerbating the risks being faced. This increase in digitisation and interconnectivity has also meant that such failures could be deliberately implemented from a remote location by means of a cyber-attack. Furthermore, the increasing complexity of cyber-attacks and the open source availability of attack-toolkits mean that effective security within critical infrastructures is a challenging task.

Developing future cyber-attack countermeasures requires real-world critical infrastructure data, which can be problematic. Real-world data is sensitive and often classified, thus companies are unwilling to part with it, even to aid researchers and students investigating cyber-security methods that may help safeguard their systems in the future.

The novel Micro-CI project, featured in this paper, aims to address the lack of access to experimental data and the hands-on experience needed to properly understand the challenges involved in an era of growing digital threats. This is achieved through the design and construction of a replicable critical infrastructure testbed for cyber-security training and research.

As such, the intended output of the project is to construct a bespoke 'bench-top' testbed for data generation; consisting of a model infrastructure system. The testbed is used for cyber-security research purposes and testing new experimental methods for enhancing the level of security in cyber-critical systems. The testbed consists of a hackable water distribution plant with control system and realistic infrastructure data output. This results in the creation of a safe and interactive environment, in which, theoretical cyber-security systems can be tested.

Software-based simulation data is often used to test theoretical cyber-security systems; however, data constructed through emulators is inherently lacking in realism and a hands-on learning experience is missed. A simulation is a representation of a mental model. This is an issue, as a tester would test the correctness of the mental model and not the real world application, which would have a negative impact. In addition, environmental concerns (e.g. temperature) might be a significant consideration during a test; typically, this is not a consideration during simulation design. Also, from an educational perspective, there are multiple modes of learning (e.g., aural, visual,) and there is a category of students that need physical hands-on experience to understand a concept.

For that reason, in this paper, the architecture for the Micro-CI testbed, which replicates a water distribution plant, is outlined. Similarly, both the physical design and construction of the testbed is detailed. The Micro-CI testbed forms the basis of the novel contribution made by this paper. A case study and evaluation, in which cyber-attacks are launched against the water distribution plant, is also presented. For this, both the Micro-CI testbed and industry-leading critical infrastructure simulation software are used to generate results, and compare the datasets produced. This then enables the assessment of the suitability of the data produced by the testbed for future cyber-security research and experimentation.

The remainder of this paper is organised as follows. Section II presents a background discussion on testbed and critical infrastructure modelling. Cyber-security and cyber-threats are also highlighted. Section III presents the novel methodology used to construct the Micro-CI testbed, the software simulation control model and an example of the data constructed from the testbed and the simulation. Section IV focuses on a case study of the impact of an attack on both the simulated and physical infrastructures. The application offered in Section IV is an example to demonstrate the effectiveness of the methodology highlighted in Section III. Section V presents a discussion ot the experiment and case study results. Finally, the paper is concluded in Section VI and future work is highlighted.

II. Background

Having a well-established critical infrastructure network is often considered a sign of civilised life. Nations can be mediated by the strength of their infrastructure network and the services provided to their citizens. Dependence on these infrastructures is also one of society's greatest weaknesses. A disruption to a single critical infrastructure can result in debilitating consequences on the population, economy and government. Operating as part of a distributed system, failures within critical infrastructures have the potential to cascade rapidly.

A. The Cyber-Threats

As dependence on these critical infrastructures increases, it is important that the ability to avoid disasters is enhanced. However, cyber-crime is becoming an increasingly concerning problem, especially with the abundance of freely available hacking toolkits. The effects of a cyber-attack can have far-reaching consequences including the availability of other dependent critical infrastructure services and the economy.

Most cyber-attacks are financially motivated, whether this is from offering the attack as a paid-for service, through selling stolen information, exploiting information captured from spear-phishing attacks or from ransom or extortion tactics. Understanding the strategies employed by cyber-attackers is crucial to counteracting the threat posed. Typically, attackers' strategies can be categorised into three different types, Reckless, Random and Opportunistic [5]. A Reckless attacker performs attacks whenever there is an opportunity to inflict maximum disruption to the services provided. A Random attacker strikes arbitrarily, to avoid detection, with the intention to cripple the target system. An Opportunistic attacker exploits the ambient noise of a system, and only attacks when the system is weak and the probability of success is high.

As mentioned previously, most attacks are financially motivated. The most common of which is paid-for Distributed Denial of Service attacks (DDoS). DDoS attacks can be used to incapacitate the host servers of a organisation and usually involve the use of illegal botnets [6]. Botnets are effectively a hidden and illegal cyber-army, which can span across the globe, without the controlling-user having to invest in their own hardware or own any physical components [7]. The popularity of this attack can be attributed to the operator having a relatively high level of anonymity. The usual form of a DDoS attack involves overloading routers and intermediate links by sending them enormous volumes of network traffic [7]. There are several different types of DDoS techniques, some of which include:

- SYN Flood: Known as a Transmission Control Protocol Synchronised Flood (SYN Flood), the attack involves exploiting the TCP connection establishment process [8]. Specifically, to establish a connection, a device sends and receives a SYN. The DDoS attack, in this case, functions by making the server unavailable and the SYN process is blocked.
- Peer-to-peer: This type of attack normally involves forcing clients of significant peer-to-peer file sharing centres to connect to a victim after disconnecting from their own network. These attacks operate differently to a botnet and the bot computers are often controlled individually.
- Permanent denial of service: Often DDoS attacks can be so severe that the target hardware needs replacement as a result. This is known as a permanent denial of service (PDoS), where backdoors are exploited and used to target device firmware which is replaced by the attackers' own firmware.

Spear-phishing is another common form of cyber-attack, which relies on human error and a lack of threat awareness to be successful. The aim is to trick victims into thinking an email-based scam is legitimate by ensuring the information inside is specific to that person or organisation. As a result of successful spear-phishing attacks, numerous military and private industry systems have been breached in recent years [9]. Each penetration is the direct result of lack of understanding about the nature of the attack, which leads to sensitive information being disclosed. Unfortunately, once attackers have gained an initial point of entry to the system, they can often freely move throughout most of the network.

The consequences of a successful spear-phishing attack are made possible through the tactical goal of achieving a foothold on the targeted system. For that reason, attacks are usually accomplished by using shellcode, code injection and capture attacks to compromise a physical component. Within a critical infrastructure setting, after a target node is compromised, the adversary refocuses the attack and employs the use of forgery, data modification, greyhole/blackhole (packet drop) and replay attacks to compromise sensors and return incorrect readings or execute incorrect commands (forgery attacks). These techniques ensure maximum damage is caused through a foothold situation. The above mentioned attacks comprise part of the background discussion as they are the most common faced by critical infrastructures. As such, they are demonstrated in the case study presented in Section IV.

B. A Cyber-Security Challenge

The control systems currently used in critical infrastructures systems are understandably closed source and not publically available. However, such systems continue to be at risk from cyber-attacks; and the facilitation of essential cyber-security research remains inherently a challenge.

Critical infrastructures tend to be civilian owned by majority. Commercial companies operate competitively with limited capital for spending on security. The result of this is that security can be put at a disadvantage. Different technologies may be used in separate infrastructures as owners are hesitant to share or co-operate with others. This is because information or strategy can be given away by the actions it takes to secure the infrastructure. Separate private ownership of infrastructures poses a challenge for access to real-world data for cyber-security research and teaching. It is this challenge that is at the core of the research put forward in this paper.

One aspect, which all critical infrastructures adopt to secure their service provision despite their separate ownership, is a Defence in Depth (DiD) approach [10]. DiD involves compartmentalising the system into various layers, each of which operates with different security technologies and Intrusion Detection Systems (IDS). This ensures that if an attacker penetrates one layer, they are not automatically able to access the next one [11]. DiD is most effective when layers are created that are independent of each other. These various levels of security would, for example, include Low levels, Medium levels and High levels. The Low levels would be accessible by general employees who require basic security clearance to the infrastructure to perform their tasks and have access to only a small amount of necessary data. Whereas, the High levels would only be accessible by management and system administrators as the contents would be of a more sensitive nature.

Inside the DiD approach, IDSs have the role of detecting hostile activities within a network, and signalling alarms when attacks are identified [12]. There are multiple types of IDS that are widely used to enhance network security [13] by providing real time identification of misuse or unauthorised use, whilst allowing the system to continue functioning. Two common types of IDSs used for the identification of intrusion attempts include anomaly detection and signature-based detection. Anomaly detection involves the detection of abnormal network activities. For example, such an anomaly may include a sudden increase in data flow to a certain part of the system, which is unexpected [14]. Signature-based detection is the use of a pattern to identify data that stands out as being an intrusion [12]. The pattern is based on the comparison of the attack with known attack signatures. Signature-based detection, however, is non-adaptive and cannot detect zero-day attacks (which do not have a pre-existing signature), making it an ineffective technique when used by itself [15]. To cover for various forms of attack, critical infrastructures typically use a combination of multiple types of IDS to maximise infrastructure protection from the many threats that can originate from external network connections.

The continued growth in scale and complexity of some critical infrastructure systems means that they are becoming increasingly enticing targets for cyber-attacks. One such example is healthcare critical infrastructure systems, which are expanding to accommodate the influx of eHealth monitoring systems spawned by smart devices and the Internet of Things (IoT) concept. Modern eHealth monitoring systems are comprised of two main infrastructure layers [16]. The first is the Physical Layer, which encompasses wireless body area networks (WBANs), smart health trackers, IoT sensors and physical equipment used by medical staff. The second is the Service Layer, which houses the cloud computing and storage facilities, and the applications, software and services offered to patients that utilise the data provided by the Physical Layer.

The Physical Layer is composed of many heterogeneous and computationally limited devices (e.g. heart rate sensors, blood oxygen sensors and blood sugar monitors), which pose many security and privacy challenges. For example, wireless communications make sensor technologies internet-accessible, which leaves them publically exposed and highly vulnerable [17].

This exposure can be used to an attacker's advantage by disseminating specific attacks to the patient-side that target both hardware and software. Attacks on medical critical infrastructure systems are increasing, with attackers aiming to cause maximum damage. This is exacerbated by the increasing number of attack vectors, such as over-the-air software update mechanisms, limited security/encryption capabilities, exploitable developer API exploitation and open source software exploitation. As an example, in over-the-air software update attacks, if updates are frequent, attackers can configure a radio to the appropriate frequency and with a demodulation technique, record updates, reverse engineer the format, craft a software containing malware and deliver it to the targeted device. Additionally, in source code analysis (through Open Source software or disassembled and decompiled binaries), stack buffer overflow vulnerabilities can be revealed. The attacker can also use fuzzing to execute stack buffer overflow attacks.

C. Current Critical Infrastructure Testbeds

Cyber-security research is hampered by a lack of realistic experimental data and opportunities to test new theories in a real-world environment [18]. Ordinarily, the production of reliable and accurate research results would require the purchase of critical infrastructure hardware, which is extremely expensive and impractical. This has led to the development of specific software-based simulators, such as Technomatix [19] and NS3 [20]; and the adaptation of existing software-based simulators such as OMNET++ [21], Simulink and Matlab [22]. These software simulators enable affordable representations of critical infrastructure systems, by modelling their behaviour, interactions and the integration of their specific protocols (e.g. MODBUS).

However, the suitability of simulation has long been disputed; with the argument that simulations do not represent real-world scenarios accurately, as they lack the ability to model the interactions of control system components. As such, this project aims to provide a testbed that is rudimentary and low-cost to build, but remains extensible. The practical nature of the testbed aims to provide users with a greater level of realism, and a more accurate representation of how different events and behaviours would manifest themselves in real-world scenarios.

As critical infrastructure testbed development for security research is an active yet relatively infantile subject area, there are several similar, yet limited, existing research projects. Some of them are outlined as follows. SCADA LAB [23] is an EU funded project to build a critical infrastructure testbed with a conjoined security lab, to facilitate security experiments. However, the primary limitation of this system is that it is a remote access system, with both the configuration and experimentation carried out by a third party. The testbed proposed in the paper is localised, where researchers/students are able to oversee and manage all aspects of their experiments directly. This means it is more tangible and users can more readily relate directly with their experimentations.

As the implementation of a working critical infrastructure testbed can be time-consuming, Farooqui *et al.* propose a hybrid approach by combining physical commercial hardware and simulation software [24]. However, our project consists of the implementation of working control devices, rather than relying on simulation software. Additionally, the testbed utilises small-scale, and therefore portable, hardware; rather than rigid commercial hardware.

Benzel *et al.* discuss the use of DETER, a cyber-DEfense Technology Experimental Research testbed for supporting the development of next-generation security technologies and experimentation [18]. The testbed is deigned to bridge the gap between small-scale and Internet-scale experiments, through combing both software and hardware components. The testbed also offers tools that aid the experimenters. The main drawback of the DETER testbed is that it is not sufficiently replicable or portable. Meaning users are unable to create their own and its operation relies on connecting to the DETER host.

In addition to the aforementioned testbed approaches, there are several existing proposals for critical infrastructure testbed architectures, which focus on specific systems, such as electricity substations [25]. However, our long-term goal is not to constrain our testbed to a single role, but to adopt a modular approach; whereby new critical infrastructure roles can be integrated at a later stage. This would make it suitable and useful to a wider audience. Specifically, the proposed system focuses on a water distribution plant; however, the design is extendable and testbeds can be extended to incorporate other infrastructure types, such as an ecologically-aware power plant.

A framework has also been proposed to address the problem of simulating large-scale critical infrastructure systems on a localised testbed by Ficco *et al.* [22]. As such, they present a framework, which acts as a glue layer between a distributed testbed and simulation of components. The drawback of such an approach is the use of a hybrid method to combine both simulation and physical systems. This results in a testbed which is not rudimentary and where simulation impacts the quality of data produced. Within the MicroCI project, we are primarily concerned with the practical realism of the data and reliability of the generated results through a real-world implementation.

The testbed proposed in by Morris *et al.* is the most similar existing research to ours in terms of its design, and pedagogical and research purposes [26]. The research put forwards proposes a testbed that focuses on cyber-security and utilises miniature hardware for a realistic representation of critical infrastructures. However, the project is only available locally at the authors' institution and is not easily replicable or portable.

A defining factor of the MicroCI project is to develop a testbed, which is cost effective and easily replicable by other institutions. The design and implementation will both be detailed in publications and made accessible during the project dissemination process.

III. Methodology and Implementation

Currently, model critical infrastructure testbeds are sparse in the UK. This project provides research opportunities for the testing and development of security enhancements in a real-life scenario. As such, the aim of the research is to have a practical output; a fully working critical infrastructure testbed. The goal is to demonstrate that the datasets generated by the Micro-CI testbed [1], are of comparable suitability to those created by industry-standard software. In this section, an outline of the architecture of the Micro-CI project is presented. This includes an explanation of how the architecture is identically replicated using both the physical Micro-CI hardware and the industry-standard simulation software.

A. Testbed Architectural Overview

The design displayed below in Figure 1 presents a water distribution plant. The specification is modest, meaning there is scope for future expansion; yet is sufficient in size to produce realistic infrastructure behaviour datasets for research purposes. As illustrated in the diagram, there are two reservoir tanks, which are fed by two pumps moving water from external sources.

The remote terminal unit (RTU) is used to monitor the outgoing flow rate and water level, to dynamically adjust the pump speed ensuring adequate replenishment of the reservoir tanks. However, vulnerabilities exist in the system, meaning that it is possible for an attacker to cut off the water supply or flood the reservoir tanks. The design is extendable to other applications, in that it can be connected to other critical infrastructure models (such as power plants, telecommunications etc.), if additional equipment is to be included. This would facilitate future research projects investigating the effect of

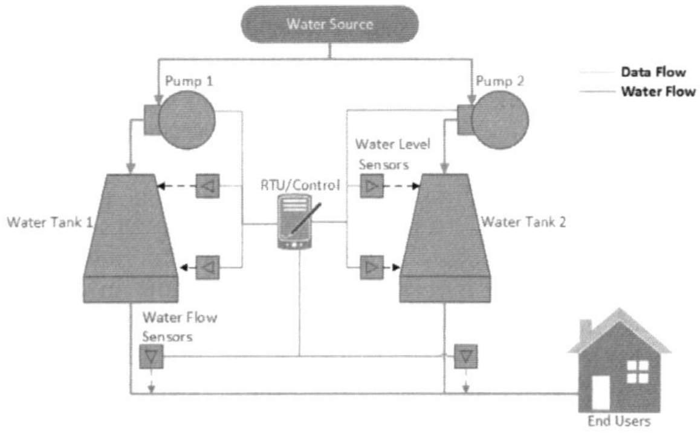

Figure 1. Water distribution plant tested architecture

cascading failures throughout a network of inter-connected critical infrastructures.

B. Practical Micro-CI implementation and data generation

To replicate the architecture illustrated in Figure 1, we will be constructing the physical Micro-CI testbed in accordance with the wiring schematics shown in Figure 2. Specifically, the physical components required include: an Arduino Uno Rev. 3 as the RTU, two 12v peristaltic pumps as the water pumps, two liquid flow meters, two water level sensors, two amplification transistors, diodes, resistors and an LCD.

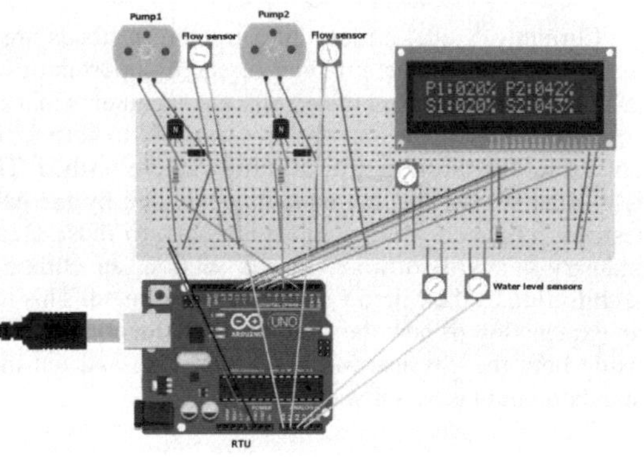

Figure 2. Physical wiring schematics

In the schematics shown in Figure 2, potentiometer symbols have been used in place of the four sensors; this is due to the limited symbols available in the modelling software. The fifth, unlabelled, potentiometer is used to control the brightness of the LCD. As the maximum output of the Arduino is only 5v, transistors amplify this to the 12v required by the pumps. Lastly, the diodes are used to ensure the current can only travel in one direction, thus preventing damage to the Arduino. The hardware specification used is modest, meaning there is scope for future expansion; yet is sufficient in size to produce realistic infrastructure behaviour datasets for research purposes.

For the purpose of this experiment, the Arduino board remains connected to a PC via a USB cable (although this could be replaced with a network connection for similar experiments). Through this USB connection, a serial connection is established to supply a real-time data feed, which is recorded and preserved by the PC (as illustrated in Figure 3). The metrics collected in this instance include: Water level sensor1/2 readings, Flow meter1/2 readings and Pump1/2 speeds. These readings are taken from each sensor every 0.25 seconds (4Hz) and written to the serial data stream.

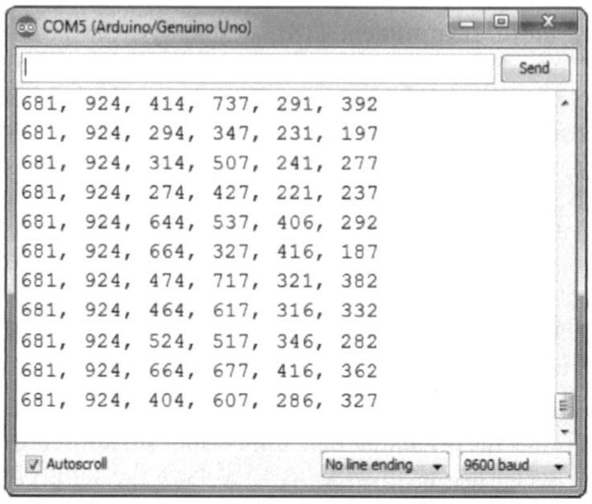

Figure 3. Example Serial Data Connection

TABLE I. Physical Testbed Data Sample (%)*

Sample (t)	P1	P2	P3	P4	P5	P6
00:10.5	65.0	69.9	47.3	55.4	81.9	85.1
00:10.7	65.0	69.9	39.4	48.5	74.1	78.8
00:11.0	65.0	69.9	39.4	53.4	74.1	83.1
00:11.2	65.0	69.9	33.6	50.5	69.0	81.1
00:11.5	65.0	69.9	41.4	39.7	76.0	70.2

*Symbol explanations are given in the Appendix

To examine the quality of the data produced by the Micro-CI implementation, a dataset was recorded over the period of 1 hour. During this time, the testbed was operating under normal parameters (i.e. no cyber-attacks were present). Essentially, this means that the pump speeds are configured to slowly continue filling the tanks at a controlled speed until full (even if no water is being used) and to cover the current rate of water consumption (if possible). The outflow (water being consumed) is a randomly applied value within a specific range (to make usage patterns more realistic). In this instance, the water source pipe is 60% smaller than the outflow pipe, which allows for a more accurate representation (and to simulate overflow). The initial configuration of the testbed was as follows: Tank1 is 65% full, Tank2 is 69.9% full, Outflow1 is functioning at 20 + (1-35)% of capacity and Outflow 2 is operating at 30 + (1-35)% of capacity. A small sample of the data obtained at 00:10.5 of run time is shown in Table I. From this dataset, we can see that there is no significant variation present in the data. We can also see that all the metrics maintain consistent trends in operation.

C. Software simulation model implementation and data generation

The simulation is constructed, in accordance with the architecture shown in Figure 1. The software is based on object-oriented modelling, where each component inserted is an

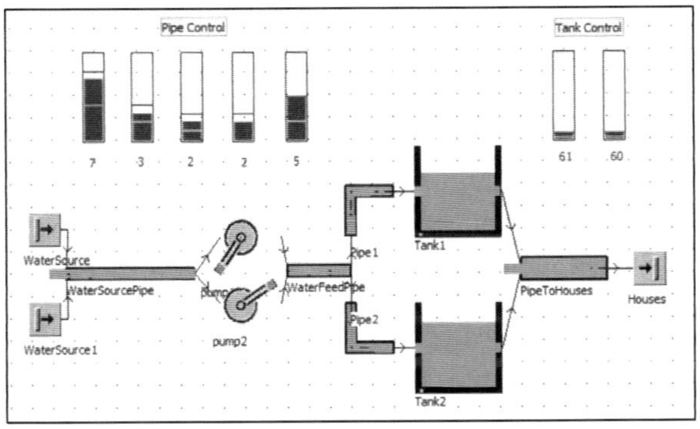

Figure 4. Case Study Simulation Testbed

individual object, which can be adjusted and used to construct data. The resulting simulation environment is displayed in Figure 4.

The figure depicts a graphical overview of the emulation, including a water source, two pumps, two tanks and network of pipes used to deliver the water throughout the system. Sensors are coded to extract data at a sampling rate of 0.25 seconds (4Hz) from each of the components within the system. The flow of water from the source to the tanks is governed by the two pumps, and the speed can be adjusted as required. During simulation run-time, the behaviour of one simulation component has a direct impact on another. When a component failure occurs, the simulation is able to keep functioning, but the effects of the fault should be visible in the dataset. The system functions smoothly and consistently. However, the output and behaviour differs slightly every time the system operates resulting in variance in the datasets.

As previously mentioned, it is clear the use of simulation has many benefits in critical infrastructure protection planning. The advantage of using simulation is that conducting experimentation can be done on a realistic representation of a system without the worry that any damage done would have a real impact. It is this aspect that is transferred over the physical testbed. However, the drawback of simulation is in the quality of data produced. As such, in the following subsection, data constructed from the simulation and the physical testbed are presented and compared in a case study put forward in Section IV.

The water distribution infrastructure in the simulation consists of 12 components. To provide a benchmark to compare the Micro-CI data against, the simulation data was again captured over the period of 1 hour of simulation, with the system functioning under normal conditions. The tables presented in the Appendix clarify the selected components presented in the table. The numbers in Table II represent the percentage of the water level in the corresponding component or the operational speed of the component. For example, at 00:10.5 component C1 is 85.7% full, whereas C2 is empty. Each of the components within the simulated system are started with the initial configuration of 0% full. This is because, unlike the Micro-CI testbed, it is a challenge to begin a simulation with the tanks partially filled. The tank water level is calculated based upon the units of water, which flow into and out of the component.

TABLE II. Simulation Data Sample (%)*

Sample (t)	C1	C2	C3	C4	C5	C6
00:10.5	85.7	0	0	100	100	83.3
00:10.7	100	100	100	48.5	100	100
00:11.0	100	100	100	100	100	100
00:11.2	100	100	100	100	100	100
00:11.5	100	100	100	100	100	100

*Symbol explanations are given in the Appendix

There is no significant change in the data during the one second sample presented above. This demonstrates that the water flow is consistent within each of the components at the given point in time.

IV. Case Study

In this section, a case study is presented, which involves conducting known cyber-attack types on both the Micro-CI testbed and the simulation. The quality of the data produced is assessed and a discussion is put forward on the suitability of both data types for cyber-security research.

In the scenario of this case study, the end users' water is supplied by a remote water distribution plant. The control of this plant is governed by an RTU, which is under a DDoS attack. The attack degraded the stability of the communication links between the RTU and its sensors. This in turn means that the availability and frequency of the sensor value measurements is degraded.

A. Testbed Data Preparation

For the first part of this case study, data for the water distribution plant is recorded whilst operating under normal conditions. This allows for the building of a behavioural norm profile for the system, in order to identify anomalies. Within the testbed, during the DDoS attack, only intermittent readings from the sensors are received, forcing it to make drastic (and therefore uncharacteristic) changes to the pump speeds, rather than gradual as when operating as normal.

In this cyber-attack dataset, a DDoS attack is launched against the RTU's communications channel, so it is only able to get sensor readings intermittently. Whilst no new values are readily available, the RTU will continue to maintain the previous pump speed.

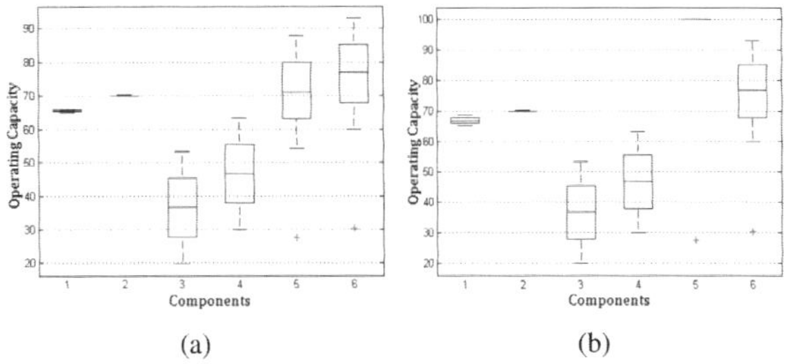

Figure 5. Testbed Normal Data Plot (a) vs Cyber-Attack Plot (b)

Figure 5 displays box plots of the testbed data for normal behaviour and when in a cyber-attack scenario. The components are displayed along the x-axis, with labels 1 to 6. The y-axis displays the operating capacity of the component. The exact behaviour induced by this experiment was relatively unknown. The results obtained showed that one tank kept filling whilst the other maintained the same level. The change in behaviour, as a result of the attack, can be seen in the average value changes in the datasets, as previously for the simulation dataset. Particularly a change in the output for P5 is visually apparent.

The data constructed during normal operation and under cyber-attack is used to assess the potential of the data to be used for cyber-security training and research. The data is evaluated using data classification techniques to identify the nature and timing of the conducted cyber-attacks. The quality of the results produced by the testbed is compared with the data constructed through simulation.

B. Simulation Data Preparation

In the simulation, each of the components has a random failure implemented and a specified time to repair. This enables the introduction of a level of realism within the dataset constructed. However, the system should not stop functioning if one of the minor components has a fault. As such, threat behaviour is constructed by causing targeted and random disruptions to the system by increasing the availability percentage in specific components. Turning components off and on, during the simulation, causes a knock-on effect throughout the rest of the system. To construct our abnormal dataset, the availability percentage was increased in each of the components, whilst ensuring the system was able to continue functioning. The Availability Percentage refers to the chances of a machine or component being ready to use at any given time taking into account failures and blockages. It is calculated using equation (1).

$$A = \frac{M}{M + F} \tag{1}$$

Here, A is the unavailability of the component, M is the Mean Time To Repair (MTTR) and F is the Mean Time Between Failures (MTBF). The implementation of random failures is intended to reflect realistic unexpected component malfunctions, which occur in all infrastructures. However, due to the fact that power plant systems are designed to be enduring, the failure percentage in the system components was kept low.

When constructing the anomalous behaviour dataset, this approach facilitates impacting system behaviour and, subsequently, the data produced. By implementing more extensive system failures, orchestrated attacks can be conducted on the simulation in order to construct a data set, which would be similar to that of a cyber-attack taking place. In order to generate attack behaviour, a number of recognised faults are introduced to the system. This facilitates an understanding of the system operating whilst under the effects of a cyber-attack. As such, significant faults are implemented in pump1 which would replicate the impact of a DDoS on an RTU component controlling the pump.

These faults are introduced to the system over a period of two hours, to create a balanced dataset for normal and attack behaviour. Figure 6 displays box plots of the simulation data for normal behaviour and when in a cyber-attack scenario.

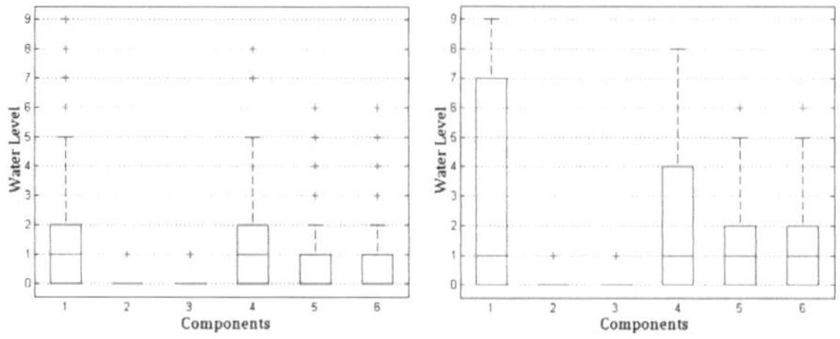

(a) (b)

Figure 6. Simulation Normal Data Plot (a) vs Cyber-Attack Plot (b)

The components are displayed along the x-axis, with labels 1 to 6. The y-axis displays the level of water within the component. The change in behaviour, as a result of the attack, can be seen in the average value changes in the datasets, and is clearer in some components, such as C1 and C4. The change in behaviour is not visually apparent in others. Changes in behaviour as a result of an attack taking place can often be subtle and hard to identify, particularly when individual components within a vast system are targeted.

C. Data Pre-Processing

Before data classification is performed, the data requires pre-processing. One of the main issues with the dataset generated by the simulation is the level of noise in the data. In order to achieve the highest possible results in the classification process, the noise needs to be reduced. This is achieved by editing or removing values from the dataset which are unwanted by the classifiers but constitute parts of the dataset which are of interest.

As a result of the behaviour of specific components in the system, there is a high level of zeros in the simulation dataset. The zeros are a result of either component failing due to introduced errors, or units of liquid in the system passing through a component faster than the sampling rate. Zeros, therefore, represent aspects such as pipes functioning normally. If the samples are consistently above zero for components, such as the water pipes, it would be the result of failures in the system. For that reason, the zero values are retained in our data set.

Data pre-processing and feature extraction are essential stages, and affect the data classification results. The features selected represent characteristics of system behaviour [27]. The process of feature selection effectively minimises the dataset and presents a representation of the behaviour taking place in the data to the classifier. Primarily, the goal of the feature selection process has three clear benefits including data comprehension, increased efficiency and prediction performance.

- Data Comprehension: Extracting features from a data set allows for a better comprehension of what the data is representing.
- Efficiency: Reducing the amount of data being classified allows for faster processing, reducing time of learning and reducing memory use.
- Prediction: The performance of the classifiers is also improved through effective feature selection. Factors

such as noise reduction and the elimination of irrelevant data enable the classifiers to be efficiently trained.

- The data manipulation process is the construction of feature vectors from significantly large normal and abnormal data sets. For this initial case study, the components themselves comprise the features, with the variables extracted every minute or 240 rows in the raw data. The data analysis is presented in the following subsection.

D. Data Analysis

In this section, data classification techniques are employed to assess the effectiveness of the data produced by the testbed for research purposed. Neural network classifiers are selected to assess the quality of the data produced. Previous research has used neural networks to successfully measure data quality [28]. Hence, we will be using neural networks as a bench mark to assess the quality of the data produced, a comparison and discussion on the datasets is put forward.

In order to perform the classification of the data, a selection of classifiers where used, these include: back-propagation trained feed-forward neural network classifier (BPXNC), levenberg-marquardt trained feed-forward neural network classifier (LMNC), automatic neural network classifier (NEURC), trainable linear perceptron classifier (PERLC), voted perception classifier (VPC) and the random neural network classifier (RNNC) [29]. The classification experiments are run 30 times on the datasets. The reason the classification experiments are conducted 30 times is to account for errors and to give consistency. Statisticians identify that experiments conducted 30 times provide an adequate realistic average [30].

In order to calculate the results, firstly, a Confusion Matrix determines the distribution of errors across all classes [31]. The estimate of the classifier is calculated as the trace of the matrix divided by the total number of entries. Additionally, a Confusion Matrix highlights where misclassification occurs in experiment. In other words, it shows true positive (a), false positive (c), true negative (d) and false negative (b) values. Diagonal elements show the performance of the classifier, while off diagonal presents errors. This is displayed in Table III.

TABLE III. Confusion Matrix

	+	-
+	a	b
-	c	d

The results are calculated mathematically, using equations (2) - (4), where a refers to True Positive, d implies True Negative and b and c refer to False Positive and False Negative respectively. N is the total number of feature vectors within the dataset.

$$\text{Sensitivity} = \frac{a}{a+c} \tag{2}$$

$$\text{Specificity} = \frac{d}{b+d} \tag{3}$$

$$\text{Accuracy} = \frac{(a+d)}{N} \tag{4}$$

Tables IV and V present the results of the classification process and include the success of the classification or Area under the Curve (AUC), sensitivity, specificity and error. Where specificity refers to normal system behaviour, sensitivity refers to abnormal (or attack behaviour) and accuracy represents the success of the classification. Each of the results are calculated using equations 2 - 4.

TABLE IV. Simulation Classification Results

Classifiers	AUC	Sensitivity	Specificity	Error
VPC	0.050	0.500	0.000	0.500
NRNC	0.850	0.769	1.000	0.150
PERLC	0.750	0.667	1.000	0.250
PBXNC	0.767	0.682	1.000	0.233
LMNC	0.833	0.750	1.000	0.167
NEURC	0.867	0.789	1.000	0.133

TABLE V. Testbed Classification Results

Classifiers	AUC	Sensitivity	Specificity	Error
VPC	0.733	0.652	1.000	0.267
NRNC	0.850	0.818	0.889	0.150
PERLC	0.800	0.875	0.750	0.200
PBXNC	0.983	1.000	0.968	0.017
LMNC	0.997	0.997	0.997	0.033
NEURC	0.933	0.933	0.933	0.063

It is clear from the results in both tables, that the classifiers are able to detect accurately both the normal and abnormal behaviours in the data set. A discussion and comparison of the results is subsequently presented in the following section.

V. Evaluation

Within the simulation classification results, the NEURC classifier is the most accurate; able to classify 86.7% of the data correctly with an error of 0.133. For the NEURC classifier 28 out of 30 normal behaviours are correctly classified. During the physical testbed classification process LMNC is to identify 99.67% of the behaviours accurately, with an error of 0.0667. In the following subsection, a discussion is put forward on the significance of the results obtained.

A. Results Comparison

Figure 7 displays a comparison of the results achieved from the neural network classification. The graphs depict that the classifiers are able to more successfully identify threat behaviours using the Micro-CI testbed, rather than through a simulation approach. This is particularly the case for the sensitivity, AUC and error. In addition to the difference between the AUC results produced by the neural network classification, the specificity results, in particular, hold significance for the evaluation of the datasets.

A comparison between the specificity results (normal behaviours) show that the simulation approach results in 5/6 classifiers being able to identify 100% of normal behaviour; with most of the misclassification occurring for the sensitivity

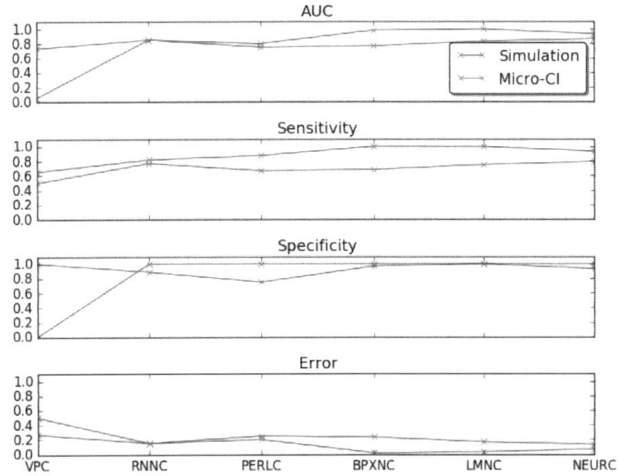

Figure 7. Simulation Results vs Testbed Results)

(the identification of abnormal/attack behaviour). Within the simulation approach, normal system behaviour is straightforward to identify, as the simulation behaviour does not have significant changes in its operation and performs as coded to perform. In a 'real-life' environment, the physical system is set up to behave in a specific way but always functions slightly differently to the anticipated. This means that any research conducted using simulation to construct data is hampered by over classification for the specificity/normal behaviour dataset.

B. Testbed Attacks Comparison

As previously discussed, one of the aims of this project is to devise a testbed, which is suitable for cyber-security training and research. As demonstrated in the previous subsection, it is our belief that the use of real-life data is more suitable for cyber-security research, than that of simulation. The second part of the case study involves a demonstration of the two further datasets constructed through launching the following cyber-attacks on the Micro-CI testbed:

- Signal injection: Falsified malicious data is injected, masquerading as one of the flow sensors. This forces the RTU to change the pumps' settings to suit the malicious data. Specifically, a signal injection attack is launched against the water flow sensor on tank 2, in which we tell it there is no water leaving tank2. The water level drops, however, it drops slowly as the tank is still on a slow refill (as it is not full).
- DoS: One of the water level sensors is rendered completely inaccessible to the RTU by means of a DoS attack. This causes the RTU to labour to accurately control the pumping station, as the crucial data needed is unavailable. Specifically, a DoS attack was launched against the water level sensor in tank1, meaning the RTU is getting a result of 0, which misleads it into thinking the tank is empty, so the tank fills up much quicker.

As such, Figure 8 below displays the resulting data output of the Micro-CI testbed pump speeds, during normal operation and when subjected to the three attacks discussed in this paper. Each of the experiments was conducted on an identical testbed.

The graphs display a clear change in behaviour as a result of the attacks taking place. The majority of the attacks are targeted at pump 2, where the separation of the datasets can be clearly identified. This is a demonstration of realistic data construction though use of the testbed. The RTU inclusion means that Micro-CI users have remote access to the functioning components. Different attack types produce diverse dataset outputs.

C. Physical Testbed Benefits

As a whole, modern education and research is becoming increasingly reliant on virtualised labs and tools [32]. Despite the numerous benefits they offer, there are many inherent limitations. Therefore, any learning or research undertaken using these tools is based around the limitations and characteristics of such tools, as well as any assumptions made by their developers. Additionally, the accuracy of data resulting from such simulations and models may be further decreased if used outside of their intended usage scenario. For example, in network reconnaissance, a Christmas tree packet (a packet set with an unusual combination of TCP headers), can cause different operating systems to respond in different ways (differing from defined IP standards). The disparity amongst these responses can be used to identify the underlying operating system. These types of unusual quirks can be utilised by attackers, and are often not something that is covered by simulation software. The practical element involved in the Micro-CI project introduces a level of realism that is difficult to match through simulation.

A recent report [33] examined the usage of both physical and virtual tools and labs. The report concluded that a virtual-based approach offers significant cost savings and a self-paced and active approach to learning. However, it also highlighted that it has several key limitations including: no hands-on experience, no real-world training with specific equipment and no experience in identifying and interpreting incorrect or uncharacteristic data.

The findings of this report echo our concerns that simulation is very effective at representing "correct" behaviour. However, critical infrastructure systems need to be protected against situations where they are exposed to extreme abnormal events. Unfortunately, in such circumstances, systems will not always behave in the way expected, fail gracefully or consistently respond in the same manner. Similarly, it is therefore difficult to accurately model how a system's erratic behaviour might affect other parts of the infrastructure. This is why we firmly believe that adopting Micro-CI's unique approach would provide an ideal solution, as it allows for the advantages of both physical and virtual tools to be combined, some of which are discussed below.

- Pedagogical benefits: The Micro-CI approach offers students and researchers with hands-on experience and first-hand knowledge of the unpredictability of a system under attack or stress. It will also help them to refine their problem solving and practical skills.
- Cost effectiveness: The Micro-CI project has been designed to be as cost effective as possible. For example, at the time of writing, we estimate that at current prices, the design presented in this paper can be replicated for around 100.

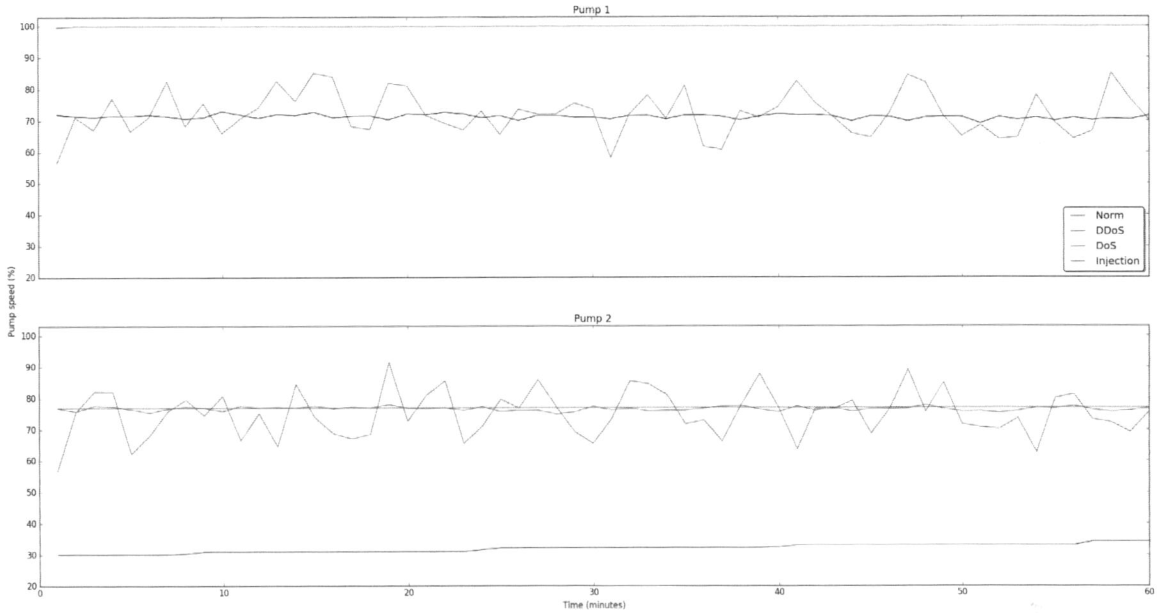

Figure 8. Simulation Attack Data Visualisation)

- Portability: As the project components are on a miniaturised bench top scale, it enables them to be packed away, stored and transported with ease. In most cases, projects can still be moved and/or stored whilst partially assembled.
- Platform independency: The Micro-CI project does not require any specific requirements, dependencies or operating systems to interact with the testbeds developed. Additionally, it is not tied or restricted by any licencing model, so it can be used on an infinite number of different machines, without incurring additional costs.

As with all solutions, there are some drawbacks to our approach. The first is that the use of low cost hardware reduces the level of accuracy that can be achieved. For example, the Arduino Uno uses an ATMega microcontroller, which is only capable of recording 4-byte precision in double values. This can present problems if precision is a crucial part of the research being undertaken. However, this can be mitigated by purchasing more expensive hardware. Another, limitation is that in comparison to simulation software, the practical approach may require a greater level of improvement to students' skillsets (which is not a detrimental attribute), and a longer initial construction time, to accomplish a working implementation.

VI. Conclusion and Future Work

One of the main challenges for governments around the globe is the need to improve the level of awareness for citizens and businesses about the threats that exist in cyberspace. The arrival of new information technologies has resulted in different types of criminal activities, which previously did not exist, with the potential to cause extensive damage to internal markets.

Given the fact that the Internet is boundary-less, it makes it difficult to identify where attacks originate from and how to counter them. Improving the level of support for security systems helps with the evolution of defences against cyber-attacks. This project supports the development of critical infrastructure security research, in the fight against a growing threat from the digital domain.

The research project will further knowledge and understanding of information systems; specifically acting as a facilitator for cyber-security research. In our future work, we will publish the constructed testbed and make the datasets available for cyber-security and critical infrastructure research. In addition, we propose to add 2-3 cheap CHIPs/ Raspberry Pi's to the testbed. In a real-world scenario, ICS systems are continually connected to a computing infrastructure. Therefore, with the addition of the PIs the following would be possible.

- Denote a Pi as the 'Corporation Firewall'. Behind the Firewall, there would be two systems: the existing ICS as well as another Pi, referred to as the 'office computer'. External to the firewall, there should be another computer called 'Target'. All three of these could be implemented using CHIPs. The additional cost of this implementation would be minimal (around 15 together).

This additional equipment would then enable further attack scenarios, such as:

- The office computer periodically surfs to the external 'target'. Now the attacker could place a payload on the external computer. This would emulate a waterhole attack, which is quite common for spear phishing.

With that, it would be possible to connect a mentioned threat to the test lab.

- As ICS are often part of a botnet, with this setup it would then also be possible to measure outgoing traffic from the ICS to the external computer. That would make the DoS scenario increasingly realistic.
- Pivoting, i.e., lateral movement after the initial breach would also be testable with this setup.

This future implementation would move the testbed from pure IC testbed to IC within a company setup testbed. Such a testbed would be invaluable for education. In addition, the forthcoming work will involve making the construction design and instructions available to other researchers and students.

REFERENCES

[1] W. Hurst, N. Shone, Q. Shi, and B. Bazli, "MICRO-CI: A Testbed for Cyber-Security Research," in Eighth International Conference on Emerging Networks and Systems Intelligence. Venice, Italy: Iaria, Oct 2016, pp. 17–22.

[2] M. Merabti, M. Kennedy, and W. Hurst, "Critical infrastructure protection: A 21st century challenge," in Proceedings of the International Conference on Communications and Information Technology (ICCIT). Jordan: IEEE, Mar 2011, pp. 1–6.

[3] G. Reichenbach, R. Gbel, H. Wolff, and S. S. von Neuforn, "Risks and Challenges for Germany, Scenarios and Key Questions," Forum on the Future of Public Safety and Security, Atlanta, GA, Tech. Rep., 2008.

[4] M. Mafuta, M. Zennaro, A. Bagula, and G. Ault, "Successful deployment of a Wireless Sensor Network for precision agriculture in Malawi," in Proceedings of the Third IEEE International Conference on Networked Embedded Systems for Every Application (NESEA). Liverpool, UK: IEEE, Dec 2012, pp. 1–7.

[5] R. Mitchell and I.-R. Chen, "Behavior Rule Specification-Based Intrusion Detection for Safety Critical Medical Cyber Physical Systems," IEEE Trans. Dependable Secur. Comput., vol. 12, no. 1, 2015, pp. 16–30.

[6] R. Poisel, M. Rybnicek, and S. Tjoa, "Game-based Simulation of Distributed Denial of Service (DDoS) Attack and Defense Mechanisms of Critical Infrastructures," in Proceedings of IEEE 27th International Conference on Advanced Information Networking and Applications. Barcelona, Spain: IEEE, Mar 2013, pp. 114–120.

[7] M. Feily, A. Shahrestani, and S. Ramadass, "A Survey of Botnet and Botnet Detection," in Proceedings of the 3rd International Conference on Emerging Security Information, Systems and Technologies. Athens, Glyfada, Greece: IEEE, Jun 2009, pp. 268–273.

[8] S. H. C. Haris, R. B. Ahmad, and M. A. H. A. Ghani, "Detecting TCP SYN Flood Attack Based on Anomaly Detection," in Proceedings of the 2nd International Conference on Network Applications, Protocols and Services. Alor Setar, Kedah, Malaysia: IEEE, Sep 2010, pp. 240–244.

[9] McAfee, "Global Energy Cyberattacks: Night Dragon," 2011, URL: http://www.mcafee.com/jp/resources/white-papers/wp-global-energy-cyberattacks-night-dragon.pdf [accessed: 2017-05-04].

[10] D. K. Hitchins, "Secure systems - Defence in Depth," in IEEE European Convention on Security and Detection. Brighton, UK: IEEE, May 1995, pp. 34–39.

[11] B. Mukherjee, L. T. Heberlein, and K. N. Levitt, "Network intrusion detection," IEEE Netw., vol. 8, no. 3, 1994, pp. 26–41.

[12] P. Nowak, B. Sakowicz, G. Anders, and A. Napieralski, "Intrusion Detection and Internet Services Failure Reporting System," in Proceedings of the Second IEEE International Conference on Dependability of Computer Systems. Szklarska, Poland: IEEE, Jun 2007, pp. 185–190.

[13] Y. Zhang, F. Deng, Z. Chen, Y. Xue, and C. Lin, "UTM-CM: A Practical Control Mechanism Solution for UTM System," in Proceedings of the 2nd IEEE International Conference on Communications and Mobile Computing. Shenzhen, China: IEEE, Apr 2010, pp. 86–90.

[14] R. Sekar, T. Bowen, and M. Segal, "On preventing intrusions by process behavior monitoring," in Proceedings of the Symposium on Operating Sytem Design and Implementation (OSDI II). Santa Clara, California: USENIX, Apr 1999, pp. 1–4.

[15] P. Li, Z. Wang, and X. Tan, "Characteristic Analysis of Virus Spreading in Ad Hoc Networks," in Proceedings of the International Conference on Computational Intelligence and Security Workshops (CISW 2007). Heilongjiang, China: IEEE, Dec 2007, pp. 538–541.

[16] A. Sawand, S. Djahel, Z. Zhang, and F. Nait-Abdesselam, "Multidisciplinary approaches to achieving efficient and trustworthy eHealth monitoring systems," in 2014 IEEE/CIC International Conference on Communications in China (ICCC). Shanghai, China: IEEE, Oct 2014, pp. 187–192.

[17] K. Hill, "The Terrifying Search Engine That Finds Internet-Connected Cameras, Traffic Lights, Medical Devices, Baby Monitors and Power Plants - Forbes," 2013, URL: http://www:forbes:com/sites/kashmirhill/2013/09/04/shodan-terrifying-search-engine/ [accessed: 2017-05-05].

[18] T. Benzel, R. Braden, D. Kim, and C. Neuman, "Experience with DETER: a testbed for security research," in Proceedings of the 2nd International Conference on Testbeds and Research Infrastructures for the Development of Networks and Communities. Barcelona, Spain: IEEE, Mar 2014, pp. 378–388.

[19] J. Stoll, B. Kemper, and G. Lanza, "Throughput analysis and simulation-based improvement of baked varnish stacking for automotive electric drives," in Proceedings of the 4th International Production Conference on Electric Drives. Nuremberg, Germany: IEEE, Sep 2014, pp. 1–6.

[20] F. Aalamifar, A. Schlogl, D. Harris, and L. Lampe, "Modelling power line communication using network simulator-3," in Proceedings of Global Communications Conference (GLOBECOM). Atlanta, GA, USA: IEEE, Dec 2013, pp. 2969–2974.

[21] C. Queiroz, A. Mahmood, J. Hu, Z. Tari, and X. Yu, "Building a SCADA Security Testbed," in Proceedings of the 3rd International Conference on Network and System Security. Gold Coast, Queensland, Australia, Australia: IEEE, Oct 2009, pp. 357–364.

[22] M. Ficco, G. Avolio, L. Battaglia, and V. Manetti, "Hybrid Simulation of Distributed Large-Scale Critical Infrastructures," Intell. Netw. Collab. Syst., vol. 35, no. 1, 2014, pp. 616–621.

[23] S. Arag, E. R. Martnez, and S. S. Clares, "SCADA Laboratory and Test-bed as a Service for Critical Infrastructure Protection," in Proceedings of the 2nd International Symposium for ICS & SCADA Cyber Security Research. St. Poelten, Austria: Learning & Development Ltd., Sep 2014, pp. 25–29.

[24] A. A. Farooqui, S. H. Zaid, A. Y. Memon, and S. Qazi, "Cyber Security Backdrop: A SCADA Testbed," in Computing Communications and IT Applications Conference (ComComAp). Beijing, China: IEEE, Oct 2014, pp. 98–103.

[25] Z. L. H. Wei, G. Yajuan, and C. Hao, "Research on information security testing technology for smart Substations," in Proceedings of the International Conference on Power System Technology (POWERCON). IEEE, Oct 2014, pp. 2492–2497.

[26] T. Morris, A. Srivastava, B. Reaves, W. Gao, K. Pavurapu, and R. Reddi, "A control system testbed to validate critical infrastructure protection concepts," Int. J. Crit. Infrastruct. Prot., vol. 4, no. 2, 2011, pp. 88–103.

[27] Z. Xu, I. King, M. R.-T. Lyu, and R. Jin, "Discriminative Semi-Supervised Feature Selection Via Manifold Regularization," IEEE Trans. Neural Networks, vol. 21, no. 7, 2010, pp. 1033–1047.

[28] A. Tchorbadjieff, "Automatic data quality control for environmental measurements," in 9th International Conference on Large-Scale Scientific Computing (LSSC). Sozopol, Bulgaria: Springer, Jun 2013, pp. 421–427.

[29] C. Hyong Jin, H. Lavretsky, R. Olmstead, M. J. Levin, M. N. Oxman, and M. R. Irwin, "Sleep Disturbance and Depression Recurrence in Community-Dwelling Older Adults: A Prospective Study," The American Journal of Psychiatry, vol. 165, no. 12, 2008, pp. 1543–1550.

[30] N. J. Salkind, Statistics for people who (think they) hate statistics, 3rd ed. Sage Publications, Jan. 2008, ISBN: 1412979595.

[31] N. Marom, L. Rokach, and A. Shmilovici, "Using the Confusion Matrix for Improving Ensemble Classifiers," in Proceedings of the Twenty-Sixth IEEE Convention of Electrical and Electronics Engineers in Israel. Eliat, Israel: IEEE, Nov 2010, pp. 555–559.

[32] L. Topham, K. Kifayat, Y. A. Younis, Q. Shi, and B. Askwith, " Cyber Security Teaching and Learning Laboratories: A Survey," Information & Security: An International Journal, vol. 35, no. 1, 2016, pp. 1–20.

[33] D. Lewis, "The pedagogical benefits and pitfalls of virtual tools for teaching and learning laboratory practices in the Biological Sciences," The Higher Education Academy, Leeds, UK, Tech. Rep., 2014, URL: https://www.heacademy.ac.uk/system/files/resources/the_pedagogical_benefits_and_pitfalls_of_virtual_tools_for_teaching_and_learning_laboratory_practices_in_the_biological_sciences.pdf [accessed: 2017-05-05].

APPENDIX

TABLE VI. Simulation Components

Abbreviation	Simulation Component Description
C1	WaterSourcePipe
C2	Pump1
C3	Pump2
C4	WaterFeedPipe
C5	Pipe1
C6	Pipe2

TABLE VII. Micro-CI Testbed Components

Abbreviation	Simulation Component Description
P1	Water Level 1
P2	Water Level 2
P3	Water Flow 1
P4	Water Flow 2
P5	Pump Speed 1
P6	Pump Speed 2

Plausibility Checks in Electronic Control Units to Enhance Safety and Security

Martin Ring and Reiner Kriesten

University of Applied Sciences Karlsruhe
76133 Karlsruhe
Germany
{martin.ring|reiner.kriesten}@hs-karlsruhe.de

Frank Kargl

Ulm University
89069 Ulm
Germany
frank.kargl@uni-ulm.de

Abstract— **Modern vehicles include a large number of Electronic Control Units interconnected by different bus systems. Attacks on these critical infrastructure elements have increased significantly over the last years, particularly since remote exploitation is possible due to increased wireless connectivity from the cars to the outside world. Many of these attacks exploit available standard communication protocols and diagnostic services implemented in cars that are often mandatory. Such services allow, for example, the activation of headlights or the turning of the steering wheel via the parking assist functionality. These services must be sufficiently secure, such that they can only be triggered when it is safe to do so, e. g., when the car is parked or driving at low speed. The validation mechanisms to determine a safe state are mainly plausibility checks, which currently often only utilize the vehicle speed, reported via the Controller Area Network bus, as an input parameter. In this paper, we motivate the need to base plausibility checks on other input values, which may be more authentic and reliable. Specifically, we propose the use of immanent signals for plausibility checks, i. e., signals derived from hard-wired sensors, which are harder to manipulate. In this paper, we propose some specific implementations of plausibility checks with immanent signals and argue how they would protect from current attacks on cars found in literature, we also discuss how the same idea may be applied to other areas, such as Industrial Control Systems.**

Keywords–Automotive Security; Vehicular Attacks; Plausibility Checks.

I. INTRODUCTION

Modern cars can be regarded as highly complex cyber physical systems. These systems are composed of up to 100 microprocessors (called Electronic Control Units (ECUs)) with up to 100 million lines of code [2]–[4]. Failures of such systems can have catastrophic consequences and come in two flavors, safety failures can be induced by a systematic or random malfunction, while security failures are induced by a malicious entitiy. These failures make the automotive systems prone to attacks. Since the introduction of bus systems to cars they were vulnerable to attacks, but these required a physical connection (e. g., car theft). With the recent introduction of ever more wireless interfaces, these attacks and many more can now be performed by remote hackers [5]. Remote attacks alone typically have little to no direct effects on the safety of cars, as they target communication units. Only combined with flaws in the internal networks can safety risks arise. Joe Weiss and the NIST share this viewpoint in that for Industrial Control Systems (ICSs) and critical infrastructures at large the principle of CIA should be replaced by AIC, thus making attacks on the availability of a system the most critical attacks, followed by attacks on its integrity and lastly its confidentiality [6]. Miller and Valasek come to the conclusion that multi stage attacks are now a realistic problem in the automotive world and argue that their work "shows that simply protecting vehicles from remote attacks isn't the only layer of defense that automakers need" [7]. A defense in depth security approach is required. One significant part of such an approach are plausibility checks, which we proposed in an earlier paper [1] and that we want to amend in this publication. In earlier publications [5], [7]–[10], most critical attacks able to compromise the safety of a car were limited to low speeds. These limitations stem from existing plausibility checks in ECUs that try to prevent the execution of the requested service in an unsafe state, like at higher speeds. However, these plausibility checks only rely on the speed of the vehicle as reported to ECUs via internal networks which can, again, be attacked. In this paper, we introduce a novel approach for enhanced validity checks that does not suffer from attackers that have infiltrated internal networks.

In the following, we will first give an introduction to plausibility checks and outline the requirements for the used signals, followed in Section II-B by an extensive overview of vulnerabilities found in cars till today. Section III then describes our approach for advanced plausibility checks and the assessment process to determine suitable functions to safeguard. Next, Section IV discusses the security of our approach and its applicability to cars and other domains like ICSs, and finally, Section V concludes this paper with an outlook.

II. STATE OF THE ART

A. Plausibility Checks

As researchers noticed in their attempts to compromise cars, most of the time the last barrier to safety critical functions is a plausibility check. These are simple checks that verify whether all prerequisites to safely execute a function are met. All checks discovered so far use the speed of the car as a signal to check against [7], [11]. All but one ECU (the Antilock Brake System (ABS)/Electronic Stability Control (ESC)-ECU) obtain this information from an internal bus

Rating	CVSS Score
None	0.0
Low	0.1 - 3.9
Medium	4.0 - 6.9
High	7.0 - 8.9
Critical	9.0 - 10.0

TABLE I. Qualitative severity rating scale [30].

system. The check only determines if the speed is below a predetermined threshold. This threshold is usually 5 mph or 8 kph depending on whether the country uses imperial or metrical units, respectively. Above these thresholds, ECUs change their internal state to one with very limited triggerable functions. The problem with this mechanism is not the general approach, but rather that it relies only on the speed of the car, which is received by spoofable bus messages that can be sent by any host with access to the network segment in most current automobiles. If no network separation is present, the signal can basically be sent by any node in the network, even by ones plugged in externally.

In order to provide the necessary protection, the signals used for plausibility checks have to be authentic and integrity protected. The modern approach [12] applies cryptographic protection, e. g., with Keyed-Hash Message Authentication Codes (HMACs), to achieve these goals. However, this type of message protection is hardly found in current production vehicles. The maximum security offered is the use of alive counters and simple checksums.

B. *Attacks on Automobiles*

In order to efficiently implement security measures, it is necessary to understand the problem in detail. For this reason, we conducted an extensive literature research that resulted in 22 published sources describing attacks on automobiles [5], [7]–[9], [11], [13]–[29]. In these 22 sources, a total of 87 attacks were found and classified according to CVSS v. 3 [30]. In the following, we present our results from an analysis and categorization of these attacks. The detailed analysis can be found in [31].

The Common Vulnerability Scoring System (CVSS) is widely accepted as the standard taxonomy to rate software vulnerabilities and is used, e.g., in the Common Vulnerabilities and Exposures (CVE) database. We classified all attacks according to the CVSS v. 3, limiting classification to the *Base Metrics*. These metrics reflect the vulnerabilities of the tested systems. The CVSS offers five severity ratings represented in Table I with their associated CVSS scores. Additional metrics are *Temporal Metrics* and *Environmental Metrics*. A *Temporal Metric* is used to classify the maturity of the available exploits, ranging from no available proof of concept to publicly available scripts ready to be used. *Environmental Metrics* are used to measure the impact to a shareholder if a vulnerable item is failing / compromised.

Figure 1 depicts the severity ratings of all examined attacks. Probably most noticeable is the fact that only one attack has a low severity. This is the attack on the WiFi pre-shared key (PSK) in a Mitsubishi [20]. This attack only compromises the confidentiality of the system. 28% of all attacks have a medium, 40% a high and 31% a critical severity rating.

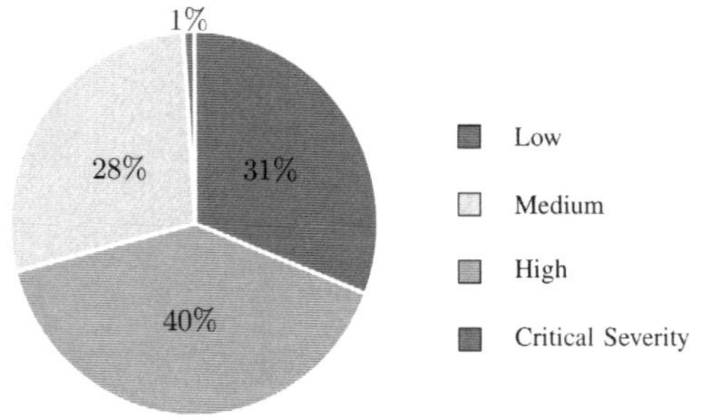

Figure 1. Severity ranking of of Vulnerabilities

Figure 2 gives an overview of the combinations of affected protection goals. The bar on the left shows all attacks that compromise a single protection goal, either confidentiality, integrity or availability (combined 26.4%). The middle bar represents the attacks that compromise a combination of two safety goals (combined 49.5%), while the right side bar represents the percentage of vulnerabilities that compromise all three protection goals (24.1%). 28% of the found vulnerabilities have a severity rating of medium, and all combinations of compromised protection goals can be found in this class. A high severity rating is determined for 40% of the found vulnerabilities. In this severity class, no attacks on the integrity of the system or the combination of confidentiality and integrity are included. 31% of all found vulnerabilities are critical, the highest severity class according to CVSS v. 3. In this class, the vulnerabilities are a combination that affect either all three protection goals (8% of all vulnerabilities) or the combination of integrity and availability (23% of all vulnerabilities). Another interesting fact is that no attack that required user interaction resulted in a critical vulnerability.

Finally, we want to investigate the attack vectors used in these attacks. The CVSS offers a distinction between four attack vectors: network, adjacent, local and physical. If a vulnerability is exploitable by network it is often referred to as *remotely exploitable*, the vulnerable component thus needs a network access and the attacker attacks through OSI layer 3. A component exploitable over an adjacent network has a network connection, but the connection only has a short range, e. g., WiFi or Bluetooth. Is a vulnerability exploitable only by local access, then the attack uses local read/write/execute commands or utilizes the user. If the vulnerability is exploitable through a physical connection, then this connection can be only brief, e. g., *evil maid attack*, or it can be a persistent connection [30].

Figure 3 shows the distribution of attack vectors for attacks on automobiles. Most vulnerabilities can be exploited by an adjacent network, for example by having access to the local Controller Area Network (CAN) network. If a malicious host is part of the local network, other hosts can be exploited. Another example is the attack on the Bluetooth implementation described in [9]. Network exploitable vulnerabilities make up 5.7 % of all possible attack vectors, an example is the exploitation of the 3G network stack described in [9] or the remote unlocking and start of cars described in [27]. Local exploitable vulnerabilities account for 15 % of all vulnerabilities.

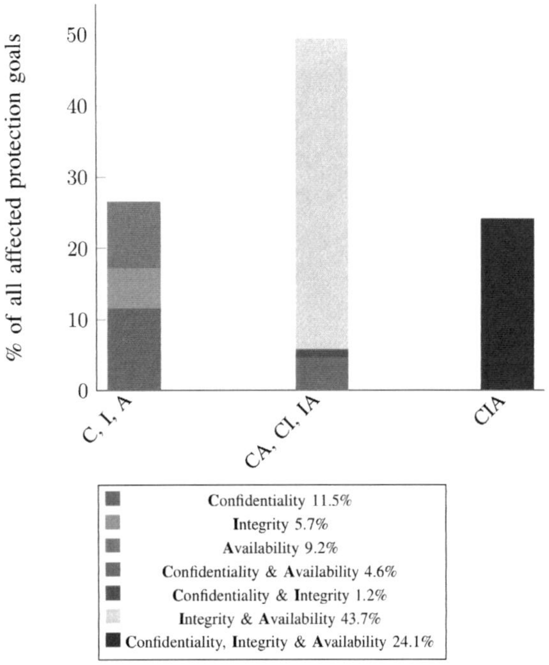

Figure 2. Overview affected protection goals

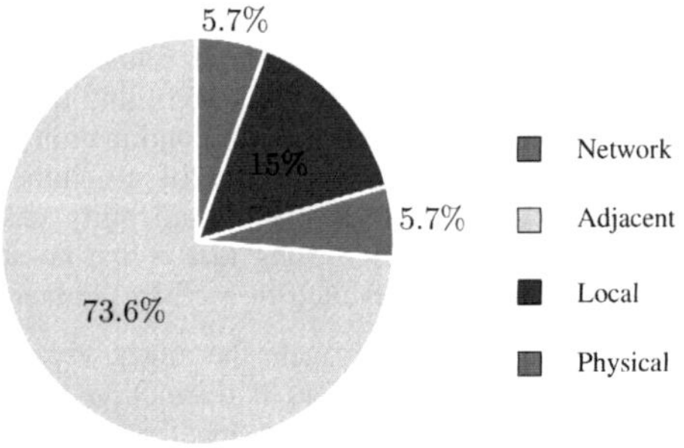

Figure 3. Distribution of attack vectors

Examples for locally exploitable vulnerabilities are, e. g., the attacks on keyless access systems described in [17], [21], [29].

Physical access was only necessary in 5.7% of all attacks, examples for such attacks are, e. g., the attack on the accelerator message in a Toyota or the dumps of the ROM of Ford ECUs in [8].

In conclusion, many of the attacks found during our literature survey rely on spoofing of messages and manipulating safety critical state (64.4%). Some attacks could only be conducted at low speeds due to simple plausibility checks being in place. However, [7] has already highlighted that such simple plausibility checks could be rendered ineffective and can be bypassed by spoofing messages that simulate a safe state, e.g., low speed. We thus conclude that more advanced and more secure plausibility checks would be required to provide better protection from such attacks. In the next section we want to present such plausibility checks.

III. Advanced Plausibility Checks

As stated before, advanced plausibility checks can be applied as part of a defense in depth concept to prevent attacks on safety critical functions. The main idea is that plausibility checks need to be based on more tamper-resistant input, because CAN messages are too easy to manipulate. In the absence of strong cryptographic protection of CAN networks in most cars, we can still resort to directly attached sensors, even if these only provide indirect evidence of the vehicles state. If, e. g., an ECU controls the steering aid and automatic steering, steering angle and forces allow it to determine whether the vehicle is driving at high speed or not, without relying on potentially spoofed remote information.

In order to allow a systematic development of such advanced plausibility checks, we have designed a systematic methodology that is shown in Figure 4 and allows to determine if our proposed approach is applicable for certain applications.

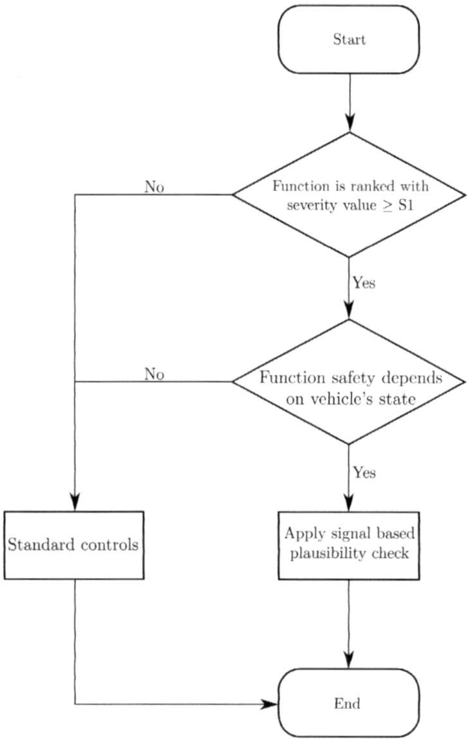

Figure 4. Methodology for applying plausibility checks

Before this assessment, a hazard and risk analysis has to be conducted. This analysis is part of every automotive development lifecycle and demanded by the functional safety standard ISO 26262 [32]. The objective of this analysis is the identification and classification of the hazards of an item ("a system that implements a function at a vehicle level" [32]). Such an item could, e. g., be the airbag. In addition, safety goals related to the prevention and mitigation of the found hazards have to be drafted. For each hazard, an Automotive Safety Integrity Level (ASIL) has to be calculated. The inputs for this calculation are the expected loss in case of an accident (*severity*) and the probability of the accident occurring (*exposure and controllability*). For this contemplation only the severity as the consequences of a malfunction are considered. With levels from S 0 to S 3, functions with a severity equal or above S 1 (light to moderate injuries) are deemed meaningful. These considerations are embodied by the first decision in the design structure chart pictured in Figure 4. The next necessary decision is to determine whether the function in question depends on the state of the vehicle.

In addition to a Hazard and Risk Analysis for the identification of *safety* risks, the overall evaluation of *security* risks is performed in a Threat Analysis and Risk Assessment (TARA) at the beginning of an automotive project [33]. Several approaches can be taken into account in order to conduct existing vulnerabilities and attacker models, e. g., starting from the entry points of possible attacks into a system. Figure 5 shows a high-level description of possible entry points for an individual ECU.

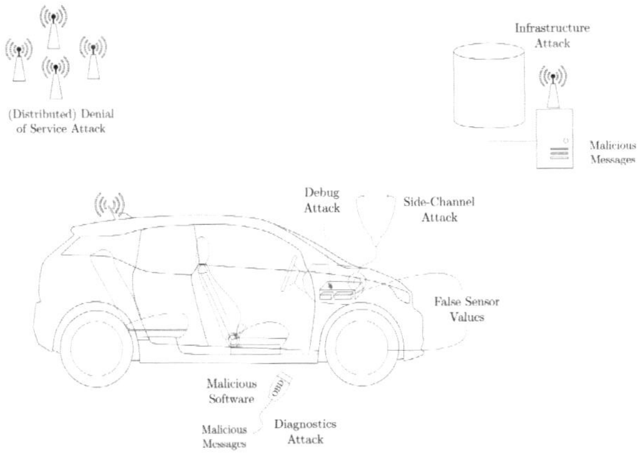

Figure 5. Possible entry Points to an ECU

The implementation of a simple plausibility check with speed evaluation is attractive to attacks, which are launched by the use of a counterfeit speed value on the on-board bus system, combined with an issuing of an (authenticated) diagnostics service request from an off-board tester unit or a wireless connection endpoint in case of diagnostics-over-the-air service possibilities. Hard-wired sensor values of an ECU are by nature resistant to protocol attacks. Thus, their use in an overall ECU security concept can be seen as complementary approach in order to derive a reliable decision on a safe state.

When the requirements as described above and pictured in Figure 4 are met, advanced plausibility checks should and can be used to safeguard functions. As mentioned before, inputs to these plausibility checks have to be authentic and their integrity should be guaranteed. These protection goals can be met by applying cryptographic functions, e. g., using HMAC [12]. This type of cryptographic measure ensures the desired protection goals with an acceptable demand for computational performance. Nevertheless, there also exist a few drawbacks using HMACs. In particular, the key management and reduced bandwidth on the bus by attaching an HMAC to each message are problematic, unless the network was planned with security in mind. If security was not a priority, or even considered during development, the necessary computational power and secure storage could be absent. This absence of relevant hardware could make a complete overhaul of the network necessary to improve security. Another point against cryptographic measures is that it is still possible to circumvent these functions by attacking other components, which is not possible when using hard-wired sensors for plausibility checks. In the next paragraphs we want to present a possible solution with a practical example based on the attacks by Miller and Valasek [7].

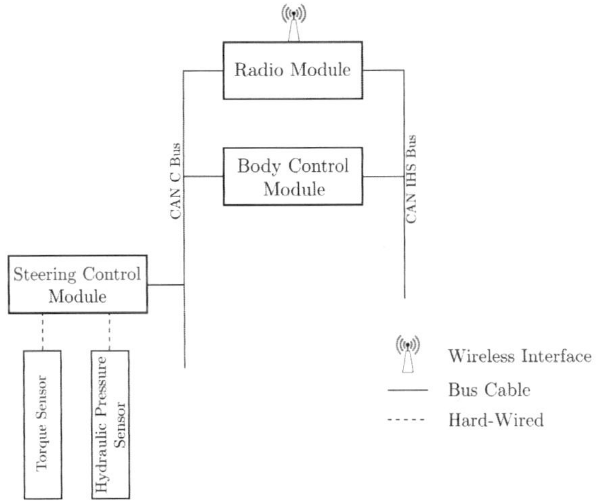

Figure 6. Sub-architecture of a Jeep Cherokee 2014 [5]

Figure 6 represents a part of a Jeep Cherokee 2014 network architecture, which was the target of the latest attacks of Miller and Valasek on a car [5], [7]. The figure shows different ECUs and gateways that are interconnected by bus systems. Furthermore, some hard-wired sensors are present, delivering relevant information about the state of the vehicle. This information can be used to derive ECU immanent signals for plausibility checks without the need for cryptographic protection.

ECU immanent signals should be used for plausibility checks whenever possible. These signals can be signals produced in the ECU, like the regulated torque in the engine ECU that is calculated by adding up all the torque demands of the engine auxiliaries and the driver requirement. The other possibility for such signals are hard-wired sensor signals, such as the rotational speed sensors for the ABS / ESC ECU. With the help of Figure 7 we want to show how an immanent signal of an ECU can be used to make a plausibility check for a requested function. This example is based on the latest hacks of Miller and Valasek. On their Jeep Cherokee [7] they spoofed the speed signal of the ABS-ECU that normally would have been used by the Steering Control Module (SCM) to make a plausibility check. In this case, the plausibility check would verify whether the car is in reverse and slower than 5 mph. The check for the driving direction is not easily possible, but we can check for the speed constraint. We can assume a known level of hydraulic pressure in the steering system, because we have a hard-wired sensor for this signal to the SCM. This module also evaluates the signal of the torque sensor. With the help of the information in Figure 7 it is possible to determine the speed of a car within small limits.

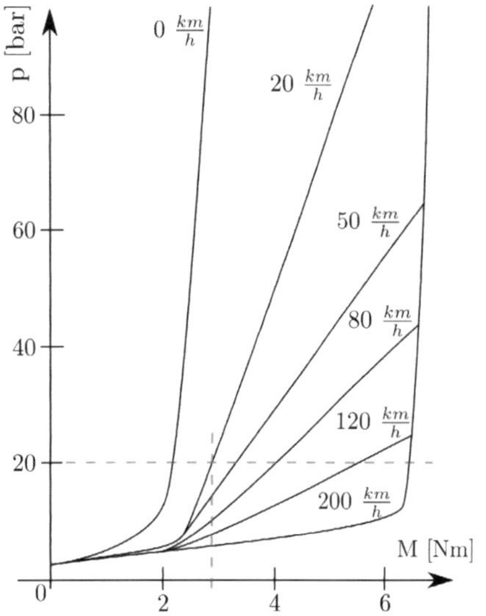

Figure 7. Plot of steering moment dependent on hydraulic pressure and vehicular speed [34]

As an example, we will show how to determine the threshold for the steering torque up to which a safe execution of safety critical functions is permissible. For easier visual evaluation we suppose a threshold of 20 kph for the safe state of the Jeep and an assumption of 20 bar for the hydraulic pressure brings us to the conclusion that a steering moment of more than 2.9 Nm is equivalent to a speed above the defined threshold and thus the execution of the requested function has to be refused.

A plausibility check like described here would have easily prevented the attack on the steering system as described in [7]. Our analysis indicates that such immanent signals can be found and utilized in almost any safety critical ECU in a car. We argue that signals from other ECUs should only be used, if local sensor signals are not available and if remote information is cryptographically protected. As mentioned before, input to plausibility checks has to fulfill some preconditions, namely being integrous and authentic. Only if these prerequisites are fulfilled, such bus messages can be used for plausibility checks of functions with a severity value of S 1 or above.

To conclude this section we want to present some limits for this method and ways to prevent them. The other attacks on the Jeep Cherokee [7] are more problematic, as they use legitimate messages to request certain functions. The *slamming on the car's brakes* is a standard function that is executed when the driver presses the switch for the electronic parking brake. While pressing the switch the pump for the ABS / ESC system is activated and provides the pressure to engage the brakes of the car. Such a brake maneuver is comparable with emergency braking. As Miller and Valasek were able to request and execute this function, it is reasonable to assume that the switch for the electronic parking brake is directly connected to the bus system of the car. The same can be concluded for their last attack, the unintended acceleration of the car. They used the standard function to enable the Apdative Cruise Control (ACC) and then increase the target speed of the cruise control. This is possible by replaying messages of the switches embedded in the steering wheel. We were able to observe the same situation in an electric vehicle produced by a German manufacturer. Therefore, safety critical functions with an ASIL of D should not be able to be activated by bus messages. For all requests of such functions direct connections should be used (peer-to-peer); although these connections can be network connections, like CAN or Ethernet, they should not be routed over gateways.

IV. DISCUSSION

A. Automotive Systems

To demonstrate the broad applicability of our proposed method, we now discuss other examples of instances where plausibility checks with immanent signals can be used. First, we further evaluate the examples in Section III. After these examples, other published attacks on safety critical functions (lighting, engine, gearbox, brakes and suspensions [5], [8], [10], [16]) and the possibility to apply plausibility checks with ECU immanent signals are evaluated. Finally, we provide a discussion of how a our approach can also be applied to other fields, like ICSs.

We start with the engine example. There are multiple attacks published on the engine of a car [8]–[10], [16]. Most attacks completely disable the engine and shut it down. To achieve this result, standard services were used to reset the ECU, deactivate fuel injectors or initiate a flash session. Every such service should use a plausibility check as the safety of its execution is widely dependent on the vehicles state. There are multiple immanent sensor values or processed signals that could be used for these plausibility checks. An extensive overview is presented in Figure 8. The easiest signal to use is the rpm-signal of the engine. If this signal is non-zero, no service that compromises the operation of the engine should be able to execute. Services that help mechanics with diagnostics of the engine in a workshop, like reading out live data, may still be allowed. Besides the aforementioned rpm-signal, there are a lot of other sensor signals, which could be used, like the readout of the air mass sensor, exhaust temperature sensor, fuel pressure sensor and more. A processed signal that could be used is the calculated torque of the engine. This torque is calculated by adding the demands of all auxiliaries of the engine, like the AC compressor, the alternator or the hydraulic steering pump, as well as the driver demand. If this signal is unequal zero, it can be concluded that the car is in use and any execution of services that compromises the operation of the engine should be considered unsafe.

The second and probably most critical point of attack is the braking system, which was also the target of multiple attacks [5], [7], [8], [16]. The executed attacks include wheel selective braking as well as disabling the braking system all together. Here, it is also possible to use ECU immanent signals. All wheel speed sensors are hard-wired to the ECU. Modern wheel speed sensors can determine speeds as low as 0.1 kph [36]. As soon as a non-zero speed is detected, all safety critical services should stop their execution. However, the speed signal is not the only one that can be used, as an alternative the hard-wired three-axis acceleration sensor can be evaluated. As soon as these sensors signals show any acceleration, the car is not in a safe state to execute safety critical functions.

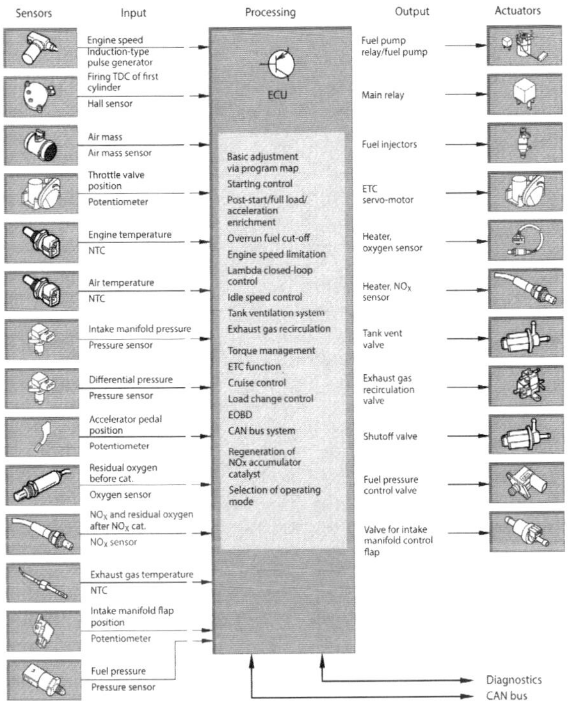

Figure 8. Engine ECU with its hard-wired sensors (green) and actuators (red) [35]

Our research also identified vulnerabilities in active suspension systems. The ECUs controlling such systems also use a vast amount of sensors and signals to control the ride of a vehicle. Two possible immanent signals of such a system are acceleration sensors or sensors for the level of each wheel. If the signals of the level sensors of the car change or an acceleration unequal to zero is detected it can be concluded that the car is in motion and thus safety critical functions should not be able to perform their task of, e. g., resetting the ECU.

A way to utilize advanced plausibility checking to ensure the safe state of the car with immanent signals of the steering system was presented in Section III. This shows that these systems could be safeguarded in their current implementation with our method. In conclusion, the presented examples show that this method allows to safeguard every ECU responsible for lateral or longitudinal behavior of a vehicle.

This method is not limited to safeguarding the movement of the car: other safety critical aspects can be secured, like the state of the lights, this is an instance where an odd sensor signal could be used [8], [10]. Attacks on the lights of a car spoofed messages of the light sensor or used diagnostic messages to deactivate the headlights of a car. The sensor signal of the light sensor is evaluated in the vehicle supply system control device. This device also powers the electric fuel pump, see, e. g., the schematic in [37]. This pump is only active when the engine is running and during a short time after unlocking the car or switching on the ignition. The signal is thus also a good indicator if it is safe to execute the inquired function. As the sensor is in the mentioned schematic hard-wired to the executing ECU it can determine if the message was spoofed or issued by the correct sender.

B. *Advanced Plausibility Checks in other Domains*

We claim that a similar approach for plausibility checking can be applied to many cyber-physical systems. The security problem in such systems is often the same. Control systems rely on insecure input to trigger actions that may be put the system in danger if executed in some situations. Often, plausibility checks are applied to prevent the system from entering unsafe states, but if attackers manage to manipulate the input to the plausibility check, there is no security gain.

So, our approach on rating the trustworthiness of all input to plausibility checks and then relying only on authentic and integrity-protected input should also be applied in such systems. Examples include ICSs or Building Automation Systems (BASs).

A simple example in a BAS may be a local controller that manages the blinds of a room depending on the instructions of a central control system. Depending on weather conditions like sun or wind, the blinds may be moved up or down. Communication can use protocols like BACnet or KNX that often provide no security features.

An attacker may now inject control messages to move blinds down during strong wind, resulting in damage to the building. While the local control may also receive wind speed via the network and thus apply plausibility checks to ignore the central controller's command in case it is unsafe to lower the blinds due to strong wind, an attacker may of course also inject false wind sensor information into the network.

Our approach would now search for local sensors data that may be used for advanced plausibility checks. For example, one may add a force-sensor to the blinds, to determine whether there is a strong wind drag and then decide to move the blinds in a safe state, i. e., up.

While researchers have studied intrusion detection and prevention for ICSs [38] and BASs [39], advanced plausibility checking and the consideration of reliability of input is not well studied so far, and should be considered as a field for future research.

V. CONCLUSION

In this paper, we have discussed the need for advanced plausibility checks to secure automotive systems from advanced attacks that have been recently demonstrated. While basic checks are already implemented in existing vehicles, they rely on bus messages of the vehicle speed, which may be forged, e. g., by the use of jamming or spoofing techniques. As these validations are one crucial part of a defense in depth approach, a more secure implementation is crucial.

With the use of immanent signals derived from hard-wired sensors a more secure way for plausibility checks can be found. We have discussed how this approach can be used in various functions of modern cars without any need to change the ECU or communication architecture; all changes depend on improved software realizations of the plausibility check and rely only on already available sensor input. We have shown that many of the recently published attacks could have been prevented by the presented approach. As discussed with building automation, similar approaches can be found in many other cyber-physical-systems.

For future work, we see a big potential in integrating remote and local input for plausibility checks. One should provide a trust rating for input to plausibility checks and determine plausibility of a system state based on these trust ratings. Furthermore, prospective future networks [40] are planned based on virtual servers, with this approach the hard wired sensor signals are not as easy to use as shown in this paper and has to be adapted.

REFERENCES

[1] M. Ring and R. Kriesten, "Plausibility Checks in Automotive Electronic Control Units to Enhance Safety and Security," in VEHICULAR 2016, 2016, accessed: 04.05.2017. [Online]. Available: https://thinkmind.org/download.php?articleid=vehicular_2016_1_30_30035

[2] R. N. Charette, "This Car Runs on Code," 2009, accessed: 12.02.2016. [Online]. Available: http://spectrum.ieee.org/transportation/systems/this-car-runs-on-code

[3] G. Serio and D. Wollschläger, "Vernetztes Automobil Verteidigungsstrategien im Kampf gegen Cyberattacken," ATZelektronik - 06/2015, 2015.

[4] SAE, "Cybersecurity Guidebook for Cyber-Physical Vehicle Systems," 2016, accessed: 12.04.2016. [Online]. Available: http://standards.sae.org/wip/j3061/

[5] C. Miller and C. Valasek, "Remote Exploitation of an Unaltered Passenger Vehicle," 2015, accessed: 13.03.2017. [Online]. Available: http://illmatics.com/Remote Car Hacking.pdf

[6] J. K. Weiss and S. N. Katzke, "Industrial Control System (ICS) Security: An Overview of Emerging Standards, Guidelines, and Implementation Activities." National Institute of Standards and Technology, Tech. Rep., accessed: 13.03.2017. [Online]. Available: http://csrc.nist.gov/groups/SMA/fisma/ics/documents/ACSAC-presentation-v2.pdf

[7] C. Miller and C. Valasek, "CAN Message Injection – OG Dynamite Edition," 2016, accessed: 13.03.2017. [Online]. Available: http://illmatics.com/can message injection.pdf

[8] C. Miller and C. Valasek, "Adventures in Automotive Networks and Control Units," 2014, accessed: 13.03.2017. [Online]. Available: http://www.ioactive.com/pdfs/IOActive_Adventures_in_Automotive_Networks_and_Control_Units.pdf/

[9] S. Checkoway, D. McCoy, B. Kantor, D. Anderson, H. Shacham, S. Savage, K. Koscher, A. Czeskis, F. Roesner, T. Kohno, and Others, "Comprehensive Experimental Analyses of Automotive Attack Surfaces," 2011.

[10] "Gehackte Mobilität," Apr. 2016, accessed: 14.06.2016. [Online]. Available: https://www.3sat.de/mediathek/?mode=play&obj=58732

[11] M. Ring, J. Dürrwang, F. Sommer, and R. Kriesten, "Survey on Vehicular Attacks – Building a Vulnerability Database," in ICVES, ser. IEEE International Conference on Vehicular Electronics and Safety (ICVES), vol. 2015. IEEE, 2015, pp. 208–212.

[12] K. Beckers, J. Dürrwang, and D. Holling, "Standard Compliant Hazard and Threat Analysis for the Automotive Domain," Information, vol. 7, no. 3, 2016, p. 36, accessed: 02.09.2016. [Online]. Available: http://www.mdpi.com/2078-2489/7/3/36

[13] Keen Security Lab of Tencent, "Car Hacking Research: Remote Attack Tesla Motors," 2016, accessed: 13.03.2017. [Online]. Available: http://keenlab.tencent.com/en/2016/09/19/Keen-Security-Lab-of-Tencent-Car-Hacking-Research-Remote-Attack-to-Tesla-Cars/

[14] T. Hunt, "Controlling vehicle features of Nissan LEAFs across the globe via vulnerable APIs," feb 2016, accessed: 13.03.2017. [Online]. Available: https://www.troyhunt.com/controlling-vehicle-features-of-nissan/

[15] R. Verdult, D. F. Garcia, and B. Ege, "Dismantling Megamos Crypto: Wirelessly Lockpicking a Vehicle Immobilizer," Supplement to the 22nd USENIX Security Symposium (USENIX Security 13), 2015, pp. 703–718, accessed: 13.03.2017. [Online]. Available: https://www.usenix.org/conference/usenixsecurity15/technical-sessions/presentation/verdult

[16] K. Koscher, A. Czeskis, F. Roesner, S. Patel, T. Kohno, S. Checkoway, D. McCoy, B. Kantor, D. Anderson, H. Shacham, and S. Savage, "Experimental Security Analysis of a Modern Automobile," 2010 IEEE Symposium on Security and Privacy, 2010, pp. 447–462, accessed: 13.03.2017. [Online]. Available: http://dx.doi.org/10.1109/SP.2010.34

[17] R. Verdult, D. F. Garcia, and J. Balasch, "Gone in 360 Seconds: Hijacking with Hitag2," Presented as part of the 21st USENIX Security Symposium (USENIX Security 12), 2012, pp. 237–252, accessed: 13.03.2017. [Online]. Available: https://www.usenix.org/conference/usenixsecurity12/technical-sessions/presentation/verdult

[18] B. Howard, "Hack the diagnostics connector, steal yourself a BMW in 3 minutes," in ExtremeTech, jul 2012, pp. 3–7, accessed: 13.03.2017. [Online]. Available: http://www.extremetech.com/extreme/132526-hack-the-diagnostics-connector-steal-yourself-a-bmw-in-3-minutes

[19] K. Poulsen, "Hacker Disables More Than 100 Cars Remotely," Wired, 2010, accessed: 13.03.2017. [Online]. Available: https://www.wired.com/2010/03/hacker-bricks-cars/

[20] D. Lodge, "Hacking the Mitsubishi Outlander PHEV hybrid — Pen Test Partners," 2016, accessed: 13.03.2017. [Online]. Available: https://www.pentestpartners.com/blog/hacking-the-mitsubishi-outlander-phev-hybrid-suv/

[21] T. Eisenbarth, T. Kasper, A. Moradi, C. Paar, M. Salmasizadeh, and M. T. M. Shalmani, "On the Power of Power Analysis in the Real World: A Complete Break of the KeeLoqCode Hopping Scheme," Advances in Cryptology - CRYPTO 2008, 28th Annual International Cryptology Conference, Santa Barbara, CA, USA, August 17-21, 2008, vol. 5157, 2008, pp. 203–220.

[22] T. Hoppe, "Prävention, Detektion und Reaktion gegen drei Ausprägungsformen automotiver Malware: eine methodische Analyse im Spektrum von Manipulationen und Schutzkonzepten," Ph.D. dissertation, 2014.

[23] A. Francillon, B. Danev, and S. Capkun, "Relay Attacks on Passive Keyless Entry and Start Systems in Modern Cars." IACR Cryptology ePrint Archive, vol. 2011, 2011, accessed: 13.03.2017. [Online]. Available: http://dx.doi.org/10.3929/ethz-a-006708714

[24] I. Rouf, R. Miller, H. Mustafa, T. Taylor, S. Oh, W. Xu, M. Gruteser, W. Trappe, and I. Seskar, "Security and Privacy Vulnerabilities of In-car Wireless Networks: A Tire Pressure Monitoring System Case Study," Proceedings of the 19th USENIX Conference on Security, 2010, p. 21, accessed: 13.03.2017. [Online]. Available: http://dl.acm.org/citation.cfm?id=1929820.1929848

[25] T. Hoppe, S. Kiltz, and J. Dittmann, "Security threats to automotive CAN networks – Practical examples and selected short-term countermeasures," Reliability Engineering & System Safety, vol. 96, no. 1, 2011, pp. 11–25, accessed: 13.03.2017. [Online]. Available: http://www.sciencedirect.com/science/article/pii/S0951832010001602

[26] D. Spaar, "Sicherheitslücken bei BMWs Connected-Drive," feb 2015, accessed: 13.03.2017. [Online]. Available: https://www.heise.de/ct/ausgabe/2015-5-Sicherheitsluecken-bei-BMWs-ConnectedDrive-2536384.html

[27] D. Bailey and M. Solnik, "Theft via text: Cars vulnerable to hack attacks," aug 2011, accessed: 13.03.2017. [Online]. Available: http://www.cbsnews.com/news/theft-via-text-cars-vulnerable-to-hack-attacks/

[28] Y. Burakova, B. Hass, L. Millar, and A. Weimerskirch, "Truck Hacking: An Experimental Analysis of the SAE J1939 Standard," 10th USENIX Workshop on Offensive Technologies (WOOT 16), aug 2016, accessed: 13.03.2017. [Online]. Available: https://www.usenix.org/conference/woot16/workshop-program/presentation/burakova

[29] F. D. Garcia, D. Oswald, T. Kasper, and P. Pavlidès, "Lock It and Still Lose It – on the (In)Security of Automotive Remote Keyless Entry Systems," in 25th USENIX Security Symposium (USENIX Security 16). Austin, TX: USENIX Association, 2016, accessed: 13.03.2017. [Online]. Available: https://www.usenix.org/conference/usenixsecurity16/technical-sessions/presentation/garcia

[30] CVSS Special Interest Group, "Common Vulnerability Scoring System," 2016, accessed: 13.03.2017. [Online]. Available: https://www.first.org/cvss/cvss-v30-specification-v1.7.pdf https://www.first.org/cvss/calculator/3.0

[31] M. Ring, "Angriffsklassifikation," 2017, accessed: 13.03.2017. [Online]. Available: http://www.mmt.hs-karlsruhe.de/downloads/IEEM/Angriffsklassifizierung.ods

[32] ISO, "ISO 26262 Road vehicles – Functional safety," 2011.

[33] M. Dowd, J. McDonald, and J. Schuh, The art of software security assessment : identifying and preventing software vulnerabilities. Upper Saddle River, NJ: Addison-Wesley, 2007, accessed: 13.03.2017. [Online]. Available: http://www.gbv.de/dms/ilmenau/toc/515753645.pdf

[34] H. Felder, "Autoelektrik – Grundlagen- und Fachwissen," accessed: 24.08.2016. [Online]. Available: http://www.fahrzeug-elektrik.de/

[35] R. H. Gscheidle, Ed., Modern automotive technology : fundamentals, service, diagnostics, 2nd ed., ser. Europa reference books for automotive technology. Haan-Gruiten: Verl. Europa-Lehrmittel, 2014.

[36] "Raddrehzahlsensoren im Kraftfahrzeug Funktion, Diagnose, Fehlersuche." Tech. Rep., accessed: 15.08.2016. [Online]. Available: http://www.hella.com/ePaper/Raddrehzalsensoren/document.pdf

[37] "STG. Bordnetz - Control Mains Power Supply," accessed: 15.08.2016. [Online]. Available: http://www.seatforum.de/uploads/DRAFT01%5B1%5D244.jpg

[38] A. Carcano, A. Coletta, M. Guglielmi, M. Masera, I. N. Fovino, and A. Trombetta, "A multidimensional critical state analysis for detecting intrusions in scada systems," IEEE Transactions on Industrial Informatics, vol. 7, no. 2, May 2011, pp. 179–186.

[39] M. Caselli, E. Zambon, J. Amann, R. Sommer, and F. Kargl, "Specification mining for intrusion detection in networked control systems," in 25th USENIX Security Symposium (USENIX Security 16). Austin, TX: USENIX Association, Aug 2016, pp. 791–806. [Online]. Available: https://www.usenix.org/conference/usenixsecurity16/technical-sessions/presentation/caselli

[40] C. Meineck, "Ethernet network-security for on-board networks," in Vector Cyber Security Symposium, 2016, accessed: 04.05.2017. [Online]. Available: https://vector.com/portal/medien/cmc/events/commercial_events/vses16/lectures/vSES16_05_Meineck.pdf